The Definitive Guide to Jython

Python for the Java™ Platform

Josh Juneau, Jim Baker, Victor Ng, Leo Soto, Frank Wierzbicki

The Definitive Guide to Jython: Python for the Java™ Platform

ISBN-13 (pbk): 978-1-4302-2527-0

ISBN-13 (electronic): 978-1-4302-2528-7

President and Publisher: Paul Manning
Lead Editors: Steve Anglin, Duncan Parkes
Technical Reviewers: Mark Ramm, Tobias Ivarsson
Editorial Board: Clay Andres, Steve Anglin, Mark Beckner, Ewan Buckingham, Gary Cornell,
    Jonathan Gennick, Jonathan Hassell, Michelle Lowman, Matthew Moodie, Duncan Parkes,
    Jeffrey Pepper, Frank Pohlmann, Douglas Pundick, Ben Renow-Clarke, Dominic Shakeshaft,
    Matt Wade, Tom Welsh
Coordinating Editor: Mary Tobin
Copy Editor: Tracy Brown Collins
Indexer: BIM Indexers and e-Services
Artist: April Milne
Cover Designer: Anna Ishchenko

Distributed to the book trade worldwide by Springer-Verlag New York, Inc., 233 Spring Street, 6th Floor, New York, NY 10013. Phone 1-800-SPRINGER, fax 201-348-4505, e-mail orders-ny@springer-sbm.com, or visit http://www.springeronline.com.

For information on translations, please e-mail info@apress.com, or visit http://www.apress.com.

Apress and friends of ED books may be purchased in bulk for academic, corporate, or promotional use. eBook versions and licenses are also available for most titles. For more information, reference our Special Bulk Sales–eBook Licensing web page at http://www.apress.com/info/bulksales.

Contents at a Glance

Contents

Foreword

I started using Python in 2003, and I fell in love with the language for a variety of reasons. The elegance of Python's whitespace based syntax, the well conceived built in data types, and a beautiful set of library functions. Since that time, many other people have discovered or rediscovered Python. At the time of this writing, the software industry is well into a resurgence of dynamically typed languages: Ruby, PHP, and Python.

It wasn't until I attended my first PyCon in 2004 that I became aware of Jython. People were glad of the ability to run Python programs on the Java Virtual Machine (JVM), but were wistful because at the time Jython was lagging behind the native C Python (CPython) interpreter in terms of supporting recent versions of the language. Jython was maintained by a series of individual developers, but the task of staying current with CPython was really too much for any single person. In December 2005, Frank Wierzbicki took over as the lead developer for Jython, and over the next few years managed to foster a community of developers for Jython. The authors of this book are some of the members of that community. In June of 2009, the Jython community released Jython 2.5, which implemented the same language as CPython 2.5. This was a major leap forward, bringing Jython much closer to feature parity with CPython, and laying a foundation for catching up the rest of the way with CPython. Jython 2.5 is able to run many of the most popular Python packages, including Django, Pylons, and SQLAlchemy.

Jython makes for a best of both worlds bridge between the elegant, expressive code of the Python world and the "enterprise ready" Java world. Developers who work in organizations where Java is already in use can now take advantage of the expressiveness and conciseness of Python by running their Python programs on Jython. Jython provides easy integration and interoperability between Python code and existing Java code.

Jython also has something to offer existing Python programmers, namely access to the very rich ecosystem of the Java Virtual Machine. There is an enormous amount of Java code out in the world. There are libraries for every task imaginable, and more. Jython gives Python programmers a way to tap into these libraries, saving both development and testing time. Web applications running on Jython can also take advantage of the scalability benefits of Java web containers such as Tomcat or GlassFish.

Things are looking very bright for Jython, and this book is a timely resource for people interested in taking advantage of the benefits that Jython has to offer.

Ted Leung

About the Authors

 **Josh Juneau** has been a software developer since the mid-1990s. He graduated from Northern Illinois University with a degree in Computer Science. His career began as an Oracle database administrator which later led into PL/SQL development and database programming. Josh began to use Java along with PL/SQL for developing web applications, and later shifted to Java as a primary base for application development. Josh has worked with Java in the form of web, GUI, and command-line programming for several years. During his tenure as a Java developer, he has worked with many frameworks including JSP, JSF, EJB, and JBoss Seam. At the same time, Josh expanded his usage of the JVM by developing applications with other JVM languages such as Jython and Groovy. Since 2006, Josh has been the editor and publisher of the *Jython Monthly* newsletter. In late 2008, he began a podcast dedicated to the Jython programming language. More modern releases of Jython have enabled Josh to begin using it as one of the primary languages for his professional development. Currently, Josh spends his days developing Java and Jython applications, and working with Oracle databases. When he is not working, he enjoys spending time with his family. Josh also sneaks in enough time to maintain the jython.org website, hack on the Jython language, and work on other such projects. He can be contacted via his blog at http://www.jj-blogger.blogspot.com.

 **Jim Baker** has over 15 years of software development experience, focusing on business intelligence, enterprise application integration, and high-performance web applications. He is a member of the Python Software Foundation and a committer on Jython. Jim has presented at Devoxx, EuroPython, JavaOne, and the Python Conference, as well as at numerous user groups. He is a graduate of both Harvard and Brown.

Victor Ng has been slinging Python code in enterprises for 10 years and has worked in the banking, adventure travel, and telecommunications industries. Victor attended the University of Waterloo where he was busy learning to cook and didn't attend too many classes. He lives just outside of Toronto, Ontario, in Canada.

 **Leonardo Soto** has been part of the Jython development team since the middle of 2008, after he successfully completed a Google Summer of Code Project that aimed to run and integrate the Django web framework with Jython. He is also finishing his thesis to get the Informatics Engineering title from the Universidad de Santiago de Chile and works on Continuum, a Chilean software boutique.

Leo has developed several software systems in the past seven years, most of which are web applications, and based on the JavaEE (formerly J2EE) platform. However, he has been spoiled by Python since the start of his professional developer career, and he has missed its power and clarity countless times, which inexorably turned him toward the Jython project.

 **Frank Wierzbicki** is the head of the Jython project and a lead software developer at Sauce Labs. He has been programming since the Commodore 64 was the king of home computers (look it up, kids!) and can't imagine why anyone would do anything else for a living. Frank's most enduring hobby is picking up new programming languages, but he has yet to find one that is more fun to work with than Python.

About the Technical Reviewers

 **Mark Ramm** is project leader of TurboGears 2, and has written myriad articles, and a book about TurboGears. He is a web developer at GeekNet (geek.net) and is the founder of Compound Thinking (compoundthinking.com), a consulting and development company focused on Python training, and web application development.

 **Tobias Ivarsson** is a software developer at Neo Technology, the commercial backer of the open source graph database Neo4j (http://neo4j.org/). Tobias is also a developer on the Jython project, with focus on the compiler.

Acknowledgments

First and foremost, I would like to thank my wife Angela for standing beside me throughout my career and writing this book. She has been my inspiration and motivation for continuing to improve my knowledge and move my career forward. She is my rock, and I dedicate this book to her. I also thank my wonderful children: Katie, Jake, Matt, and our new addition Zachary, for always making me smile and for understanding on those weekend mornings when I was writing this book instead of playing games. I hope that one day they can read this book and understand why I spent so much time in front of my computer.

I'd like to thank my parents and grandparents for allowing me to follow my ambitions throughout my childhood. My family, including my in-laws, have always supported me throughout my career and authoring this book and I really appreciate it. I look forward to discussing this book with my family at future gatherings as I'm sure they will all read it soon.

My co-workers, especially Roger Slisz, Necota Smith, and Matt Arena, who showed me the ropes in IT. Without that knowledge I wouldn't have ventured into learning about Oracle and PL/SQL, which ultimately led to this! I'd like to especially thank Roger Slisz and Kent Collins for trusting me to guide and develop the applications for our department, and for allowing me the freedom to manage my projects and provide the necessary time and resource toward our applications and databases.

I'd really like to thank Jim Baker for providing me with the opportunity to become the lead author for this book. I appreciate that he believed in me to provide the leadership and knowledge to make this book a reality. Jim Baker is a great person and a scholar; without him, this book may not have been written.

Jim and I collaborated to find the other great authors that helped us write this book. In the end, I believe that the team of authors that was chosen provides the perfect blend of knowledge and skills that went into authoring this book. I thank each of the authors for devoting their time and effort towards this book; I think that it will be a great asset to the community! Thanks for everything, I look forward to writing the second edition soon!

I owe a huge thanks to Duncan Parkes of Apress for providing excellent support and advice. I also wish to thank all of our technical reviewers and our Apress project coordinator, Mary Tobin. All of their efforts helped to make this book complete and we couldn't have done it without you.

Last, but definitely not least, I'd like to thank the Jython developers and the community as a whole. The developers work hard to provide us with this great technology allowing us to write Python on the JVM. Frank Wierzbicki has done an excellent job in leading the core of Jython developers to produce 2.5.1, and I know that he'll continue to do a great job leading into the future. Thanks to the community for using Jython and providing great ideas and support via the mailing lists; without this help I could not provide the newsletter and podcast.

Josh J. Juneau

This book is dedicated to my kids, Zack and Zoe, who are just about the best children a dad could hope for: happy, loving, and fun to be with. Fundamentally, what I love to do is create, so it's wonderful watching you grow!

Three years ago, we had this audacious idea of reviving Jython. We would jump to supporting the 2.5 version of the Python language. And we would focus on making it a suitable platform for running the increasingly large apps that are being developed. This meant a renewed focus on compatibility for Jython. Fortunately, we could leverage the new reality that developers of Python applications, frameworks, and libraries increasingly have a commitment to strong testing. Our problem was tractable because we could use this testing to converge on a robust implementation.

This book documents how we, in fact, achieved this goal, while still preserving the ability to interactively explore and script the Java platform. In other words, Jython has grown up, but it hasn't forgotten what made it both useful and fun in the first place.

To my good friend Frank Wierzbicki, we made it happen; Charlie Nutter, for his commitment to collaboration; Albert Wenger and Bruce Eckel, who both convinced me that working on Jython was important; Leslie Hawthorn of the Google Open Source Programs Office; Dorene Beaver; Brian Goetz, John Rose, and Ted Leung at Sun, for their support of alternative languages on the JVM; Chris Perkins, Glyph Lefkowitz, Jacob Kaplan-Moss, Mark Ramm, and Raymond Hettinger for their support of a robust Python ecosystem; my fellow Jython developers, Alan Kennedy, Charlie Groves, Josh Juneau, Nicholas Riley, Oti Humbel, and Phil Jenvey, not to mention many other contributors. And especially to my Google Summer of Code students, now also Jython committers, Leo Soto and Tobias Ivarsson: it's been wonderful watching you grow as both developers and individuals.

Jim Baker

Thanks to Liz and Rosie for putting up with far too many side projects this year. Special thanks to everyone in the Jython and Python developer community for making life as a programmer much less painful than it could be.

Victor Ng

First, thanks to my family for having patience with me when I took on yet another challenge which decreases the amount of time I can spend with them. Especially Eliana, my mother, who has endured a large part of that sacrifice, and also Nicolás, my brother, who gives encouragement in his own particular way. They and Leocadio, my father, who rests in peace, forged my personality and share credit on every goal I achieve.

Thanks to all my friends for sharing my happiness when starting this project and following with encouragement when it seemed too difficult to be completed. I would have probably given up without their support and example on what to do when you really want something.

Speaking of encouragement, I must mention that Jim Baker was responsible for having me on the team who wrote this book: first by mentoring me on Jython and later by insisting that I should share part of what I have learned on this book. He is a great person and I can only be grateful to have met him.

Thanks to Josh Juneau, our lead author. He coordinated our numerous team members and made sure we all were on the right track. He did that while also working on a lot of chapters and also handling the paperwork. I have no idea how he managed to do it. All I know is that he rocks.

Thanks to Duncan Parkes, our editor, and all the technical reviewers who worked on this book. Not only by catching mistakes but also by suggesting those additions that can seem obvious in hindsight but that would never have occurred to you.

On the first half of the Django chapter, I received a lot of help from Jacob Fenwick who discovered some problems on specific platforms and offered valuable suggestions to overcome them. Thanks to him, many readers won't experience the frustration caused when the code shown on the book doesn't work on their environment. By the way, while working on Django integration with Jython, I've met a lot of nice people in the Django community. Special thanks to Jacob Kaplan-Moss for his outstanding support when I was working on that area.

And thanks to the Jython community! Starting with our leader, Frank Wierzbicki, who has played a crucial role to move Jython forward in recent years. The core Jython developers are also really awesome people and I'm immensely happy to work with them on the project. And every person of the Jython community I've talked to has been nice and even when criticizing they know how to be constructive. I'm grateful to work with this community and hope their members will find this book useful!

Leo Soto

First and foremost, I want to thank my wife, Jill Fitzgibbons, for all of the support she has given through all of these years of Jython work. Most of that work occurred on weekends, nights, while on vacation, and other times inconvenient to my family. My daughter, Lily, who is five at the time of writing, has also needed to show patience when her dad was working on Jython and on this book. I want to thank my parents, who brought a Commodore 64 into the house when I was still impressionable enough to get sucked into a life of programming. I also want to thank all of the contributors and users of Jython. They make my work on Jython and this book worth doing.

Frank Wierzbicki

Introduction

Jython brings the power of the Python language to the JVM. It provides Java developers the ability to write productive and dynamic code using an elegant syntax. Likewise, it allows Python developers to harness the plethora of useful Java libraries and APIs that the JVM has to offer. We wrote this book in an effort to provide a complete guide for developers from both parties. Whether you are a seasoned Java developer looking to add a mature dynamic language to your arsenal, or a connoisseur of the Python language, this book provides useful information in an easy-to-read fashion, which will help you become a professional Jython developer.

This book is organized so that each chapter is encapsulated as its own entity and can be read separately from the others. This provides the ability to jump around the book if you'd like, or read it from start to finish. Some chapters contain references to other parts of the book and this book builds upon itself to guide a novice or a seasoned developer into becoming an expert Jython programmer. Since this is a multi-author book, each of the chapters was written by an individual author or a pair of authors, and because of this you may find that the chapters each contain a unique touch, but they are orchestrated in such a way that they work very well together.

Part I of this book will take a look at the Python language and provide a tutorial to guide you through learning the language from the ground up. It contains Python language basics, as well as Jython-specific portions for those who already know Python. Until now, using Jython in Java applications has not been very well documented. Part II addresses this topic, teaches you how to use Python and Java techniques for working with databases, and even shows how to develop Jython using both the Eclipse and Netbeans IDEs. The second part of the book is all about making use of Jython. Part III delves into developing full applications with Jython, deploying them in different environments, and also testing them to ensure stability. In this part, you'll learn how to use the Django and Pylons web frameworks to develop sophisticated web applications, and you'll also learn how to develop robust desktop applications using the Java Swing API along with Jython. Lastly, Part IV covers some concepts for making your application development more productive, and ensuring that your Jython code is efficient. You'll learn how to run tests against your Jython code and set up continuous integration using Hudson. Advanced threading and concurrency concepts are covered in Part IV to ensure that you have the knowledge to build Jython code that performs well and runs efficiently. In the end, this book is great to read from start to finish, but also very useful as a reference guide to using Jython with different technologies.

This book is available online under the Creative Commons Attribution Share-Alike license (http://creativecommons.org/licenses/by-sa/3.0/). You can read the open source book at http://jythonbook.com. I'd like to personally thank James Gardner, author of the *Definitive Guide to Pylons* from Apress, for assisting us in transforming our book into restructured text format, which is used to generate the Open Source online version.

Throughout the book, you will find a number of code examples. Many of the examples are Python code; however, there are also plenty of Java examples as well as those working with web markup languages. All code examples will be in the code font. The examples are available on the Apress website at http://www.apress.com as well as at the Open Source site http://jythonbook.com.

This book will continue to evolve and we will continually update both the online version and the printed copy. We'd like to thank members of the Jython community for contributing to the book, especially Andrea Aime and others who wrote to the mailing lists providing comments and feedback for book content. We would like to advocate that the community continues to stay involved with the book. If you would like to post comments or suggestions for the book or if you find errors, please submit them via apress.com.

Thanks for reading this book, and for developing with the Jython language. We had a great time working on this book and hope that you enjoy reading it just as much. We look forward to continually updating this book, and seeing what the future will hold for Jython. Surely if Jython remains as active as it is today, we will all enjoy it long into the future.

PART 1

■■■

Jython Basics: Learning the Language

CHAPTER 1

■■■

Language and Syntax

Elegant is an adjective that is often used to describe the Python language. The word elegant is defined as "pleasingly graceful and stylish in appearance or manner." *Uncomplicated* and *powerful* could also be great words to assist in the description of this language. It is a fact that Python is an elegant language that lets one create powerful applications in an uncomplicated manner. The ability to make reading and writing complex software easier is the objective of all programming languages, and Python does just that.

While we've easily defined the goal of programming languages in a broad sense in paragraph one, we have left out one main advantage of learning the Python programming language: Python has been extended to run on the Java platform, and so it can run anywhere with a JVM. There are also C and .NET versions of Python with multiplatform support. So, Python can run nearly everywhere. In this book, we focus on Jython, the language implementation that takes the elegance, power, and ease of Python and runs it on the JVM.

The Java platform is an asset to the Jython language much like the C libraries are for Python. Jython is able to run just about everywhere, which gives lots of flexibility when deciding how to implement an application. Not only does the Java platform allow for flexibility with regards to application deployment, but it also offers a vast library containing thousands of APIs that are available for use by Jython. Add in the maturity of the Java platform and it becomes easy to see why Jython is such an attractive programming language. The goal, if you will, of any programming language is to grant its developers the same experience that Jython does. Simply put, learning Jython will be an asset to any developer.

As I've mentioned, the Jython language implementation takes Python and runs it on the JVM, but it does much more than that. Once you have experienced the power of programming on the Java platform, it will be difficult to move away from it. Learning Jython not only allows you to run on the JVM, but it also allows you to learn a new way to harness the power of the platform. The language increases productivity as it has an easily understood syntax that reads almost as if it were pseudocode. It also adds dynamic abilities that are not available in the Java language itself.

In this chapter you will learn how to install and configure your environment, and you will also get an overview of those features that the Python language has to offer. This chapter is not intended to delve so deep into the concepts of syntax as to bore you, but rather to give you a quick and informative introduction to the syntax so that you will know the basics and learn the language as you move on through the book. It will also allow you the chance to compare some Java examples with those which are written in Python so you can see some of the advantages this language has to offer.

By the time you have completed this chapter, you should know the basic structure and organization that Python code should follow. You'll know how to use basic language concepts such as defining variables, using reserved words, and performing basic tasks. It will give you a taste of using statements and expressions. As every great program contains comments, you'll learn how to document single lines of code as well as entire code blocks. As you move through the book, you will use this chapter as a reference to the basics. This chapter will not cover each feature in completion, but it will give you enough basic knowledge to start using the Python language.

The Difference between Jython and Python

Jython is an implementation of the Python language for the Java platform. Throughout this book, you will be learning how to use the Python language, and along the way we will show you where the Jython implementation differs from CPython, which is the canonical implementation of Python written in the C language. It is important to note that the Python language syntax remains consistent throughout the different implementations. At the time of this writing, there are three mainstream implementations of Python. These implementations are: CPython, Jython for the Java platform, and IronPython for the .NET platform. At the time of this writing, CPython is the most prevalent of the implementations. Therefore if you see the word Python somewhere, it could well be referring to that implementation.

This book will reference the Python language in sections regarding the language syntax or functionality that is inherent to the language itself. However, the book will reference the name Jython when discussing functionality and techniques that are specific to the Java platform implementation. No doubt about it, this book will go in-depth to cover the key features of Jython and you'll learn concepts that only adhere the Jython implementation. Along the way, you will learn how to program in Python and advanced techniques.

Developers from all languages and backgrounds will benefit from this book. Whether you are interested in learning Python for the first time or discovering Jython techniques and advanced concepts, this book is a good fit. Java developers and those who are new to the Python language will find specific interest in reading through Part I of this book as it will teach the Python language from the basics to more advanced concepts. Seasoned Python developers will probably find more interest in Part II and Part III as they focus more on the Jython implementation specifics. Often in this reference, you will see Java code compared with Python code.

Installing and Configuring Jython

Before we delve into the basics of the language, we'll learn how to obtain Jython and configure it for your environment. To get started, you will need to obtain a copy of Jython from the official website www.jython.org. Because this book focuses on release 2.5.x, it would be best to visit the site now and download the most recent version of that release. You will see that there are previous releases that are available to you, but they do not contain many of the features which have been included in the 2.5.x series.

Jython implementation maintains consistent features which match those in the Python language for each version. For example, if you download the Jython 2.2.1 release, it will include all of the features that the Python 2.2 release contains. Similarly, when using the 2.5 release you will have access to the same features which are included in Python 2.5. There are also some extra pieces included with the 2.5 release which are specific to Jython. We'll discuss more about these extra features throughout the book.

Please grab a copy of the most recent version of the Jython 2.5 release. You will see that the release is packaged as a cross-platform executable JAR file. Right away, you can see the obvious advantage of running on the Java platform. . .one installer that works for various platforms. It doesn't get much easier than that! In order to install the Jython language, you will need to have Java 5 or greater installed on your machine. If you do not have Java 5 or greater then you'd better go and grab that from www.java.com and install it before trying to initiate the Jython installer.

You can initiate the Jython installer by simply double-clicking on the JAR file. It will run you through a series of standard installation questions. At one point you will need to determine which features you'd like to install. If you are interested in looking through the source code for Jython, or possibly developing code for the project then you should choose the "All" option to install everything. . .including source. However, for most Jython developers and especially for those who are just beginning to learn the language, I would recommend choosing the "Standard" installation option. Once you've chosen your options and supplied an installation path then you will be off to the races.

In order to run Jython, you will need to invoke the jython.bat executable file on Windows or the jython.sh file on *NIX machines and Mac OS X. That being said, you'll have to traverse into the directory that you've installed Jython where you will find the file. It would be best to place this directory within your PATH environment variable on either Windows, *NIX, or OS X machines so that you can fire up Jython from within any directory on your machine. Once you've done this then you should be able to open up a terminal or command prompt and type "jython" then hit enter to invoke the interactive interpreter. This is where our journey begins! The Jython interactive interpreter is a great place to evaluate code and learn the language. It is a real-time testing environment that allows you to type code and instantly see the result. As you are reading through this chapter, I recommend you open up the Jython interpreter and follow along with the code examples.

Identifiers and Declaring Variables

Every programming language needs to contain the ability to capture or calculate values and store them. Python is no exception, and doing so is quite easy. Defining variables in Python is very similar to other languages such as Java, but there are a few differences that you need to note.

To define a variable in the Python language, you simply name it using an identifier. An identifier is a name that is used to identify an object. The language treats the variable name as a label that points to a value. It does not give any type for the value. Therefore, this allows any variable to hold any type of data. It also allows the ability of having one variable contain of different data types throughout the life cycle of a program. So a variable that is originally assigned with an integer, can later contain a String. Identifiers in Python can consist of any ordering of letters, numbers, or underscores. However, an identifier must always begin with a non-numeric character value. We can use identifiers to name any type of variable, block, or object in Python. As with most other programming languages, once an identifier is defined, it can be referenced elsewhere in the program.

Once declared, a variable is untyped and can take any value. This is one difference between using a statically typed language such as Java, and using dynamic languages like Python. In Java, you need to declare the type of variable which you are creating, and you do not in Python. It may not sound like very much at first, but this ability can lead to some extraordinary results. Consider the following two listings, lets define a value 'x' below and we'll give it a value of zero.

Listing 1-1. Java – Declare Variable

```
int x = 0;
```

Listing 1-2. Python – Declare Variable

```
x = 0
```

As you see, we did not have to give a type to this variable. We simply choose a name and assign it a value. Since we do not need to declare a type for the variable, we can change it to a different value and type later in the program.

Listing 1-3.

```
x = 'Hello Jython'
```

We've just changed the value of the variable 'x' from a numeric value to a String without any consequences. What really occurred is that we created a new variable 'Hello Jython' and assigned it to the identifier 'x', which in turn lost its reference to 0. This is a key to the dynamic language philosophy. . .change should not be difficult.

Let us take what we know so far and apply it to some simple calculations. Based upon the definition of a variable in Python, we can assign an integer value to a variable, and change it to a float at a later point. For instance:

Listing 1-4.

```
>>> x = 6
>>> y = 3.14
>>> x = x * y
>>> print x
18.84
```

In the previous example, we've demonstrated that we can dynamically change the type of any given variable by simply performing a calculation upon it. In other languages such as Java, we would have had to begin by assigning a float type to the 'x' variable so that we could later change its value to a float. Not here, Python allows us to bypass type constriction and gives us an easy way to do it.

Reserved Words

There are a few more rules to creating identifiers that we must follow in order to adhere to the Python language standard. Certain words are not to be used as identifiers as the Python language reserves them for performing a specific role within our programs. These words which cannot be used are known as reserved words. If we try to use one of these reserved words as an identifier, we will see a SyntaxError thrown as Python wants these reserved words as its own.

There are no symbols allowed in identifiers. Yes, that means the Perl developers will have to get used to defining variables without the $.

Table 1-1 lists all of the Python language reserved words:

Table 1-1. Reserved Words

and	assert	break	class	continue
def	del	elif	else	except
exec	finally	for	from	global
or	pass	print	raise	return
try	while	with	yield	

It is important to take care when naming variables so that you do not choose a name that matches one of the module names from the standard library.

Coding Structure

Another key factor in which Python differs from other languages is its coding structure. Back in the day, we had to develop programs based upon a very strict structure such that certain pieces must begin and end within certain punctuations. Python uses indentation rather than punctuation to define the structure of code. Unlike languages such as Java that use brackets to open or close a code block, Python uses spacing as to make code easier to read and also limit unnecessary symbols in your code. It strictly enforces ordered and organized code but it lets the programmer define the rules for indentation, although a standard of four characters exists.

For instance, let's jump ahead and look at a simple 'if' statement. Although you may not yet be familiar with this construct, I think you will agree that it is easy to determine the outcome. Take a look at the following block of code written in Java first, and then we'll compare it to the Python equivalent.

Listing 1-5. Java if-statement

```java
x = 100;
if(x > 0){
    System.out.println("Wow, this is Java");
} else {
    System.out.println("Java likes curly braces");
}
```

Now, let's look at a similar block of code written in Python.

Listing 1-6. Python if-statement

```python
x = 100
if x > 0:
    print 'Wow, this is elegant'
else:
    print 'Organization is the key'
```

Okay, this is cheesy but we will go through it nonetheless as it is demonstrating a couple of key points to the Python language. As you see, the Python program evaluates if the value of the variable 'x' is greater than zero. If so, it will print 'Wow, this is elegant.' Otherwise, it will print 'Organization is the key.' Look at the indentation which is used within the 'if' block. This particular block of code uses four spaces to indent the 'print' statement from the initial line of the block. Likewise, the 'else' jumps back to the first space of the line and its corresponding implementation is also indented by four spaces. This technique must be adhered to throughout an entire Python application. By doing so, we gain a couple of major benefits: easy-to-read code and no need to use curly braces. Most other programming languages such as Java use a bracket "[" or curly brace "{" to open and close a block of code. There is no need to do so when using Python as the spacing takes care of this for you. Less code = easier to read and maintain. It is also worth noting that the Java code in the example could have been written on one line, or worse, but we chose to format it nicely.

Python ensures that each block of code adheres to its defined spacing strategy in a consistent manner. What is the defined spacing strategy? You decide. As long as the first line of a code block is out-dented by at least one space, the rest of the block can maintain a consistent indentation, which makes code easy to read. Many argue that it is the structuring technique that Python adheres to which makes them so easy to read. No doubt, adhering to a standard spacing throughout an application makes for organization. As mentioned previously, the Python standard spacing technique is to use four characters for indentation. If you adhere to these standards then your code will be easy to read and maintain in the future. Your brain seems hard-wired to adhering to some form of indentation, so Python and your brain are wired up the same way.

Operators

The operators that are used by Python are very similar to those used in other languages...straightforward and easy to use. As with any other language, you have your normal operators such as +, -, *, and /, which are available for performing calculations. As you can see from the following examples, there is no special trick to using any of these operators.

Listing 1-7. Performing Integer-based Operations

```
>>> x = 9
>>> y = 2
>>> x + y
11
>>> x - y
7
>>> x * y
18
>>> x / y
4
```

Perhaps the most important thing to note with calculations is that if you are performing calculations based on integer values then you will receive a rounded result. If you are performing calculations based upon floats then you will receive float results, and so on.

Listing 1-8. Performing Float-based Operations

```
>>> x = 9.0
>>> y = 2.0
>>> x + y
11.0
>>> x - y
7.0
>>> x * y
18.0
>>> x / y
4.5
```

It is important to note this distinction because as you can see from the differences in the results of the division (/) operations in Listings 1-7 and 1-8, we have rounding on the integer values and not on the float. A good rule of thumb is that if your application requires precise calculations to be defined, then it is best to use float values for all of your numeric variables, or else you will run into a rounding issue. In Python 2.5 and earlier, integer division always rounds down, producing the floor as the result. In Python 2.2, the // operator was introduced which is another way to obtain the floor result when dividing integers or floats. This operator was introduced as a segue way for changing integer division in future releases so that the result would be a *true* division. In Chapter 3, we'll discuss division using a technique that always performs *true* division.

Expressions

Expressions are just what they sound like. They are a piece of Python code that can be evaluated and produces a value. Expressions are not instructions to the interpreter, but rather a combination of values and operators that are evaluated. If we wish to perform a calculation based upon two variables or numeric values then we are producing an expression.

Listing 1-9. Examples of Expressions

```
>>> x + y
>>> x - y
>>> x * y
>>> x / y
```

The examples of expressions that are shown above are very simplistic. Expressions can be made to be very complex and perform powerful computations. They can be combined together to produce complex results.

Functions

Oftentimes it is nice to take suites of code that perform specific tasks and extract them into their own unit of functionality so that the code can be reused in numerous places without retyping each time. A common way to define a reusable piece of code is to create a function. Functions are named portions of code that perform that usually perform one or more tasks and return a value. In order to define a function we use the *def* statement.

The *def* statement will become second nature for usage throughout any Python programmer's life. The *def* statement is used to define a function. Here is a simple piece of pseudocode that shows how to use it.

Listing 1-10.

```
def my_function_name(parameter_list):
    implementation
```

The pseudocode above demonstrates how one would use the *def* statement, and how to construct a simple function. As you can see, *def* precedes the function name and parameter list when defining a function.

Listing 1-11.

```
>>> def my_simple_function():
...     print 'This is a really basic function'
...
>>> my_simple_function()
This is a really basic function
```

This example is about the most basic form of function that can be created. As you can see, the function contains one line of code which is a print statement. We will discuss the print statement in more detail later in this chapter; however, all you need to know now is that it is used to print some text to the screen. In this case, we print a simple message whenever the function is called.

Functions can accept parameters, or other program variables, that can be used within the context of the function to perform some task and return a value.

Listing 1-12.

```
>>> def multiply_nums(x, y):
...     return x * y
...
>>> multiply_nums(25, 7)
175
```

As seen above, parameters are simply variables that are assigned when the function is called. Specifically, we assign 25 to x and 7 to y in the example. The function then takes x and y, performs a calculation and returns the result.

Functions in Python are just like other variables and they be passed around as parameters to other functions if needed. Here we show a basic example of passing one function to another function. We'll pass the *multiply_nums* function into the function below and then use it to perform some calculations.

Listing 1-13.

```
>>> def perform_math(oper):
...     return oper(5, 6)
...
>>> perform_math(multiply_nums)
30
```

Although this example is very basic, you can see that another function can be passed as a parameter and then used within another function. For more detail on using *def* and functions, please take a look at Chapter 4, which is all about functions.

Classes

Python is an object-oriented programming language. which means that everything in the language is an object of some type. Much like building blocks are used for constructing buildings, each object in Python can be put together to build pieces of programs or entire programs. This section will give you a brief introduction to Python classes, which are one of the keys to object orientation in this language.

Classes are defined using the *class* keyword. Classes can contain functions, methods, and variables. Methods are just like functions in that the *def* keyword is used to create them, and they accept parameters. The only difference is that methods take a parameter known as *self* that refers to the object to which the method belongs. Classes contain what is known as an initializer method, and it is called automatically when a class is instantiated. Let's take a look at a simple example and then explain it.

Listing 1-14. Simple Python Class

```
>>> class my_object:
...     def __init__(self, x, y):
...         self.x = x
...         self.y = y
...
...     def mult(self):
...         print self.x * self.y
...
...     def add(self):
...         print self.x + self.y
...
>>> obj1 = my_object(7, 8)
>>> obj1.mult()
56
>>> obj1.add()
15
```

In this class example, we define a class named *my_object*. The class accepts two parameters, *x* and *y*. A class initializer method is named *__init__()*, and it is used to initialize any values that may be used in the class. An initializer also defines what values can be passed to a class in order to create an object. You can see that each method and function within the class accepts the *self* argument. The *self* argument is used to refer to the object itself, this is how the class shares variables and such. The *self* keyword is similar to *this* in Java code. The *x* and *y* variables in the example are named *self.x* and *self.y* in the initializer, that means that they will be available for use throughout the entire class. While working with code within the object, you can refer to these variables as *self.x* and *self.y*. If you create the object and assign a name to it such as *obj1*, then you can refer to these same variables as *obj1.x* and *obj1.y*.

As you can see, the class is called by passing the values 7 and 8 to it. These values are then assigned to *x* and *y* within the class initializer method. We assign the class object to an identifier that we call *obj1*. The *obj1* identifier now holds a reference to *my_object()* with the values we've passed it. The *obj1* identifier can now be used to call methods and functions that are defined within the class.

For more information on classes, please see Chapter 6, which covers object orientation in Python. Classes are very powerful and the fundamental building blocks for making larger programs.

Statements

When we refer to statements, we are really referring to a line of code that contains an instruction that does something. A statement tells the Python interpreter to perform a task. Ultimately, programs are made up of a combination of expressions and statements. In this section, we will take a tour of statement keywords and learn how they can be used.

Let's start out by listing each of these different statement keywords, and then we will go into more detail about how to use each of them with different examples. I will not cover every statement keyword in this section as some of them are better left for later in the chapter or the book, but you should have a good idea of how to code an action which performs a task after reading through this section. While this section will provide implementation details about the different statements, you should refer to later chapters to find advanced uses of these features.

Table 1-2. Statement Keywords

if-elif-else	for
while	continue
break	try-except-finally
assert	def
print	del
raise	import

Now that we've taken a look at each of these keywords, it is time to look at each of them in detail. It is important to remember that you cannot use any of these keywords for variable names.

if-elif-else Statement

The if statement simply performs an evaluation on an expression and does different things depending on whether it is *True* or *False*. If the expression evaluates to *True* then one set of statements will be executed, and if it evaluates to *False* a different set of statements will be executed. If statements are quite often used for branching code into one direction or another based upon certain values which have been calculated or provided in the code.

Pseudocode would be as follows:

Listing 1-15.

```
if <an expression to test>:
    perform an action
else:
    perform a different action
```

Any number of *if/else* statements can be linked together in order to create a logical code branch. When there are multiple expressions to be evaluated in the same statement, then the *elif* statement can be used to link these expressions together. Note that each set of statements within an *if-elif*-else statement must be indented with the conditional statement out-dented and the resulting set of statements indented. Remember, a consistent indentation must be followed throughout the course of the program. The *if* statement is a good example of how well the consistent use of indention helps readability of a program. If you are coding in Java for example, you can space the code however you'd like as long as you use the curly braces to enclose the statement. This can lead to code that is very hard to read…the indentation which Python requires really shines through here.

Listing 1-16. Example of if statement

```
>>> x = 3
>>> y = 2
>>> if x == y:
...     print 'x is equal to y'
... elif x > y:
...     print 'x is greater than y'
... else:
...     print 'x is less than y'
...
x is greater than y
```

While the code is simple, it demonstrates that using an *if* statement can result in branching code logic.

print Statement

The *print* statement is used to display program output onto the screen (you've already seen it in action several times). It can be used for displaying messages, which are printed from within a program, and also for printing values, which may have been calculated. In order to display variable values within a print statement, we need to learn how to use some of the formatting options that are available to Python. This section will cover the basics of using the print statement along with how to display values by formatting your strings of text.

In the Java language, we need to make a call to the System library in order to print something to the command line. In Python, this can be done with the use of the *print* statement. The most basic use of the *print* statement is to display a line of text. In order to do so, you simply enclose the text that you want to display within single or double quotes. Take a look at the following example written in Java, and compare it to the example immediately following which is rewritten in Python. I think you'll see why the *print* statement in Python makes life a bit easier.

Listing 1-17. Java Print Output Example

```
System.out.println("This text will be printed to the command line");
```

Listing 1-18. Python Print Output Example

```
print 'This text will be printed to the command line'
```

As you can see from this example, printing a line of text in Python is very straightforward. We can also print variable values to the screen using the *print* statement.

Listing 1-19.

```
>>> my_value = 'I love programming in Jython'
>>> print my_value
I love programming in Jython
```

Once again, very straightforward in terms of printing values of variables. Simply place the variable within a print statement. We can also use this technique in order to append the values of variables to a line of text. In order to do so, just place the concatenation operator (+) in between the String of text which you would like to append to, and the variable you'd like to append.

Listing 1-20.

```
>>> print 'I like programming in Java, but ' + my_value
I like programming in Java, but I love programming in Jython
```

This is great and all, but really not useful if you'd like to properly format your text or work with *int* values. After all, the Python parser is treating the (+) operator as a concatenation operator in this case...not as an addition operator. Python bases the result of the (+) operator on the type of the first operand. If you try to append a numeric value to a String you will end up with an error.

Listing 1-21.

```
>>> z = 10
>>> print 'I am a fan of the number: ' + z
Traceback (most recent call last):
  File "<stdin>", line 1, in <module>
TypeError: cannot concatenate 'str' and 'int' objects
```

As you can see from this example, Python does not like this trick very much. So in order to perform this task correctly we will need to use some of the aforementioned Python formatting options. This is easy and powerful to do, and it allows one to place any content or value into a print statement. Before you see an example, let's take a look at some of the formatting operators and how to choose the one that you need.

- %s - String

- %d - Decimal

- %f - Float

If you wish to include the contents of a variable or the result of an expression in your *print* statement, you'll use the following syntax:

Listing 1-22.

```
print 'String of text goes here %d %s %f' % (decimalValue, stringValue, floatValue)
```

In the pseudocode above (if we can really have pseudocode for print statements), we wish to print the string of text, which is contained within the single quotes, but also have the values of the variables contained where the formatting operators are located. Each of the formatting operators, which are included in the string of text, will be replaced with the corresponding values from those variables at the end of the print statement. The % symbol between the line of text and the list of variables tells Python that it should expect the variables to follow, and that the value of these variables should be placed within the string of text in their corresponding positions.

Listing 1-23.

```
>>> string_value = 'hello world'
>>> float_value = 3.998
>>> decimal_value = 5
>>> print 'Here is a test of the print statement using the values: %d, %s, and %f' %
(decimal_value, string_value, float_value)
Here is a test of the print statement using the values: 5, hello world, and 3.998000
```

As you can see this is quite easy to use and very flexible. The next example shows that we also have the option of using expressions as opposed to variables within our statement.

Listing 1-24.

```
>>> x = 1
>>> y = 2
>>> print 'The value of x + y is: %d' % (x + y)
The value of x + y is: 3
```

The formatting operator that is used determines how the output looks, it does not matter what type of input is passed to the operator. For instance, we could pass an integer or float to %s and it would print just fine, but it will in effect be turned into a string in its exact format. If we pass an integer or float to %d or %f, it will be formatted properly to represent a decimal or float respectively. Take a look at the following example to see the output for each of the different formatting operators.

Listing 1-25.

```
>>> x = 2.3456
>>> print '%s' % x
2.3456
>>> print '%d' % x
2
>>> print '%f' % x
2.345600
```

Another useful feature of the print statement is that it can be used for debugging purposes. If we simply need to find out the value of a variable during processing then it is easy to display using the *print* statement. Using this technique can often really assist in debugging and writing your code.

try-except-finally

The *try-except-finally* is the supported method for performing error handling within a Python application. The idea is that we try to run a piece of code and if it fails then it is caught and the error is handled in a proper fashion. We all know that if someone is using a program that displays an ugly long error message, it is not usually appreciated. Using the *try-except-finally* statement to properly catch and handle our errors can mitigate an ugly program dump.

This approach is the same concept that is used within many languages, including Java. There are a number of defined *error types* within the Python programming language and we can leverage these error types in order to facilitate the *try-except-finally* process. When one of the defined error types is caught, then a suite of code can be coded for handling the error, or can simply be logged, ignored, and so on.

The main idea is to avoid those ugly error messages and handle them neatly by displaying a formatted error message or performing another process.

Listing 1-26.

```
>>> # Suppose we've calculated a value and assigned it to x
>>> x
8.97
>>> y = 0
>>> try:
...     print 'The rocket trajectory is: %f' % (x/y)
... except:
...     print 'Houston, we have a problem.
...
Houston, we have a problem.
```

If there is an exception that is caught within the block of code and we need a way to perform some cleanup tasks, we would place the cleanup code within the *finally* clause of the block. All code within the *finally* clause is always invoked before the exception is raised. The details of this topic can be read about more in Chapter 7. In the next section, we'll take a look at the raise statement, which we can use to raise exceptions at any point in our program.

raise Statement

As mentioned in the previous section, the *raise* statement is used to throw or "raise" an exception in Python. We know that a *try*-except clause is needed if Python decides to raise an exception, but what if you'd like to raise an exception of your own? You can place a *raise* statement anywhere that you wish to raise a specified exception. There are a number of defined exceptions within the language which can be raised. For instance, NameError is raised when a specific piece of code is undefined or has no name. For a complete list of exceptions in Python, please visit Chapter 7.

Listing 1-27.

```
>>> raise NameError
Traceback (most recent call last):
  File "<stdin>", line 1, in <module>
NameError
```

If you wish to specify your own message within a *raise* then you can do so by raising a generic Exception, and then specifying your message on the statement as follows.

Listing 1-28.

```
>>> raise Exception('Custom Exception')
Traceback (most recent call last):
  File "<stdin>", line 1, in <module>
Exception: Custom Exception
```

import Statement

A program can be made up of one or more suites of code. In order to save a program so that it can be used later, we place the code into files on our computer. Files that contain Python code should contain a *.py* suffix such as my_code.py and so forth. These files are known as modules in the Python world. The *import* statement is used much like it is in other languages, it brings external modules or code into a program so that it can be used. This statement is ultimately responsible for reuse of code in multiple locations. The *import* statement allows us to save code into a flat file or script, and then use it in an application at a later time.

If a class is stored in an external module that is named the same as the class itself, the *import* statement can be used to explicitly bring that class into an application. Similarly, if you wish to import only a specific identifier from another module into your current module, then the specific code can be named within using the syntax *from <<module>> import <<specific code>>*. Time to see some examples.

Listing 1-29.

```
#  Import a module named TipCalculator
import TipCalculator

#  Import a function tipCalculator from within a module called ExternalModule.py

from ExternalModule import tipCalculator
```

When importing modules into your program, you must ensure that the module being imported does not conflict with another name in your current program. To import a module that is named the same as another identifier in your current program, you can use the *as* syntax. In the following example, let's assume that we have defined an external module with the name of *tipCalculator.py* and we want to use it's functionality in our current program. However, we already have a function named *tipCalculator()* within the current program. Therefore, we use the *as* syntax to refer to the *tipCalculator* module.

Listing 1-30.

```
import tipCalculator as tip
```

This section just touches the surface of importing and working with external modules. For a more detailed discussion, please visit Chapter 7 which covers this topic specifically.

Iteration

The Python language has several iteration structures which are used to traverse through a series of items in a list, database records, or any other type of collection. A list in Python is a container that holds objects or values and can be indexed. For instance, we create a list of numbers in the following example. We then obtain the second element in the list by using the index value of 1 (indexing starts at zero, so the first element of the list is my_numbers[0]).

Listing 1-31.

```
>>> my_numbers = [1, 2, 3, 4, 5]
>>> my_numbers
[1, 2, 3, 4, 5]
>>> my_numbers[1]
2
```

For more information on lists, please see Chapter 2 that goes into detail about lists and other containers that can be used in Python.

The most commonly used iteration structure within the language is probably the *for* loop, which is known for its easy syntax and practical usage.

Listing 1-32.

```
>>> for value in my_numbers:
...     print value
...
1
2
3
4
5
```

However, the *while* loop still plays an important role in iteration, especially when you are not dealing with collections of data, but rather working with conditional expressions. In this simple example, we use a *while* loop to iterate over the contents of *my_numbers*. Note that the *len()* function just returns the number of elements that are contained in the list.

Listing 1-33.

```
>>> x = 0
>>> while x < len(my_numbers):
...     print my_numbers[x]
...     x = x + 1
...
1
2
3
4
5
```

This section will take you though each of these two iteration structures and touch upon the basics of using them. The *while* loop is relatively basic in usage, whereas there are many different implementations and choices when using the *for* loop. I will only touch upon the *for* loop from a high-level perspective in this introductory chapter, but if you wish to go more in-depth then please visit Chapter 3.

While Loop

The *while* loop construct is used in order to iterate through code based upon a provided conditional statement. As long as the condition is true, then the loop will continue to process. Once the condition evaluates to false, the looping ends. The pseudocode for *while* loop logic reads as follows:

```
while True
    perform operation
```

The loop begins with the declaration of the *while* and conditional expression, and it ends once the conditional has been met and the expression is *True*. The expression is checked at the beginning of each looping sequence, so normally some value that is contained within the expression is changed within the suite of statements inside the loop. Eventually the value is changed in such a way that it makes the expression evaluate to False, otherwise an infinite loop would occur. Keep in mind that we need to indent each of the lines of code that exist within the *while* loop. This not only helps the code to maintain readability, but it also allows Python to do away with the curly braces!

Listing 1-34. Example of a Java While Loop

```java
int x = 9;
int y = 2;
int z = x - y;
while (y < x){
    System.out.println("y is " + z + " less than x");
    y = y++;
}
```

Now, let's see the same code written in Python.

Listing 1-35. Example of a Python While Loop

```python
>>> x = 9
>>> y = 2
>>> while y < x:
...     print 'y is %d less than x' % (x-y)
...     y += 1
...
y is 7 less than x
y is 6 less than x
y is 5 less than x
y is 4 less than x
y is 3 less than x
y is 2 less than x
y is 1 less than x
```

In this example, you can see that the conditional $y < x$ is evaluated each time the loop passes. Along the way, we increment the value of y by one each time we iterate, so that eventually y is no longer less than x and the loop ends.

For Loop

We will lightly touch upon *for* loops in this chapter, but you can delve deeper into the topic in chapter two or three when lists, dictionaries, tuples, and ranges are discussed. For now, you should know that a *for* loop is used to iterate through a defined set of values. The *for* loop is very useful for performing iteration through values because this is a concept which is used in just about any application. For instance, if you retrieve a list of database values, you can use a *for* loop to iterate through them and print each one out.

The pseudocode to *for* loop logic is as follows:

```
for each value in this defined set:
    perform suite of operations
```

As you can see with the pseudocode, I've indented in a similar fashion to the way in which the other expression constructs are indented. This uniform indentation practice is consistent throughout the Python programming language. We'll compare the *for* loop in Java to the Python syntax below so that you can see how the latter makes code more concise.

Listing 1-36. Example of Java For Loop

```java
for (x = 0; x <= 10; x++){
    System.out.println(x);
}
```

Now, the same code implemented in Python:

Listing 1-37. Example of Python For Loop

```python
>>> for x in range(10):
...     print x
...
0
1
2
3
4
5
6
7
8
9
```

In this example, we use a construct which has not yet been discussed. A range is a built-in function for Python which simply provides a range from one particular value to another. In the example, we pass the value 10 into the range which gives us all values between 0 and 10, inclusive of the zero at the front and exclusive at the end. We see this in the resulting print out after the expression.

Basic Keyboard Input

The Python language has a couple of built-in functions to take input from the keyboard as to facilitate the process of writing applications that allow user input. Namely, *raw_input()*, and *input()* can be used to prompt and accept user input from the command-line. Not only is this useful for creating command-line applications and scripts, but it also comes in handy for writing small tests into your applications.

The *raw_input()* function accepts keyboard entry and converts it to a string, stripping the trailing newline character. Similarly, the *input()* function accepts keyboard entry as *raw_input()*, but it then evaluates it as an expression. The *input()* function should be used with caution as it expects a valid Python expression to be entered. It will raise a *SyntaxError* if this is not the case. Using *input()* could result in a security concern as it basically allows your user to run arbitrary Python code at will. It is best to steer clear of using *input()* in most cases and just stick to using raw_input. Let's take a look at using each of these functions in some basic examples.

Listing 1-38. Using raw_input() and input()

```
# The text within the function is optional, and it is used as a prompt to the user
>>> name = raw_input("Enter Your Name:")
Enter Your Name:Josh
>>> print name
Josh

# Use the input function to evaluate an expression entered in by the user
>>> val = input ('Please provide an expression: ')
Please provide an expression: 9 * 3
>>> val
27

# The input function raises an error if an expression is not provided
>>> val = input ('Please provide an expression: ')
Please provide an expression: My Name is Josh
Traceback (most recent call last):
  File "<stdin>", line 1, in <module>
  File "<string>", line 1
    My Name is Josh
           ^
SyntaxError: invalid syntax
```

There will be examples provided later in the book for different ways of using the *raw_input()* function. Now let's take a look at some of the other Python statements that have not yet been covered in this chapter.

Other Python Statements

There are some other Python statements that can be used within applications as well, but they are probably better meant to be discussed within a later chapter as they provide more advanced functionality. The following is a listing of other Python statements which you will read more about later on:

exec—Execute Python code in a dynamic fashion

global—References a variable a global (Chapter 4)

with—New feature in 2.5 using __future__

class—Create or define a new class object (Chapter 6)

yield—Used with generators, returns a value (Chapter 4)

Documenting Code

Code documentation: an annoyingly important part of every application developer's life. Although many of us despise code documentation, it must exist for any application that is going to be used for production purposes. Not only is proper code documentation a must for manageability and long-term understanding of Python code fragments, but it also plays an important role in debugging some code as we will see in some examples below.

Sometimes we wish to document an entire function or class, and other times we wish to document only a line or two. Whatever the case, Python provides a way to do it in a rather unobtrusive manner. Much like many of the other programming languages that exist today, we can begin a comment on any part of any code line. We can also comment spanning multiple lines if we wish. Just on a personal note, we rather like the Python documentation symbol (#) or hash, as it provides for clear-cut readability. There are not many places in code that you will use the (#) symbol unless you are trying to perform some documentation. Many other languages use symbols such as (/) which can make code harder to read as those symbols are evident in many other non-documenting pieces of code. Okay, it is time to get off my soap box on Python and get down to business.

In order to document a line of code, you simply start the document or comment with a (#) symbol. This symbol can be placed anywhere on the line and whatever follows it is ignored by the Python compiler and treated as a comment or documentation. Whatever precedes the symbol will be parsed as expected.

Listing 1-39.

```
>>> # This is a line of documentation
>>> x = 0  # This is also documentation
>>> y = 20
>>> print x + y
20
```

As you can see, the Python parser ignores everything after the #, so we can easily document or comment as needed.

One can easily document multiple lines of code using the # symbol as well by placing the hash at the start of each line. It nicely marks a particular block as documentation. However, Python also provides a multi-line comment using the triple-quote ("') designation at the beginning and end of a comment. This type of multi-line comment is also referred to as a doc string and it is only to be used at the start of a module, class, or function. While string literals can be placed elsewhere in code, they will not be treated as docstrings unless used at the start of the code. Let's take a look at these two instances of multi-line documentation in the examples that follow.

Listing 1-40. Multiple Lines of Documentation Beginning With #

```
# This function is used in order to provide the square
# of any value which is passed in.  The result will be
# passed back to the calling code.
def square_val(value):
    return value * value
...
>>> print square_val(3)
9
```

Listing 1-41. Multiple Lines of Documentation Enclosed in Triple Quotes (''')

```
def tip_calc(value, pct):
    ''' This function is used as a tip calculator based on a percentage
        which is passed in as well as the value of the total amount.  In
        this function, the first parameter is to be the total amount of a
        bill for which we will calculate the tip based upon the second
        parameter as a percentage '''
    return value * (pct * .01)
...
>>> print tip_calc(75,15)
11.25
```

Okay, as we can see, both of these documentation methods can be used to get the task of documenting or comment code done. In Listing 1-40, we used multiple lines of documentation beginning with the # symbol in order to document the *square_val* function. In Listing 1-41, we use the triple-quote method in order to span multiple lines of documentation. Both of them appear to work as defined. However, the second option provides a greater purpose as it allows one to document specific named code blocks and retrieve that documentation by calling the *help(function)* function. For instance, if we wish to find out what the *square_val* code does, we need to visit the code and either read the multi-line comment or simply parse the code. However, if we wish to find out what the tip_calc function does, we can call the help(tip_calc) function and the multi-line comment will be returned to us. This provides a great tool to use for finding out what code does without actually visiting the code itself.

Listing 1-42. Printing the Documentation for the tip_calc Function

```
>>> help(tip_calc)
Help on function tip_calc in module __main__:

tip_calc(value, pct)
    This function is used as a tip calculator based on a percentage
    which is passed in as well as the value of the total amount.  In
    this function, the first parameter is to be the total amount of a
    bill for which we will calculate the tip based upon the second

    parameter as a percentage
```

These examples and short explanations should give you a pretty good feel for the power of documentation that is provided by the Python language. As you can see, using the multi-line triple-quote method is very suitable for documenting classes or functions. Commenting with the # symbol provides a great way to organize comments within source and also for documenting those lines of code which may be "not so easy" to understand.

Python Help

Getting help when using the Jython interpreter is quite easy. Built into the interactive interpreter is an excellent *help()* option which provides information on any module, keyword, or topic available to the Python language. By calling the *help()* function without passing in the name of a function, the Python help system is invoked. While making use of the *help()* system, you can either use the interactive help which is invoked within the interpreter by simply typing *help()*, or as we have seen previously you can obtain the docstring for a specific object by typing *help(object)*.

It should be noted that while using the help system in the interactive mode, there is a plethora of information available at your fingertips. If you would like to see for yourself, simply start the Jython interactive interpreter and type *help()*. After you are inside the interactive help, you can exit at any time by typing *quit*. In order to obtain a listing of modules, keywords, or topics you just type either "*modules*," "*keywords*," or "*topics*", and you will be provided with a complete listing. You will also receive help for using the interactive help system. . .or maybe this should be referred to as *meta-help*!

Although the Jython interactive help system is great, you may still need further assistance. There are a large number of books published on the Python language that will be sure to help you out. Make sure that you are referencing a book that provides you with information for the specific Python release that you are using as each version contains some differences. As mentioned previously in the chapter, the Jython version number contains is consistent with its CPython counterpart. Therefore, each feature that is available within CPython 2.5, for instance, should be available within Jython 2.5 and so on.

Summary

This chapter has covered lots of basic Python programming material. It should have provided a basic foundation for the fundamentals of programming in Python. This chapter shall be used to reflect upon while delving deeper into the language throughout the remainder of this book.

We began by discussing some of the differences between CPython and Jython. There are many good reasons to run Python on the JVM, including the availability of great Java libraries and excellent deployment targets. Once we learned how to install and configure Jython, we dove into the Python language. We learned about the declaration of variables and explained the dynamic tendencies of the language. We then went on to present the reserved words of the language and then discussed the coding structure which must be adhered to when developing a Python application. After that, we discussed operators and expressions. We learned that expressions are generally pieces of code that are evaluated to produce a value. We took a brief tour of Python functions as to cover their basic syntax and usage. Functions are a fundamental part of the language and most Python developers use functions in every program. A short section introducing classes followed, it is important to know the basics of classes early even though there is much more to learn in Chapter 6. We took a look at statements and learned that they consist of instructions that allow us to perform different tasks within our applications. Each of the Python statements were discussed and examples were given. Iteration constructs were then discussed so that we could begin to use our statements and program looping tasks.

Following the language overview, we took a brief look at using keyboard input. This is a feature for many programs, and it is important to know for building basic programs. We then learned a bit about documentation, it is an important part of any application and Python makes it easy to do. Not only did we learn how to document lines of code, but also documenting entire modules, functions and classes. We touched briefly on the Python help() system as it can be a handy feature to use while learning the language. It can also be useful for advanced programmers who need to look up a topic that they may be a bit rusty on.

Throughout the rest of the book, you will learn more in-depth and advanced uses of the topics that we've discussed in this chapter. You will also learn concepts and techniques that you'll be able to utilize in your own programs to make them more powerful and easy to maintain.

CHAPTER 2

■■■

Data Types and Referencing

Programming languages and applications need data. We define applications to work with data, and we need to have containers that can be used to hold it. This chapter is all about defining containers and using them to work with application data. Whether the data we are using is coming from a keyboard entry or if we are working with a database, there needs to be a way to temporarily store it in our programs so that it can be manipulated and used. Once we're done working with the data then these temporary containers can be destroyed in order to make room for new constructs.

We'll start by taking a look at the different data types that are offered by the Python language, and then we'll follow by discussing how to use that data once it has been collected and stored. We will compare and contrast the different types of structures that we have in our arsenal, and we'll give some examples of which structures to use for working with different types of data. There are a multitude of tasks that can be accomplished through the use of lists, dictionaries, and tuples and we will try to cover many of them. Once you learn how to define and use these structures, then we'll talk a bit about what happens to them once they are no longer needed by our application.

Let's begin our journey into exploring data types and structures within the Python programming language. . .these are skills that you will use in each and every practical Jython program.

Python Data Types

As we've discussed, there is a need to store and manipulate data within programs. In order to do so then we must also have the ability to create containers used to hold that data so that the program can use it. The language needs to know how to handle data once it is stored, and we can do that by assigning data type to our containers in Java. However, in Python it is not a requirement to do so because the interpreter is able to determine which type of data we are storing in a dynamic fashion.

Table 2-1 lists each data type and gives a brief description of the characteristics that define each of them.

Table 2-1. Python Data Types

Data Type	Characteristics
None	NULL value object
int	Plain integer (e.g., 32)
long	Long integer. Integer literal with an 'L' suffix, too long to be a plain integer

Table 2-1. *Python Data Types (continued)*

Data Type	Characteristics
float	Floating-point number. Numeric literal containing decimal or exponent sign
complex	Complex number. Expressed as a sum of a numeric literal with a real and imaginary part
Boolean	True or False value (also characterized as numeric values of 1 and 0 respectively)
Sequence	Includes the following types: string, unicode string, basestring, list, tuple
Mapping	Includes the dictionary type
Set	Unordered collection of distinct objects; includes the following types: set, frozenset
File	Used to make use of file system objects
Iterator	Allows for iteration over a container. See section on Iterators for more details

Given all of that information and the example above, we should officially discuss how to declare a variable in the Python language. Let's take a look at some examples of defining variables in the following lines of code.

Listing 2-1. Defining Variables in Jython

```
# Defining a String
x = 'Hello World'
x = "Hello World Two"

#  Defining an integer
y = 10

#  Float
z = 8.75

# Complex
i = 1 + 8.07j
```

An important point to note is that there really are no types in Jython. Every object is an instance of a class. In order to find the type of an object, simply use the *type()* function.

Listing 2-2.

```
# Return the type of an object using the type function
>>> i = 1 + 8.07j
>>> type(i)
<type 'complex'>
```

```
>>> a = 'Hello'
>>> type(a)
<type 'str'>
```

A nice feature to note is multiple assignment. Quite often it is necessary to assign a number of values to different variables. Using multiple assignment in Python, it is possible to do this in one line.

Listing 2-3. Multiple Assignment

```
>>> x, y, z = 1, 2, 3
>>> print x
1
>>> print z
3
>>>
```

Strings and String Methods

Strings are a special type within most programming languages because they are often used to manipulate data. A string in Python is a sequence of characters, which is immutable. An immutable object is one that cannot be changed after it is created. The opposite would be a mutable object, which can be altered after creation. This is very important to know as it has a large impact on the overall understanding of strings. However, there are quite a few string methods that can be used to manipulate the contents of a particular string. We never actually manipulate the contents though, these methods return a manipulated copy of the string. The original string is left unchanged.

Prior to the release of Jython 2.5.0, CPython and Jython treated strings a bit differently. There are two types of string objects in CPython, these are known as *Standard* strings and *Unicode* strings. There is a lot of documentation available that specifically focuses on the differences between the two types of strings, this reference will only cover the basics. It is worth noting that Python contains an abstract string type known as *basestring* so that it is possible to check any type of string to ensure that it is a string instance.

Prior to the release of Jython 2.5.0 there was only one string type. The string type in Jython supported full two-byte Unicode characters and all functions contained in the string module were Unicode-aware. If the u'' string modifier is specified, it is ignored by Jython. Since the release of 2.5.0, strings in Jython are treated just like those in CPython, so the same rules will apply to both implementations. If you are interested in learning more about String encoding, there are many great references available on the topic. It is also worth noting that Jython uses character methods from the Java platform. Therefore properties such as isupper and islower, which we will discuss later in the section, are based upon the Java methods, although they actually work the same way as their CPython counterparts

In the remainder of this section, we will go through each of the many string functions that are at our disposal. These functions will work on both Standard and Unicode strings. As with many of the other features in Python and other programming languages, at times there is more than one way to accomplish a task. In the case of strings and string manipulation, this holds true. However, you will find that in most cases, although there are more than one way to do things, Python experts have added functions which allow us to achieve better performing and easier to read code.

Table 2-2 lists all of the string methods that have been built into the Python language as of the 2.5 release. Because Python is an evolving language, this list is sure to change in future releases. Most often, additions to the language will be made, or existing features are enhanced. Following the table, we will give numerous examples of the methods and how they are used. Although we cannot provide an example of how each of these methods work (that would be a book in itself), they all function in the same manner so it should be rather easy to pick up.

Table 2-2. String Methods

Method	Description of Functionality
capitalize()	Returns a capitalized copy of string
center (width[,fill])	Returns a repositioned string with specified width and provide optional padding filler character
count(sub[,start[,end]])	Count the number of distinct times the substring occurs within the string
decode([encoding[,errors]])	Decodes and returns Unicode string
encode([encoding[,errors]])	Returns an encoded version of a string
endswith(suffix[,start[,end]])	Returns a boolean to state whether the string ends in a given pattern
expandtabs([tabsize])	Converts tabs within a string into spaces
find(sub[,start[,end]])	Returns the index of the position where the first occurrence of the given substring begins
index(sub[,start[,end]])	Returns the index of the position where the first occurrence of the given substring begins. Raises a *ValueError* with the substring is not found.
isalnum()	Returns a boolean to state whether the string contain only alphabetic and numeric characters
isalpha()	Returns a boolean to state whether the string contains all alphabetic characters
isdigit()	Returns a boolean to state whether the string contains all numeric characters
islower()	Returns a boolean to state whether a string contains all lowercase characters
isspace()	Returns a boolean to state whether the string consists of all whitespace
istitle()	Returns a boolean to state whether the first character of each word in the string is capitalized
isupper()	Returns a boolean to state whether all characters within the string are uppercase

Table 2-2. String Methods (continued)

Method	Description of Functionality
join(sequence)	Returns a copy of sequence joined together with the original string placed between each element
ljust(width[,fillchar])	Returns a string of the specified width along with a copy of the original string at the leftmost bit. (Optionally padding empty space with fillchar)
lower()	Returns a copy of the original string with all characters in the string converted to lowercase
lstrip([chars])	Removes the first found characters in the string from the left that match the given characters. Also removes whitespace from the left. Whitespace removal is default when specified with no arguments.
partition(separator)	Returns a partitioned string starting from the left using the provided separator
replace(old,new[,count])	Returns a copy of the original string replacing the portion of string given in *old* with the portion given in *new*
rfind(sub[,start[,end]])	Searches string from right to left and finds the first occurrence of the given string and returns highest index where sub is found
rindex(sub[,start[,end]])	Searches string from right to left and finds the first occurrence of the given string and either returns highest index where sub is found or raises an exception
rjust(width[,fillchar])	Returns copy of string Aligned to the right by width
rpartition(separator)	Returns a copy of stringPartitioned starting from the right using the provided separator object
rsplit([separator[,maxsplit]])	Returns list of words in string and splits the string from the right side and uses the given separator as a delimiter. If maxsplit is specified then at most maxsplit splits are done (from the right).
rstrip([chars])	Returns copy of string removing the first found characters in the string from the right that match those given. Also removes whitespace from the right when no argument is specified.
split([separator[,maxsplit]])	Returns a list of words in string and splits the string from the left side and uses the given separator as a delimiter.

Table 2-2. String Methods (continued)

Method	Description of Functionality
splitlines([keepends])	Splits the string into a list of lines. Keepends denotes if newline delimiters are removed. Returns the list of lines in the string.
startswith(prefix[,start[,end]])	Returns a boolean to state whether the string starts with the given prefix
strip([chars])	Returns a copy of string with the given characters removed from the string. If no argument is specified then whitespace is removed.
swapcase()	Returns a copy of the string the case of each character in the string converted.
title()	Returns a copy of the string with the first character in each word uppercase.
translate(table[,deletechars])	Returns a copy of the string using the given character translation table to translate the string. All characters occurring in optional deletechars argument are removed.
upper()	Returns a copy of string with all of the characters in the string converted to uppercase
zfill(width)	Returns a numeric string padded from the left with zeros for the specified width.

Now let's take a look at some examples so that you get an idea of how to use the string methods. As stated previously, most of them work in a similar manner.

Listing 2-4. Using String Methods

```
our_string='python is the best language ever'
# Capitalize first character of a String
>>> our_string.capitalize()
'Python is the best language ever'

# Center string
>>> our_string.center(50)
'          python is the best language ever          '
>>> our_string.center(50,'-')
'---------python is the best language ever---------'

# Count substring within a string
>>> our_string.count('a')
```

```
2
# Count occurrences of substrings
>>> state = 'Mississippi'
>>> state.count('ss')
2

# Partition a string returning a 3-tuple including the portion of string
# prior to separator, the separator
# and the portion of string after the separator
>>> x = "Hello, my name is Josh"
>>> x.partition('n')
('Hello, my ', 'n', 'ame is Josh')

# Assuming the same x as above, split the string using 'l' as the separator

>>> x.split('l')
['He', '', 'o, my name is Josh']

# As you can see, the tuple returned does not contain the separator value
# Now if we add maxsplits value of 1, you can see that the right-most split is
# taken.  If we specify maxsplits value of 2, the two right-most splits are taken
>>> x.split('l',1)
['He', 'lo, my name is Josh']
>>> x.split('l',2)
['He', '', 'o, my name is Josh']
```

String Formatting

You have many options when printing strings using the *print* statement. Much like the C programming language, Python string formatting allows you to make use of a number of different conversion types when printing.

Listing 2-5. Using String Formatting

```
# The two syntaxes below work the same
>>> x = "Josh"
>>> print "My name is %s" % (x)
My name is Josh
>>> print "My name is %s" % x
My name is Josh

# An example using more than one argument
>>> name = 'Josh'
>>> language = 'Python'
>>> print "My name is %s and I speak %s" % (name, language)
My name is Josh and I speak Python

# And now for some fun, here's a different conversion type
# Mind you, I'm not sure where in the world the temperature would
# fluctuate so much!
>>> day1_temp = 65
>>> day2_temp = 68
```

```
>>> day3_temp = 84
>>> print "Given the temparatures %d, %d, and %d, the average would be %f" % (day1_temp,
day2_temp, day3_temp, (day1_temp + day2_temp + day3_temp)/3)
Given the temperatures 65, 68, and 83, the average would be 72.333333
```

Table 2-3 lists the conversion types.

Table 2-3. Conversion Types

Type	Description
d	signed integer decimal
i	signed integer
o	unsigned octal
u	unsigned decimal
x	unsigned hexidecimal (lowercase)
X	unsigned hexidecimal (uppercase letters)
E	floating point exponential format (uppercase 'E')
e	floating point exponential format (lowercase 'e')
f	floating point decimal format (lowercase)
F	floating point decimal format (same as 'f')
g	floating point exponential format if exponent < -4, otherwise float
G	floating point exponential format (uppercase) if exponent < -4, otherwise float
c	single character
r	string (converts any python object using repr())
s	string (converts any python object using str())
%	no conversion, results in a percent (%) character if specified twice

Listing 2-6.

```
>>> x = 10
>>> y = 5.75
>>> print 'The expression %d * %f results in %f' % (x, y, x*y)
The expression 10 * 5.750000 results in 57.500000

# Example of using percentage
>>> test1 = 87
>>> test2 = 89
>>> test3 = 92
>>> "The gradepoint average of three students is %d%%" % (avg)
'The gradepoint average of three students is 89%'
```

Lists, Dictionaries, Sets, and Tuples

Lists, dictionaries, sets, and tuples all offer similar functionality and usability, but they each have their own niche in the language. We'll go through several examples of each since they all play an important role under certain circumstances. Unlike strings, all of the containers discussed in this section (except tuples) are mutable objects, so they can be manipulated after they have been created.

Because these containers are so important, we'll go through an exercise at the end of this chapter, which will give you a chance to try them out for yourself.

Lists

Perhaps one of the most used constructs within the Python programming language is the list. Most other programming languages provide similar containers for storing and manipulating data within an application. The Python list provides an advantage over those similar constructs that are available in statically typed languages. The dynamic tendencies of the Python language help the list construct to harness the great feature of having the ability to contain values of different types. This means that a list can be used to store any Python data type, and these types can be mixed within a single list. In other languages, this type of construct is often defined as a typed object, which locks the construct to using only one data type.

The creation and usage of Python lists is just the same as the rest of the language. . .very simple and easy to use. Simply assigning a set of empty square brackets to a variable creates an empty list. We can also use the built-in **list**() function to create a list. The list can be constructed and modified as the application runs, they are not declared with a static length. They are easy to traverse through the usage of loops, and indexes can also be used for positional placement or removal of particular items in the list. We'll start out by showing some examples of defining lists, and then go through each of the different avenues which the Python language provides us for working with lists.

Listing 2-7. Defining Lists

```
# Define an empty list
my_list = []
my_list = list()  # rarely used

# Single Item List
>>> my_list = [1]
>>> my_list          # note that there is no need to use print to display a variable in the
>>> # interpreter
```

```
[1]

# Define a list of string values
my_string_list = ['Hello', 'Jython' ,'Lists']

# Define a list containing mulitple data types
multi_list = [1, 2, 'three', 4, 'five', 'six']

# Define a list containing a list
combo_list = [1, my_string_list, multi_list]

# Define a list containing a list inline
>>> my_new_list = ['new_item1', 'new_item2', [1, 2, 3, 4], 'new_item3']
>>> print my_new_list
['new_item1', 'new_item2', [1, 2, 3, 4], 'new_item3']
```

As stated previously, in order to obtain the values from a list we can make use of indexes. Much like the Array in the Java language, using the *list[index]* notation will allow us to access an item. If we wish to obtain a range or set of values from a list, we can provide a *starting* index, and/or an *ending* index. This technique is also known as *slicing*. What's more, we can also return a set of values from the list along with a stepping pattern by providing a *step* index as well. One key to remember is that while accessing a list via indexing, the first element in the list is contained within the 0 index. Note that when slicing a list, a new list is always returned. One way to create a shallow copy of a list is to use slice notation without specifying an upper or lower bound. The lower bound defaults to zero, and the upper bound defaults to the length of the list.

Note that a shallow copy constructs a new compound object (list or other object containing objects) and then inserts references into it to the original objects. A deep copy constructs a new compound object and then inserts copies into it based upon the objects found in the original.

Listing 2-8. Accessing a List

```
# Obtain elements in the list
>>> my_string_list[0]
'Hello'

>>> my_string_list[2]
'Lists'

# Negative indexes start with the last element in the list and work back towards the first
# item
>>> my_string_list[-1]
'Lists'
>>> my_string_list[-2]
'Jython'

# Using slicing (Note that slice includes element at starting index and excludes the end)
>>> my_string_list[0:2]
['Hello', 'Jython']

# Create a shallow copy of a list using slice
>>> my_string_list_copy = my_string_list[:]
>>> my_string_list_copy
['Hello', 'Jython', 'Lists']
```

```
# Return every other element in a list
>>> new_list=[2, 4, 6, 8, 10, 12, 14, 16, 18, 20]
# Using a third parameter in the slice will cause a stepping action to take place
# In this example we step by one
>>> new_list[0:10:1]
[2, 4, 6, 8, 10, 12, 14, 16, 18, 20]

# And here we step by two
>>> new_list[0:10:2]
[2, 6, 10, 14, 18]

# Leaving a positional index blank will also work as the default is 0 for the start, and the
length of the string for the end.
>>> new_list[::2]
[2, 6, 10, 14, 18]
```

Modifying a list is much the same, you can use the index in order to insert or remove items from a particular position. There are also many other ways that you can insert or remove elements from the list. Python provides each of these different options as they provide different functionality for your operations.

Listing 2-9.

```
# Modify an element in a list.  In this case we'll modify the element in the 9th position
>>> new_list[9] = 25
>>> new_list
[2, 4, 6, 8, 10, 12, 14, 16, 18, 25]
```

You can make use of the *append()* method in order to add an item to the end of a list. The *extend()* method allows you to add copy of an entire list or sequence to the end of a list. Lastly, the *insert()* method allows you to place an item or another list into a particular position of an existing list by utilizing positional indexes. If another list is inserted into an existing list then it is not combined with the original list, but rather it acts as a separate item contained within the original list. You will find examples of each method below.

Similarly, we have plenty of options for removing items from a list. The *del* statement, as explained in Chapter 1, can be used to remove or delete an entire list or values from a list using the index notation. You can also use the *pop()* or *remove()* method to remove single values from a list. The *pop()* method will remove a single value from the end of the list, and it will also return that value at the same time. If an index is provided to the *pop()* function, then it will remove and return the value at that index. The *remove()* method can be used to find and remove a particular value in the list. In other words, *remove()* will delete the first matching element from the list. If more than one value in the list matches the value passed into the *remove()* function, the first one will be removed. Another note about the *remove()* function is that the value removed is not returned. Let's take a look at these examples of modifying a list.

Listing 2-10. Modifying a List

```
# Adding values to a list using the append method
>>> new_list=['a','b','c','d','e','f','g']
>>> new_list.append('h')
>>> print new_list
['a', 'b', 'c', 'd', 'e', 'f', 'g', 'h']

# Add another list to the existing list
>>> new_list2=['h','i','j','k','l','m','n','o','p']
>>> new_list.extend(new_list2)
>>> print new_list
['a', 'b', 'c', 'd', 'e', 'f', 'g', 'h','h', 'i', 'j', 'k', 'l', 'm', 'n', 'o', 'p']

# Insert a value into a particular location via the index.
# In this example, we add a 'c' into the third position in the list
# (Remember that list indicies start with 0, so the second index is actually the third
# position)
>>> new_list.insert(2,'c')
>>> print new_list
['a', 'b', 'c', 'c', 'd', 'e', 'f', 'g', 'h', 'h','i', 'j', 'k', 'l', 'm', 'n', 'o', 'p']

# Insert a list into a particular postion via the index
>>> another_list = ['a', 'b', 'c']
>>> another_list.insert(2, new_list)
>>> another_list
['a', 'b', [2, 4, 8, 10, 12, 14, 16, 18, 25], 'c']

# Use the slice notation to overwrite part of a list or sequence
>>> new_listA=[100,200,300,400]
>>> new_listB=[500,600,700,800]
>>> new_listA[0:2]=new_listB
>>> print new_listA
[500, 600, 700, 800, 300, 400]
# Assign a list to another list using the empty slice notation
>>> one = ['a', 'b', 'c', 'd']
>>> two = ['e', 'f']
>>> one
['a', 'b', 'c', 'd']
>>> two
['e', 'f']

# Obtain an empty slice from a list by using the same start and end position.
# Any start and end position will work, as long as they are the same number.
>>> one[2:2]
[]
# In itself, this is not very interesting - you could have made an empty list
# very easily. The useful thing about this is that you can assign to this empty slice
# Now, assign the 'two' list to an empty slice for the 'one' list which essentially
# inserts the 'two' list into the 'one' list
>>> one[2:2] = two        # the empty list between elements 1 and 2 of list 'one' is
>>>                       # replaced by the list 'two'
```

```
>>> one
['a', 'b', 'c', 'd', 'e', 'f']

# Use the del statement to remove a value or range of values from a list
# Note that all other elements are shifted to fill the empty space
>>> new_list3=['a','b','c','d','e','f']
>>> del new_list3[2]
>>> new_list3
['a', 'b', 'd', 'e', 'f']
>>> del new_list3[1:3]
>>> new_list3
['a', 'e', 'f']

# Use the del statement to delete a list
>>> new_list3=[1,2,3,4,5]
>>> print new_list3
[1, 2, 3, 4, 5]
>>> del new_list3
>>> print new_list3
Traceback (most recent call last):
  File "<stdin>", line 1, in <module>
NameError: name 'new_list3' is not defined



# Remove values from a list using pop and remove functions
>>> print new_list
['a', 'b', 'c', 'c', 'd', 'e', 'f', 'g', 'h','h', 'i', 'j', 'k', 'l', 'm', 'n', 'o', 'p']
# pop the element at index 2
>>> new_list.pop(2)
'c'
>>> print new_list
['a', 'b', 'c', 'd', 'e', 'f', 'g', 'h','h', 'i', 'j', 'k', 'l', 'm', 'n', 'o', 'p']
# Remove the first occurrence of the letter 'h' from the list
>>> new_list.remove('h')
>>> print new_list
['a', 'b', 'c', 'd', 'e', 'f', 'g', 'h', 'i', 'j', 'k', 'l', 'm', 'n', 'o', 'p']

# Useful example of using pop() function
>>> x = 5
>>> times_list = [1,2,3,4,5]
>>> while times_list:
...     print x * times_list.pop(0)
...
5
10
15
20
25
```

Now that we know how to add and remove items from a list, it is time to learn how to manipulate the data within them. Python provides a number of different methods that can be used to help us manage our lists. See Table 2-4 for a list of these functions and what they can do.

Table 2-4. Python List Methods

Method	Tasks Performed
index	Returns the index of the first value in the list which matches a given value.
count	Returns the number of items in the list which equal a given value.
sort	Sorts the items contained within the list and returns the list
reverse	Reverses the order of the items contained within the list, and returns the list

Let's take a look at some examples of how these functions can be used on lists.

Listing 2-11. Utilizing List Functions

```
# Returning the index for any given value
>>> new_list=[1,2,3,4,5,6,7,8,9,10]
>>> new_list.index(4)
3

#  Change the value of the element at index 4
>>> new_list[4] = 30
>>> new_list
[1, 2, 3, 4, 30, 6, 7, 8, 9, 10]
# Ok, let's change it back
>>> new_list[4] = 5
>>> new_list
[1, 2, 3, 4, 5, 6, 7, 8, 9, 10]

# Add a duplicate value into the list and then return the index
# Note that index returns the index of the first matching value it encounters
>>> new_list.append(6)
>>> new_list
[1, 2, 3, 4, 5, 6, 7, 8, 9, 10, 6]
>>> new_list.index(6)
5

# Using count() function to return the number of items which  equal a given value
>>> new_list.count(2)
1
>>> new_list.count(6)
2

# Sort the values in the list
>>> new_list.sort()
>>> new_list
[1, 2, 3, 4, 5, 6, 6, 7, 8, 9, 10]

# Reverse the order of the value in the list
```

```
>>> new_list.reverse()
>>> new_list
[10, 9, 8, 7, 6, 6, 5, 4, 3, 2, 1]
```

Traversing and Searching Lists

Moving around within a list is quite simple. Once a list is populated, often times we wish to traverse through it and perform some action against each element contained within it. You can use any of the Python looping constructs to traverse through each element within a list. While there are plenty of options available, the *for* loop works especially well. This is because of the simple syntax that the Python *for* loop uses. This section will show you how to traverse a list using each of the different Python looping constructs. You will see that each of them has advantages and disadvantages.

Let's first take a look at the syntax that is used to traverse a list using a *for* loop. This is by far one of the easiest modes of going through each of the values contained within a list. The *for* loop traverses the list one element at a time, allowing the developer to perform some action on each element if so desired.

Listing 2-12. Traversing a List Using a 'for' Loop

```
>>> ourList=[1,2,3,4,5,6,7,8,9,10]
>>> for elem in ourList:
...     print elem
...
1
2
3
4
5
6
7
8
9
10
```

As you can see from this simple example, it is quite easy to go through a list and work with each item individually. The *for* loop syntax requires a variable to which each element in the list will be assigned for each pass of the loop.

It is also possible to combine slicing with the use of the *for* loop. In this case, we'll simply use a list slice to retrieve the exact elements we want to see. For instance, take a look a the following code which traverses through the first 5 elements in our list.

Listing 2-13.

```
>>> for elem in ourList[:5]:
...     print elem
...
1
2
3
4
5
```

As you can see, doing so is quite easy by simply making use of the built-in features that Python offers.

List Comprehensions

As we've seen in the previous section, we can create a copy of a list using the slicing. Another more powerful way to do so is via the list comprehension. There are some advanced features for lists that can help to make a developer's life easier. One such feature is known as a *list comprehension*. While this concept may be daunting at first, it offers a good alternative to creating many separate lists manually. List comprehensions take a given list, and then iterate through it and apply a given expression against each of the objects in the list.

Listing 2-14. Simple List Comprehension

```
# Multiply each number in a list by 2 using a list comprehension
# Note that list comprehension returns a new list
>>> num_list = [1, 2, 3, 4]
>>> [num * 2 for num in num_list]
[2, 4, 6, 8]
# We could assign a list comprehension to a variable
>>> num_list2 = [num * 2 for num in num_list]
>>> num_list2
[2, 4, 6, 8]
```

As you can see, this allows one to quickly take a list and alter it via the use of the provided expression. Of course, as with many other Python methods the list comprehension returns an altered copy of the list. The list comprehension produces a new list and the original list is left untouched. Let's take a look at the syntax for a list comprehension. They are basically comprised of an expression of some kind followed by a *for* statement and then optionally more *for* or *if* statements. The basic functionality of a list comprehension is to iterate over the items of a list, and then apply some expression against each of the list's members. Syntactically, a list comprehension reads as follows:

Iterate through a list and optionally perform an expression on each element, then either return a new list containing the resulting elements or evaluate each element given an optional clause.
[list-element (optional expression) for list-element in list (optional clause)]

Listing 2-15. Using an If Clause in a List Comprehension

```
# The following example returns each element
# in the list that is greater than the number 4
>>> nums = [2, 4, 6, 8]
>>> [num for num in nums if num > 4]
[6, 8]
```

Let's take a look at some more examples. Once you've seen list comprehensions in action you are sure to understand them and see how useful they can be.

Listing 2-16. Python List Comprehensions

```
# Create a list of ages and add one to each of those ages using a list comprehension
>>> ages=[20,25,28,30]
>>> [age+1 for age in ages]
[21, 26, 29, 31]
```

```
# Create a list of names and convert the first letter of each name to uppercase as it should
be
>>> names=['jim','frank','vic','leo','josh']
>>> [name.title() for name in names]
['Jim', 'Frank', 'Vic', 'Leo', 'Josh']

# Create a list of numbers and return the square of each EVEN number
>>> numList=[1,2,3,4,5,6,7,8,9,10,11,12]
>>> [num*num for num in numList if num % 2 == 0]
[4, 16, 36, 64, 100, 144]

# Use a list comprehension with a range
>>> [x*5 for x in range(1,20)]
[5, 10, 15, 20, 25, 30, 35, 40, 45, 50, 55, 60, 65, 70, 75, 80, 85, 90, 95]


# Use a for clause to perform calculations against elements of two different lists
>>> list1 = [5, 10, 15]
>>> list2 = [2, 4, 6]
>>> [e1 + e2 for e1 in list1 for e2 in list2]
[7, 9, 11, 12, 14, 16, 17, 19, 21]
```

List comprehensions can make code much more concise and allows one to apply expressions or functions to list elements quite easily. Let's take a quick look at an example written in Java for performing the same type of work as an list comprehension. It is plain to see that list comprehensions are much more concise.

Listing 2-17. Java Code to Take a List of Ages and Add One Year to Each Age

```
int[] ages = {20, 25, 28, 30};
int[] ages2 = new int[ages.length];
// Use a  Java for loop to go through each element in the array
for (int x = 0; x <= ages.length; x++){
    ;
    ages2[x] = ages[x]+1;

}
```

Tuples

Tuples are much like lists; however, they are immutable. Once a tuple has been defined, it cannot be changed. They contain indexes just like lists, but again, they cannot be altered once defined. Therefore, the index in a tuple may be used to retrieve a particular value and not to assign or modify. While tuples may appear similar to lists, they are quite different in that tuples usually contain heterogeneous elements, whereas lists oftentimes contain elements that are related in some way. For instance, a common use case for tuples is to pass parameters to a function, method, and so on.

Since tuples are a member of the sequence type, they can use the same set of methods an operations available to all sequence types.

Listing 2-18. Examples of Tuples

```
# Creating an empty tuple
>>> myTuple = ()

# Creating tuples and using them
>>> myTuple2 = (1, 'two',3, 'four')
>>> myTuple2
(1, 'two', 3, 'four')

# To create a single-item tuple, include a trailing comma
>>> myteam = 'Bears',
>>> myteam
('Bears',)
```

As mentioned previously, tuples can be quite useful for passing to functions, methods, classes, and so on. Oftentimes, it is nice to have an immutable object for passing multiple values. One such case would be using a tuple to pass coordinates in a geographical information system or another application of the kind. They are also nice to use in situations where an immutable object is warranted. Because they are immutable, their size does not grow once they have been defined, so tuples can also play an important role when memory allocation is a concern.

Dictionaries

A Python dictionary is a key-value store container. A dictionary is quite different than a typical list in Python as there is no automatically populated index for any given element within the dictionary. When you use a list, you need not worry about assigning an index to any value that is placed within it. A dictionary allows the developer to assign an index or "key" for every element that is placed into the construct. Therefore, each entry into a dictionary requires two values, the *key* and the *element*.

The beauty of the dictionary is that it allows the developer to choose the data type of the key value. Therefore, if one wishes to use a string or any other hashable object such as an int or float value as a key then it is entirely possible. Dictionaries also have a multitude of methods and operations that can be applied to them to make them easier to work with. Table 2-5 lists dictionary methods and functions.

Listing 2-19. Basic Dictionary Examples

```
# Create an empty dictionary and a populated dictionary
>>> myDict={}
>>> myDict.values()
[]
# Assign key-value pairs to dictionary
>>> myDict['one'] = 'first'
>>> myDict['two'] = 'second'
>>> myDict
{'two': 'second', 'one': 'first'}
```

Table 2-5. *Dictionary Methods and Functions*

Method or Function	Description
len(dictionary)	Function that returns number of items within the given dictionary.
dictionary [key]	Returns the item from the dictionary that is associated with the given key.
dictionary[key] = value	Sets the associated item in the dictionary to the given value.
del dictionary[key]	Deletes the given key/value pair from the dictionary.
dictionary.clear()	Method that removes all items from the dictionary.
dictionary.copy()	Method that creates a shallow copy of the dictionary.
has_key(key)	Function that returns a boolean stating whether the dictionary contains the given key. (Deprecated in favor of using in')
key in d	Returns a boolean stating whether the given key is found in the dictionary
key not in d	Returns a boolean stating whether the given key is not found in the dictionary
items()	Returns a list of tuples including a copy of the key/value pairs within the dictionary.
keys()	Returns the a list of keys within the dictionary.
update([dictionary2])	Updates dictionary with the key/value pairs from the given dictionary. Existing keys will be overwritten.
fromkeys(sequence[,value])	Creates a new dictionary with keys from the given sequence. The values will be set to the value given.
values()	Returns the values within the dictionary as a list.
get(key[, b])	Returns the value associated with the given key. If the key does not exist, then returns b.
setdefault(key[, b])	Returns the value associated with the given key. If the key does not exist, then the key value is set to b (mydict[key] = b)
pop(key[, b])	Returns and removes the key/value pair associated with the given key. If the key does not exist then returns b.

Table 2-5. *Dictionary Methods and Functions (continued)*

Method or Function	Description
popItem()	An arbitrary key/value pair is popped from the dictionary
iteritems()	Returns an iterator over the key/value pairs in the dictionary.
iterkeys()	Returns an iterator over the keys in the dictionary.
itervalues()	Returns an iterator over the values in the dictionary.

Now we will take a look at some dictionary examples. This reference will not show you an example of using each of the dictionary methods and functions, but it should provide you with a good enough base understanding of how they work.

Listing 2-20. *Working with Python Dictionaries*

```
# Create an empty dictionary and a populated dictionary

>>> mydict = {}
# Try to find a key in the dictionary
>>> 'firstkey' in mydict
False

# Add key/value pair to dictionary
>>> mydict['firstkey'] = 'firstval'
>>> 'firstkey' in mydict
True

# List the values in the dictionary
>>> mydict.values()
['firstval']

# List the keys in the dictionary
>>> mydict.keys()
['firstkey']

# Display the length of the dictionary (how many  key/value pairs are in it)
>>> len(mydict)
1

# Print the contents of the dictionary
>>> mydict
{'firstkey': 'firstval'}
>>>

# Replace the original dictionary with a dictionary containing string-based keys
# The following dictionary represents a hockey team line
```

```
>>> myDict =
{'r_wing':'Josh','l_wing':'Frank','center':'Jim','l_defense':'Leo','r_defense':'Vic'}
>>> myDict.values()
['Josh', 'Vic', 'Jim', 'Frank', 'Leo']
>>> myDict.get('r_wing')
'Josh'
>>> myDict['r_wing']
'Josh'

# Try to obtain the value for a key that does not exist
>>> myDict['goalie']
Traceback (most recent call last):
  File "<stdin>", line 1, in <module>
KeyError: 'goalie'

# Try to obtain a value for a key that does not exist using get()
>>> myDict.get('goalie')

# Now use a default message that will be displayed if the key does not exist
>>> myDict.get('goalie','Invalid Position')
'Invalid Position'

# Iterate over the items in the dictionary

>>> for player in myDict.iterItems():
...     print player
...
('r_wing', 'Josh')
('r_defense', 'Vic')
('center', 'Jim')
('l_wing', 'Frank')
('l_defense', 'Leo')

# Assign keys and values to separate objects and then print
>>> for key,value in myDict.iteritems():
...     print key, value
...
r_wing Josh
r_defense Vic
center Jim
l_wing Frank
l_defense Leo
```

Sets

Sets are unordered collections of unique elements. What makes sets different than other sequence types is that they contain no indexing or duplicates. They are also unlike dictionaries because there are no key values associated with the elements. They are an arbitrary collection of unique elements. Sets cannot contain mutable objects, but sets themselves can be mutable. Another thing to note is that sets are note available to use by default, you must import set from the Sets module before using.

Listing 2-21. Examples of Sets

```
# In order to use a Set, we must first import it
>>> from sets import Set
# To create a set use the following syntax
>>> myset = Set([1,2,3,4,5])
>>> myset
Set([5, 3, 2, 1, 4])
# Add a value to the set - See Table 2-7 for more details
>>> myset.add(6)
>>> myset
Set([6, 5, 3, 2, 1, 4])
# Try to add a duplicate
>>> myset.add(4)
>>> myset
Set([6, 5, 3, 2, 1, 4])
```

There are two different types of sets, namely *set* and *frozenset*. The difference between the two is quite easily conveyed from the name itself. A regular *set* is a mutable collection object, whereas a *frozen* set is immutable. Remember, immutable objects cannot be altered once they have been created whereas mutable objects can be altered after creation. Much like sequences and mapping types, sets have an assortment of methods and operations that can be used on them. Many of the operations and methods work on both mutable and immutable sets. However, there are a number of them that only work on the mutable set types. In Tables 2-6 and 2-7, we'll take a look at the different methods and operations.

Table 2-6. Set Type Methods and Functions

Method or Operation	Description
len(set)	Returns the number of elements in a given set
copy()	Returns a new shallow copy of the set
difference(set2)	Returns a new set that contains all elements that are in the calling set, but not in set2
intersection(set2)	Returns a new set that contains all elements that the calling set and set2 have in common
issubbset(set2)	Returns a Boolean stating whether all elements in calling set are also in set2
issuperset(set2)	Returns a Boolean stating whether all elements in set2 are contained in calling set
symmetric_difference(set2)	Returns a new set containing elements either from the calling set or set2 but not from both (set1 ^ set2)

Table 2-6. Set Type Methods and Functions (continued)

Method or Operation	Description
x in set	Tests whether x is contained in the set, returns boolean
x not in set	Tests whether x is not contained in the set, returns boolean
union(set2)	Returns a new set containing elements that are contained in both the calling set and set2

Listing 2-22. Using Set Type Methods and Functions

```
# Create two sets
>>> s1 = Set(['jython','cpython','ironpython'])
>>> s2 = Set(['jython','ironpython','pypy'])
# Make a copy of a set
>>> s3 = s1.copy()
>>> s3
Set(['cpython', 'jython', 'ironpython'])
# Obtain a new set containing all elements that are in s1 but not s2
>>> s1.difference(s2)
Set(['cpython'])
# Obtain a new set containing all elements from each set
>>> s1.union(s2)
Set(['cpython', 'pypy', 'jython', 'ironpython'])
# Obtain a new set containing elements from either set that are not contained in both
>>> s1.symmetric_difference(s2)
Set(['cpython', 'pypy'])
```

Table 2-7. Mutable Set Type Methods

Method or Operation	Description
add(item)	Adds an item to a set if it is not already in the set
clear()	Removes all items in a set
difference_update(set2)	Returns the set with all elements contained in set2 removed
discard(element)	Removes designated element from set if present
intersection_update(set2)	Returns the set keeping only those elements that are also in set2
pop()	Return an arbitrary element from the set
remove(element)	Remove element from set if present, if not then KeyError is raised

Table 2-7. Mutable Set Type Methods (continued)

Method or Operation	Description
symmetric_difference_update(set2)	Replace the calling set with a set containing elements from either the calling set or set2 but not both, and return it
update(set2)	Returns set including all elements from set2

Listing 2-23. More Using Sets

```
# Create three sets
>>> s1 = Set([1, 2, 3, 4, 5, 6, 7, 8, 9, 10])
>>> s2 = Set([5, 10, 15, 20])
>>> s3 = Set([2, 4, 6, 8, 10])

# Remove arbitrary element from s2
>>> s2.pop()
20
>>> s2
Set([5, 15, 10])

# Discard the element that equals 3 from s1 (if exists)
>>> s1.discard(3)
>>> s1
Set([6, 5, 7, 8, 2, 9, 10, 1, 4])

# Update s1 to include only those elements contained in both s1 and s2
>>> s1.intersection_update(s2)
>>> s1
Set([5, 10])
>>> s2
Set([5, 15, 10])

# Remove all elements in s2
>>> s2.clear()
>>> s2
Set([])

# Updates set s1 to include all elements in s3
>>> s1.update(s3)
>>> s1
Set([6, 5, 8, 2, 10, 4])
```

Ranges

The range is a special function that allows one to iterate between a range of numbers or list a specific range of numbers. It is especially helpful for performing mathematical iterations, but it can also be used for simple iterations.

The format for using the range function includes an optional starting number, an ending number, and an optional stepping number. If specified, the starting number tells the range where to begin, whereas the ending number specifies where the range should end. The starting index is inclusive whereas the ending index is not. The optional step number tells the range how many numbers should be placed between each number contained within the range output. The step number is added to the previous number and if that number exceeds the end point then the range stops.

Range Format
`range([start], stop, [step])`

Listing 2-24. Using the Range Function

```
#Simple range starting with zero, note that the end point is not included in the range
>>>range(0,10)
[0, 1, 2, 3, 4, 5, 6, 7, 8, 9]
>>> range(50, 65)
[50, 51, 52, 53, 54, 55, 56, 57, 58, 59, 60, 61, 62, 63, 64]

>>>range(10)
[0, 1, 2, 3, 4, 5, 6, 7, 8, 9]
# Include a step of two in the range
>>>range(0,10,2)
[0, 2, 4, 6, 8]
# Including a negative step performs the same functionality...the step is added to the
previously
# number in the range
>>> range(100,0,-10)
[100, 90, 80, 70, 60, 50, 40, 30, 20, 10]
```

One of the most common uses for this function is in a *for* loop. The following example displays a couple ways of using the range function within a *for* loop context.

Listing 2-25. Using the Range Function Within a For Loop

```
>>> for i in range(10):
...         print i
...
0
1
2
3
4
5
6
7
8
9

# Multiplication Example
>>> x = 1
>>> for i in range(2, 10, 2):
...         x = x + (i * x)
...         print x
```

```
...
3
15
105
945
```

As you can see, a range can be used to iterate through just about any number set. . .be it going up or down, positive or negative in step. Ranges are also a good way to create a list of numbers. In order to do so, simply pass a range to *list()* as shown in the following example.

Listing 2-26. Create a List from a Range

```
>>> my_number_list = list(range(10))
>>> my_number_list
[0, 1, 2, 3, 4, 5, 6, 7, 8, 9]
```

As you can see, not only are ranges useful for iterative purposes but they are also a good way to create numeric lists.

Jython-specific Collections

There are a number of Jython-specific collection objects that are available for use. Most of these collection objects are used to pass data into Java classes and so forth, but they add additional functionality into the Jython implementation that will assist Python newcomers that are coming from the Java world. Nonetheless, many of these additional collection objects can be quite useful under certain situations.

In the Jython 2.2 release, Java collection integration was introduced. This enables a bidirectional interaction between Jython and Java collection types. For instance, a Java ArrayList can be imported in Jython and then used as if it were part of the language. Prior to 2.2, Java collection objects could act as a Jython object, but Jython objects could not act as Java objects. For instance, it is possible to use a Java ArrayList in Jython and use methods such as *add()*, *remove()*, and *get()*. You will see in the example below that using the *add()* method of an ArrayList will add an element to the list and return a boolean to signify the success or failure of the addition. The *remove()* method acts similarly, except that it removes an element rather than adding it.

Listing 2-27. Example of Using Java Oriented Collection in Jython

```
# Import and use a Java ArrayList
>>> import java.util.ArrayList as ArrayList
>>> arr = ArrayList()
#  Add method will add an element to the list and return a boolean to signify successsful
addition
>>> arr.add(1)
True
>>> arr.add(2)
True
>>> print arr
[1, 2]
```

Ahead of the integration of Java collections, Jython also had implemented the *jarray* object which basically allows for the construction of a Java array in Jython. In order to work with a *jarray*, simply define a sequence type in Jython and pass it to the *jarray* object along with the type of object contained within the sequence. The *jarray* is definitely useful for creating Java arrays and then passing them into java objects, but it is not very useful for working in Jython objects. Moreover, all values within a jarray must be the same type. If you try to pass a sequence containing multiple types to a jarray then you'll be given a *TypeError* of one kind or another. See Table 2-8 for a listing of character typecodes used with jarray.

Table 2-8. *Character Typecodes for Use With Jarray*

Character	Java Equivalent
z	boolean
b	byte
c	char
d	Double
f	Float
h	Short
i	Int
l	Long

Listing 2-28. Jarray Usage

```
>>> my_seq = (1,2,3,4,5)
>>> from jarray import array
>>> array(my_seq,'i')
array('i', [1, 2, 3, 4, 5])

>>> myStr = "Hello Jython"
>>> array(myStr,'c')
array('c', 'Hello Jython')
```

Another useful feature of the jarray is that we can create empty arrays if we wish by using the *zeros()* method. The *zeros()* method works in a similar fashion to the *array()* method which we've already demonstrated. In order to create an array that is empty, simply pass the length of the array along with the type to the *zeros()* method. Let's take a quick look at an example.

Listing 2-29. Create an Empty Boolean Array

```
>>> arr = zeros(10,'z')
>>> arr
array('z', [False, False, False, False, False, False, False, False, False, False])
```

Listing 2-30. Create an Empty Integer Array

```
>>> arr2 = zeros(6, 'i')
>>> arr2
array('i', [0, 0, 0, 0, 0, 0])
```

In some circumstances when working with Java objects, you will need to call a Java method that requires a Java array as an argument. Using the jarray object allows for a simple way of creating Java arrays when needed.

Files

File objects are used to read and write data to a file on disk. The file object is used to obtain a reference to the file on disk and open it for reading, writing, appending, or a number of different tasks. If we simply use the *open(filename[, mode])* function, we can return a file object and assign it to a variable for processing. If the file does not yet exist on disk, then it will automatically be created. The *mode* argument is used to tell what type of processing we wish to perform on the file. This argument is optional and if omitted then the file is opened in read-only mode. See Table 2-9.

Table 2-9. Modes of Operations for File Types

Mode	Description
'r'	read only
'w'	write (Note: This overwrites anything else in the file, so use with caution)
'a'	append
'r+'	read and write
'rb'	binary file read
'wb'	binary file write
'r+b'	binary file read and write

Listing 2-31.

```
# Open a file and assign it to variable f
>>> f = open('newfile.txt','w')
```

There are plenty of methods that can be used on file objects for manipulation of the file content. We can call *read([size])* on a file in order to read its content. Size is an optional argument here and it is used to tell how much content to read from the file. If it is omitted then the entire file content is read. The *readline()* method can be used to read a single line from a file. *readlines([size])* is used to return a list containing all of the lines of data that are contained within a file. Again, there is an optional *size* parameter that can be used to tell how many bytes from the file to read. If we wish to place content into the file, the *write(string)* method does just that. The *write()* method writes a string to the file.

When writing to a file it is oftentimes important to know exactly what position in the file you are going to write to. There are a group of methods to help us out with positioning within a file using integers to represent bytes in the file. The *tell()* method can be called on a file to give the file object's current position. The integer returned is in a number of bytes and is an offset from the beginning of the file. The *seek(offset, from)* method can be used to change position in a file. The *offset* is the number in bytes of the position you'd like to go, and *from* represents the place in the file where you'd like to calculate the *offset* from. If *from* equals 0, then the offset will be calculated from the beginning of the file. Likewise, if it equals 1 then it is calculated from the current file position, and 2 will be from the end of the file. The default is 0 if *from* is omitted.

Lastly, it is important to allocate and de-allocate resources efficiently in our programs or we will incur a memory overhead and leaks. Resources are usually handled a bit differently between CPython and Jython because garbage collection acts differently. In CPython, it is not as important to worry about de-allocating resources as they are automatically de-allocated when they go out of scope. The JVM does note immediately garbage collect, so proper de-allocation of resources is more important. The *close()* method should be called on a file when we are through working with it. The proper methodology to use when working with a file is to open, process, and then close each time. However, there are more efficient ways of performing such tasks. In Chapter 7 we will discuss the use of context managers to perform the same functionality in a more efficient manner.

Listing 2-32. File Manipulation in Python

```
# Create a file, write to it, and then read its content

>>> f = open('newfile.txt','r+')
>>> f.write('This is some new text for our file\n')
>>> f.write('This should be another line in our file\n')
#  No lines will be read because we are at the end of the written content
>>> f.read()
''
>>> f.readlines()
[]
>>> f.tell()
75L
# Move our position back to the beginning of the file
>>> f.seek(0)
>>> f.read()
'This is some new text for our file\nThis should be another line in our file\n'
>>> f.seek(0)
>>> f.readlines()
['This is some new text for our file\n', 'This should be another line in our file\n']
```

```
# Closing the file to de-allocate
>>> f.close()
```

Iterators

The iterator was introduced into Python back in version 2.2. It allows for iteration over Python containers. All iterable containers have built-in support for the iterator type. For instance, sequence objects are iterable as they allow for iteration over each element within the sequence. If you try to return an iterator on an object that does not support iteration, you will most likely receive an *AttributeError* which tells you that __iter__ has not been defined as an attribute for that object. It is important to note that Python method names using double-underscores are special methods. For instance, in Python a class can be initialized using the *__init__()* method. . .much like a Java constructor. For more details on classes and special class methods, please refer to Chapter 7.

Iterators allow for easy access to sequences and other iterable containers. Some containers such as dictionaries have specialized iteration methods built into them as you have seen in previous sections. Iterator objects are required to support two main methods that form the iterator protocol. Those methods are defined below in Table 2-10.

Table 2-10. Iterator Protocol

Method	Description
iterator.__iter__()	Returns the iterator object on a container. Required to allow use with *for* and *in* statements
iterator.next()	Returns the next item from a container.

To return an iterator on a container, just assign *container.__iter__()* to some variable. That variable will become the iterator for the object. This affords one the ability to pass iterators around, into functions and the like. The iterator is then itself like a changing variable that maintains its state. We can use work with the iterator without affecting the original object. If using the *next()* call, it will continue to return the next item within the list until all items have been retrieved. Once this occurs, a *StopIteration* exception is issued. The important thing to note here is that we are actually creating a copy of the list when we return the iterator and assign it to a variable. That variable returns and removes an item from that copy each time the *next()* method is called on it. If we continue to call *next()* on the iterator variable until the *StopIteration* error is issued, the variable will no longer contain any items and is empty. For instance, if we created an iterator from a list then called the *next()* method on it until it had retrieved all values then the iterator would be empty and the original list would be left untouched.

Listing 2-33. Create an Iterator from a List and Use It

```
>>> hockey_roster = ['Josh', 'Leo', 'Frank', 'Jim', 'Vic']
>>> hockey_itr = hockey_roster.__iter__()
>>> hockey_itr = hockey_roster.__iter__()
>>> hockey_itr.next()
'Josh'
>>> for x in hockey_itr:
...     print x
...
```

```
Leo
Frank
Jim
Vic
# Try to call next() on iterator after it has already used all of its elements
>>> hockey_itr.next()
Traceback (most recent call last):
  File "<stdin>", line 1, in <module>
StopIteration
```

Listing 2-34. *Iteration Over Sequence and List*

```
# Iterate over a string and a list
>>> str_a = 'Hello'
>>> list_b = ['Hello','World']
>>> for x in str_a:
...     print x
...
H
e
l
l
o
>>> for y in list_b:
...     print y + '!'
...
Hello!
World!
```

Referencing and Copies

Creating copies and referencing items in the Python language is fairly straightforward. The only thing you'll need to keep in mind is that the techniques used to copy mutable and immutable objects differ a bit.

In order to create a copy of an immutable object, you simply assign it to a different variable. The new variable is an exact copy of the object. If you attempt to do the same with a mutable object, you will actually just create a reference to the original object. Therefore, if you perform operations on the "copy" of the original then the same operation will actually be performed on the original. This occurs because the new assignment references the same mutable object in memory as the original. It is kind of like someone calling you by a different name. One person may call you by your birth name and another may call you by your nickname, but both names will reference you of course.

Listing 2-35. Working with Copies

```
# Strings are immutable, so when you assign a string to another variable, it creates a real
copy
>>> mystring = "I am a string, and I am an immutable object"
>>> my_copy = mystring
>>> my_copy
'I am a string, and I am an immutable object'
>>> mystring
'I am a string, and I am an immutable object'
```

```
>>> my_copy = "Changing the copy of mystring"
>>> my_copy
'Changing the copy of mystring'
>>> mystring
'I am a string, and I am an immutable object'

# Lists are mutable objects, so assigning a list to a variable
# creates a reference to that list. Changing one of these variables will also
# change the other one - they are just references to the same object.

>>> listA = [1,2,3,4,5,6]
>>> print listA
[1, 2, 3, 4, 5, 6]
>>> listB = listA
>>> print listB
[1, 2, 3, 4, 5, 6]
>>> del listB[2]
# Oops, we've altered the original list!
>>> print listA
[1, 2, 4, 5, 6]

# If you want a new list which contains the same things, but isn't just a reference
# to your original list, you need the copy module
>>> import copy
>>> a = [[]]
>>> b = copy.copy(a)
>>> b
[[]]
# b is not the same list as a, just a copy
>>> b is a
False

# But the list b[0] is the same the same list as the list a[0], and changing one will
# also change the other. This is what is known as a shallow copy - a and b are
# different at the top level, but if you go one level down, you have references to
# the same things - if you go deep enough, it's not a copy,
# it's the same object.
>>> b[0].append('test')
>>> a
[['test']]
>>> b
[['test']]
```

To effectively create a copy of a mutable object, you have two choices. You can either create what is known as a *shallow* copy or a *deep* copy of the original object. The difference is that a shallow copy of an object will create a new object and then populate it with references to the items that are contained in the original object. Hence, if you modify any of those items then each object will be affected since they both reference the same items.

A deep copy creates a new object and then recursively copies the contents of the original object into the new copy. Once you perform a deep copy of an object then you can perform operations on any object contained in the copy without affecting the original. You can use the *deepcopy* function in the copy module of the Python standard library to create such a copy. Let's look at some more examples of creating copies in order to give you a better idea of how this works.

Listing 2-36.

```
# Create an integer variable, copy it, and modify the copy
>>> a = 5
>>> b = a
>>> print b
5
>>> b = a * 5
>>> b
25
>>> a
5


# Create a deep copy of the list and modify it
>>> import copy
>>> listA = [1,2,3,4,5,6]
>>> listB = copy.deepcopy(listA)

>>> print listB
[1, 2, 3, 4, 5, 6]
>>> del listB[2]
>>> print listB
[1, 2, 4, 5, 6]
>>> print listA
[1, 2, 3, 4, 5, 6]
```

Garbage Collection

This is one of those major differences between CPython and Jython. In CPython, an object is garbage collected when it goes out of scope or is no longer needed. This occurs automatically and rarely needs to be tracked by the developer. Behind the scenes, CPython uses a reference counting technique to maintain a count on each object which effectively determines if the object is still in use. Unlike CPython, Jython does not implement a reference counting technique for aging out or garbage collection unused objects. Instead, Jython makes use of the garbage collection mechanisms that the Java platform provides. When a Jython object becomes stale or unreachable, the JVM may or may not reclaim it. One of the main aspects of the JVM that made developers so happy in the early days is that there was no longer a need to worry about cleaning up after your code. In the C programming language, one must maintain an awareness of which objects are currently being used so that when they are no longer needed the program would perform some clean up. Not in the Java world, the gc thread on the JVM takes care of all garbage collection and cleanup for you.

Even though we haven't spoken about classes in detail yet, you saw a short example of how them in Chapter 1. It is a good time to mention that Python provides a mechanism for object cleanup. A finalizer method can be defined in any class in order to ensure that the garbage collector performs specific tasks. Any cleanup code that needs to be performed when an object goes out of scope can be placed within this finalizer method. It is important to note that the finalizer method cannot be counted on as a method which will always be invoked when an object is stale. This is the case because the finalizer method is invoked by the Java garbage collection thread, and there is no way to be sure when and if the garbage collector will be called on an object. Another issue of note with the finalizer is that they incur a performance penalty. If you're coding an application that already performs poorly then it may not be a good idea to throw lots of finalizers into it.

The following is an example of a Python finalizer. It is an instance method that must be named __del__.

Listing 2-37. Python Finalizer Example

```
class MyClass:
    def __del__(self):
        pass    # Perform some cleanup here
```

The downside to using the JVM garbage collection mechanisms is that there is really no guarantee as to when and if an object will be reclaimed. Therefore, when working with performance intensive objects it is best to not rely on a finalizer to be called. It is always important to ensure that proper coding techniques are used in such cases when working with objects like files and databases. Never code the close() method for a file into a finalizer because it may cause an issue if the finalizer is not invoked. Best practice is to ensure that all mandatory cleanup activities are performed before a finalizer would be invoked.

Summary

A lot of material was covered in this chapter. You should be feeling better acquainted with Python after reading through this material. We began the chapter by covering the basics of assignment an assigning data to particular objects or data types. You learned that working with each type of data object opens different doors as the way we work with each type of data object differs. Our journey into data objects began with numbers and strings, and we discussed the many methods available to the string object. We learned that strings are part of the sequence family of Python collection objects along with lists and tuples. We covered how to create and work with lists, and the variety of options available to us when using lists. You discovered that list comprehensions can help create copies of a given list and manipulate their elements according to an expression or function. After discussing lists, we went on to discuss dictionaries, sets and tuples.

After discussing the collection types, we learned that Jython has its own set of collection objects that differ from those in Python. We can leverage the advantage of having the Java platform at our fingertips and use Java collection types from within Jython. We finished up by discussing referencing, copies, and garbage collection. Creating different copies of objects does not always give you what you'd expect, and that Jython garbage collection differs quite a bit from that of Python.

The next chapter will help you to combine some of the topics you've learned about in this chapter as you will learn how to define expressions and work with control flow.

CHAPTER 3

■ ■ ■

Operators, Expressions, and Program Flow

The focus of this chapter is an in-depth look at each of the ways that we can evaluate code, and write meaningful blocks of conditional logic. We'll cover the details of many operators that can be used in Python expressions. This chapter will also cover some topics that have already been discussed in more meaningful detail such as the looping constructs, and some basic program flow.

We'll begin by discussing details of expressions. If you'll remember from Chapter 1, an expression is a piece of code that evaluates to produce a value. We have already seen some expressions in use while reading through the previous chapters. In this chapter, we'll focus more on the internals of operators used to create expressions, and also different types of expressions that we can use. This chapter will go into further detail on how we can define blocks of code for looping and conditionals.

This chapter will also go into detail on how you write and evaluate mathematical expressions, and Boolean expressions. And last but not least, we'll discuss how you can use augmented assignment operations to combine two or more operations into one.

Types of Expressions

An expression in Python is a piece of code that produces a result or value. Most often, we think of expressions that are used to perform mathematical operations within our code. However, there are a multitude of expressions used for other purposes as well. In Chapter 2, we covered the details of String manipulation, sequence and dictionary operations, and touched upon working with sets. All of the operations performed on these objects are forms of expressions in Python. Other examples of expressions could be pieces of code that call methods or functions, and also working with lists using slicing and indexing.

Mathematical Operations

The Python contains all of your basic mathematical operations. This section will briefly touch upon each operator and how it functions. You will also learn about a few built-in functions which can be used to assist in your mathematical expressions.

Assuming that this is not the first programming language you are learning, there is no doubt that you are at least somewhat familiar with performing mathematical operations within your programs. Python is no different than the rest when it comes to mathematics, as with most programming languages, performing mathematical computations and working with numeric expressions is straightforward. Table 3-1 lists the numeric operators.

Table 3-1. *Numeric Operators*

Operator	Description
+	Addition
-	Subtraction
*	Multiplication
/	Division
//	Truncating Division
%	Modulo (Remainder of Division)
**	Power Operator
+var	Unary Plus
-var	Unary Minus

Most of the operators in Table 3-1 work exactly as you would expect, so for example:

Listing 3-1. Mathematical Operator

```
# Performing basic mathematical computations
>>> 10 - 6
4
>>> 9 * 7
63
```

However, division, truncating division, modulo, power, and the unary operators could use some explanation. Truncating division will automatically truncate a division result into an integer by rounding down, and modulo will return the remainder of a truncated division operation. The power operator does just what you'd expect as it returns the result of the number to the left of the operator multiplied by itself n times, where n represents the number to the right of the operator.

Listing 3-2. Truncating Division and Powers

```
>>> 36 // 5
7
# Modulo returns the remainder
>>> 36 % 5
1
# Using powers, in this case 5 to the power of 2
>>> 5**2
25
```

```
# 100 to the power of 2
>>> 100**2
10000
```

Division itself is an interesting subject as its current implementation is somewhat controversial in some situations. The problem 10/5 = 2 definitely holds true. However, in its current implementation, division rounds numbers in such a way that sometimes yields unexpected results. There is a new means of division available in Jython 2.5 by importing from __future__. In a standard division for 2.5 and previous releases, the quotient returned is the floor (nearest integer after rounding down) of the quotient when arguments are ints or longs. However, a reasonable approximation of the division is returned if the arguments are floats or complex. Often times this solution is not what was expected as the quotient should be the reasonable approximation or "true division" in any case. When we import *division* from the __future__ module then we alter the return value of division by causing true division when using the / operator, and floor division only when using the , // operator. In an effort to not break backward compatibility, the developers have placed the repaired division implementation in a module known as __future__. The __future__ module actually contains code that is meant to be included as a part of the standard language in some future revision. In order to use the new repaired version of division, it is important that you always import from __future__ prior to working with division. Take a look at the following piece of code.

Listing 3-3. Division Rounding Issues

```
# Works as expected
>>> 14/2
7
>>> 10/5
2
>>> 27/3
9
# Now divide some numbers that should result in decimals
# Here we would expect 1.5
>>> 3/2
1
# The following should give us 1.4
>>> 7/5
1
# In the following case, we'd expect 2.3333
>>> 14/6
2
```

As you can see, when we'd expect to see a decimal value we are actually receiving an integer value. The developers of this original division implementation have acknowledged this issue and repaired it using the new __future__ implementation.

Listing 3-4. Working With __future__ Division

```
# We first import division from __future__
from __future__ import division

# We then work with division as usual and see the expected results
>>> 14/2
7.0
>>> 10/5
```

```
2.0
>>> 27/3
9.0
>>> 3/2
1.5
>>> 7/5
1.4
>>> 14/6
2.3333333333333335
```

It is important to note that the Jython implementation differs somewhat from CPython in that Java provides extra rounding in some cases. The differences are in display of the rounding only as both Jython and CPython use the same IEEE float for storage. Let's take a look at one such case.

Listing 3-5. Subtle Differences Between Jython and CPython Division

```
# CPython 2.5 Rounding
>>> 5.1/1
5.0999999999999996

# Jython 2.5
>>> 5.1/1
5.1
```

Unary operators can be used to evaluate positive or negative numbers. The unary plus operator multiplies a number by positive 1 (which generally doesn't change it at all), and a unary minus operator multiplies a number by negative 1.

Listing 3-6. Unary Operators

```
# Unary minus
>>> -10 + 5
-5
>>> +5 - 5
0
>>> -(1 + 2)
-3
```

As stated at the beginning of the section, there are a number of built-in mathematical functions that are at your disposal. Table 3-2 lists the built-in mathematical functions.

Table 3-2. Mathematical Built-in Functions

Function	Description
abs(var)	Absolute value
pow(x, y)	Can be used in place of ** operator
pow(x,y,modulo)	Ternary power-modulo (x **y) % modulo
round(var[, n])	Returns a value rounded to the nearest 10^{-n} or (10^{**-n}), where n defaults to 0)
divmod(x, y)	Returns a tuple of the quotient and the remainder of division

Listing 3-7. Mathematical Built-ins

```
#  The following code provides some examples for using mathematical built-ins
# Absolute value of 9
>>> abs(9)
9
# Absolute value of -9
>>> abs(-9)
9
# Divide 8 by 4 and return quotient, remainder tuple
>>> divmod(8,4)
(2, 0)
# Do the same, but this time returning a remainder (modulo)
>>> divmod(8,3)
(2, 2)

# Obtain 8 to the power of 2
>>> pow(8,2)
64

# Obtain 8 to the power of 2 modulo 3   ((8 **2) % 3)
>>> pow(8,2,3)
1
# Perform rounding
>>> round(5.67,1)
5.7
>>> round(5.67)
6.00
```

Comparison Operators

Comparison operators can be used for comparison of two or more expressions or variables. As with the mathematical operators described above, these operators have no significant difference to that of Java. See Table 3-3.

Table 3-3. Comparison Operators

Operator	Description
>	Greater than
<	Less than
>=	Greater than or equal
<=	Less than or equal
!=	Not equal
==	Equal

Listing 3-8. Examples of Comparison Operators

```
# Simple comparisons
>>> 8 > 10
False
>>> 256 < 725
True
>>> 10 == 10
True

# Use comparisons in an expression
>>> x = 2*8
>>> y = 2
>>> while x != y:
...     print 'Doing some work...'
...     y = y + 2
...
Doing some work...
Doing some work...
Doing some work...
Doing some work...
Doing some work...
Doing some work...
Doing some work...

# Combining comparisons
>>> 3<2<3
False
>>> 3<4<8
True
```

Bitwise Operators

Bitwise operators in Python are a set of operators that are used to work on numbers in a two's complement binary fashion. That is, when working with bitwise operators numbers are treated as a string of bits consisting of 0s and 1s. If you are unfamiliar with the concept of two's complement, a good place to start would be at the Wikipedia page discussing the topic: (http://en.wikipedia.org/wiki/Two's_complement). It is important to know that bitwise operators can only be applied to integers and long integers. Let's take a look at the different bitwise operators that are available to us (Table 3-4), and then we'll go through a few examples.

Table 3-4. Bitwise Operators

Operator	Description
&	Bitwise and operator copies a bit to the result if a bit appears in both operands
|	Bitwise or operator copies a bit to the result if it exists in either of the operands
^	Bitwise xor operator copies a bit to the result if it exists in only one operand
~	Bitwise negation operator flips the bits, and returns the exact opposite of each bit

Suppose we have a couple of numbers in binary format and we would like to work with them using the bitwise operators. Let's work with the numbers 14 and 27. The binary (two's complement) representation of the number 14 is 00001110, and for 27 it is 00011011. The bitwise operators look at each 1 and 0 in the binary format of the number and perform their respective operations, and then return a result. Python does not return the bits, but rather the integer value of the resulting bits. In the following examples, we take the numbers 14 and 27 and work with them using the bitwise operators.

Listing 3-9. Bitwise Operator Examples

```
>>> 14 & 27
10
>>> 14 | 27
31
>>> 14 ^ 27
21
>>> ~14
-15
>>> ~27
-28
```

To summarize the examples above, let's work through the operations using the binary representations for each of the numbers.

    14 & 27 = 00001110 and 00011011 = 00001010 (The integer 10)
    14 | 27 = 00001110 or 000110011 = 00011111 (The integer 31)
    14 ^ 27 = 00001110 xor 000110011 = 00010101 (The integer 21)
    ~14 = 00001110 = 11110001 (The integer -15)

The shift operators (see Table 3-5) are similar in that they work with the binary bit representation of a number. The left shift operator moves the left operand's value to the left by the number of bits specified by the right operand. The right shift operator does the exact opposite as it shifts the left operand's value to the right by the number of bits specified by the right operand. Essentially this translates to the left shift operator multiplying the operand on the left by the number two as many times as specified by the right operand. The opposite holds true for the right shift operator that divides the operand on the left by the number two as many times as specified by the right operand.

Table 3-5. Shift Operators

x<<n	Shift left (The equivalent of multiplying the number x by 2, n times)
x>>n	Shift right (The equivalent of dividing the number x by 2, n times)

More specifically, the left shift operator (<<) will multiply a number by two *n* times, *n* being the number that is to the right of the shift operator. The right shift operator will divide a number by two n times, n being the number to the right of the shift operator. The __future__ division import does not make a difference in the outcome of such operations.

Listing 3-10. Shift Operator Examples

```
# Shift left, in this case  3*2
>>> 3<<1
6
# Equivalent of 3*2*2
>>> 3<<2
12
# Equivalent of 3*2*2*2*2*2
>>> 3<<5
96

# Shift right
# Equivalent of 3/2
>>> 3>>1
1
# Equivalent of 9/2
>>> 9>>1
4
# Equivalent of 10/2
>>> 10>>1
5
# Equivalent of 10/2/2
>>> 10>>2
2
```

While bitwise operators are not the most commonly used operators, they are good to have on hand. They are especially important if you are working in mathematical situations.

Augmented Assignment

Augmented assignment operators (see Table 3-6) combine an operation with an assignment. They can be used to do things like assign a variable to the value it previously held, modified in some way. While augmented assignment can assist in coding concisely, some say that too many such operators can make code more difficult to read.

Listing 3-11. *Augmented Assignment Code Examples*

```
>>> x = 5
>>> x
5
# Add one to the value of x and then assign that value to x
>>> x+=1
>>> x
6
# Multiply the value of x by 5 and then assign that value to x
>>> x*=5
>>> x
30
```

Table 3-6. *Augmented Assignment Operators*

Operator	Equivalent
a += b	a = a + b
a -= b	a = a – b
a *= b	a = a * b
a /= b	a = a / b
a %= b	a = a % b
a //= b	a = a // b
a **= b	a = a** b
a &= b	a = a & b
a |= b	a = a | b
a ^= b	a = a ^ b
a >>= b	a = a >> b
a <<= b	a = a << b

Boolean Expressions

Evaluating two or more values or expressions also uses a similar syntax to that of other languages, and the logic is quite the same. Note that in Python, *True* and *False* are very similar to constants in the Java language. *True* actually represents the number *1*, and *False* represents the number *0*. One could just as easily code using 0 and 1 to represent the Boolean values, but for readability and maintenance the *True* and *False* "constants" are preferred. Java developers, make sure that you capitalize the first letter of these two words as you will receive an ugly *NameError* if you do not.

Boolean properties are not limited to working with int and bool values, but they also work with other values and objects. For instance, simply passing any non-empty object into a Boolean expression will evaluate to *True* in a Boolean context. This is a good way to determine whether a string contains anything. See Table 3-7.

Listing 3-12. Testing a String

```
>>> mystr = ''
>>> if mystr:
...     'Now I contain the following: %s' % (mystr)
... else:
...     'I do not contain anything'
...
'I do not contain anything'
>>> mystr = 'Now I have a value'
>>> if mystr:
...     'Now I contain the following: %s' % (mystr)
... else:
...     'I do not contain anything'
...
'Now I contain the following: Now I have a value'
```

***Table 3-7.** Boolean Conditionals*

Conditional	Logic
and	In an x and y evaluation, if *x* evaluates to false then its value is returned, otherwise *y* is evaluated and the resulting value is returned
or	In an *x or y* evaluation, if x evaluates to true then its value is returned, otherwise y is evaluated and the resulting value is returned
not	In a *not x* evaluation, if *not x*, we mean the opposite of x

As with all programming languages, there is an order of operations for deciding what operators are evaluated first. For instance, if we have an expression a + b *c, then which operation would take place first? The order of operations for Python is shown in Table 3-8 with those operators that receive the highest precedence shown first, and those with the lowest shown last. Repeats of the same operator are grouped from left to the right with the exception of the power (**) operator.

Table 3-8. Python Order of Operations

Operator Precedence from Highest to Lowest	Name
+var, -var, ~var	Unary Operations
**	Power Operations
*, /, //, %	Multiplication, Division, Floor Division, Modulo
+, -	Addition, Subtraction
<<, >>	Left and Right Shift
&	Bitwise And
^	Bitwise Exclusive Or
|	Bitwise Or
<, >, <=. >= , <>	Comparison Operators
==, != , is, is not, in, not in	Equality and Membership
and, or, not	Boolean Conditionals

An important note is that when working with Boolean conditionals, *'and'* and *'or'* group from the left to the right. Let's take a look at a few examples.

Listing 3-13. Order of Operations Examples

```
# Define a few variables
>>> x = 10
>>> y = 12
>>> z = 14

# (y*z) is evaluated first, then x is added
>>> x + y * z
178

# (x * y) is evaluated first, then z is subtracted from the result
>>> x * y - z
106

# When chaining comparisons, a logical 'and' is implied.  In this
# case, x < y and y <= z and z > x
>>> x < y <= z > x
True
```

```
# (2 * 0) is evaluated first and since it is False or zero, it is returned
>>> 2 * 0 and 5 + 1
0
# (2 * 1) is evaluated first, and since it is True or not zero, the (5 + 1) is evaluated and
# returned
>>> 2 * 1 and 5 + 1
6

# x is returned if it is True, otherwise y is returned if it is False.  If neither
# of those two conditions occur, then z is returned.
>>> x or (y and z)
10

# In this example, the (7 - 2) is evaluated and returned because of the 'and' 'or'
# logic
>>> 2 * 0 or ((6 + 8) and (7 - 2))
5

# In this case, the power operation is evaluated first, and then the addition
>>> 2 ** 2 + 8
12
```

Conversions

There are a number of conversion functions built into the language in order to help conversion of one data type to another (see Table 3-9). While every data type in Jython is actually a class object, these conversion functions will really convert one class type into another. For the most part, the built-in conversion functions are easy to remember because they are primarily named after the type to which you are trying to convert.

Table 3-9. Conversion Functions

Function	Description
chr(value)	Converts integer to a character
complex(real [,imag])	Produces a complex number
dict(sequence)	Produces a dictionary from a given sequence of (key, value) tuples
eval(string)	Evaluates a string to return an object...useful for mathematical computations. *Note: This function should be used with extreme caution as it can pose a security hazard if not used properly.*
float(value)	Converts number to float

Table 3-9. Conversion Functions (continued)

frozenset(set)	Converts a set into a frozen set
hex(value)	Converts an integer into a string representing that number in hex
int(value [, base])	Converts to an integer using a base if a string is given
list(sequence)	Converts a given sequence into a list
long(value [, base])	Converts to a long using a base if a string is given
oct(value)	Converts an integer to a string representing that number as an octal
ord(value)	Converts a character into its integer value
repr(value)	Converts object into an expression string. Same as enclosing expression in reverse quotes (`` `x + y` ``). Returns a string containing a printable and evaluable representation of the object
set(sequence)	Converts a sequence into a set
str(value)	Converts an object into a string Returns a string containing a printable representation of the value, but not an evaluable string
tuple(sequence)	Converts a given sequence to a tuple
unichr(value)	Converts integer to a Unicode character

Listing 3-14. Conversion Function Examples

```
# Return the character representation of the integers
>>> chr(4)
'\x04'
>>> chr(10)
'\n'

# Convert intger to float

>>> float(8)
8.0

# Convert character to its integer value
>>> ord('A')
65
>>> ord('C')
67
```

```
>>> ord('z')
122

# Use repr() with any object
>>> repr(3.14)
'3.14'
>>> x = 40 * 5
>>> y = 2**8
>>> repr((x, y, ('one','two','three')))
"(200, 256, ('one', 'two', 'three'))"
```

The following is an example of using the *eval()* functionality as it is perhaps the one conversion function for which an example helps to understand. Again, please note that using the *eval()* function can be dangerous and impose a security threat if used incorrectly. If using the *eval()* function to accept text from a user, standard security precautions should be set into place to ensure that the string being evaluated is not going to compromise security.

Listing 3-15. Example of eval()

```
# Suppose keyboard input contains an expression in string format (x * y)
>>> x = 5
>>> y = 12
>>> keyboardInput = 'x * y'
# We should provide some security checks on the keyboard input here to
# ensure that the string is safe for evaluation. Such a task is out of scope
# for this chapter, but it is good to note that comparisons on the keyboard
# input to check for possibly dangerous code should be performed prior to
# evaluation.
>>> eval(keyboardInput)
60
```

Using Expressions to Control Program Flow

As you've learned in previous references in this book, the statements that make up programs in Python are structured with attention to spacing, order, and technique. Each section of code must be consistently spaced as to set each control structure apart from others. One of the great advantages to Python's syntax is that the consistent spacing allows for delimiters such as the curly braces {} to go away. For instance, in Java one must use curly braces around a *for* loop to signify a start and an end point. Simply spacing a *for* loop in Python correctly takes place of the braces. Convention and good practice adhere to using four spaces of indentation per statement throughout the entire program. For more information on convention, please see PEP 8, Style Guide for Python Code (www.python.org/dev/peps/pep-0008/). Follow this convention along with some control flow and you're sure to develop some easily maintainable software.

if-elif-else Statement

The standard Python if-elif-else conditional statement is used in order to evaluate expressions and branch program logic based upon the outcome. An if-elif-else statement can consist of any expressions we've discussed previously. The objective is to write and compare expressions in order to evaluate to a *True* or *False* outcome. As shown in Chapter 1, the logic for an *if-elif-else* statement follows one path if an expression evaluates to *True*, or a different path if it evaluates to *False*.

You can chain as many *if-else* expressions together as needed. The combining *if-else* keyword is *elif*, which is used for every expression in between the first and the last expressions within a conditional statement.

The *elif* portion of the statement helps to ensure better readability of program logic. Too many *if* statements nested within each other can lead to programs that are difficult to maintain. The initial *if* expression is evaluated, and if it evaluates to *False*, the next *elif* expression is evaluated, and if it evaluates to *False* then the process continues. If any of the *if* or *elif* expressions evaluate to *True* then the statements within that portion of the *if* statement are processed. Eventually if all of the expressions evaluate to *False* then the final *else* expression is evaluated.

These next examples show a few ways for making use of a standard *if-elif-else* statement. Note that any expression can be evaluated in an *if-elif-else* construct. These are only some simplistic examples, but the logic inside the expressions could become as complex as needed.

Listing 3-16. Standard if-elif-else

```
# terminal symbols are left out of this example so that you can see the precise indentation
pi =3.14
x = 2.7 * 1.45
if x == pi:
    print 'The number is pi'
elif x > pi:
    print 'The number is greater than pi'
else:
    print 'The number is less than pi'
```

Empty lists or strings will evaluate to *False* as well, making it easy to use them for comparison purposes in an *if-elif-else* statement.

Listing 3-17. Evaluate Empty List

```
# Use an if-statement to determine whether a list is empty
# Suppose mylist is going to be a list of names
>>> mylist = []
>>> if mylist:
...     for person in mylist:
...         print person
... else:
...     print 'The list is empty'
...
The list is empty
```

while Loop

Another construct that we touched upon in Chapter 1 was the loop. Every programming language provides looping implementations, and Python is no different. To recap, the Python language provides two main types of loops known as the *while* and the *for* loop.

The *while* loop logic follows the same semantics as the *while* loop in Java. The while loop evaluates a given expression and continues to loop through its statements until the results of the expression no longer hold true and evaluate to False. Most while loops contain a comparison expression such as $x <= y$ or the like, in this case the expression would evaluate to False when x becomes greater than y. The loop will continue processing until the expression evaluates to *False*. At this time the looping ends and that would be it for the Java implementation. Python on the other hand allows an *else* clause which is executed when the loop is completed.

Listing 3-18. Python while Statement

```
>>> x = 0
>>> y = 10
>>> while x <= y:
...     print 'The current value of x is: %d' % (x)
...     x += 1
... else:
...     print 'Processing Complete...'
...
The current value of x is: 0
The current value of x is: 1
The current value of x is: 2
The current value of x is: 3
The current value of x is: 4
The current value of x is: 5
The current value of x is: 6
The current value of x is: 7
The current value of x is: 8
The current value of x is: 9
The current value of x is: 10
Processing Complete...
```

This *else* clause can come in handy while performing intensive processing so that we can inform the user of the completion of such tasks. It can also be handy when debugging code, or when some sort of cleanup is required after the loop completes

Listing 3-19. Resetting Counter Using with-else

```
>>> total = 0
>>> x = 0
>>> y = 20
>>> while x <= y:
...     total += x
...     x += 1
... else:
...     print total
...     total = 0
...
210
```

continue Statement

The *continue* statement is to be used when you are within a looping construct, and you have the requirement to tell Python to *continue* processing past the rest of the statements in the current loop. Once the Python interpreter sees a *continue* statement, it ends the current iteration of the loop and goes on to continue processing the next iteration. The *continue* statement can be used with any *for* or *while* loop.

Listing 3-20. Continue Statement

```
# Iterate over range and print out only the positive numbers
>>> x = 0

>>> while x < 10:

...     x += 1

...     if x % 2 != 0:

...         continue

...     print x

...

2

4

6

8

10
```

        In this example, whenever *x* is odd, the 'continue' causes execution to move on to the next iteration
of the loop. When x is even, it is printed out.

break Statement

Much like the *continue* statement, the *break* statement can be used inside of a loop. We use the *break*
statement in order to stop the loop completely so that a program can move on to its next task. This
differs from *continue* because the *continue* statement only stops the current iteration of the loop and
moves onto the next iteration. Let's check it out:

Listing 3-21. Break Statement

```
>>> x = 10
>>> while True:
...     if x == 0:
...         print 'x is now equal to zero!'
...         break
...     if x % 2 == 0:
...         print x
...     x -= 1
...
10
8
6
4
```

```
2
x is now equal to zero!
```

In the previous example, the loop termination condition is always True, so execution only leaves the loop when a break is encountered. If we are working with a break statement that resides within a loop that is contained in another loop (nested loop construct), then only the inner loop will be terminated.

for Loop

The *for* loop can be used on any iterable object. It will simply iterate through the object and perform some processing during each pass. Both the *break* and *continue* statements can also be used within the *for* loop. The *for* statement in Python also differs from the same statement in Java because in Python we also have the *else* clause with this construct. Once again, the *else* clause is executed when the *for* loop processes to completion without any *break* intervention or raised exceptions. Also, if you are familiar with pre-Java 5 *for* loops then you will love the Python syntax. In Java 5, the syntax of the *for* statement was adjusted a bit to make it more in line with syntactically easy languages such as Python.

Listing 3-22. Comparing Java and Python for-loop

Example of Java for-loop (pre Java 5)

```
for(x = 0; x <= myList.size(); x++){
    // processing statements iterating through myList
    System.out.println("The current index is: " + x);
}
```

Listing 3-23. Example of Python for-loop

```
my_list = [1,2,3,4,5]
>>> for value in my_list:
...        # processing statements using value as the current item in my_list
...        print 'The current value is %s' % (value)
...
The current value is 1
The current value is 2
The current value is 3
The current value is 4
The current value is 5
```

As you can see, the Python syntax is a little easier to understand, but it doesn't really save too many keystrokes at this point. We still have to manage the index (*x* in this case) by ourselves by incrementing it with each iteration of the loop. However, Python does provide a built-in function that can save us some keystrokes and provides a similar functionality to that of Java with the automatically incrementing index on the *for* loop. The *enumerate(sequence)* function does just that. It will provide an index for our use and automatically manage it for us.

Listing 3-24. Enumerate() Functionality

```
>>> myList = ['jython','java','python','jruby','groovy']
>>> for index, value in enumerate(myList):
```

```
...     print index, value
...
0 jython
1 java
2 python
3 jruby
4 groovy
```

If we do not require the use of an index, it can be removed and the syntax can be cleaned up a bit.

```
>>> myList = ['jython', 'java', 'python', 'jruby', 'groovy']
>>> for item in myList:
...     print item
...
jython
java
python
jruby
groovy
```

Now we have covered the program flow for conditionals and looping constructs in the Python language. However, good programming practice will tell you to keep it as simple as possible or the logic will become too hard to follow. In practicing proper coding techniques, it is also good to know that lists, dictionaries, and other containers can be iterated over just like other objects. Iteration over containers using the *for* loop is a very useful strategy. Here is an example of iterating over a dictionary object.

Listing 3-25. Iteration Over Containers

```
# Define a dictionary and then iterate over it to print each value
>>> my_dict = {'Jython':'Java', 'CPython':'C', 'IronPython':'.NET', 'PyPy':'Python'}
>>> for key in my_dict:
...     print key
...
Jython
IronPython
CPython
PyPy
```

It is useful to know that we can also obtain the values of a dictionary object via each iteration by calling *my_dict.values()*.

Example Code

Let's take a look at an example program that uses some of the program flow which was discussed in this chapter. The example program simply makes use of an external text file to manage a list of players on a sports team. You will see how to follow proper program structure and use spacing effectively in this example. You will also see file utilization in action, along with utilization of the *raw_input()* function.

Listing 3-26. # import os module

```
import os
```

```python
# Create empty dictionary
player_dict = {}
# Create an empty string
enter_player = ''

# Enter a loop to enter inforation from keyboard
while enter_player.upper() != 'X':

    print 'Sports Team Administration App'

    # If the file exists, then allow us to manage it, otherwise force creation.
    if os.path.isfile('players.txt'):
        enter_player = raw_input("Would you like to create a team or manage an existing
team?\n (Enter 'C' for create, 'M' for manage, 'X' to exit) ")
    else:
        # Force creation of file if it does not yet exist.
        enter_player = 'C'

    # Check to determine which action to take.  C = create, M = manage, X = Exit and Save
    if enter_player.upper() == 'C':

    # Enter a player for the team
        print 'Enter a list of players on our team along with their position'
        enter_cont = 'Y'

        #  While continuing to enter new player's, perform the following
        while enter_cont.upper() == 'Y':
            # Capture keyboard entry into name variable
            name = raw_input('Enter players first name: ')
            # Capture keyboard entry into position variable
            position = raw_input('Enter players position: ')
            # Assign position to a dictionary key of the player name
            player_dict[name] = position
            enter_cont = raw_input("Enter another player? (Press 'N' to exit or 'Y' to
continue)")
        else:
            enter_player = 'X'

    # Manage player.txt entries
    elif enter_player.upper() == 'M':

        # Read values from the external file into a dictionary object
        print
        print 'Manage the Team'
        # Open file and assign to playerfile
        playerfile = open('players.txt','r')
        # Use the for-loop to iterate over the entries in the file
        for player in playerfile:
            # Split entries into key/value pairs and add to list
            playerList = player.split(':')
            # Build dictionary using list values from file
            player_dict[playerList[0]] = playerList[1]
        # Close the file
        playerfile.close()
```

```
        print 'Team Listing'
        print '++++++++++++'

        # Iterate over dictionary values and print key/value pairs
        for i, player in enumerate(player_dict):
            print 'Player %s Name: %s -- Position: %s' %(i, player, player_dict[player])

else:
    # Save the external file and close resources
    if player_dict:

        print 'Saving Team Data...'
        # Open the file
        playerfile = open('players.txt','w')
        # Write each dictionary element to the file
        for player in player_dict:
            playerfile.write('%s:%s\n' % (player.strip(),player_dict[player].strip()))
        # Close file
        playerfile.close()
```

This example is packed full of concepts that have been discussed throughout the first three chapters of the book. As stated previously, the concept is to create and manage a list of sport players and their relative positions. The example starts by entering a *while()* loop that runs the program until the user enters the exit command. Next, the program checks to see if the 'players.txt' file exists. If it does, then the program prompts the user to enter a code to determine the next action to be taken. However, if the file does not exist then the user is forced to create at least one player/position pair in the file.

Continuing on, the program allows the user to enter as many player/position pairs as needed, or exit the program at any time. If the user chooses to manage the player/position list, the program simply opens the 'players.txt' file, uses a *for()* loop to iterate over each entry within the file. A dictionary is populated with the current player in each iteration of the loop. Once the loop has completed, the file is closed and the dictionary is iterated and printed. Exiting the program forces the *else()* clause to be invoked, which iterates over each player in the dictionary and writes them to the file.

Unfortunately, this program is quite simplistic and some features could not be implemented without knowledge of functions (Chapter 4) or classes (Chapter 6). A good practice would be to revisit this program once those topics have been covered and simplify as well as add additional functionality.

Summary

All programs are constructed out of statements and expressions. In this chapter we covered details of creating expressions and using them. Expressions can be composed of any number of mathematical operators and comparisons. In this chapter we discussed the basics of using mathematical operators in our programs. The __future__ division topic introduced us to using features from the __future__. We then delved into comparisons and comparison operators.

We ended this short chapter by discussing proper program flow and properly learned about the *if* statement as well as how to construct different types of loops in Python. In the next chapter you will learn how to write functions, and the use of many built-in functions will be discussed.

CHAPTER 4

■ ■ ■

Defining Functions and Using Built-ins

Functions are the fundamental unit of work in Python. A function in Python performs a task and returns a result. In this chapter, we will start with the basics of functions. Then we look at using the built-in functions. These are the core functions that are always available, meaning they don't require an explicit import into your namespace. Next we will look at some alternative ways of defining functions, such as lambdas and classes. We will also look at more advanced types of functions, namely closures and generator functions.

As you will see, functions are very easy to define and use. Python encourages an incremental style of development that you can leverage when writing functions. So how does this work out in practice? Often when writing a function it may make sense to start with a sequence of statements and just try it out in a console. Or maybe just write a short script in an editor. The idea is to just to prove a path and answer such questions as, "Does this API work in the way I expect?" Because top-level code in a console or script works just like it does in a function, it's easy to later isolate this code in a function body and then package it as a function, maybe in a library, or as a method as part of a class. The ease of doing this style of development is one aspect that makes Python such a joy use. And of course in the Jython implementation, it's easy to use this technique within the context of any Java library.

An important thing to keep in mind is that functions are first-class objects in Python. They can be passed around just like any other variable, resulting in some very powerful solutions. We'll see some examples of using functions in such a way later in this chapter.

Function Syntax and Basics

Functions are usually defined by using the *'def'* keyword, the name of the function, its parameters (if any), and the body of code. We will start by looking at this example function:

Listing 4-1.

```
def times2(n):
    return n * 2
```

In this example, the function name is *times2* and it accepts a parameter *n*. The body of the function is only one line, but the work being done is the multiplication of the parameter by the number 2. Instead of storing the result in a variable, this function simply returns it to the calling code. An example of using this function would be as follows.

Listing 4-2.

```
>>> times2(8)
16
>>> x = times2(5)
>>> x
10
```

Normal usage can treat function definitions as being very simple. But there's subtle power in every piece of the function definition, due to the fact that Python is a dynamic language. We'll look at these pieces from both a simple (the more typical case) and a more advanced perspective. We will also look at some alternative ways of creating functions in a later section.

The *def* Keyword

Using *'def'* for *define* seems simple enough, and this keyword certainly can be used to declare a function just like you would in a static language. You should write most code that way in fact.

However, a function definition can occur at any level in your code and be introduced at any time. Unlike the case in a language like C or Java, function definitions are not declarations. Instead they are *executable statements*. You can nest functions, and we'll describe that more when we talk about nested scopes. And you can do things like conditionally define them.

This means it's perfectly valid to write code like the following:

Listing 4-3.

```
if variant:
    def f():
        print "One way"
 else:
    def f():
        print "or another"
```

Please note, regardless of when and where the definition occurs, including its variants as above, the function definition will be compiled into a *function object* at the same time as the rest of the module or script that the function is defined in.

Naming the Function

We will describe this more in a later section, but the `dir` built-in function will tell us about the names defined in a given namespace, defaulting to the module, script, or console environment we are working in. With this new `times2` function defined above, we now see the following (at least) in the console namespace:

Listing 4-4.

```
>>> dir()
['__doc__', '__name__', 'times2']
```

We can also just look at what is bound to that name:

Listing 4-5.

```
>>> times2
<function times2 at 0x1>
```

(This object is further introspectable. Try `dir(times2)` and go from there.) We can reference the function by supplying the function name such as we did in the example above. However, in order to call the function and make it perform some work, we need to supply the () to the end of the name.

We can also redefine a function at any time:

Listing 4-6.

```
>>> def f(): print "Hello, world"
...
>>> def f(): print "Hi, world"
...
>>> f()
Hi, world
```

This is true not just of running it from the console, but any module or script. The original version of the function object will persist until it's no longer referenced, at which point it will be ultimately be garbage collected. In this case, the only reference was the name f, so it became available for GC immediately upon rebind.

What's important here is that we simply rebound the name. First it pointed to one function object, then another. We can see that in action by simply setting another name (equivalently, a variable) to `times2`.

Listing 4-7.

```
>>> t2 = times2
>>> t2(5)
10
```

This makes passing a function as a parameter very easy, for a callback for example. A callback is a function that can be invoked by a function to perform a task and then turn around and invoke the calling function, thus the callback. Let's take a look at function parameters in more detail.

FUNCTION METAPROGRAMMING

A given name can only be associated with one function at a time, so can't overload a function with multiple definitions. If you were to define two or more functions with the same name, the last one defined is used, as we saw.

However, it is possible to overload a function, or otherwise genericize it. You simply need to create a dispatcher function that then dispatches to your set of corresponding functions. Another way to genericize a function is to make use of the simplegeneric module which lets you define simple single-dispatch generic functions. For more information, please see the simplegeneric package in the Python Package Index.

Function Parameters and Calling Functions

When defining a function, you specify the parameters it takes. Typically you will see something like the following. The syntax is familiar:

def tip_calc(amt, pct)

As mentioned previously, calling functions is also done by placing parentheses after the function name. For example, for the function x with parameters a,b,c that would be x(a,b,c). Unlike some other dynamic languages like Ruby and Perl, the use of parentheses is required syntax (due the function name being just like any other name).

Objects are strongly typed, as we have seen. But function parameters, like names in general in Python, are not typed. This means that any parameter can refer to any type of object.

We see this play out in the times2 function. The * operator not only means multiply for numbers, it also means repeat for sequences (like strings and lists). So you can use the times2 function as follows:

Listing 4-8.

```
>>> times2(4)
8
>>> times2('abc')
'abcabc'
>>> times2([1,2,3])
[1, 2, 3, 1, 2, 3]
```

All parameters in Python are passed by reference. This is identical to how Java does it with object parameters. However, while Java does support passing unboxed primitive types by value, there are no such entities in Python. Everything is an object in Python. It is important to remember that immutable objects cannot be changed, and therefore, if we pass a string to a function and alter it, a copy of the string is made and the changes are applied to the copy.

Listing 4-9.

```
# The following function changes the text of a string by making a copy
# of the string and then altering it.  The original string is left
# untouched as it is immutable.
>>> def changestr(mystr):
...      mystr = mystr + '_changed'
...      print 'The string inside the function: ', mystr
...      return
>>> mystr = 'hello'
>>> changestr(mystr)
The string inside the function:  hello_changed
>>> mystr
'hello'
```

Functions are objects too, and they can be passed as parameters:

Listing 4-10.

```
# Define a function that takes two values and a mathematical function
>>> def perform_calc(value1, value2, func):
...      return func(value1, value2)
```

```
...
# Define a mathematical function to pass
>>> def mult_values(value1, value2):
...     return value1 * value2
...
>>> perform_calc(2, 4, mult_values)
8

# Define another mathematical function to pass
>>> def add_values(value1, value2):
...     return value1 + value2
...
>>> perform_calc(2, 4, add_values)
6
>>>
```

If you have more than two or so arguments, it often makes more sense to call a function by named values, rather than by the positional parameters. This tends to create more robust code. So if you have a function draw_point(x,y), you might want to call it as draw_point(x=10,y=20).

Defaults further simplify calling a function. You use the form of param=default_value when defining the function. For instance, you might take our times2 function and generalize it.

Listing 4-11.

```
def times_by(n, by=2):
    return n * by
```

This function is equivalent to times2 when called with just one argument—it uses the default value for the second argument by.

There's one point to remember that often trips up developers. The default value is initialized exactly once, when the function is defined. That's certainly fine for immutable values like numbers, strings, tuples, frozensets, and similar objects. But you need to ensure that if the default value is mutable, that it's being used correctly. So a dictionary for a shared cache makes sense. But this mechanism won't work for a list where we expect it is initialized to an empty list upon invocation. If you're doing that, you need to write that explicitly in your code. As a best practice, use None as the default value rather than a mutable object, and check at the start of the body of your function for the case *value = None* and set the variable to your mutable object there.

Lastly, a function can take an unspecified number of ordered arguments, through *args, and keyword args, through **kwargs. These parameter names (args and kwargs) are conventional, so you can use whatever name makes sense for your function. The markers * and ** are used to determine that this functionality should be used. The single * argument allows for passing a sequence of values, and a double ** argument allows for passing a dictionary of names and values. If either of these types of arguments is specified, they must follow any single arguments in the function declaration. Furthermore, the double ** must follow the single *.

Definition of a function that takes a sequence of numbers:

Listing 4-12.

```
def sum_args(*nums):
    return sum(nums)
```
Calling the function using a sequence of numbers:

```
>>> seq = [6,5,4,3]
>>> sum_args(*seq)
18
# we can also call the function without using the *
>>> sum_args(1,2,3,4)
10
```

Recursive Function Calls

It is also quite common to see cases in which a function calls itself from inside the function body. This type of function call is known as a recursive function call. Let's take a look at a function that computes the factorial of a given argument. This function calls itself passing in the provided argument decremented by 1 until the argument reaches the value of 0 or 1.

Listing 4-13.

```
def fact(n):
    if n in (0, 1):
        return 1
    else:
        return n * fact(n - 1)
```

It is important to note that Jython is like CPython in that it is ultimately stack based. Stacks are regions of memory where data is added and removed in a last-in first-out manner. If a recursive function calls itself too many times then it is possible to exhaust the stack, which results in an *OutOfMemoryError*. Therefore, be cautious when developing software using deep recursion.

Function Body

This section will break down the different components that comprise the body of a function. The body of a function is the part that performs the work. Throughout the next couple of sub-sections, you will see that a function body can be comprised of many different parts.

Documenting Functions

First, you should specify a document string for the function. The docstring, if it exists, is a string that occurs as the first value of the function body.

Listing 4-14.

```
def times2(n):
    """Given n, returns n * 2"""
    return n * 2
```

As mentioned in Chapter 1, by convention we use triple-quoted strings, even if your docstring is not multiline. If it is multiline, this is how we recommend you format it. For more information, please take a look at PEP 257 (www.python.org/dev/peps/pep-0257).

Listing 4-15.

```
def fact(n):
    """Returns the factorial of n

    Computes the factorial of n recursively. Does not check its
    arguments if nonnegative integer or if would stack
    overflow. Use with care!
    """

    if n in (0, 1):
        return 1
    else:
        return n * fact(n - 1)
```

Any such docstring, but with leading indentation stripped, becomes the __doc__ attribute of that function object. Incidentally, docstrings are also used for modules and classes, and they work exactly the same way.

You can now use the help built-in function to get the docstring, or see them from various IDEs like PyDev for Eclipse and nbPython for NetBeans as part of the auto-complete.

Listing 4-16.

```
>>> help(fact)
Help on function fact in module __main__:

fact(n)
    Returns the factorial of n

>>>
```

Returning Values

All functions return some value. In times2, we use the return statement to exit the function with that value. Functions can easily return multiple values at once by returning a tuple or other structure. The following is a simple example of a function that returns more than one value. In this case, the tip calculator returns the result of a tip based upon two percentage values.

Listing 4-17.

```
>>> def calc_tips(amount):
...     return (amount * .18), (amount * .20)
...
>>> calc_tips(25.25)
(4.545, 5.050000000000001)
```

A function can return at any time, and it can also return any object as its value. So you can have a function that looks like the following:

Listing 4-18.

```
>>> def check_pos_perform_calc(num1, num2, func):
...     if num1 > 0 and num2 > 0:
...         return func(num1, num2)
...     else:
...         return 'Only positive numbers can be used with this function!'
...
>>> def mult_values(value1, value2):
...     return value1 * value2
...
>>> check_pos_perform_calc(3, 4, mult_values)
12
>>> check_pos_perform_calc(3, -44, mult_values)
'Only positive numbers can be used with this function!'
```

   If a return statement is not used, the value None is returned. There is no equivalent to a void method in Java, because every function in Python returns a value. However, the Python console will not show the return value when it's None, so you need to explicitly print it to see what is returned.

Listing 4-19.

```
>>> do_nothing()
>>> print do_nothing()
None
```

Introducing Variables

A function introduces a scope for new names, such as variables. Any names that are created in the function are only visible within that scope. In the following example, the sq variable is defined within the scope of the function definition itself. If we try to use it outside of the function then we'll receive an error.

Listing 4-20.

```
>>> def square_num(num):
...     """ Return the square of a number"""
...     sq = num * num
...     return sq
...
>>> square_num(35)
1225
>>> sq
Traceback (most recent call last):
  File "<stdin>", line 1, in <module>
NameError: name 'sq' is not defined
```

GLOBAL VARIABLES

The global keyword is used to declare that a variable name is from the module scope (or script) containing this function. Using global is rarely necessary in practice, since it is not necessary if the name is called as a function or an attribute is accessed (through dotted notation).

This is a good example of where Python is providing a complex balancing between a complex idea—the lexical scoping of names, and the operations on them—and the fact that in practice it is doing the right thing.

Here is an example of using a global variable in the same *square_num()* function.

Listing 4-21.

```
>>> sq = 0
>>> def square_num(n):
...     global sq
...     sq = n * n
...     return sq
...
>>> square_num(10)
100
>>> sq
100
```

Other Statements

What can go in a function body? Pretty much any statement, including material that we will cover later in this book. So you can define functions or classes or use even import, within the scope of that function.

In particular, performing a potentially expensive operation like import as least as possible, can reduce the startup time of your app. It's even possible it will be never needed too.

There are a couple of exceptions to this rule. In both cases, these statements must go at the beginning of a module, similar to what we see in a static language like Java:

- Compiler directives. Python supports a limited set of compiler directives that have the provocative syntax of from __future__ import X; see PEP 236. These are features that will eventually be made available, generally in the next minor revision (such as 2.5 to 2.6). In addition, it's a popular place to put Easter eggs, such as from __future__ import braces. (Try it in the console, which also relaxes what it means to be performed at the beginning.)

- Source encoding declaration. Although technically not a statement—it's in a specially parsed comment—this must go in the first or second line.

Empty Functions

It is also possible to define an empty function. Why have a function that does nothing? As in math, it's useful to have an operation that stands for doing nothing, like "add zero" or "multiply by one." These identity functions eliminate special cases. Likewise, as see with empty_callback, we may need to specify a callback function when calling an API, but nothing actually needs to be done. By passing in an empty function—or having this be the default—we can simplify the API. An empty function still needs something in its body. You can use the pass statement.

Listing 4-22.

```
def do_nothing():
    pass # here's how to specify an empty body of code
```

Or you can just have a docstring for the function body as in the following example.

```
def empty_callback(*args, **kwargs):
    """Use this function where we need to supply a callback,
    but have nothing further to do.
    """
```

Miscellaneous Information for the Curious Reader

As you already know, Jython is an interpreted language. That is, the Python code that we write for a Jython application is ultimately compiled down into Java bytecode when our program is run. So oftentimes it is useful for Jython developers to understand what is going on when this code is interpreted into Java bytecode.

What do functions look like from Java? They are instances of an object named PyObject, supporting the __call__ method.

Additional introspection is available. If a function object is just a standard function written in Python, it will be of class PyFunction. A built-in function will be of class PyBuiltinFunction. But don't assume that in your code, because many other objects support the function interface (__call__), and these potentially could be proxying, perhaps several layers deep, a given function. You can only assume it's a PyObject.

Much more information is available by going to the Jython wiki. You can also send questions to the jython-dev mailing list for more specifics.

Built-in Functions

Built-in functions are those functions that are always in the Python namespace. In other words, these functions—and built-in exceptions, boolean values, and some other objects—are the only truly globally defined names. If you are familiar with Java, they are somewhat like the classes from java.lang.

Built-ins are rarely sufficient, however; even a simple command line script generally needs to parse its arguments or read in from its standard input. So for this case you would need to import sys. And in the context of Jython, you will need to import the relevant Java classes you are using, perhaps with import java. But the built-in functions are really the core function that almost all Python code uses.

The documentation for covering all of the built-in functions that are available is extensive. However, it has been included in this book as Appendix C. It should be easy to use Appendix C as a reference when using a built-in function, or for choosing which built-in function to use.

Alternative Ways to Define Functions

The '*def*' keyword is not the only way to define a function. Here are some alternatives:

- Lambda Functions: '*lambda*' functions. The '*lambda*' keyword creates an unnamed function. Some people like this because it requires minimal space, especially when used in a callback.

- Classes: In addition, we can also create objects with classes whose instance objects look like ordinary functions. Objects supporting the __call__ protocol. For Java developers, this is familiar. Classes implement such single-method interfaces as Callable or Runnable.

- Bound Methods: Instead of calling x.a(), I can pass x.a as a parameter or bind to another name. Then I can invoke this name. The first parameter of the method will be passed the bound object, which in OO terms is the receiver of the method. This is a simple way of creating callbacks. (In Java you would have just passed the object of course, then having the callback invoke the appropriate method such as *call* or *run*.)

Lambda Functions

As stated in the introduction, a lambda function is an anonymous function. In other words, a lambda function is not required to be bound to any name. This can be useful when you are trying to create compact code or when it does not make sense to declare a named function because it will only be used once.

A lambda function is usually written inline with other code, and most often the body of a lambda function is very short in nature. A lambda function is comprised of the following segments:
lambda <<argument(s)>> : <<function body>>

A lambda function accepts arguments just like any other function, and it uses those arguments within its function body. Also, just like other functions in Python a value is always returned. Let's take a look at a simple lambda function to get a better understanding of how they work.

Listing 4-23. Example of using a lambda function to combine two strings. In this case, a first and last name

```
>>> name_combo = lambda first,last: first + ' ' + last
>>> name_combo('Jim','Baker')
'Jim Baker'
```

In the example above, we assigned the function to a name. However, a lambda function can also be defined in-line with other code. Oftentimes a lambda function is used within the context of other functions, namely built-ins.

Generator Functions

Generators are special functions that are an example of iterators, which will be discussed in Chapter 6. Generators advance to the next point by calling the special method next. Usually that's done implicitly, typically through a loop or a consuming function that accepts iterators, including generators. They return values by using the *yield* statement. Each time a *yield* statement is encountered then the current iteration halts and a value is returned. Generators have the ability to remember where they left off. Each time *next()* is called, the generator resumes where it had left off. A *StopIteration* error will be raised once the generator has been terminated.

Over the next couple of sections, we will take a closer look at generators and how they work. Along the way, you will see many examples for creating and using generators.

Defining Generators

A generator function is written so that it consists of one or more yield points, which are marked through the use of the *yield* statement. As mentioned previously, each time the yield statement is encountered, a value is returned.

Listing 4-24.

```
def g():
    print "before yield point 1"
    # The generator will return a value once it encounters the yield statement
    yield 1
    print "after 1, before 2"
    yield 2
    yield 3
```

In the previous example, the generator function *g()* will halt and return a value once the first *yield* statement is encountered. In this case, a 1 will be returned. The next time *g.next()* is called, the generator will continue until it encounters the next yield statement. At that point it will return another value, the 2 in this case. Let's see this generator in action. Note that calling the generator function simply creates your generator, it does not cause any yields. In order to get the value from the first yield, we must call *next()*.

Listing 4-25.

```
# Call the function to create the generator
>>> x = g()
# Call next() to get the value from the yield
>>> x.next()
before the yield point 1
1
>>> x.next()
after 1, before 2
2
>>> x.next()
3
>>> x.next()
Traceback (most recent call last):
  File "<stdin>", line 1, in <module>
StopIteration
```

Let's take a look at another more useful example of a generator. In the following example, the *step_to()* function is a generator that increments based upon a given factor. The generator starts at zero and increments each time *next()* is called. It will stop working once it reaches the value that is provided by the *stop* argument.

Listing 4-26.

```
>>> def step_to(factor, stop):
...     step = factor
...     start = 0
```

```
...         while start <= stop:
...             yield start
...             start += step
...
>>> for x in step_to(1, 10):
...     print x
...
0
1
2
3
4
5
6
7
8
9
10
>>> for x in step_to(2, 10):
...     print x
...
0
2
4
6
8
10
>>>
```

If the yield statement is seen in the scope of a function, then that function is compiled as if it's a generator function. Unlike other functions, you use the return statement only to say, "I'm done," that is, to exit the generator, and not to return any values. You can think of return as acting like a break in a for-loop or while-loop. Let's change the step_to function just a bit to check and ensure that the factor is less than the stopping point. We'll add a return statement to exit the generator if the factor is greater or equal to the stop.

Listing 4-27

```
>>> def step_return(factor, stop):
...     step = factor
...     start = 0
...     if factor >= stop:
...         return
...     while start <= stop:
...         yield start
...         start += step
...
>>> for x in step_return(1,10):
...     print x
...
0
1
2
```

```
3
4
5
6
7
8
9
10
>>> for x in step_return(3,10):
...     print x
...
0
3
6
9
>>> for x in step_return(3,3):
...     print x
...
```

If you attempt to return an argument then a syntax error will be raised.

Listing 4-28.

```
def g():
    yield 1
    yield 2
    return None

for i in g():
    print i

SyntaxError: 'return' with argument inside generator
```

Many useful generators actually will have an infinite loop around their yield expression, instead of ever exiting, explicitly or not. The generator will essentially work each time *next()* is called throughout the life of the program.

Listing 4-29. Pseudocode for generator using infinite loop

```
while True:
    yield stuff
```

This works because a generator object can be garbage collected as soon as the last reference to the generator is used. The fact that it uses the machinery of function objects to implement itself doesn't matter.

HOW IT ACTUALLY WORKS

Generators are actually compiled differently from other functions. Each yield point saves the state of unnamed local variables (Java temporaries) into the frame object, then returns the value to the function that had called next (or send in the case of a coroutine which will be discussed later in this chapter). The generator is then indefinitely suspended, just like any other iterator. Upon calling *next* again, the generator is resumed by restoring these local variables, then executing the next bytecode instruction following the yield point. This process continues until the generator is either garbage collected or it exits.

Generators can also be resumed from any thread, although some care is necessary to ensure that underlying system state is shared (or compatible).

Generator Expressions

Generator expressions are an alternative way to create the generator object. Please note that this is not the same as a generator function! It's the equivalent to what a generator function yields when called. Generator expressions basically create an unnamed generator.

Listing 4-30.

```
>>> x = (2 * x for x in [1,2,3,4])
>>> x
<generator object at 0x1>
>>> x()
Traceback (most recent call last):
  File "<stdin>", line 1, in <module>
TypeError: 'generator' object is not callable
    Let's see this generator expression in action:
>>> for v in x:
...     print v
...
2
4
6
8
>>>
```

Typically generator expressions tend to be more compact but less versatile than generator functions. They are useful for getting things done in a concise manner.

Namespaces, Nested Scopes, and Closures

Note that you can introduce other namespaces into your function definition. It is possible to include import statements directly within the body of a function. This allows such imports to be valid only within the context of the function. For instance, in the following function definition the imports of *A* and *B* are only valid within the context of *f()*.

Listing 4-31.

```
def f():
    from NS import A, B
```

At first glance, including import statements within your function definitions may seem unnecessary. However, if you think of a function as an object then it makes much more sense. We can pass functions around just like other objects in Python such as variables. As mentioned previously, functions can even be passed to other functions as arguments. Function namespaces provide the ability to treat functions as their own separate piece of code. Oftentimes, functions that are used in several different places throughout an application are stored in a separate module. The module is then imported into the program where needed.

Functions can also be nested within each other to create useful solutions. Since functions have their own namespace, any function that is defined within another function is only valid within the parent function. Let's take a look at a simple example of this before we go any further.

Listing 4-32.

```
>>> def parent_function():
...     x = [0]
...     def child_function():
...         x[0] += 1
...         return x[0]
...     return child_function
...
>>> p = parent_function()
>>> p()
1
>>> p()
2
>>> p()
3
>>> p()
4
```

While this example is not extremely useful, it allows you to understand a few of the concepts for nesting functions. As you can see, the *parent_function* contains a function named *child_function*. The *parent_function* in this example returns the *child_function*. What we have created in this example is a simple *Closure* function. Each time the function is called, it executes the inner function and increments the variable *x* which is only available within the scope of this closure.

In the context of Jython, using closures such as the one defined previously can be useful for integrating Java concepts as well. It is possible to import Java classes into the scope of your function just as it is possible to work with other Python modules. It is sometimes useful to import in a function call in order to avoid circular imports, which is the case when function A imports function B, which in turn contains an import to function A. By specifying an import in a function call you are only using the import where it is needed. You will learn more about using Java within Jython in Chapter 10.

Function Decorators

Decorators are a convenient syntax that describes a way to transform a function. They are essentially a metaprogramming technique that enhances the action of the function that they decorate. To program a function decorator, a function that has already been defined can be used to decorate another function, which basically allows the decorated function to be passed into the function that is named in the decorator. Let's look at a simple example.

Listing 4-33.

```
def plus_five(func):
    x = func()
    return x + 5

@plus_five
def add_nums():
    return 1 + 2
```

In this example, the *add_nums()* function is decorated with the *plus_five()* function. This has the same effect as passing the *add_nums* function into the *plus_five* function. In other words, this decorator is syntactic sugar that makes this technique easier to use. The decorator above has the same functionality as the following code.

Listing 4-34.

```
add_nums = plus_five(add_nums)
```

In actuality, *add_nums* is now no longer a function, but rather an integer. After decorating with *plus_five* you can no longer call *add_nums()*, we can only reference it as if it were an integer. As you can see, *add_nums* is being passed to *plus_five* at import time. Normally, we'd want to have *add_nums* finish up as a function so that it is still callable. In order to make this example more useful, we'll want to make *add_nums* callable again and we will also want the ability to change the numbers that are added. To do so, we need to rewrite the decorator function a bit so that it includes an inner function that accepts arguments from the decorated function.

Listing 4-35.

```
def plus_five(func):
    def inner(*args, **kwargs):
        x = func(*args, **kwargs) + 5
        return x
    return inner

@plus_five
def add_nums(num1, num2):
    return num1 + num2
```

Now we can call the add_nums() function once again and we can also pass two arguments to it. Because it is decorated with the plus_five function it will be passed to it and then the two arguments will be added together and the number five will be added to that sum. The result will then be returned.

Listing 4-36.

```
>>> add_nums(2,3)
10
>>> add_nums(2,6)
13
```

Now that we've covered the basics of function decorators it is time to take a look at a more in-depth example of the concept. In the following decorator function example, we are taking a twist on the old tip_calculator function and adding a sales tax calculation. As you see, the original *calc_bill* function takes a sequence of amounts, namely the amounts for each item on the bill. The *calc_bill* function then simply sums the amounts and returns the value. In the given example, we apply the *sales_tax* decorator to the function which then transforms the function so that it not only calculates and returns the sum of all amounts on the bill, but it also applies a standard sales tax to the bill and returns the tax amount and total amounts as well.

Listing 4-37.

```
def sales_tax(func):
    ''' Applies a sales tax to a given bill calculator '''
    def calc_tax(*args, **kwargs):
        f = func(*args, **kwargs)
        tax = f * .18
        print "Total before tax: $ %.2f" % (f)
        print "Tax Amount: $ %.2f" % (tax)
        print "Total bill: $ %.2f" % (f + tax)
    return calc_tax

@sales_tax
def calc_bill(amounts):
    ''' Takes a sequence of amounts and returns sum '''
    return sum(amounts)
```

The decorator function contains an inner function that accepts two arguments, a sequence of arguments and a dictionary of keyword args. We must pass these arguments to our original function when calling from the decorator to ensure that the arguments that we passed to the original function are applied within the decorator function as well. In this case, we want to pass a sequence of amounts to *calc_bill*, so passing the *args, and **kwargs arguments to the function ensures that our amounts sequence is passed within the decorator. The decorator function then performs simple calculations for the tax and total dollar amounts and prints the results. Let's see this in action:

Listing 4-38.

```
>>> amounts = [12.95,14.57,9.96]
>>> calc_bill(amounts)
Total before tax: $ 37.48
Tax Amount: $ 6.75
Total bill: $ 44.23
```

It is also possible to pass arguments to decorator functions when doing the decorating. In order to do so, we must nest another function within our decorator function. The outer function will accept the arguments to be passed into the decorator function, the inner function will accept the decorated function, and the inner most function will perform the work. We'll take another spin on the tip calculator example and create a decorator that will apply the tip calculation to the *calc_bill* function.

Listing 4-39.

```
def tip_amount(tip_pct):
    def calc_tip_wrapper(func):
```

```
        def calc_tip_impl(*args, **kwargs):
            f = func(*args, **kwargs)
            print "Total bill before tip: $ %.2f" % (f)
            print "Tip amount: $ %.2f" % (f * tip_pct)
            print "Total with tip: $ %.2f" % (f + (f * tip_pct))
        return calc_tip_impl
    return calc_tip_wrapper
```

Now let's see this decorator function in action. As you'll notice, we pass a percentage amount to the decorator itself and it is applied to the decorator function.

Listing 4-40.

```
>>> @tip_amount(.18)
... def calc_bill(amounts):
...     ''' Takes a sequence of amounts and returns sum '''
...     return sum(amounts)
...
>>> amounts = [20.95, 3.25, 10.75]
>>> calc_bill(amounts)
Total bill before tip: $ 34.95
Tip amount: $ 6.29
Total with tip: $ 41.24
```

As you can see, we have a similar result as was produced with the sales tax calculator, except that with this decorator solution we can now vary the tip percentage. All of the amounts in the sequence of amounts are summed up and then the tip is applied. Let's take a quick look at what is actually going on if we do not use the decorator @ syntax.

Listing 4-41.

```
calc_bill = tip_amount(.18)(calc_bill)
```

At import time, the *tip_amount()* function takes both the tip percentage and the *calc_bill* function as arguments, and the result becomes the new calc_bill function. By including the decorator, we're actually decorating *calc_bill* with the function which is returned by *tip_amount(.18)*. In the larger scale of the things, if we applied this decorator solution to a complete application then we could accept the tip percentage from the keyboard and pass it into the decorator as we've shown in the example. The tip amount would then become a variable that can fluctuate based upon a different situation. Lastly, if we were dealing with a more complex decorator function, we have the ability to change the inner-working of the function without adjusting the original decorated function at all. Decorators are an easy way to make our code more versatile and manageable.

Coroutines

Coroutines are often compared to generator functions in that they also make use of the *yield* statement. However, a coroutine is exactly the opposite of a generator in terms of functionality. A coroutine actually treats a *yield* statement as an expression, and it accepts data instead of returning it. Coroutines are oftentimes overlooked as they may at first seem like a daunting topic. However, once it is understood that coroutines and generators are not the same thing then the concept of how they work is a bit easier to grasp.

A coroutine is a function that receives data and does something with it. We will take a look at a simple coroutine example and then break it down to study the functionality.

Listing 4-42.

```
def co_example(name):
    print 'Entering coroutine %s' % (name)
    my_text = []
    while True:
        txt = (yield)
        my_text.append(txt)
        print my_text
```

Here we have a very simplistic coroutine example. It accepts a value as the "name" of the coroutine. It then accepts strings of text, and each time a string of text is sent to the coroutine, it is appended to a list. The *yield* statement is the point where text is being entered by the user. It is assigned to the *txt* variable and then processing continues. It is important to note that the my_text list is held in memory throughout the life of the coroutine. This allows us to append values to the list with each yield. Let's take a look at how to actually use the coroutine.

Listing 4-43.

```
>>> ex = co_example("example1")
>>> ex.next()
Entering coroutine example1
```

In this code, we assign the name "example1" to this coroutine. We could actually accept any type of argument for the coroutine and do whatever we want with it. We'll see a better example after we understand how this works. Moreover, we could assign this coroutine to multiple variables of different names and each would then be its own coroutine object that would function independently of the others. The next line of code calls *next()* on the function. The *next()* must be called once to initialize the coroutine. Once this has been done, the function is ready to accept values.

Listing 4-44.

```
>>> ex.send("test1")
['test1']
>>> ex.send("test2")
['test1', 'test2']
>>> ex.send("test3")
['test1', 'test2', 'test3']
```

As you can see, we use the *send()* method to actually send data values into the coroutine. In the function itself, the text we *send* is inserted where the *(yield)* expression is placed. We can really continue to use the coroutine forever, or until our JVM is out of memory. However, it is a best practice to *close()* the coroutine once it is no longer needed. The *close()* call will cause the coroutine to be garbage collected.

Listing 4-45.

```
>>> ex.close()
>>> ex.send("test1")
Traceback (most recent call last):
  File "<stdin>", line 1, in <module>
StopIteration
```

If we try to send more data to the function once it has been closed then a *StopIteration* error is raised. Coroutines can be very helpful in a number of situations. While the previous example doesn't do much, there are a number of great applications to which we can apply the use of coroutines and we will see a more useful example in a later section.

Decorators in Coroutines

While the initialization of a coroutine by calling the *next()* method is not difficult to do, we can eliminate this step to help make things even easier. By applying a decorator function to our coroutine, we can automatically initialize it so it is ready to receive data.

Let's define a decorator that we can apply to the coroutine in order to make the call to *next()*.

Listing 4-46.

```
def coroutine_next(f):
    def initialize(*args,**kwargs):
        coroutine = f(*args,**kwargs)
        coroutine.next()
        return coroutine
    return initialize
```

Now we will apply our decorator to the coroutine function and then make use of it.

```
>>> @coroutine_next
... def co_example(name):
...     print 'Entering coroutine %s' % (name)
...     my_text = []
...     while True:
...         txt = (yield)
...         my_text.append(txt)
...         print my_text
...
>>> ex2 = co_example("example2")
Entering coroutine example2
>>> ex2.send("one")
['one']
>>> ex2.send("two")
['one', 'two']
>>> ex2.close()
```

As you can see, while it is not necessary to use a decorator for performing such tasks, it definitely makes things easier to use. If we chose not to use the syntactic sugar of the @ syntax, we could do the following to initialize our coroutine with the *coroutine_next()* function.

Listing 4-47.

```
co_example = coroutine_next(co_example)
```

Coroutine Example

Now that we understand how coroutines are used, let's take a look at a more in-depth example. Hopefully after reviewing this example you will understand how useful such functionality can be.

In this example, we will pass the name of a file to the coroutine on initialization. After that, we will send strings of text to the function and it will open the text file that we sent to it (given that the file resides in the correct location), and search for the number of matches per a given word. The numeric result for the number of matches will be returned to the user.

Listing 4-48.

```
def search_file(filename):
    print 'Searching file %s' % (filename)
    my_file = open(filename, 'r')
    file_content = my_file.read()
    my_file.close()
    while True:
        search_text = (yield)
        search_result = file_content.count(search_text)
        print 'Number of matches: %d' % (search_result)
```

The coroutine above opens the given file, reads its content, and then searches and returns the number of matches for any given *send* call.

Listing 4-49.

```
>>> search = search_file("example4_3.txt")
>>> search.next()
Searching file example4_3.txt
>>> search.send('python')
Number of matches: 0
>>> search.send('Jython')
Number of matches: 1
>>> search.send('the')
Number of matches: 4
>>> search.send('This')
Number of matches: 2
>>> search.close();
```

Summary

In this chapter, we have covered the use of functions in the Python language. There are many different use-cases for functions and we have learned techniques that will allow us to apply the functions to many situations. Functions are first-class objects in Python, and they can be treated as any other object. We started this chapter by learning the basics of how to define a function. After learning about the basics, we began to evolve our knowledge of functions by learning how to use parameters and make recursive function calls.

There are a wide variety of built-in functions available for use. If you take a look at Appendix C of this book you can see a listing of these built-ins. It is a good idea to become familiar with what built-ins are available. After all, it doesn't make much sense to rewrite something that has already been written.

This chapter also discussed some alternative ways to define functions including the lambda notation, as well as some alternative types of functions including decorators, generators and coroutines. Wrapping up this chapter, you should now be familiar with Python functions and how to create and use them. You should also be familiar with some of the advanced techniques that can be applied to functions.

In the next chapter, you will learn a bit about input and output with Jython and the basics of Python I/O. Later in this book, we will build upon object-orientation and learn how to use classes in Python.

CHAPTER 5

■ ■ ■

Input and Output

A program means very little if it does not take input of some kind from the program user. Likewise, if there is no form of output from a program then one may ask why we have a program at all. Input and output operations can define the user experience and usability of any program. This chapter is all about how to put information or data into a program, and then how to display it or save it to a file. This chapter does not discuss working with databases, but rather, working at a more rudimentary level with files. Throughout this chapter you will learn such techniques as how to input data for a program via a terminal or command line, likewise, you will learn how to read input from a file and write to a file. After reading this chapter, you should know how to persist Python objects to disk using the *pickle* module and also how to retrieve objects from disk and use them.

Input from the Keyboard

As stated, almost every program takes input from a user in one form or another. Most basic applications allow for keyboard entry via a terminal or command line environment. Python makes keyboard input easy, and as with many other techniques in Python there are more than one way to enable keyboard input. In this section, we'll cover each of those different ways to perform this task, along with a couple of use-cases. In the end you should be able to identify the most suitable method of performing input and output for your needs.

sys.stdin and raw_input

Making use of std.stdin is by far the most widely used method to read input from the command line or terminal. This procedure consists of importing the sys package, then writing a message prompting the user for some input, and lastly reading the input by making a call to *sys.stdin.readln()* and assigning the returned value to a variable. The process looks like the code that is displayed in Listing 5-1.

Listing 5-1. Using sys.stdin

```
# Obtain a value from the command line and store it into a variable

>>> import sys
>>> fav_team = sys.stdin.readline()
Cubs
>>> sys.stdout.write("My favorite team is: %s" % fav_team)
My favorite team is: Cubs
```

You can see that the usage of sys modules is quite easy. However, another approach to performing this same task is to make use of the *raw_input* function. This function uses a more simplistic syntax in order to perform the same procedure. It basically generates some text on the command line or terminal, accepts user input, and assigns it to a variable. Let's take a look at the same example from above using the *raw_input* syntax. Note that there is another function that performs a similar task named the *input* function. However, the *input* function needs to be used with great care as it could be a potential security risk. The *raw_input* function always returns content passed in as a string whereas the *input* function returns content and evaluates it as an expression. It is safest to stay away from using *input* whenever possible.

Listing 5-2. Using raw_input

```
# Obtain a value using raw_input and store it into a variable
>>> fav_team = raw_input("Enter your favorite team: ")
Enter your favorite team: Cubs
```

Obtaining Variables from Jython Environment

It is possible to retrieve values directly from the Jython environment for use within your applications. For instance, we can obtain system environment variables or the strings that have been passed into the command line or terminal when running the program.

To use environment variable values within your Jython application, simply import the *os* module and use it's *environ* dictionary to access them. Since this is a dictionary object, you can obtain a listing of all environment variables by simply typing *os.environ*.

Listing 5-3. Obtaining and Altering System Environment Variables

```
>>> import os
>>> os.environ["HOME"]

'/Users/juneau'

# Change home directory for the Python session
>>> os.environ["HOME"] = "/newhome"
>>> os.environ["HOME"]
/newhome'
```

When you are executing a Jython module from the command prompt or terminal, you can make use of the *sys.argv* list that takes values from the command prompt or terminal after invoking the Jython module. For instance, if we are interested in having our program user enter some arguments to be used by the module, they can simply invoke the module and then type all of the text entries followed by spaces, using quotes if you wish to pass an argument that contains a space. The number of arguments can be any size (I've never hit an upper bound anyways), so the possibilities are endless.

Listing 5-4. Using sys.argv

```
# sysargv_print.py - Prints all of the arguments provided at the command line
import sys
for sysargs in sys.argv:
    print sysargs

# Usage
>>> jython sysargv_print.py test test2 "test three"
sysargv_print.py
test
test2
```

```
test three
```

As you can see, the first entry in sys.argv is the script name, and then each additional argument provided after the module name is then added to the sys.argv list. This is quite useful for creating scripts to use for automating tasks, etc.

File I/O

You learned a bit about the *File* data type in Chapter 2. In that chapter, we briefly discussed a few of the operations that can be performed using this type. In this section, we will go into detail on what we can do with a *File* object. We'll start with the basics, and move into more detail. To begin, you should take a look at Table 5-1 that lists all of the methods available to a *File* object and what they do.

Table 5-1. File Object Methods

Method	Description
close()	Close file
fileno()	Returns integer file descriptor
flush()	Used to flush or clear the output buffers and write content to the file
isatty()	If the file is an interactive terminal, returns 1
next()	This allows the file to be iterated over. Returns the next line in the file. If no line is found, raises StopIteration
read(x)	Reads x bytes
readline(x)	Reads single line up to x characters, or entire line if x is omitted
readlines(size)	Reads all lines in file into a list. If *size* > 0, reads that number of characters
seek()	Moves cursor to a new position in the file
tell()	Returns the current position of the cursor
truncate(size)	Truncates file's size. Size defaults to current position unless specified
write(string)	Writes a string to the file object
writelines(seq)	Writes all strings contained in a sequence with no separator

We'll start by creating a file for use. As discussed in Chapter 2, the *open(filename[, mode])* built-in function creates and opens a specified file in a particular manner. The *mode* specifies what mode we will open the file into, be it read, read-write, and so on.

Listing 5-5. Creating, Opening, and Writing to a File

```
>>> my_file = open('mynewfile.txt','w')
>>> first_string = "This is the first line of text."
>>> my_file.write(first_string)
>>> my_file.close()
```

In this example, the file "mynewfile.txt" did not exist until the *open* function was called. If it did exist already, the previous version is overwritten by the new version and it is now empty. The file was created in *write* mode and then we do just that, write a string to the file. Now, it is important to make mention that the *first_string* is not actually written to the file until it is closed or *flush()* is performed. It is also worth mentioning that if we were to close the file, reopen it, and perform a subsequent *write()* operation on the file then the previous contents of the file would be overwritten by content of the new write.

Now we'll step through each of the file functions in an example. The main focus of this example is to provide you with a place to look for actual working file I/O code.

Listing 5-6.

```
# Write lines to file, flush, and close
>>> my_file = open('mynewfile.txt','w')
>>> my_file.write('This is the first line of text.\n')
>>> my_file.write('This is the second line of text.\n')
>>> my_file.write('This is the last line of text.\n')
>>> my_file.flush()  # Optional, really unneccesary if closing the file but useful to clear
>>>          #buffer
>>> my_file.close()

# Open file in read mode
>>> my_file = open('mynewfile.txt','r')
>>> my_file.read()
'This is the first line of text.\nThis is the second line of text.\nThis is the last line of
text.\n'

# If we read again, we get a '' because cursor is at the end of text
>>> my_file.read()
''


# Seek back to the beginning of file and perform read again
>>> my_file.seek(0)
>>> my_file.read()
'This is the first line of text.This is the second line of text.This is the last line of
text.'

# Seek back to beginning of file and perform readline()
>>> my_file.seek(0)
>>> my_file.readline()
'This is the first line of text.\n'
>>> my_file.readline()
'This is the second line of text.\n'
>>> my_file.readline()
'This is the last line of text.\n'
>>> my_file.readline()
''
```

```
# Use tell() to display current cursor position
>>> my_file.tell()
93L
>>> my_file.seek(0)
>>> my_file.tell()
0L

# Loop through lines of file
>>> for line in my_file:
...     print line
...
This is the first line of text.

This is the second line of text.

This is the last line of text.
```

There are a handful of read-only attributes that we can use to find out more information about file objects. For instance, if we are working with a file and want to see if it is still open or if it has been closed, we could view the *closed* attribute on the file to return a boolean stating whether the file is closed. Table 5-2 lists each of these attributes and what they tell us about a file object.

Table 5-2. File Attributes

Attribute	Description
closed	Returns a boolean to indicate if the file is closed
encoding	Returns a string indicating encoding on file
mode	Returns the I/O mode for a file(i.e., 'r', 'w', 'r+','rb', etc.)
name	Returns the name of the file
newlines	Returns the newline representation in the file. This keeps track of the types of newlines encountered while reading the file. Allows for universal newline support.

Listing 5-7. File Attribute Usage

```
>>> my_file.closed
False
>>> my_file.mode
'r'
>>> my_file.name
'mynewfile.txt'
```

Pickle

One of the most popular modules in the Python language is the *pickle* module. The goal of this module is basically to allow for the serialization and persistence of Python objects to disk in file format. A *pickled* object can be written to disk using this module, and it can also be read back in and utilized in object format. Just about any Python object can be persisted using *pickle*.

To write an object to disk, we call the *pickle()* function. The object will be written to file in a format that may be unusable by anything else, but we can then read that file back into our program and use the object as it was prior to writing it out. In the following example, we'll create a *Player* object and then persist it to file using *pickle*. Later, we will read it back into a program and make use of it. We will make use of the *File* object when working with the *pickle* module.

Listing 5-8. Write an Object to Disk Using Pickle

```
>>> import pickle
>>> class Player(object):
...     def __init__(self, first, last, position):
...         self.first = first
...         self.last = last
...         self.position = position
...
>>> player = Player('Josh','Juneau','Forward')
>>> pickle_file = open('myPlayer','wb')
>>> pickle.dump(player, pickle_file)
>>> pickle_file.close()
```

In the example above, we've persisted a *Player* object to disk using the *dump(object, file)* method in the *pickle* module. Now let's read the object back into our program and print it out.

Listing 5-9. Read and Use a Pickled Object

```
>>> pickle_file = open('myPlayer','rb')
>>> player1 = pickle.load(pickle_file)
>>> pickle_file.close()
>>> player1.first
'Josh'
>>> player1.last, player1.position
('Juneau', 'Forward')
```

Similarly, we read the pickled file back into our program using the *load(file)* method. Once read and stored into a variable, we can close the file and work with the object. If we had to perform a sequence of *dump* or *load* tasks, we could do so one after the other without issue. You should also be aware that there are different *pickle* protocols that can be used in order to make *pickle* work in different Python environments. The default protocol is 0, but protocols 1 and 2 are also available for use. It is best to stick with the default as it works well in most situations, but if you run into any trouble using *pickle* with binary formats then please give the others a try.

If we had to store objects to disk and reference them at a later time, it may make sense to use the *shelve* module which acts like a dictionary for pickled objects. With the *shelve* technique, you basically *pickle* an object and store it using a string-based key value. You can later retrieve the object by passing the key to the opened file object. This technique is very similar to a filing cabinet for our objects in that we can always reference our objects by key value. Let's take a look at this technique and see how it works.

Listing 5-10. Using the Shelve Technique

```
# Store different player objects
>>> import shelve
>>> player1 = Player('Josh','Juneau','forward')
>>> player2 = Player('Jim','Baker','defense')
>>> player3 = Player('Frank','Wierzbicki','forward')
>>> player4 = Player('Leo','Soto','defense')
>>> player5 = Player('Vic','Ng','center')
>>> data = shelve.open("players")
>>> data['player1'] = player1
>>> data['player2'] = player2
>>> data['player3'] = player3
>>> data['player4'] = player4
>>> data['player5'] = player5
>>> player_temp = data['player3']
>>> player_temp.first, player_temp.last, player_temp.position
('Frank', 'Wierzbicki', 'forward')
>>> data.close()
```

In the scenario above, we used the same *Player* object that was defined in the previous examples. We then opened a new *shelve* and named it "players", this shelve actually consists of a set of three files that are written to disk. These three files can be found on disk named "players.bak", "players.dat", and "players.dir" once the objects were persisted into the *shelve* and when close() was called on the object. As you can see, all of the *Player* objects we've instantiated have all been stored into this *shelve* unit, but they exist under different keys. We could have named the keys however we wished, as long as they were each unique. In the example, we persist five objects and then, at the end, one of the objects is retrieved and displayed. This is quite a nice technique to make a small data store.

Output Techniques

We basically covered the *print* statement in Chapter 2 very briefly when discussing string formatting. The *print* statement is by far the most utilized form of output in most Python programs. Although we covered some basics such as conversion types and how to format a line of output in Chapter 2, here we will go into a bit more depth on some different variations of the *print* statement as well as other techniques for generating output. There are basically two formats that can be used with the *print* statement. We covered the first in Chapter 2, and it makes use of a string and some conversion types embedded within the string and preceded by a percent (%) symbol. After the string, we use another percent(%) symbol followed by a parenthesized list of arguments that will be substituted in place of the embedded conversion types in our string in order. Check out the examples of each depicted in the example below.

Listing 5-11. Output With the Print Statement

```
# Using the % symbol
>>> x = 5
>>> y = 10
>>> print 'The sum of %d and %d is %d' % (x, y, (x + y))
The sum of 5 and 10 is 15

>>> adjective = "awesome"
>>> print 'Jython programming is %s' % (adjective)
```

```
Jython programming is awesome
```

You can also format floating-point output using the conversion types that are embedded in your string. You may specify a number of decimal places you'd like to print by using a ".# of places" syntax in the embedded conversion type.

Listing 5-12. Formatting Floating-Point Arithmetic

```
>>> pi = 3.14
>>> print 'Here is some formatted floating point arithmetic: %.2f' % (pi + y)
Here is some formatted floating point arithmetic: 13.14
>>> print 'Here is some formatted floating point arithmetic: %.3f' % (pi + y)
Here is some formatted floating point arithmetic: 13.140
```

Summary

It goes without saying that Python has its share of input and output strategies. This chapter covered most of those techniques starting with basic terminal or command line I/O and then onto file manipulation. We learned how to make use of the *open* function for creating, reading, or writing a file. The command line sys.argv arguments are another way that we can grab input, and environment variables can also be used from within our programs. Following those topics, we took a brief look at the *pickle* module and how it can be used to persist Python objects to disk. The *shelve* module is another twist on using *pickle* that allows for multiple objects to be indexed and stored within the same file. Finally, we discussed a couple of techniques for performing output in our programs.

Although there are some details that were left out as I/O could consume an entire book, this chapter was a solid starting point into the broad topic of I/O in Python. As with much of the Python language specifics discussed in this book, there are many resources available on the web and in book format that will help you delve deeper into the topics if you wish. A good resource is *Beginning Python: From Novice to Professional* by: Magnus Lie Hetland. You may also wish to look at the Python documentation which can be found at www.python.org/doc/.

CHAPTER 6

■ ■ ■

Object-Oriented Jython

This chapter is going to cover the basics of object-oriented programming. We'll start with covering the basic reasons why you would want to write object-oriented code in the first place, and then cover all the basic syntax, and finally we'll show you a non-trivial example.

Object-oriented programming is a method of programming where you package your code up into bundles of data and behavior. In Jython, you can define a template for this bundle with a class definition. With this first class written, you can then create instances of that class that include instance-specific data, as well as bits of code called methods that you can call to do things based on that data. This helps you organize your code into smaller, more manageable bundles.

With the release of Jython 2.5, the differences in syntax between the C version of Python and Jython are negligible. So, although everything here covers Jython, you can assume that all of the same code will run on the C implementation of Python, as well. Enough introduction though—let's take a look at some basic syntax to see what this is all about.

Basic Syntax

Writing a class is simple. It is fundamentally about managing some kind of "state" and exposing some functions to manipulate that state. In object jargon, we call those functions "methods."

Let's start by creating a Car class. The goal is to create an object that will manage its own location on a two-dimensional plane. We want to be able to tell it to turn and move forward, and we want to be able to interrogate the object to find out where its current location is. Place the following code in a file named "car.py."

Listing 6-1.

```
class Car(object):

    NORTH = 0
    EAST = 1
    SOUTH = 2
    WEST = 3

    def __init__(self, x=0, y=0):
        self.x = x
        self.y = y
        self.direction = self.NORTH

    def turn_right(self):
        self.direction += 1
        self.direction = self.direction % 4
```

```
    def turn_left(self):
        self.direction -= 1
        self.direction = self.direction % 4

    def move(self, distance):
        if self.direction == self.NORTH:
            self.y += distance
        elif self.direction == self.SOUTH:
            self.y -= distance
        elif self.direction == self.EAST:
            self.x += distance
        else:
            self.x -= distance

    def position(self):
        return (self.x, self.y)
```

We'll go over that class definition in detail but right now, let's just see how to create a car, move it around, and ask the car where it is.

Listing 6-2.

```
from car import Car

def test_car():
    c = Car()
    c.turn_right()
    c.move(5)
    assert (5, 0) ==  c.position()

    c.turn_left()
    c.move(3)
    assert (5, 3) == c.position()
```

In Jython there are things that are "callables." Functions are one kind of callable; classes are another. So one way to think of a class is that it's just a special kind of function, one that creates object instances.

Once we've created the car instance, we can simply call functions that are attached to the Car class and the object will manage its own location. From the point of view of our test code, we do not need to manage the location of the car—nor do we need to manage the direction that the car is pointing in. We just tell it to move, and it does the right thing.

Let's go over the syntax in detail to see exactly what's going on here.

In Line 1 of car.py, we declare that our Car object is a subclass of the root "object" class. Jython, like many object-oriented languages, has a "root" object that all other objects are based off of. This "object" class defines basic behavior that all classes can reuse.

Jython actually has two kinds of classes: "new style" and old style. The old way of declaring classes didn't require you to type "object;" you'll occasionally see the old-style class usage in some Jython code, but it's not considered good practice. Just subclass "object" for any of your base classes and your life will be simpler.

Lines 3 to 6 declare class attributes for the direction that any car can point to. These are *class* attributes, so they can be shared across all object instances of the Car object. Class attributes can be referenced without having to create an object instance.

Now for the good stuff.

Lines 8-11 declare the object initializer method. This method is called immediately after your object is created and memory for it has been allocated. In some languages, you might be familiar with a constructor; in Jython, we have an initializer which is run after construction. Valid method names in Jython are similar to many other C style languages. Generally, use method names that start with a letter; you can use numbers in the rest of the method name if you really want, but don't use any spaces. Jython classes have an assortment of special "magic" methods as well. These methods all start with a double underscore and end with a double underscore. These methods are reserved by the language and they have special meaning. So for our initializer "__init__," the Jython runtime will automatically invoke that method once you've called your constructor with "Car()." There are other reserved method names to let you customize your classes further, and we'll get into those later.

In our initializer, we are setting the initial position of the car to (0, 0) on a two-dimensional plane, and then the direction of the car is initialized to pointing north. When we initialize the object, we don't have to pass in the position explicitly. The function signature uses Jython's default argument list feature, so we don't have to explicitly set the initial location to (0,0). Default arguments for methods work just the same as the default function arguments that were covered in Chapter 4. When the method is created, Jython binds the default values into the method so that, if nothing is passed in, the signature's values will be used. There's also a new argument introduced called "self." This is a reference to the current object, the Car object. If you're familiar with other C style languages, you might have called the reference "this."

Remember, your class definition is creating instances of objects. Once your object is created, it has its own set of internal variables to manage. Your object will inevitably need to access these, as well as any of the class internal methods. Jython will pass a reference to the current object as the first argument to all your instance methods.

If you're coming from some other object-oriented language, you're probably familiar with the "this" variable. Unlike C++ or Java, Jython doesn't magically introduce the reference into the namespace of accessible variables, but this is consistent with Jython's philosophy of making things explicit for clarity.

When we want to assign the initial x, y position, we just need to assign values on to the name "x", and "y" on the object. Binding the values of x and y to self makes the position values accessible to any code that has access to self; namely, the other methods of the object. One minor detail here: in Jython, you can technically name the arguments however you want. There's nothing stopping you from calling the first argument "this" instead of "self," but the community standard is to use "self." One of Jython's strengths is its legibility and community standards around style.

Lines 13 to 19 declare two methods to turn the vehicle in different directions. Notice how the direction is never directly manipulated by the caller of the Car object. We just asked the car to turn, and the car changed its own internal "direction" state. In Jython, you can specify private attributes by using a preceding double underscore, so self.direction would change to self.__direction. Once your object is instantiated, your methods can continue to access private attributes using the double underscore name, but external callers would not be able to easily access those private attributes. The attribute name will be mangled for external callers into "obj._Car__direction". In practice, we don't suggest using private attributes, because you cannot possibly know all the use cases your code may have to satisfy. If you want to provide a hint to other programmers that an attribute should be considered private, you can use a single underscore.

Lines 21 to 29 define where the car should move to when we move the car forward. The internal direction variable informs the car how it should manipulate the x and y position. Notice how the caller of the Car object never needs to know precisely what direction the car is pointing in. The caller only needs to tell the object to turn and move forward. The particular details of how that message is used is abstracted away.

That's not too bad for a couple dozen lines of code.

This concept of hiding internal details is called encapsulation. This is a core concept in object-oriented programming. As you can see from even this simple example, it allows you to structure your code so that you can provide a simplified interface to the users of your code.

Having a simplified interface means that we could have all kinds of behavior happening behind the function calls to turn and move, but the caller can ignore all those details and concentrate on *using* the car instead of managing the car.

As long as the method signatures don't change, the caller really doesn't need to care about any of that.

Let's extend the class definition now to add persistence so we can save and load the car's state to disk. The goal here is to add it without breaking the existing interface to our class.

First, pull in the pickle module. Pickle will let us convert Jython objects into byte strings that can be restored to full objects later.

Import pickle

Now, just add two new methods to load and save the state of the object.

Listing 6-3.

```
def save(self, filename):
    state = (self.direction, self.x, self.y)
    pickle.dump(state, open(filename,'wb'))

def load(self, filename):
    state = pickle.load(open(filename,'rb'))
    (self.direction, self.x, self.y) = state
```

Simply add calls to save() at the end of the turn and move methods and the object will automatically save all the relevant internal values to disk.

There's a slight problem here: we need to have different files for each of our cars; our load and save methods have explicit filename arguments but our objects themselves don't have any notion of a name. Let's modify the intializer so that we always have a name bound into the object. Change __init__ to accept a name argument.

Listing 6-4.

```
    def __init__(self, name, x=0, y=0):
        self.name = name
        self.x = x
        self.y = y
        self.direction = self.NORTH
```

People who use the Car object don't even need to know that it's saving to disk, because the car object handles it behind the scenes.

Listing 6-5.

```
def turn_right(self):
    self.direction += 1
    self.direction = self.direction % 4
    self.save(self.name)

def turn_left(self):
    self.direction -= 1
```

```
    self.direction = self.direction % 4
    self.save(self.name)

def move(self, distance):
    if self.direction == self.NORTH:
        self.y += distance
    elif self.direction == self.SOUTH:
        self.y -= distance
    elif self.direction == self.EAST:
        self.x += distance
    else:
        self.x -= distance
    self.save(self.name)
```

Now, when you call the turn, or move methods, the car will automatically save itself to disk. If you want to reconstruct the car object's state from a previously saved pickle file, you can simply call the load() method and pass in the string name of your car.

Object Attribute Lookups

If you've been paying attention, you're probably wondering how the NORTH, SOUTH, EAST and WEST variables got bound to self. We never actually assigned them to the self variable during object initialization—so what's going on when we call move()? How is Jython actually resolving the value of those four variables?

Now seems like a good time to show how Jython resolves name lookups.

The direction names actually got bound to the car class. The Jython object system does a little bit of magic when you try accessing any *name* against an object, it first searches for anything that was bound to "self." If Jython can't resolve any attribute on self with that name, it goes up the object graph to the class definition. The direction attributes NORTH, SOUTH, EAST, WEST were bound to the class definition, so the name resolution succeeds and we get the value of the class attribute.

A very short example will help clarify this.

Listing 6-6.

```
>>> class Foobar(object):
...     def __init__(self):
...         self.somevar = 42
...     class_attr = 99
...
>>>
>>> obj = Foobar()
>>> obj.somevar
42
>>> obj.class_attr
99
>>> obj.not_there
Traceback (most recent call last):
  File "<stdin>", line 1, in <module>
AttributeError: 'Foobar' object has no attribute 'not_there'
>>>
```

So the key difference here is *what* you bind a value to. The values you bind to self are available only to a single object. Values you bind to the class definition are available to all instances of the class. The sharing of class attributes among all instances is a critical distinction, because mutating a class attribute will affect all instances. This may cause unintended side effects if you're not paying attention as a variable may change value on you when you aren't expecting it to.

Listing 6-7.

```
>>> other = Foobar()
>>> other.somevar
42
>>> other.class_attr
99
>>> # obj and other can have different values for somevar
>>> obj.somevar = 77
>>> obj.somevar
77
>>> other.somevar
42
>>> # If we assign to other.class_attr, that makes an instance attribute of other called
class_attr.
>>> other.class_attr = 66
>>> other.class_attr
66
>>> # And doesn't change the class_attribute class_attr for other objects
>>> obj.class_attr
99
>>> # You can still get at the class attribute from other by looking at
other.__class__.class_attr
>>> other.__class__.class_attr
99
>>> # and if you remove the instance attribute other.class_attr,
>>> then other.class_attr goes back to referring to the class attribute
>>> del other.class_attr

>>> other.class_attr

99

>>> # But if the class_attribute is mutable, when you change it, you change it for every
instance
>>> Foobar.class_list = []

>>> obj.class_list

[]

>>> other.class_list

[]

>>> obj.class_list.append(1)
```

```
>>> obj.class_list
```

```
[1]
```

```
>>> other.class_list
```

```
[1]
```

We think it's important to stress just how transparent Jython's object system really is. Object attributes are just stored in a plain Jython dictionary. You can directly access this dictionary by looking at the __dict__ attribute.

Listing 6-8.

```
>>> obj = Foobar()
>>> obj.__dict__
{'somevar': 42}
```

Notice that there are no references to the methods of the class (in this case, just our initializer), or the class attribute 'class_attr'. The __dict__ only shows the local attributes and methods of the object. We'll cover inheritance shortly, and you'll see how attributes and methods are looked up in the case where you specialize classes through subclassing.

The same trick can be used to inspect all the attributes of the class, just look into the __dict__ attribute of the class definition and you'll find your class attributes and all the methods that are attached to your class definition:

Listing 6-9.

```
>>> Foobar.__dict__
{'__module__': '__main__',
    'class_attr': 99,
    '__dict__': <attribute '__dict__' of 'Foobar' objects>,
    '__init__': <function __init__ at 1>}
```

This transparency can be leveraged with dynamic programming techniques using closures and binding new functions into your class definition at runtime. We'll revisit this later in the chapter when we look at generating functions dynamically and finally with a short introduction to metaprogramming.

Inheritance and Overloading

In the car example, we subclass from the root object type. You can also subclass your own classes to specialize the behavior of your objects. You may want to do this if you notice that your code naturally has a structure where you have many different classes that all share some common behavior.

With objects, you can write one class, and then reuse it using inheritance to automatically gain access to the pre-existing behavior and attributes of the parent class. Your "base" objects will inherit behavior from the root "object" class, but any subsequent subclasses will inherit from your own classes.

Let's take a simple example of using some animal classes to see how this works. Define a module "animals.py" with the following code:

Listing 6-10.

```
class Animal(object):
    def sound(self):
        return "I don't make any sounds"
class Goat(Animal):
    def sound(self):
        return "Bleeattt!"
class Rabbit(Animal):
    def jump(self):
        return "hippity hop hippity hop"
class Jackalope(Goat, Rabbit):
    pass
```

Now you should be able to explore that module with the jython interpreter:

Listing 6-11.

```
>>> from animals import *
>>> animal = Animal()
>>> goat = Goat()
>>> rabbit = Rabbit()
>>> jack = Jackalope()
>>> animal.sound()
"I don't make any sounds"
>>> animal.jump()
Traceback (most recent call last):
  File "<stdin>", line 1, in <module>
AttributeError: 'Animal' object has no attribute 'jump'
>>> rabbit.sound()
"I don't make any sounds"
>>> rabbit.jump()
'hippity hop hippity hop'
>>> goat.sound()
'Bleeattt!'
>>> goat.jump()
Traceback (most recent call last):
  File "<stdin>", line 1, in <module>
AttributeError: 'Goat' object has no attribute 'jump'
>>> jack.jump()
'hippity hop hippity hop'
>>> jack.sound()
'Bleeattt!'
```

Inheritance is a very simple concept, when you declare your class, you simply specify which parent classes you would like to reuse. Your new class can then automatically access all the methods and attributes of the super class. In this example, the Goat object has no method jump, and its super class Animal has no method jump, so the attempt to invoke the jump method fails. Invoking the sound method on the rabbit actually calls the super class's sound method.

This is the key idea: if an attribute lookup fails on the local object instance, the lookup is then propagated up the inheritance tree to the super class. Notice how the Jackalope had access to methods from both the rabbit and the goat because it can use two super classes to resolve methods.

With single inheritance—when your class simply inherits from one parent class—the rules for resolving where to find an attribute or a method are very straightforward. Jython just looks up to the parent if the current object doesn't have a matching attribute.

It's important to point out now that the Rabbit class is a type of Animal: the Jython runtime can tell you that programmatically by using the isinstance function:

Listing 6-12.

```
>>> isinstance(bunny, Rabbit)
True
>>> isinstance(bunny, Animal)
True
>>> isinstance(bunny, Goat)
False
```

For many classes, you may want to extend the behavior of the parent class instead of just completely overriding it. For this, you'll want to use the super() function. Let's specialize the Rabbit class like this:

Listing 6-13.

```
class EasterBunny(Rabbit):
    def sound(self):
        orig = super(EasterBunny, self).sound()
        return "%s - but I have eggs!" % orig
```

If you now try making this rabbit speak, it will extend the original sound() method from the base Rabbit class. Calling the super() function lets you access the super class's implementation of the sound method. In this example, it's useful because the EasterBunny class is reusing and extending the basic Rabbit class's sound() method.

Listing 6-14.

```
>>> bunny = EasterBunny()
>>> bunny.sound()
"I don't make any sounds - but I have eggs!"
```

That wasn't so bad. For these examples, we only demonstrated that inherited methods can be invoked, but you can do exactly the same thing with attributes that are bound to the self.

For multiple inheritance, things get complicated quickly. Jython uses "left first, depth first" search to resolve attribute lookups. In a nutshell, if you were to draw your inheritance diagram, Jython would look down the left side of your graph looking for attributes going from the bottom up, left to right. If any super class is inherited by two or more subclasses, then the super class is used for lookup only after all attribute lookups have been exhausted on the subclasses.

Underscore Methods

Abstraction using plain classes is wonderful and all, but it's even better if your code seems to naturally fit into the syntax of the language. Jython supports a variety of underscore methods: methods that start and end with double "_" signs that let you overload the behavior of your objects. This means that your objects will seem to integrate more tightly with the language itself. You have already seen one such method: __init__.

With the underscore methods, you can give you objects behavior for logical and mathematical operations. You can even make your objects behave more like standard builtin types like lists, sets or dictionaries. Let's start with adding simple unicode extensions to a SimpleObject to see the most simple example of this. Then we'll move on to building customized container classes.

Listing 6-15.

```
from __future__ import with_statement
from contextlib import closing
with closing(open('simplefile','w')) as fout:
    fout.writelines(["blah"])
with closing(open('simplefile','r')) as fin:
    print fin.readlines()
```

This snippet of code just opens a file, writes a little bit of text, and then we read the contents out. Not terribly exciting. Most objects in Jython are serializable to strings using the pickle module. The pickle module lets us convert our live Jython objects into byte streams that can be saved to disk and later restored into objects. Let's see the functional version of this:

Listing 6-16.

```
from __future__ import with_statement
from contextlib import closing
from pickle import dumps, loads

def write_object(fout, obj):
    data = dumps(obj)
    fout.write("%020d" % len(data))
    fout.write(data)

def read_object(fin):
    length = int(fin.read(20))
    obj = loads(fin.read(length))
    return obj

class Simple(object):
    def __init__(self, value):
        self.value = value
    def __unicode__(self):
        return "Simple[%s]" % self.value

with closing(open('simplefile','wb')) as fout:
    for i in range(10):
        obj = Simple(i)
        write_object(fout, obj)

print "Loading objects from disk!"
print '=' * 20

with closing(open('simplefile','rb')) as fin:
```

```
for i in range(10):
    print read_object(fin)
```

This should output something like this:

Listing 6-17.

```
Loading objects from disk!
====================
Simple[0]
Simple[1]
Simple[2]
Simple[3]
Simple[4]
Simple[5]
Simple[6]
Simple[7]
Simple[8]
Simple[9]
```

So now we're doing something interesting. Let's look at exactly what happening here.

First, you'll notice that the Simple object is rendering nicely: the Simple object can render itself using the __unicode__ method. This is clearly an improvement over the earlier rendering of the object with angle brackets and a hex code.

The write_object function is fairly straightforward, we're just converting our objects into strings using the pickle module, computing the length of the string and then writing the length and the actual serialized object to disk.

This is fine, but the read side is a bit clunky. We don't really know when to stop reading. We can fix this using the iteration protocol. Which bring us to one of my favorite reasons to use objects at all in Jython.

Protocols

In Jython, we have "duck typing." If it walks like a duck, quacks like a duck, and looks like a duck, it's a duck. This is in stark contrast to more rigid languages like C# or Java which have formal interface definitions. One of the nice benefits of having duck typing is that Jython has the notion of object protocols.

If you happen to implement the right methods, Jython will recognize your object as a certain type of 'thing'.

Iterators are objects that look like lists that let you read the next object. Implementing an iterator protocol is straightforward: just implement a next() method and a __iter__ method, and you're ready to rock and roll. Let's see this in action:

Listing 6-18.

```
class PickleStream(object):
    """
    This stream can be used to stream objects off of a raw file stream
    """
    def __init__(self, file):
        self.file = file
```

```
    def write(self, obj):
        data = dumps(obj)
        length = len(data)
        self.file.write("%020d" % length)
        self.file.write(data)

    def __iter__(self):
        return self

    def next(self):
        data = self.file.read(20)
        if len(data) == 0:
            raise StopIteration
        length = int(data)
        return loads(self.file.read(length))

    def close(self):
        self.file.close()
```

This class will let you wrap a simple file object and you can now send it raw Jython objects to write to a file, or you can read objects out as if the stream was just a list of objects. Writing and reading becomes much simpler:

Listing 6-19.

```
with closing(PickleStream(open('simplefile','wb'))) as stream:
    for i in range(10):
        obj = Simple(i)
        stream.write(obj)

with closing(PickleStream(open('simplefile','rb'))) as stream:
    for obj in stream:
        print obj
```

Abstracting out the details of serialization into the PickleStream lets us "forget" about the details of how we are writing to disk. All we care about is that the object will do the right thing when we call the write() method.

The iteration protocol can be used for much more advanced purposes, but even with this example, it should be obvious how useful it is. While you could implement the reading behavior with a read() method, just using the stream as something you can loop over makes the code much easier to understand.

Let's step back now and look at some of the other underscore methods. Two of the most common uses of underscore methods are to implement proxies and to implement your own container-like classes. Proxies are very useful in many programming problems. You use a proxy to act as an intermediary between a caller and a callee. The proxy class can add in extra behavior in a manner that is transparent to the caller. In Jython, you can use the __getattr__ method to implement attribute lookups if a method or attribute does not seem to exist.

Listing 6-20.

```
class SimpleProxy(object):
    def __init__(self, parent):
        self._parent = parent

    def __getattr__(self, key):
        return getattr(self._parent, key)
```

That represents the simplest (and not very useful) proxy. Any lookup for an attribute that doesn't exist on SimpleProxy will automatically invoke the __getattr__ method, and the lookup will then be delegated to the parent object. Note that this works for attributes that are **not** underscore attributes. Let's look at a simple example to make this clearer.

Listing 6-21.

```
>>> class TownCrier(object):
...     def __init__(self, parent):
...         self._parent = parent
...     def __getattr__(self, key):
...         print "Accessing : [%s]" % key
...         return getattr(self._parent, key)
...
>>> class Calc(object):
...     def add(self, x, y):
...         return x + y
...     def sub(self, x, y):
...         return x - y
...
>>> calc = Calc()
>>> crier = TownCrier(calc)
>>> crier.add(5,6)
Accessing : [add]
11
>>> crier.sub(3,6)
Accessing : [sub]
-3
```

Here, we can see that our TownCrier class is delegating control to the Calculator object whenever a method is invoked, but we are also adding in some debug messages along the way. Unlike a language like Java where you would need to implement a specific interface (if one even exists), in Jython, creating a proxy is nearly free. The __getattr__ method is automatically invoked if attribute lookups fail using the normal lookup mechanism. Proxies provide a way for you to inject new behavior by using a delegation pattern. The advantage here is that you can add new behavior without having to know anything about the delegate's implementation; something that you'd have to deal with if you used subclassing.

The second common use of underscore methods we'll cover is implementing your own container class. We'll take a look at implementing a small dictionary-like class. Suppose we have class that behaves like a regular dictionary, but it logs all read access to a file. To get the basic behavior of a dictionary, we need to be able to get, set and delete key/value pairs, check for key existence and count the number of records in the dictionary. To get all of that behavior, we will need to implement the following methods:

Listing 6-22.

```
__getitem__(self, key)
__setitem__(self, key, value)
__delitem__(self, key)
__contains__(self, item)
__len__(self)
```

The method names are fairly self-explanatory. __gettiem__, __setitem__ and __delitem__ all manipulate key/value pairs in our dictionary. We can implement this behavior on top of a regular list object to get a naïve implementation. Put the following code into a file named "foo.py."

Listing 6-23.

```
class SimpleDict(object):
    def __init__(self):
        self._items = []

    def __getitem__(self, key):
        # do a brute force key lookup and return the value
        for k, v in self._items:
            if k == key:
                return v
        raise LookupError, "can't find key: [%s]" % key

    def __setitem__(self, key, value):
        # do a brute force search and replace
        # for the key if it exists. Otherwise append
        # a new key/value pair.
        for i, (k , v) in enumerate(self._items):
            if k == key:
                self._items[i][1] = v
                return
        self._items.append((key, value))

    def __delitem__(self, key):
        # do a brute force search and delete
        for i, (k , v) in enumerate(self._items):
            if k == key:
                del self._items[i]
                return
        raise LookupError, "Can't find [%s] to delete" % key
```

The implementations listed previously are naïve, but they should illustrate the basic pattern of usage. Once you have just those three methods implemented, you can start using dictionary style attribute access.

Listing 6-24.

```
>>> from foo import *
>>> x = SimpleDict()
>>> x[0] = 5
```

```
>>> x[15]= 32
>>> print x[0]
5
>>> print x[15]
32
```

To get two remaining behaviors, key existence and dictionary size, we fill in the __contains__ and __len__ methods.

Listing 6-25.

```
def __contains__(self, key):
    return key in [k for (k, v) in self._items]

def __len__(self):
    return len(self._items)
```

Now this implementation of a dictionary will behave almost identically to a standard dictionary, we're still missing some "regular" methods like items(), keys() and values(), but accessing the SimpleDict using square brackets will work the way you expect a dictionary to work. While this implementation was intentionally made to be simple, it is easy to see that we could have saved our items into a text file, a database backend or any other backing storage. The caller would be blind to these changes; all they would interact with is the dictionary interface.

Default Arguments

One particular snag that seems to catch every Jython programmer is when you use default values in a method signature.

Listing 6-26.

```
>>> class Tricky(object):
...     def mutate(self, x=[]):
...         x.append(1)
...         return x
...
>>> obj = Tricky()
>>> obj.mutate()
[1]
>>> obj.mutate()
[1, 1]
>>> obj.mutate()
[1, 1, 1]
```

What's happening here is that the instance method "mutate" is an object. The method object stores the default value for "x" in an attribute *inside* the method object. To complicate things further, method objects are bound to your class definition. So when you go and mutate the list, you're actually changing the value of an attribute of the method itself. Each of your object instances point to the same class definition, and the same method. Your default arguments will change for all of your instances!

Runtime Binding of Methods

One interesting feature of Jython is that instance methods are actually just attributes hanging off of the class definition; the functions are just attributes like any other variable, except that they happen to be "callable."

It's even possible to create and bind in functions to a class definition at runtime using the new module to create instance methods. In the following example, you can see that it's possible to define a class with nothing in it, and then bind methods to the class definition at runtime.

Listing 6-27.

```
>>> def some_func(self, x, y):
...     print "I'm in object: %s" % self
...     return x * y
...
>>> import new
>>> class Foo(object): pass
...
>>> f = Foo()
>>> f
<__main__.Foo object at 0x1>
>>> Foo.mymethod = new.instancemethod(some_func, f, Foo)
>>> f.mymethod(6,3)
I'm in object: <__main__.Foo object at 0x1>
18
```

When you invoke the mymethod method, the same attribute lookup machinery is being invoked. Jython looks up the name against the "self" object. When it can't find anything there, it goes to the class definition. When it finds it there, the instancemethod object is returned. The function is then called with two arguments and you get to see the final result.

The special function new.instancemethod is doing some magic so that when some_func is invoked, the Jython runtime will automatically pass in the object instance as the first argument. That's the self attribute we saw earlier in this chapter. Functions that are bound to an object in this manner are appropriately called "bound methods." Without this binding behavior, the object instance will not be passed in as the first argument. In this case, the method would be called an "unbound method."

This kind of dynamism in Jython is extremely powerful. You can write code that generates functions at program runtime, and then bind those functions to objects. You can do all of this because in Jython, classes and functions are what are known as "first-class objects." The class definition itself is an actual object, just like any other object. Manipulating classes is as easy as manipulating any other object.

The practical use of this kind of technique is when you are building tools that generate code. Instead of statically code generating functions and methods, you can "grow" your methods depending on runtime features of your objects. This is how most of the Python database toolkits work. You define classes that represent objects in your database, and the toolkit will inspect your objects and enhance the classes with persistence behavior. Using dynamic programming techniques, like creating new methods at runtime, opens up the possibility of literally post-processing your classes.

Caching Attribute Access

Suppose we have some method that requires intensive computational resources to run, but the results do not vary much over time. Wouldn't it be nice if we could cache the results so that the computation wouldn't have to run each and every time? We can leverage the decorator pattern in Chapter 4 and add write the results of our computations as new attributes of our objects.

Here's our class with a slow computation method. The slow_compute() method really doesn't do anything interesting; it just sleeps and eats up one second of time. We're going to wrap the method up with a caching decorator so that we don't have to wait the one second every time we invoke the method.

Listing 6-28.

```
import time
class Foobar(object):
    def slow_compute(self, *args, **kwargs):
        time.sleep(1)
        return args, kwargs, 42
```

Now let's cache the value using a decorator function. Our strategy is that for any function named X with some argument list, we want to create a unique name and save the final computed value to that name. We want our cached value to have a human readable name, we want to reuse the original function name, as well as the arguments that were passed in the first time.

Let's get to some code!

Listing 6-29.

```
import hashlib
def cache(func):
    """
    This decorator will add a _cache_functionName_HEXDIGEST
    attribute after the first invocation of an instance method to
    store cached values.
    """
    # Obtain the function's name
    func_name = func.func_name
    # Compute a unique value for the unnamed and named arguments
    arghash = hashlib.sha1(str(args) + str(kwargs)).hexdigest()
    cache_name = '_cache_%s_%s' % (func_name, arghash)

    def inner(self, *args, **kwargs):
        if hasattr(self, cache_name):
            # If we have a cached value, just use it
            print "Fetching cached value from : %s" % cache_name
            return getattr(self, cache_name)
        result = func(self, *args, **kwargs)
        setattr(self, cache_name, result)
        return result
    return inner
```

There are only two new tricks that are in this code.

1. We're using the hashlib module to convert the arguments to the function into a unique single string.

2. We're using getattr, hasattr, and setattr to manipulate the cached value on the instance object.

The three functions getattr, setattr, and hasattr allow you to get, set, and test for attributes on an object by using string names instead of symbols. So accessing foo.bar is equivalent to invoking getattr(foo, 'bar'). In the previous case, we're using the attribute functions to bind the result of the slow calculation function into an attribute of an instance of Foobar.

The next time the decorated method is invoked, the hasattr test will find the cached value and we return the precomputed value.

Now, if we want to cache the slow method, we just throw on a @cache line above the method declaration.

Listing 6-30.

```
@cache
def slow_compute(self, *args, **kwargs):
    time.sleep(1)
    return args, kwargs, 42
```

Fantastic! We can reuse this cache decorator for any method we want now. Let's suppose now that we want our cache to invalidate itself after every N number of calls. This practical use of currying is only a slight modification to the original caching code. The goal is the same; we are going to store the computed result of a method as an attribute of an object. The name of the attribute is determined based on the actual function name, and is concatenated with a hash string computed by using the arguments to the method.

In the code sample, we'll save the function name into the variable "func_name" and we'll save the argument hash value into "arghash."

Those two variables will also be used to compute the name of a counter attribute. When the counter reaches N, we'll clear out the precomputed value so that the calculation can run again.

Listing 6-31.

```
import hashlib
def cache(loop_iter):
    def function_closure(func):
        func_name = func.func_name

        def closure(self, loop_iter, *args, **kwargs):
            arghash = hashlib.sha1(str(args) + str(kwargs)).hexdigest()
            cache_name = '_cache_%s_%s' % (func_name, arghash)
            counter_name = '_counter_%s_%s' % (func_name, arghash)

            if hasattr(self, cache_name):
                # If we have a cached value, just use it
                print "Fetching cached value from : %s" % cache_name
                loop_iter -= 1
                setattr(self, counter_name, loop_iter)
                result = getattr(self, cache_name)

                if loop_iter == 0:
                    delattr(self, counter_name)
                    delattr(self, cache_name)
                    print "Cleared cached value"
                return result

            result = func(self, *args, **kwargs)
            setattr(self, cache_name, result)
```

```
        setattr(self, counter_name, loop_iter)
        return result

    return closure

return function_closure
```

Now we're free to use @cache for any slow method and caching will come in for free, including automatic invalidation of the cached value. Just use it like this:

Listing 6-32.

```
@cache(10)
def slow_compute(self, *args, **kwargs):
    # TODO: stuff goes here...
    pass
```

Summary

Now, we're going to ask you to use your imagination a little. We've covered quite a bit of ground really quickly.

We can:

- look up attributes in an object (use the __dict__ attribute);

- check if an object belongs to a particular class hierarchy (use the isinstance function);

- build functions out of other functions using currying and even bind those functions to arbitrary names.

This is fantastic. We now have all the basic building blocks we need to generate complex methods based on the attributes of our class. Imagine a simplified addressbook application with a simple contact.

Listing 6-33.

```
class Contact(object):
    first_name = str
    last_name = str
    date_of_birth = datetime.Date
```

Assuming we know how to save and load to a database, we can use the function generation techniques to automatically generate load() and save() methods and bind them into our Contact class. We can use our introspection techniques to determine what attributes need to be saved to our database. We could even grow special methods onto our Contact class so that we could iterate over all of the class attributes and magically grow 'searchby_first_name' and 'searchby_last_name' methods.

Jython's flexible object system allows you to write code that has a deep ability to introspect itself by simply looking up information in dictionaries like __dict__. You also have the ability to rewrite parts of your classes using decorators and even creating new instance methods at runtime. These techniques can be combined together to write code that effectively rewrites itself. This technique is called 'metaprogramming'. This technique is very powerful: we can write extremely minimal code, and we can code generate all of our specialized behavior. In the case of our contact, it would "magically" know how to save itself, load itself, and delete itself from a database. This is precisely how the database mappers in Django and SQLAlchemy work: they rewrite parts of your program to talk to a database. We urge you to open up the source code to those libraries to see how you can apply some of these techniques in real world settings.

CHAPTER 7

■ ■ ■

Exception Handling and Debugging

Any good program makes use of a language's exception handling mechanisms. There is no better way to frustrate an end-user then by having them run into an issue with your software and displaying a big ugly error message on the screen, followed by a program crash. Exception handling is all about ensuring that when your program encounters an issue, it will continue to run and provide informative feedback to the end-user or program administrator. Any Java programmer becomes familiar with exception handling on day one, as some Java code won't even compile unless there is some form of exception handling put into place via the try-catch-finally syntax. Python has similar constructs to that of Java, and we'll discuss them in this chapter.

After you have found an exception, or preferably before your software is distributed, you should go through the code and debug it in order to find and repair the erroneous code. There are many different ways to debug and repair code; we will go through some debugging methodologies in this chapter. In Python as well as Java, the *assert* keyword can help out tremendously in this area. We'll cover *assert* in depth here and learn the different ways that it can be used to help you out and save time debugging those hard-to-find errors.

Exception Handling Syntax and Differences with Java

Java developers are very familiar with the *try-catch-finally* block as this is the main mechanism that is used to perform exception handling. Python exception handling differs a bit from Java, but the syntax is fairly similar. However, Java differs a bit in the way that an exception is *thrown* in code. Now, realize that I just used the term *throw*…this is Java terminology. Python does not *throw* exceptions, but instead it *raises* them. Two different terms which mean basically the same thing. In this section, we'll step through the process of handling and raising exceptions in Python code, and show you how it differs from that in Java.

For those who are unfamiliar, I will show you how to perform some exception handling in the Java language. This will give you an opportunity to compare the two syntaxes and appreciate the flexibility that Python offers.

Listing 7-1. Exception Handling in Java

```
try {
    // perform some tasks that may throw an exception
} catch (ExceptionType messageVariable) {
    // perform some exception handling
} finally {
    // execute code that must always be invoked
}
```

Now let's go on to learn how to make this work in Python. Not only will we see how to handle and raise exceptions, but you'll also learn some other great techniques such as using assertions later in the chapter.

Catching Exceptions

How often have you been working in a program and performed some action that caused the program to abort and display a nasty error message? It happens more often than it should because most exceptions can be caught and handled nicely. By nicely, I mean that the program will not abort and the end user will receive a descriptive error message stating what the problem is, and in some cases how it can be resolved. The exception handling mechanisms within programming languages were developed for this purpose.

Listing 7-2. try-except Example

```
# This function uses a try-except clause to provide a nice error
# message if the user passes a zero in as the divisor
>>> from __future__ import division
>>> def divide_numbers(x, y):
...     try:
...         return x/y
...     except ZeroDivisionError:
...         return 'You cannot divide by zero, try again'
...
# Attempt to divide 8 by 3
>>> divide_numbers(8,3)
2.6666666666666665
# Attempt to divide 8 by zero
>>> divide_numbers(8, 0)
'You cannot divide by zero, try again'
```

Table 7-1 lists of all exceptions that are built into the Python language along with a description of each. You can write any of these into an *except* clause and try to handle them. Later in this chapter I will show you how you and *raise* them if you'd like. Lastly, if there is a specific type of exception that you'd like to throw that does not fit any of these, then you can write your own exception type object. It is important to note that Python exception handling differs a bit from Java exception handling. In Java, many times the compiler forces you to catch exceptions, such is known as checked exceptions. Checked exceptions are basically exceptions that a method *may* throw while performing some task. The developer is forced to handle these checked exceptions using a try/catch or a throws clause, otherwise the compiler complains. Python has no such facility built into its error handling system. The developer decides when to handle exceptions and when not to do so. It is a best practice to include error handling wherever possible even though the interpreter does not force it.

Exceptions in Python are special classes that are built into the language. As such, there is a class hierarchy for exceptions and some exceptions are actually subclasses of another exception class. In this case, a program can handle the superclass of such an exception and all subclassed exceptions are handled automatically. Table 7-1 lists the exceptions defined in the Python language, and the indentation resembles the class hierarchy.

Table 7-1. Exceptions

Exception	Description
BaseException	This is the root exception for all others
GeneratorExit	Raised by close() method of generators for terminating iteration
KeyboardInterrupt	Raised by the interrupt key
SystemExit	Program exit
Exception	Root for all non-exiting exceptions
StopIteration	Raised to stop an iteration action
StandardError	Base class for all built-in exceptions
ArithmeticError	Base for all arithmetic exceptions
FloatingPointError	Raised when a floating-point operation fails
OverflowError	Arithmetic operations that are too large
ZeroDivisionError	Division or modulo operation with zero as divisor
AssertionError	Raised when an assert statement fails
AttributeError	Attribute reference or assignment failure
EnvironmentError	An error occurred outside of Python
IOError	Error in Input/Output operation
OSError	An error occurred in the os module
EOFError	input() or raw_input() tried to read past the end of a file
ImportError	Import failed to find module or name
LookupError	Base class for IndexError and KeyError
IndexError	A sequence index goes out of range
KeyError	Referenced a non-existent mapping (dict) key
MemoryError	Memory exhausted
NameError	Failure to find a local or global name
UnboundLocalError	Unassigned local variable is referenced
ReferenceError	Attempt to access a garbage-collected object
RuntimeError	Obsolete catch-all error
NotImplementedError	Raised when a feature is not implemented
SyntaxError	Parser encountered a syntax error
IndentationError	Parser encountered an indentation issue
TabError	Incorrect mixture of tabs and spaces
SystemError	Non-fatal interpreter error
TypeError	Inappropriate type was passed to an operator or function
ValueError	Argument error not covered by TypeError or a more precise error
Warning	Base for all warnings

The *try-except-finally* block is used in Python programs to perform the exception-handling task. Much like that of Java, code that may or may not raise an exception can be placed in the *try* block. Differently though, exceptions that may be caught go into an *except* block much like the Java *catch* equivalent. Any tasks that must be performed no matter if an exception is thrown or not should go into the *finally* block. All tasks within the *finally* block are performed if an exception is raised either within the *except* block or by some other exception. The tasks are also performed before the exception is raised to ensure that they are completed. The *finally* block is a great place to perform cleanup activity such as closing open files and such.

Listing 7-3. try-except-finally Logic

```
try:
    # perform some task that may raise an exception
except Exception, value:
    # perform some exception handling
finally:
    # perform tasks that must always be completed (Will be performed before the exception is
    # raised.)
```

Python also offers an optional *else* clause to create the *try-except-else* logic. This optional code placed inside the *else* block is run if there are no exceptions found in the block.

Listing 7-4. try-finally logic

```
try:
    # perform some tasks that may raise an exception
finally:
    # perform tasks that must always be completed (Will be performed before the exception is
    # raised.)
```

The *else* clause can be used with the exception handling logic to ensure that some tasks are only run if no exceptions are raised. Code within the *else* clause is only initiated if no exceptions are thrown, and if any exceptions are raised within the *else* clause the control does not go back out to the *except*. Such activities to place in inside an *else* clause would be transactions such as a database commit. If several database transactions were taking place inside the *try* clause you may not want a commit to occur unless there were no exceptions raised.

Listing 7-5. try-except-else logic:

```
try:
    # perform some tasks that may raise an exception
except:
    # perform some exception handling
else:
    # perform some tasks thatwill only be performed if no exceptions are thrown
```

You can name the specific type of exception to catch within the *except* block, or you can generically define an exception handling block by not naming any exception at all. Best practice of course states that you should always try to name the exception and then provide the best possible handling solution for the case. After all, if the program is simply going to spit out a nasty error then the exception handling block is not very user friendly and is only helpful to developers. However, there are some rare cases where it would be advantageous to not explicitly refer to an exception type when we simply wish to ignore errors and move on. The *except* block also allows us to define a variable to which the exception message will be assigned. This allows us the ability to store that message and display it somewhere within our exception handling code block. If you are calling a piece of Java code from within Jython and the Java code throws an exception, it can be handled within Jython in the same manner as Jython exceptions.

Listing 7-6. Exception Handling in Python

```
# Code without an exception handler
>>> x = 10
>>> z = x / y
Traceback (most recent call last):
  File "<stdin>", line 1, in <module>
NameError: name 'y' is not defined

# The same code with an exception handling block
>>> x = 10
>>> try:
...     z = x / y
... except NameError, err:
...     print "One of the variables was undefined: ", err
...
One of the variables was undefined:  name 'y' is not defined
```

It is important to note that Jython 2.5.x uses the Python 2.5.x exception handling syntax. This syntax will be changing in future releases of Jython. Take note of the syntax that is being used for defining the variable that holds the exception. Namely, the *except ExceptionType, value* statement syntax in Python and Jython 2.5 differs from that beyond 2.5. In Python 2.6, the syntax changes a bit in order to ready developers for Python 3, which exclusively uses the new syntax.

Listing 7-7. Jython and Python 2.5 and Prior

```
try:
    # code
except ExceptionType, messageVar:
    # code
```

Listing 7-8. Jython 2.6 (Not Yet Implemented) and Python 2.6 and Beyond

```
try:
    # code
except ExceptionType as messageVar:
    # code
```

We had previously mentioned that it was simply bad programming practice to not explicitly name an exception type when writing exception handling code. This is true, however Python provides us with another a couple of means to obtain the type of exception that was thrown. The easiest way to find an exception type is to simply catch the exception as a variable as we've discussed previously. You can then find the specific exception type by using the *type(error_variable)* syntax if needed.

Listing 7-9. Determining Exception Type

```
# In this example, we catch a general exception and then determine the type later

>>> try:
...      8/0
... except Exception, ex1:
...      'An error has occurred'
...
'An error has occurred'
>>> ex1
ZeroDivisionError('integer division or modulo by zero',)
>>> type(ex1)
<type 'exceptions.ZeroDivisionError'>
>>>
```

There is also a function provided in the *sys* package known as *sys.exc_info()* that will provide us with both the exception type and the exception message. This can be quite useful if we are wrapping some code in a *try-except* block but we really aren't sure what type of exception may be thrown. Below is an example of using this technique.

Listing 7-10. Using sys.exc_info()

```
# Perform exception handling without explicitly naming the exception type
>>> x = 10
>>> try:
...      z = x / y
... except:
...      print "Unexpected error: ", sys.exc_info()[0], sys.exc_info()[1]
...
Unexpected error:  <type 'exceptions.NameError'> name 'y' is not defined
```

Sometimes you may run into a situation where it is applicable to catch more than one exception. Python offers a couple of different options if you need to do such exception handling. You can either use multiple *except clauses*, which does the trick and works well if you're interested in performing different tasks for each different exception that occurs, but may become too wordy. The other preferred option is to enclose your exception types within parentheses and separated by commas on your *except* statement. Take a look at the following example that portrays the latter approach using Listing 7-6.

Listing 7-11. Handling Multiple Exceptions

```
# Catch NameError, but also a ZeroDivisionError in case a zero is used in the equation

>>> try:
...      z = x/y
... except(NameError, ZeroDivisionError), err:
...      "An error has occurred, please check your values and try again"
...
'An error has occurred, please check your values and try again'
```

```
# Using multiple except clauses
>>> x = 10
>>> y = 0
>>> try:
...     z = x / y
... except NameError, err1:
...     print err1
... except ZeroDivisionError, err2:
...     print 'You cannot divide a number by zero!'
...
You cannot divide a number by zero!
```

As mentioned previously, an exception is simply a class in Python. There are superclasses and subclasses for exceptions. You can catch a superclass exception to catch any of the exceptions that subclass that exception are thrown. For instance, if a program had a specific function that accepted either a list or dict object, it would make sense to catch a *LookupError* as opposed to finding a *KeyError* or *IndexError* separately. Look at the following example to see one way that this can be done.

Listing 7-12. Catching a Superclass Exceptions

```
# In the following example, we define a function that will return
# a value from some container.  The function accepts either lists
# or dictionary objects.  The LookupError superclass is caught
# as opposed to checking for each of it's subclasses...namely KeyError and IndexError.

>>> def find_value(obj, value):
...     try:
...         return obj[value]
...     except LookupError, ex:
...         return 'An exception has been raised, check your values and try again'
...

# Create both a dict and a list and test the function by looking for a value that does
# not exist in either container

>>> mydict = {'test1':1,'test2':2}
>>> mylist = [1,2,3]
>>> find_value(mydict, 'test3')
'An exception has been raised, check your values and try again'
>>> find_value(mylist, 2)
3
>>> find_value(mylist, 3)
'An exception has been raised, check your values and try again'
>>>
```

If multiple exception blocks have been coded, the first matching exception is the one that is caught. For instance, if we were to redesign the *find_value* function that was defined in the previous example, but instead raised each exception separately then the first matching exception would be raised. . .the others would be ignored. Let's see how this would work.

Listing 7-13. Catching the First Matching Exceptions

```
# Redefine the find_value() function to check for each exception separately
# Only the first matching exception will be raised, others will be ignored.
# So in these examples, the except LookupError code is never run.

>>> def find_value(obj, value):
...     try:
...         return obj[value]
...     except KeyError:
...         return 'The specified key was not in the dict, please try again'
...     except IndexError:
...         return 'The specified index was out of range, please try again'
...     except LookupError:
...         return 'The specified key was not found, please try again'
...
>>> find_value(mydict, 'test3')
'The specified key was not in the dict, please try again'
>>> find_value(mylist, 3)
'The specified index was out of range, please try again'
>>>
```

The *try-except* block can be nested as deep as you'd like. In the case of nested exception handling blocks, if an exception is thrown then the program control will jump out of the inner most block that received the error, and up to the block just above it. This is very much the same type of action that is taken when you are working in a nested loop and then run into a *break* statement, your code will stop executing and jump back up to the outer loop. The following example shows an example for such logic.

Listing 7-14. Nested Exception Handling Blocks

```
# Perform some division on numbers entered by keyboard
 try:
     # do some work
     try:
         x = raw_input ('Enter a number for the dividend:  ')
         y = raw_input('Enter a number to divisor: ')
         x = int(x)
         y = int(y)
     except ValueError:
         # handle exception and move to outer try-except
         print 'You must enter a numeric value!'
     z = x / y
 except ZeroDivisionError:
    # handle exception
    print 'You cannot divide by zero!'
 except TypeError:
    print 'Retry and only use numeric values this time!'
 else:
    print 'Your quotient is: %d' % (z)
```

In the previous example, we nested the different exception blocks. If the first *ValueError* were raised, it would give control back to the outer exception block. Therefore, the *ZeroDivisionError* and *TypeError* could still be raised. Otherwise, if those last two exceptions are not thrown then the tasks within the *else* clause would be run.

As stated previously, it is a common practice in Jython to handle Java exceptions. Oftentimes we have a Java class that throws exceptions, and these can be handled or displayed in Jython just the same way as handling Python exceptions.

Listing 7-15. Handling Java Exceptions in Jython

```java
// Java Class TaxCalc
public class TaxCalc {

    public static void main(String[] args) {
        double cost = 0.0;
        int pct   = 0;
        double tip = 0.0;
        try {
            cost = Double.parseDouble(args[0]);
            pct = Integer.parseInt(args[1]);
            tip = (cost * (pct * .01));
            System.out.println("The total gratutity based on " + pct + " percent would be "
+
                    tip);
            System.out.println("The total bill would be " + (cost + tip) );
        } catch (NumberFormatException ex){
            System.out.println("You must pass number values as arguments.  Exception: " +
ex);
        } catch (ArrayIndexOutOfBoundsException ex1){
            System.out.println("You must pass two values to this utility.  Format:
TaxCalc(cost, percentage)  Exception: " + ex1);
        }
    }
}
```

Using Jython:

```
# Now lets bring the TaxCalc Java class into Jython and use it
>>> import TaxCalc
>>> calc = TaxCalc()

# pass strings within a list to the TaxCalc utility and the Java exception will be thrown
>>> vals = ['test1','test2']
>>> calc.main(vals)
You must pass number values as arguments.  Exception: java.lang.NumberFormatException: For
input string: "test1"

# Now pass numeric values as strings in a list, this works as expected (except for the bad
# rounding)
>>> vals = ['25.25', '20']
>>> calc.main(vals)
The total gratutity based on 20 percent would be 5.050000000000001
The total bill would be 30.3
```

You can also throw Java exceptions in Jython by simply importing them first and then using then raising them just like Python exceptions.

Raising Exceptions

Often you will find reason to raise your own exceptions. Maybe you are expecting a certain type of keyboard entry, and a user enters something incorrectly that your program does not like. This would be a case when you'd like to raise your own exception. The *raise* statement can be used to allow you to raise an exception where you deem appropriate. Using the *raise* statement, you can cause any of the Python exception types to be raised, you could raise your own exception that you define (discussed in the next section). The *raise* statement is analogous to the *throw* statement in the Java language. In Java we may opt to throw an exception if necessary. However, Java also allows you to apply a *throws* clause to a particular method if an exception may possibly be thrown within instead of using try-catch handler in the method. Python does not allow you do perform such techniques using the *raise* statement.

Listing 7-16. raise Statement Syntax

```
raise ExceptionType or String[, message[, traceback]]
```

As you can see from the syntax, using *raise* allows you to become creative in that you could use your own string when raising an error. However, this is not really looked upon as a best practice as you should try to raise a defined exception type if at all possible. You can also provide a short message explaining the error. This message can be any string. Let's take a look at an example.

Listing 7-17. raising Exceptions Using Message

```
>>> raise Exception("An exception is being raised")
Traceback (most recent call last):
  File "<stdin>", line 1, in <module>
Exception: An exception is being raised

>>> raise TypeError("You've specified an incorrect type")
Traceback (most recent call last):
  File "<stdin>", line 1, in <module>
TypeError: You've specified an incorrect type
```

Now you've surely seen some exceptions raised in the Python interpreter by now. Each time an exception is raised, a message appears that was created by the interpreter to give you feedback about the exception and where the offending line of code may be. There is always a *traceback* section when any exception is raised. This really gives you more information on where the exception was raised. Lastly, let's take a look at raising an exception using a different format. Namely, we can use the format *raise Exception, "message"*.

Listing 7-18. Using the raise Statement with the Exception, "message" Syntax

```
>>> raise TypeError,"This is a special message"
Traceback (most recent call last):
  File "<stdin>", line 1, in <module>
TypeError: This is a special message
```

Defining Your Own Exceptions

You can define your own exceptions in Python by creating an exception class. You simply define a class that inherits from the base *Exception* class. The easiest defined exception can simply use a pass statement inside the class. Exception classes can accept parameters using the initializer, and return the exception using the *__str__* method. Any exception you write should accept a message. It is also a good practice to name your exception giving it a suffix of *Error* if the exception is referring to an error of some kind.

Listing 7-19. Defining a Basic Exception Class

```
class MyNewError(Exception):
    pass
```

This example is the simplest type of exception you can create. This exception that was created above can be raised just like any other exception now.

```
raise MyNewError("Something happened in my program")
```

A more involved exception class may be written as follows.

Listing 7-20. Exception Class Using Initializer

```
class MegaError(Exception):
    """ This is raised when there is a huge problem with my program"""
    def __init__(self, val):
        self.val = val
    def __str__(self):
        return repr(self.val)
```

Issuing Warnings

Warnings can be raised at any time in your program and can be used to display some type of warning message, but they do not necessarily cause execution to abort. A good example is when you wish to deprecate a method or implementation but still make it usable for compatibility. You could create a warning to alert the user and let them know that such methods are deprecated and point them to the new definition, but the program would not abort. Warnings are easy to define, but they can be complex if you wish to define rules on them using filters. Warning filters are used to modify the behavior of a particular warning. Much like exceptions, there are a number of defined warnings that can be used for categorizing. In order to allow these warnings to be easily converted into exceptions, they are all instances of the *Exception* type. Remember that exceptions are not necessarily errors, but rather alerts or messages. For instance, the *StopIteration* exception is raised by a program to stop the iteration of a loop…not to flag an error with the program.

To issue a warning, you must first import the *warnings* module into your program. Once this has been done then it is as simple as making a call to the *warnings.warn()* function and passing it a string with the warning message. However, if you'd like to control the type of warning that is issued, you can also pass the warning class. Warnings are listed in Table 7-2.

Listing 7-21. Issuing a Warning

```python
# Always import the warnings module first
import warnings

# A couple of examples for setting up warnings
warnings.warn("this feature will be deprecated")
warnings.warn("this is a more involved warning", RuntimeWarning)

# Using A Warning in a Function

# Suppose that use of the following function has been deprecated,
# warnings can be used to alert the function users

# The following function calculates what the year will be if we
# add the specified number of days to the current year.  Of course,
# this is pre-Y2K code so it is being deprecated.  We certainly do not
# want this code around when we get to year 3000!
>>> def add_days(current_year, days):
...     warnings.warn("This function has been deprecated as of version x.x",
DeprecationWarning)
...     num_years = 0
...     if days > 365:
...         num_years = days/365
...     return current_year + num_years
...

# Calling the function will return the warning that has been set up,
# but it does not raise an error...the expected result is still returned.
>>> add_days(2009, 450)
__main__:2: DeprecationWarning: This function has been deprecated as of version x.x
2010
```

Table 7-2. Python Warning Categories

Warning	Description
Warning	Root warning class
UserWarning	A user-defined warning
DeprecationWarning	Warns about use of a deprecated feature
SyntaxWarning	Syntax issues
RuntimeWarning	Runtime issues
FutureWarning	Warns that a particular feature will be changing in a future release

Importing the warnings module into your code gives you access to a number of built-in warning functions that can be used. If you'd like to filter a warning and change its behavior then you can do so by creating a filter. Table 7-3 lists functions that come with the *warnings* module.

Table 7-3. Warning Functions

Function	Description
warn(message[, category[, stacklevel]])	Issues a warning. Parameters include a message string, the optional category of warning, and the optional stack level that tells which stack frame the warning should originate from, usually either the calling function or the source of the function itself.
warn_explicit(message, category, filename, lineno[, module[, registry]])	This offers a more detailed warning message and makes category a mandatory parameter. filename, lineno, and module tell where the warning is located. registry represents all of the current warning filters that are active.
showwarning(message, category, filename, lineno[, file])	Gives you the ability to write the warning to a file.
formatwarning(message, category, filename, lineno)	Creates a formatted string representing the warning.
simplefilter(action[, category[, lineno[, append]]])	Inserts simple entry into the ordered list of warnings filters. Regular expressions are not needed for simplefilter as the filter always matches any message in any module as long as the category and line number match. filterwarnings() described below uses a regular expression to match against warnings.
resetwarnings()	Resets all of the warning filters.
filterwarnings(action[, message[, category[, module[, lineno[, append]]]]])	This adds an entry into a warning filter list. Warning filters allow you to modify the behavior of a warning. The action in the warning filter can be one from those listed in Table 7-4, message is a regular expression, category is the type of a warning to be issued, module can be a regular expression, lineno is a line number to match against all lines, append specifies whether the filter should be appended to the list of all filters.

Table 7-4. Python Filter Actions

Filter Actions	
'always'	Always print warning message
'default'	Print warning once for each location where warning occurs
'error'	Converts a warning into an exception
'ignore'	Ignores the warning
'module'	Print warning once for each module in which warning occurs
'once'	Print warning only one time

Let's take a look at a few ways to use warning filters in the examples below.

Listing 7-22. Warning Filter Examples

```
# Set up a simple warnings filter to raise a warning as an exception

>>> warnings.simplefilter('error', UserWarning)
>>> warnings.warn('This will be raised as an exception')
Traceback (most recent call last):
  File "<stdin>", line 1, in <module>
  File "/Applications/Jython/jython2.5.1rc2/Lib/warnings.py", line 63, in warn
    warn_explicit(message, category, filename, lineno, module, registry,
  File "/Applications/Jython/jython2.5.1rc2/Lib/warnings.py", line 104, in warn_explicit
    raise message
UserWarning: This will be raised as an exception

# Turn off all active filters using resetwarnings()
>>> warnings.resetwarnings()
>>> warnings.warn('This will not be raised as an exception')
__main__:1: UserWarning: This will not be raised as an exception

# Use a regular expression to filter warnings
# In this case, we ignore all warnings containing the word "one"
>>> warnings.filterwarnings('ignore', '.*one*.',)
>>> warnings.warn('This is warning number zero')
__main__:1: UserWarning: This is warning number zero
>>> warnings.warn('This is warning number one')
>>> warnings.warn('This is warning number two')
__main__:1: UserWarning: This is warning number two
>>>
```

There can be many different warning filters in use, and each call to the *filterwarnings()* function will append another warning to the ordered list of filters if so desired. The specific warning is matched against each filter specification in the list in turn until a match is found. In order to see which filters are currently in use, issue the command *print warnings.filters*. One can also specify a warning filter from the command line by use of the –W option. Lastly, all warnings can be reset to defaults by using the *resetwarnings*() function.

It is also possible to set up a warnings filter using a command-line argument. This can be quite useful for filtering warnings on a per-script or per-module basis. For instance, if you are interested in filtering warnings on a per-script basis then you could issue the -*W* command line argument while invoking the script.

Listing 7-23. -W command-line option

```
-Waction:message:category:module:lineno
```

Listing 7-24. Example of using W command line option

```
# Assume we have the following script test_warnings.py
# and we are interested in running it from the command line
import warnings
def test_warnings():
    print "The function has started"
    warnings.warn("This function has been deprecated", DeprecationWarning)
    print "The function has been completed"

if __name__ == "__main__":
    test_warnings()

# Use the following syntax to start and run jython as usual without
# filtering any warnings
jython test_warnings.py
The function has started
test_warnings.py:4: DeprecationWarning: This function has been deprecated
  warnings.warn("This function has been deprecated", DeprecationWarning)
The function has been completed

# Run the script and ignore all deprecation warnings
jython -W "ignore::DeprecationWarning::0" test_warnings.py
The function has started
The function has been completed

# Run the script one last time and treat the DeprecationWarning
# as an exception.  As you see, it never completes
jython -W "error::DeprecationWarning::0" test_warnings.py
The function has started
Traceback (most recent call last):
  File "test_warnings.py", line 8, in <module>
    test_warnings()
  File "test_warnings.py", line 4, in test_warnings
    warnings.warn("This function has been deprecated", DeprecationWarning)
  File "/Applications/Jython/jython2.5.1rc2/Lib/warnings.py", line 63, in warn
    warn_explicit(message, category, filename, lineno, module, registry,
  File "/Applications/Jython/jython2.5.1rc2/Lib/warnings.py", line 104, in warn_explicit
    raise message
DeprecationWarning: This function has been deprecated
```

Warnings can be very useful in some situations. They can be made as simplistic or sophisticated as need be.

Assertions and Debugging

Debugging can be an easy task in Python via use of the *assert* statement. In CPython, the __debug__ variable can also be used, but this feature is currently not usable in Jython as there is no *optimization* mode for the interpreter. . Assertions are statements that can print to indicate that a particular piece of code is not behaving as expected. The assertion checks an expression for a True or False value, and if it evaluates to False in a Boolean context then it issues an *AssertionError* along with an optional message. If the expression evaluates to True then the assertion is ignored completely.

```
assert expression [, message]
```

By effectively using the *assert* statement throughout your program, you can easily catch any errors that may occur and make debugging life much easier. Listing 7-25 will show you the use of the assert statement.

Listing 7-25. Using assert

```
#  The following example shows how assertions are evaluated
>>> x = 5
>>> y = 10
>>> assert x < y, "The assertion is ignored"
>>> assert x > y, "The assertion raises an exception"
Traceback (most recent call last):
  File "<stdin>", line 1, in <module>
AssertionError: The assertion raises an exception

# Use assertions to validate parameters# Here we check the type of each parameter to ensure
# that they are integers
>>> def add_numbers(x, y):
...     assert type(x) is int, "The arguments must be integers, please check the first
argument"
...     assert type(y) is int, "The arguments must be integers, please check the second
argument"
...     return x + y
...
# When using the function, AssertionErrors are raised as necessary
>>> add_numbers(3, 4)
7
>>> add_numbers('hello','goodbye')
Traceback (most recent call last):
  File "<stdin>", line 1, in <module>
  File "<stdin>", line 2, in add_numbers
AssertionError: The arguments must be integers, please check the first argument
```

Context Managers

Ensuring that code is written properly in order to manage resources such as files or database connections is an important topic. If files or database connections are opened and never closed then our program could incur issues. Often times, developers elect to make use of the *try-finally* blocks to ensure that such resources are handled properly. While this is an acceptable method for resource management, it can sometimes be misused and lead to problems when exceptions are raised in programs. For instance, if we are working with a database connection and an exception occurs after we've opened the connection, the program control may break out of the current block and skip all further processing. The connection may never be closed in such a case. That is where the concept of context management becomes an important new feature in Jython. Context management via the use of the *with* statement is new to Jython 2.5, and it is a very nice way to ensure that resources are managed as expected.

In order to use the *with* statement, you must import from __future__. The *with* statement basically allows you to take an object and use it without worrying about resource management. For instance, let's say that we'd like to open a file on the system and read some lines from it. To perform a file operation you first need to open the file, perform any processing or reading of file content, and then close the file to free the resource. Context management using the *with* statement allows you to simply open the file and work with it in a concise syntax.

Listing 7-26. Python with Statement Example

```
#  Read from a text file named players.txt
>>> from __future__ import with_statement
>>> with open('players.txt','r') as file:
...     x = file.read()
...
>>> print x
Sports Team Management
---------------------------------
Josh - forward
Jim - defense
```

In this example, we did not worry about closing the file because the context took care of that for us. This works with object that extends the context management protocol. In other words, any object that implements two methods named *__enter__()* and *__exit__()* adhere to the context management protocol. When the *with* statement begins, the *__enter__()* method is executed. Likewise, as the last action performed when the *with* statement is ending, the *__exit__()* method is executed. The __enter__() method takes no arguments, whereas the __exit__() method takes three optional arguments *type, value,* and *traceback*. The *__exit__()* method returns a *True* or *False* value to indicate whether an exception was thrown. The *as variable* clause on the *with* statement is optional as it will allow you to make use of the object from within the code block. If you are working with resources such as a lock then you may not need the optional clause.

If you follow the context management protocol, it is possible to create your own objects that can be used with this technique. The *__enter__()* method should create whatever object you are trying to work if needed.

Listing 7-27. Creating a Simple Object That Follows Context Management Protocol

```
# In this example, my_object facilitates the context management protocol
# as it defines an __enter__ and __exit__ method

class my_object:
    def __enter__(self):
        # Perform setup tasks
        return object

    def __exit__(self, type, value, traceback):
        # Perform cleanup
```

If you are working with an immutable object then you'll need to create a copy of that object to work with in the *__enter__()* method. The *__exit__()* method on the other hand can simply return *False* unless there is some other type of cleanup processing that needs to take place. If an exception is raised somewhere within the context manager, then __exit__() is called with three arguments representing type, value, and traceback. However, if there are no exceptions raised then __exit__() is passed three None arguments. If __exit__() returns *True*, then any exceptions are "swallowed" or ignored, and execution continues at the next statement after the with-statement.

Summary

In this chapter, we discussed many different topics regarding exceptions and exception handling within a Python application. First, you learned the exception handling syntax of the *try-except-finally* code block and how it is used. We then discussed why it may be important to *raise* your own exceptions at times and how to do so. That topic led to the discussion of how to define an exception and we learned that in order to do so we must define a class that extends the *Exception* type object.

After learning about exceptions, we went into the warnings framework and discussed how to use it. It may be important to use warnings in such cases where code may be deprecated and you want to warn users, but you do not wish to *raise* any exceptions. That topic was followed by assertions and how assertion statement can be used to help us debug our programs. Lastly, we touched upon the topic of context managers and using the *with* statement that is new in Jython 2.5.

In the next chapter you will delve into the arena of building larger programs, learning about modules and packages.

■ ■ ■

Modules and Packages for Code Reuse

Up until this chapter, we have been looking at code at the level of the interactive console and simple scripts. This works well for small examples, but when your program gets larger, it becomes necessary to break programs up into smaller units. In Jython, the basic building block for these units in larger programs is the module.

Imports for Reuse

Breaking code up into modules helps to organize large code bases. Modules can be used to logically separate code that belongs together, making programs easier to understand. Modules are helpful for creating libraries that can be imported and used in different applications that share some functionality. Jython's standard library comes with a large number of modules that can be used in your programs right away.

Import Basics

The following is a very simple program that we can use to discuss imports.

breakfast.py

```
import search.scanner as scanner
import sys

class Spam(object):

    def order(self, number):
        print "spam " * number

def order_eggs():
    print " and eggs!"

s = Spam()
s.order(3)
order_eggs()
```

We'll start with a couple of definitions. A **namespace** is a logical grouping of unique identifiers. In other words, a namespace is that set of names that can be accessed from a given bit of code in your program. For example, if you open up a Jython prompt and type dir(), the names in the interpreter's namespace will be displayed.

```
>>> dir()
['__doc__', '__name__']
```

The interpreter namespace contains __doc__ and __name__. The __doc__ property contains the top level docstring, which is empty in this case. We'll get to the __name__ property in a moment. First we need to talk about Jython **modules**. A **module** in Jython is a file containing Python definitions and statements which in turn define a namespace. The module name is the same as the file name with the suffix .py removed, so in our current example the Python file "breakfast.py" defines the module "breakfast."

Now we can talk about the __name__ property. When a module is run directly, as in jython breakfast.py, __name__ will contain '__main__'. If a module is imported, __name__ will contain the name of the module, so "import breakfast" results in the breakfast module containing a __name__ of "breakfast". Again from a basic Jython prompt:

```
>>> dir()
['__doc__', '__name__']
>>> __name__
'__main__'
```

Let's see what happens when we import breakfast:

```
>>> import breakfast
spam spam spam
 and eggs!
>>> dir()
['__doc__', '__name__', 'breakfast']
>>> import breakfast
>>>
```

Checking the dir() after the import shows that breakfast has been added to the top level namespace. Notice that the act of importing actually executed the code in breakfast.py. This is the expected behavior in Jython. When a module is imported, the statements in that module are actually executed. This includes class and function definitions. It is important to note that this only happens the first time you import a module. Note the last statement where we issue "import breakfast" again, resulting in no output. Most of the time, we wouldn't want a module to execute print statements when imported. To avoid this, but allow the code to execute when it is called directly, we typically check the __name__ property. If the __name__ property is '__main__', we know that the module was called directly instead of being imported from another module.

```
class Spam(object):

    def order(self, number):
        print "spam " * number

    def order_eggs():
        print " and eggs!"

if __name__ == '__main__':
    s = Spam()
    s.order(3)
```

```
order_eggs()
```

Now if we import breakfast (remember to close and reopen the interpreter so that the module is actually reimported!), we will not get the output:

```
>>> import breakfast
```

This is because in this case the __name__ property will contain 'breakfast,' the name of the module. If we call breakfast.py from the commandline like "jython breakfast.py" we would then get the output again, because breakfast would be executing as __main__:

```
$ jython breakfast.py
spam spam spam
 and eggs!
```

The Import Statement

In Java, the Import statement is strictly a compiler directive that must occur at the top of the source file. In Jython, the import statement is an expression that can occur anywhere in the source file, and can even be conditionally executed.

As an example, a common idiom is to attempt to import something that may not be there in a try block, and in the except block define the thing in some other way, or import it from a module that is known to be there.

```
>>> try:
...    from blah import foo
...    print "imported normally"
... except ImportError:
...    print "defining foo in except block"
...    def foo():
...      return "hello from backup foo"
...
defining foo in except block
>>> foo()
'hello from backup foo'
>>>
```

If a module named "blah" had existed, the definition of foo would have been taken from there and we would have seen "imported normally" printed out. Because no such module existed, foo was defined in the except block, "defining foo in except block" was printed, and when we called foo, the 'hello from backup foo' string was returned.

An Example Program

Here is the layout of a contrived but simple program that we will use to describe some aspects of importing in Jython.

```
chapter8/
        greetings.py
        greet/
                __init__.py
                hello.py
```

```
people.py
```

This example contains one package: greet, which is a package because it is a directory containing the special __init__.py file. Note that the directory chapter8 itself is not a package because it does not contain an __init__.py. There are three modules in the example program: greetings, greet.hello, and greet.people. The code for this program can be downloaded at http://kenai.com/projects/jythonbook/sources/jython-book/show/src/chapter8.

greetings.py

```
print "in greetings.py"
import greet.hello

g = greet.hello.Greeter()
g.hello_all()
```

greet/__init__.py

```
print "in greet/__init__.py"
```

greet/hello.py

```
print "in greet/hello.py"
import greet.people as people

class Greeter(object):
    def hello_all(self):
        for name in people.names:
            print "hello %s" % name
```

greet/people.py

```
print "in greet/people.py"

names = ["Josh", "Jim", "Victor", "Leo", "Frank"]
```

Trying Out the Example Code

If you run greetings.py in its own directory you get the following output:

```
$ jython greetings.py
in greetings.py
in greet/__init__.py
in greet/hello.py
in greet/people.py
hello Josh
hello Jim
hello Victor
hello Leo
hello Frank
```

There is a print statement at the top of each of the .py files to show the order of execution for the modules. When run, the module greetings is loaded, printing out "in greetings.py." Next it imports greet.hello:

```
import greet.hello
```

Because this is the first time that the greet package has been imported, the code in __init__.py is executed, printing "in greet/__init__.py". Then the greet.hello module is executed, printing out "in greet/hello.py." The greet.hello module then imports the greet.people module, printing out "in greet/people.py." Now all of the imports are done, and greetings.py can create a greet.hello.Greeter class and call its hello_all method.

Types of Import Statements

The import statement comes in a variety of forms that allow much finer control over how importing brings named values into your current module.

```
import module
from module import submodule
from . import submodule
```

We will discuss each of the import statement forms in turn starting with:

```
import module
```

This most basic type of import imports a module directly. Unlike Java, this form of import binds the left-most module name, so if you import a nested module like:

import greet.hello

you need to refer to it as "greet.hello" and not just "hello" in your code.

import greet.hello as foo

The "as foo" part of the import allows you to relabel the "greet.hello" module as "foo" to make it more convenient to call. The example program uses this method to relabel "greet.hello" as "hello." Note that it is not important that "hello" was the name of the subpackage except that it might aid in reading the code. You would also use this technique if the identifier of the thing you wanted to import was already in use in this namespace: if you already had a variable called foo, and you wanted to import something else called foo, you could do import foo as bar.

From Import Statements

```
from module import name
```

This form of import allows you to import modules, classes or functions nested in other modules. This allows you to import code like this:

```
from greet import hello
```

In this case, it *is* important that "hello" is actually a submodule of greet. This is not a relabeling but actually gets the submodule named "hello" from the greet namespace. You can also use the from style of import to import all of the names in a module (except for those that start with an underscore) into your current module using a *. This form of import is discouraged in the Python community, and is particularly troublesome when importing from Java packages (in some cases it does not work) so you should avoid its use. It looks like this:

```
from module import *
```

If you are not importing from a Java package, it is sometimes convenient to use this form to pull in everything from another module.

Relative Import Statements

A new kind of import introduced in Python 2.5 is the explicit relative import. These import statements use dots to indicate how far back you will walk from the current nesting of modules, with one dot meaning the current module.

```
from . import module
from .. import module
from .module import submodule
from ..module import submodule
```

Even though this style of importing has just been introduced, its use is discouraged. Explicit relative imports are a reaction to the demand for implicit relative imports. If we had wanted to import the Greeter class out of greet.hello so that it could be instantiated with just Greeter() instead of greet.hello.Greeter we could have imported it like this:

```
from greet.hello import Greeter
```

If you wanted to import Greeter into the greet.people module, you could get away with:

```
from hello import Greeter
```

This is a relative import. Because greet.people is a sibling module of greet.hello, the "greet" can be left out. This relative import style is deprecated and should not be used. Some developers like this style so that imports will survive module restructuring, but these relative imports can be error prone because of the possibility of name clashes. There is a new syntax that provides an explicit way to use relative imports, though they too are still discouraged. The previous import statement would look like this:

```
from .hello import Greeter
```

Aliasing Import Statements

Any of the above imports can add an "as" clause to import a module but give it a new name.

```
import module as alias
from module import submodule as alias
from . import submodule as alias
```

This gives you enormous flexibility in your imports, so to go back to the greet.hello example, you could issue:

```
import greet.hello as foo
```

And use foo in place of greet.hello.

Hiding Module Names

Typically when a module is imported, all of the names in the module are available to the importing module. There are a couple of ways to hide these names from importing modules. Starting any name with an underscore (_) will document these names as private. The names are still accessible, they are just not imported when you import the names of a module with "from module import *". The second way to hide module names is to define a list named __all__, which should contain only those names that you wish to have your module to expose. As an example here is the value of __all__ at the top of Jython's OS module:

```
__all__ = ["altsep", "curdir", "pardir", "sep", "pathsep",
           "linesep", "defpath", "name", "path",
           "SEEK_SET", "SEEK_CUR", "SEEK_END"]
```

Note that you can add to __all__ inside of a module to expand the exposed names of that module. In fact, the os module in Jython does just this to conditionally expose names based on the operating system that Jython is running on.

Module Search Path, Compilation, and Loading

Understanding Jython's process of locating, compiling, and loading packages and modules is very helpful in getting a deeper understanding of how things really work in Jython.

Java Import Example

We'll start with a Java class which is on the CLASSPATH when Jython is started:

```
package com.foo;
public class HelloWorld {
    public void hello() {
        System.out.println("Hello World!");
    }
    public void hello(String name) {
        System.out.printf("Hello %s!", name);
    }
}
```

Here we manipulate that class from the Jython interactive interpreter:

```
>>> from com.foo import HelloWorld
>>> h = HelloWorld()
>>> h.hello()
Hello World!
>>> h.hello("frank")
Hello frank!
```

It's important to note that, because the HelloWorld program is located on the Java CLASSPATH, it did not go through the sys.path process we talked about before. In this case the Java class gets loaded directly by the ClassLoader. Discussions of Java ClassLoaders are beyond the scope of this book. To read more about ClassLoader see execution section of the Java language specification:

http://java.sun.com/docs/books/jls/second_edition/html/execution.doc.html.

Module Search Path and Loading

Understanding the process of module search and loading is more complicated in Jython than in either CPython or Java, because Jython can search both Java's CLASSPATH and Python's path. We'll start by looking at Python's path and sys.path. When you issue an import, sys.path defines the path that Jython will use to search for the name you are trying to import. The objects within the sys.path list tell Jython where to search for modules. Most of these objects point to directories, but there are a few special items that can be in sys.path for Jython that are not just pointers to directories. Trying to import a file that does not reside anywhere in the sys.path (and also cannot be found in the CLASSPATH) raises an ImportError exception. Let's fire up a command line and look at sys.path.

```
>>> import sys
>>> sys.path
['', '/Users/frank/jython/Lib', '__classpath__', '__pyclasspath__/',
'/Users/frank/jython/Lib/site-packages']
```

The first blank entry (") tells Jython to look in the current directory for modules. The second entry points to Jython's Lib directory that contains the core Jython modules. The third and fourth entries are special markers that we will discuss later, and the last points to the site-packages directory where new libraries can be installed when you issue setuptools directives from Jython (see Appendix A for more about setuptools). The module that gets imported is the first one that is found along this path. Once a module is found, no more searching is done.

```
>>> import sys
>>> sys.path.append("/Users/frank/lib/mysql-connector-java-5.1.6.jar")
>>> import com.mysql
*sys-package-mgr*: processing new jar, '/Users/frank/lib/mysql-connector-java-5.1.6.jar'
>>> dir(com.mysql)
['__name__', 'jdbc']
```

In this example, we added the mysql jar to the sys path, then when we tried to find com.mysql, the jar was scanned. Note that "com.mysql" is a Java package that is found in mysql-connector-java-5.1.6.jar.

Java Package Scanning

Although you can ask the Java SDK to give you a list of all of the packages known to a ClassLoader using:

```
java.lang.ClassLoader#getPackages()
```

there is no corresponding

```
java.lang.Package#getClasses()
```

This is unfortunate for Jython, because Jython users expect to be able to introspect the code they use in powerful ways. For example, users expect to be able to call dir() on Java packages to see what they contain:

```
>>> import java.util.zip
>>> dir(java.util.zip)
['Adler32', 'CRC32', 'CheckedInputStream', 'CheckedOutputStream', 'Checksum',
'DataFormatException', 'Deflater', 'DeflaterOutputStream', 'GZIPInputStream',
'GZIPOutputStream', 'Inflater', 'InflaterInputStream', 'ZipEntry', 'ZipException',
'ZipFile', 'ZipInputStream', 'ZipOutputStream', '__name__']
```

And the same can be done on Java classes to see what they contain:

```
>>> import java.util.zip
>>> dir(java.util.zip.ZipInputStream)
['__class__', '__delattr__', '__doc__', '__eq__', '__getattribute__', '__hash__',
'__init__', '__ne__', '__new__', '__reduce__', '__reduce_ex__', '__repr__', '__setattr__',
'__str__', 'available', 'class', 'close', 'closeEntry', 'equals', 'getClass',
'getNextEntry', 'hashCode', 'mark', 'markSupported', 'nextEntry', 'notify', 'notifyAll',
'read', 'reset', 'skip', 'toString', 'wait']
```

Making this sort of introspection possible in the face of merged namespaces requires some major effort the first time that Jython is started (and when jars or classes are added to Jython's path at runtime). If you have ever run a new install of Jython before, you will recognize the evidence of this system at work:

```
*sys-package-mgr*: processing new jar, '/Users/frank/jython/jython.jar'
*sys-package-mgr*: processing new jar,
'/System/Library/Frameworks/JavaVM.framework/Versions/1.5.0/Classes/classes.jar'
*sys-package-mgr*: processing new jar,
'/System/Library/Frameworks/JavaVM.framework/Versions/1.5.0/Classes/ui.jar'
*sys-package-mgr*: processing new jar,
'/System/Library/Frameworks/JavaVM.framework/Versions/1.5.0/Classes/laf.jar'
...
*sys-package-mgr*: processing new jar,
'/System/Library/Frameworks/JavaVM.framework/Versions/1.5.0/Home/lib/ext/sunjce_provider.jar
'
*sys-package-mgr*: processing new jar,
'/System/Library/Frameworks/JavaVM.framework/Versions/1.5.0/Home/lib/ext/sunpkcs11.jar'
```

This is Jython scanning all of the jar files that it can find to build an internal representation of the package and classes available on your JVM. This has the unfortunate side effect of making the first startup on a new Jython installation painfully slow.

How Jython Finds the Jars and Classes to Scan

There are two properties that Jython uses to find jars and classes. These settings can be given to Jython using commandline settings or the registry (see Appendix A). The two properties are:

```
python.packages.paths
python.packages.directories
```

These properties are comma separated lists of further registry entries that actually contain the values the scanner will use to build its listing. You probably should not change these properties. The properties that get pointed to by these properties are more interesting. The two that potentially make sense to manipulate are:

```
java.class.path
java.ext.dirs
```

For the java.class.path property, entries are separated as the classpath is separated on the operating system you are on (that is, ";" on Windows and ":" on most other systems). Each of these paths are checked for a .jar or .zip and if they have these suffixes they will be scanned.

For the java.ext.dirs property, entries are separated in the same manner as java.class.path, but these entries represent directories. These directories are searched for any files that end with .jar or .zip, and if any are found they are scanned.

To control the jars that are scanned, you need to set the values for these properties. There are a number of ways to set these property values, see Appendix A for more.

If you only use full class imports, you can skip the package scanning altogether. Set the system property python.cachedir.skip to true or (again) pass in your own postProperties to turn it off.

Compilation

Despite the popular belief that Jython is "interpreted, not compiled," in reality all Jython code is turned into Java bytecode before execution. This Java bytecode is not always saved to disk, but when you see Jython execute any code, even in an eval or an exec, you can be sure that bytecode is getting fed to the JVM. The sole exception to this that we know of is the experimental pycimport module that we will describe in the section on sys.meta_path below, which interprets CPython bytecodes instead of producing Java bytecodes.

Python Modules and Packages versus Java Packages

The basic semantics of importing Python modules and packages versus the semantics of importing Java packages into Jython differ in some important respects that need to be kept carefully in mind.

sys.path

When Jython tries to import a module, it will look in its sys.path in the manner described in the previous section until it finds one. If the module it finds represents a Python module or package, this import will display a "winner take all" semantic. That is, the first Python module or package that gets imported blocks any other module or package that might subsequently get found on any lookups. This means that if you have a module foo that contains only a name bar early in the sys.path, and then another module also called foo that only contains a name baz, then executing "import foo" will **only** give you foo.bar and not foo.baz.

This differs from the case when Jython is importing Java packages. If you have a Java package org.foo containing bar, and a Java package org.foo containing baz later in the path, executing "import org.foo" will **merge** the two namespaces so that you will get both org.foo.bar and org.foo.baz.

Just as important to keep in mind, if there is a Python module or package of a particular name in your path that conflicts with a Java package in your path this will also have a winner-take-all effect. If the Java package is first in the path, then that name will be bound to the merged Java packages. If the Python module or package wins, no further searching will take place, so the Java packages with the clashing names will never be found.

Naming Python Modules and Packages

Developers coming from Java will often make the mistake of modeling their Jython package structure the same way that they model Java packages. **Do not do this**. The reverse url convention of Java is a great, we would even say a brilliant convention for Java. It works very well indeed in the world of Java where these namespaces are merged. In the Python world however, where modules and packages display the winner-take-all semantic, this is a disastrous way to organize your code.

If you adopt this style for Python, say you are coming from "acme.com," you would set up a package structure like "com.acme." If you try to use a library from your vendor xyz that is set up as "com.xyz," then the first of these on your path will take the "com" namespace, and you will not be able to see the other set of packages.

Proper Python Naming

The Python convention is to keep namespaces as shallow as you can, and make your top level namespace reasonably unique, whether it is a module or a package. In the case of acme and company xyz, you might start your package structures with "acme" and "xyz" if you wanted to have these entire codebases under one namespace (not necessarily the right way to go — better to organize by product instead of by organization, as a general rule).

■ **Note** There are at least two sets of names that are particularly bad choices for naming modules or packages in Jython. The first is any top level domain like org, com, net, us, name. The second is any of the domains that Java the language has reserved for its top level namespaces: java, javax.

Advanced Import Manipulation

This section describes some advanced tools for dealing with the internal machinery of imports. It is pretty advanced stuff that is rarely needed, but when you need it, you **really** need it.

Import Hooks

To understand the way that Jython imports Java classes you have to understand a bit about the Python import protocol. We won't get into every detail, for that you would want to look at PEP 302 http://www.python.org/dev/peps/pep-0302/.

Briefly, we first try any custom importers registered on sys.meta_path. If one of them is capable of importing the requested module, allow that importer to handle it. Next, we try each of the entries on sys.path. For each of these, we find the first hook registered on sys.path_hooks that can handle the path entry. If we find an import hook and it successfully imports the module, we stop. If this did not work, we try the builtin import logic. If that also fails, an ImportError is thrown. So let's look at Jython's path_hooks.

sys.path_hooks

```
>>> import sys
>>> sys.path_hooks
[<type 'org.python.core.JavaImporter'>, <type 'zipimport.zipimporter'>,
<type 'ClasspathPyImporter'>]
```

Each of these path_hooks entries specifies a path_hook that will attempt to import special files. JavaImporter, as its name implies, allows the dynamic loading of Java packages and classes that are specified at runtime. For example, if you want to include a jar at runtime you can execute the following code:

```
>>> import sys
>>> sys.path.append("mysql-connector-java-5.1.6.jar")
>>> import com.mysql
*sys-package-mgr*: processing new jar, 'mysqlconnector-java-5.1.6.jar'
>>> dir(com.mysql)
['__name__', 'jdbc']
```

Note how the package scanning gets kicked off when "com.mysql" is imported, as evidenced by the line starting with *sys-package-mgr*. Upon import, the JavaImporter scanned the new jar and allowed the import to succeed.

sys.meta_path

Adding entries to sys.meta_path allows you to add import behaviors that will occur before any other import is attempted, even the default builtin importing behavior. This can be a very powerful tool, allowing you to do all sorts of interesting things. As an example, we will talk about an experimental module that ships with Jython 2.5. That module is pycimport. If you start up Jython and issue

```
>>> import pycimport
```

Jython will start scanning for .pyc files in your path and, if it finds one, it will use the .pyc file to load your module.pyc files. These are the files that CPython produces when it compiles Python source code. So, after you have imported pycimport (which adds a hook to sys.meta_path) then issue:

```
>>> import foo
```

Jython will scan your path for a file named foo.pyc, and if it finds one it will import the foo module using the CPython bytecodes. It does this by creating a special class that defines a find_module method that specifies how to load in a pyc file. This class is then added to the meta search path with the sys.meta_path.insert method. The find_module method calls into other parts of pycimport and looks for .pyc files. If it finds one, it knows how to parse and execute those files and adds the corresponding module to the runtime. Pretty cool, eh?

Summary

In this chapter, you have learned how to divide code up into modules to for the purpose of organization and reuse. We have learned how to write modules and packages, and how the Jython system interacts with Java classes and packages. This ends Part I. We have now covered the basics of the Jython language and are now ready to learn how to use Jython.

PART II

■■■

Using the Language

CHAPTER 9

■ ■ ■

Scripting With Jython

In this chapter, we will look at scripting with Jython. For our purposes, we will define "scripting" as the writing of small programs to help out with daily tasks. These tasks are things like deleting and creating directories, managing files and programs, and anything else that feels repetitive that you might be able to express as a small program. In practice, however, scripts can become so large that the line between a script and a full sized program can blur.

We'll start with some very small examples to give you a feel for the sorts of tasks you might script from Jython. Then we'll cover a medium-sized task to show the use of a few of these techniques together.

Getting the Arguments Passed to a Script

All but the simplest of scripts will take some arguments from the command line. We'll start our look at scripting by printing out any args passed to our script.

Listing 9-1.

```
import sys

for arg in sys.argv:
    print arg
```

Let's try running our script with some random arguments:

Listing 9-2.

```
$ jython args.py a b c 1 2 3
args.py
a
b
c
1
2
3
```

The first value in sys.argv is the name of the script itself (args.py), the rest is the items passed in on the command line.

Searching for a File

Many scripting tasks take the form of "find a bunch of files and do something with them." So let's take a look at how you might find some files from a Jython program. We'll start with a simple script that finds any files in your current directory that match a passed in string:

Listing 9-3.

```
import sys
import os

for f in os.listdir(sys.argv[1]):
    if f.find(sys.argv[2]) != -1:
        print f
```

At the top of the script, we import the sys and os modules. Then we run a for loop over the results of os.listdir(sys.argv[1]). The os module is a good place to look if you are trying to accomplish the sorts of tasks you might do on a command prompt, such as listing the files in a directory, deleting a file, renaming a file, and the like. The listdir function of the os module takes one argument: a string that will be used as the path. The entries of the directory on that path are returned as a list. In this case, if we run this in its own directory (by passing in "." for the current directory), we see:

Listing 9-4.

```
$ ls
args.py
search.py
$ jython list.py . py
args.py
search.py
$ jython list.py . se
search.py
```

In the first call to list.py, we list all files that contain "py", listing "args.py" and "search.py." In the second call, we list all files that contain the string "se", so only "search.py" is listed.

The os module contains many useful functions and attributes that can be used to get information about your operating environment. Next we can open up a Jython prompt and try out a few os features:

Listing 9-5.

```
>>> import os
>>> os.getcwd()
'/Users/frank/Desktop/frank/hg/jythonbook~jython-book/src/chapter8'
>>> os.chdir("/Users/frank")
>>> os.getcwd()
'/Users/frank'
```

We just printed out our current working directory with os.getcwd(), changed our current working directory to "/Users/frank," and then printed out the new directory with another call to os.getcwd(). It is important to note that the JVM does not expose the ability to actually change the current working directory of the process running Jython. For this reason, Jython keeps track of its own current working directory. As long as you stay within Jython's standard library, the current working directory will behave as you expect (it will be changed with os.chdir()). However, if you import Java library functions that depend on a current working directory, it will always reflect the directory that Jython was started in.

Listing 9-6.

```
>>> import os
>>> os.getcwd()
'/Users/frank/Desktop/frank/hg/jythonbook~jython-book/src/chapter8'
>>> from java.io import File
>>> f = File(".")
>>> for x in f.list():
...     print x
...
args.py
search.py
>>> os.chdir("/Users/frank")
>>> os.getcwd()
'/Users/frank'
>>> os.listdir(".")
['Desktop', 'Documents', 'Downloads', 'Dropbox', 'Library', 'Movies', 'Music', 'Pictures',
'Public', 'Sites']
>>> g = File(".")
>>> for x in g.list():
...     print x
...
args.py
search.py
```

Quite a bit went on in that last example, we'll take it step by step. We imported os and printed the current working directory, which is chapter8. We imported the File class from java.io. We then printed the contents of "." from the Java side of the world. We then changed directories with os.chdir() to the home directory, and listed the contents of "." from Jython's perspective, and listed "." from the Java perspective. The important thing to note is that "." from Java will always see the chapter8 directory because we cannot change the real working directory of the Java process—we can only keep track of a working directory so that Jython's working directory behaves the way Python programmers expect. Too many Python tools (like distutils and setuptools) depend on the ability to change working directories to ignore.

Manipulating Files

Listing files is great, but a more interesting scripting problem is actually doing something to the files you are working with. One of these problems that comes up for me from time to time is that of changing the extensions of a bunch of files. If you need to change one or two extensions, it isn't a big deal to do it manually. If you want to change hundreds of extensions, things get very tedious. Splitting extensions can be handled with the splitext function from the os.path module. The splitext function takes a file name and returns a tuple of the base name of the file and the extension.

Listing 9-7.

```
>>> import os
>>> for f in os.listdir("."):
...    print os.path.splitext(f)
...
('args', '.py')
('builder', '.py')

('HelloWorld', '.java')
('search', '.py')
```

Now that we can get the extensions, we just need to be able to rename the files. Luckily, the os module has exactly the function we need, rename:

Listing 9-8.

```
>>> import os
>>> os.rename('HelloWorld.java', 'HelloWorld.foo')
>>> os.listdir('.')
['args.py', 'builder.py', 'HelloWorld.foo', 'search.py']
    If you are manipulating any important files, be sure to put the names back!
>>> os.rename('HelloWorld.foo', 'HelloWorld.java')
>>> os.listdir('.')
['args.py', 'builder.py', 'HelloWorld.java', 'search.py']
```

Now that you know how to get extensions and how to rename files, we can put them together into a script (chext.py) that changes extensions:

Listing 9-9.

```
import sys
import os

for f in os.listdir(sys.argv[1]):
    base, ext = os.path.splitext(f)
    if ext[1:] == sys.argv[2]:
        os.rename(f, "%s.%s" % (base, sys.argv[3]))
```

Making a Script a Module

If you wanted to turn chext.py into a module that could also be used from other modules, you could put this code into a function and separate its use as a script like this:

Listing-9-10.

```
import sys
import os

def change_ext(directory, old_ext, new_ext):
    for f in os.listdir(sys.argv[1]):
        base, ext = os.path.splitext(f)
        if ext[1:] == sys.argv[2]:
            os.rename(f, "%s.%s" % (base, sys.argv[3]))

if __name__ == '__main__':
    if len(sys.argv) < 4:
        print "usage: %s directory old_ext new_ext" % sys.argv[0]
        sys.exit(1)
    change_ext(sys.argv[1], sys.argv[2], sys.argv[3])
```

This new version can be used from an external module like this:

Listing 9-11.

```
import chext

chext.change_ext(".", "foo", "java")
```

We have also used this change to introduce a little error checking, if we haven't supplied enough arguments, the script prints out a usage message.

Parsing Commandline Options

Many scripts are simple one-offs that you write once, use, and forget. Others become part of your weekly or even daily use over time. When you find that you are using a script over and over again, you often find it helpful to pass in command line options. There are three main ways that this is done in Jython. The first way is to hand parse the arguments that can be found from sys.argv as we did above in chext.py, the second is the getopt module, and the third is the newer, more flexible optparse module.

If you are going to do more than just feed the arguments to your script directly, then parsing these arguments by hand can get pretty tedious, and you'll be much better off using getopt or optparse. The optparse module is the newer, more flexible option, so we'll cover that one. The getopt module is still useful since it requires a little less code for simpler expected arguments. Here is a basic optparse script:

Listing 9-12.

```
# script foo3.py
from optparse import optionparser
parser = optionparser()
parser.add_option("-f", "--foo", help="set foo option")
parser.add_option("-b", "--bar", help="set bar option")
(options, args) = parser.parse_args()
print "options: %s" % options
print "args: %s" % args
```

running the above:

Listing 9-13.

```
$ jython foo3.py -b a --foo b c d
$ options: {'foo': 'b', 'bar': 'a'}
$ args: ['c', 'd']
```

In this example, we have created an optionparser and added two options with the add_option method. The add_option method takes at least one string as an option argument ("-f" in the first case) and an optional long version ("--foo" in the previous case). You can then pass in optional keyword options like the "help" option that sets the help string that will be associated with the script. We'll come back to the optparse module with a more concrete example later in this chapter.

Compiling Java Source

While compiling Java source is not strictly a typical scripting task, it is a task that we'd like to show off in a bigger example starting in the next section. The API we are about to cover was introduced in jdk 6, and is optional for jvm vendors to implement. We know that it works on the jdk 6 from Sun (the most common JDK in use) and on the jdk 6 that ships with mac os x. For more details of the javacompiler api, a good starting point is here: http://java.sun.com/javase/6/docs/api/javax/tools/javacompiler.html.

The following is a simple example of the use of this API from Jython:

Listing 9-14.

```
from javax.tools import (ForwardingJavaFileManager, ToolProvider,
        DiagnosticCollector,)
names = ["HelloWorld.java"]
compiler = ToolProvider.getSystemJavaCompiler()
diagnostics = DiagnosticCollector()
manager = compiler.getStandardFileManager(diagnostics, none, none)
units = manager.getJavaFileObjectsFromStrings(names)
comp_task = compiler.getTask(none, manager, diagnostics, none, none, units)
success = comp_task.call()
manager.close()
```

First we import some Java classes from the javax.tools package. Then we create a list containing just one string, "HelloWorld.java." Then we get a handle on the system Java compiler and call it "compiler." A couple of objects that need to get passed to our compiler task, "diagnostics" and "manager" are created. We turn our list of strings into "units" and finally we create a compiler task and execute its call method. If we wanted to do this often, we'd probably want to roll up all of this into a simple method.

Example Script: Builder.py

So we've discussed a few of the modules that tend to come in handy when writing scripts for Jython. Now we'll put together a simple script to show off what can be done. We've chosen to write a script that will help handle the compilation of java files to .class files in a directory, and clean the directory of .class files as a separate task. We will want to be able to create a directory structure, delete the directory structure for a clean build, and of course compile our java source files.

Listing 9-15.

```
import os
import sys
import glob

from javax.tools import (forwardingjavafilemanager, toolprovider,
        diagnosticcollector,)

tasks = {}

def task(func):
    tasks[func.func_name] = func

@task
def clean():
    files = glob.glob("*.class")
    for file in files:
        os.unlink(file)

@task
def compile():
    files = glob.glob("*.java")
    _log("compiling %s" % files)
    if not _compile(files):
        quit()
    _log("compiled")

def _log(message):
    if options.verbose:
        print message

def _compile(names):
    compiler = toolprovider.getsystemjavacompiler()
    diagnostics = diagnosticcollector()
    manager = compiler.getstandardfilemanager(diagnostics, none, none)
    units = manager.getjavafileobjectsfromstrings(names)
    comp_task = compiler.gettask(none, manager, diagnostics, none, none, units)
    success = comp_task.call()
    manager.close()
    return success

if __name__ == '__main__':
    from optparse import optionparser
    parser = optionparser()
    parser.add_option("-q", "--quiet",
            action="store_false", dest="verbose", default=true,
            help="don't print out task messages.")
    parser.add_option("-p", "--projecthelp",
            action="store_true", dest="projecthelp",
            help="print out list of tasks.")
    (options, args) = parser.parse_args()
```

```
    if options.projecthelp:
        for task in tasks:
            print task
        sys.exit(0)

    if len(args) < 1:
        print "usage: jython builder.py [options] task"
        sys.exit(1)

    try:
        current = tasks[args[0]]
    except KeyError:
        print "task %s not defined." % args[0]
        sys.exit(1)
    current()
```

The script defines a "task" decorator that gathers the names of the functions and puts them in a dictionary. We have an optionparser class that defines two options --projecthelp and --quiet. By default the script logs its actions to standard out. The option --quiet turns this logging off, and --projecthelp lists the available tasks. We have defined two tasks, "compile" and "clean." The "compile" task globs for all of the .java files in your directory and compiles them. The "clean" task globs for all of the .class files in your directory and deletes them. Do be careful! The .class files are deleted without prompting!

So let's give it a try. If you create a Java class in the same directory as builder.py, say the classic "Hello World" program:

HelloWorld.java

Listing 9-16.

```
public class HelloWorld {
    public static void main(String[] args) {
        System.out.println("Hello, World");
    }
}
```

You could then issue these commands to builder.py with these results:

Listing 9-17.

```
[frank@pacman chapter8]$ jython builder.py --help
Usage: builder.py [options]

Options:
  -h, --help        show this help message and exit
  -q, --quiet       Don't print out task messages.
  -p, --projecthelp  Print out list of tasks.
[frank@pacman chapter8]$ jython builder.py --projecthelp
compile
clean
```

```
[frank@pacman chapter8]$ jython builder.py compile
compiling ['HelloWorld.java']
compiled
[frank@pacman chapter8]$ ls
HelloWorld.java HelloWorld.class builder.py
[frank@pacman chapter8]$ jython builder.py clean
[frank@pacman chapter8]$ ls
HelloWorld.java builder.py
[frank@pacman chapter8]$ jython builder.py --quiet compile
[frank@pacman chapter8]$ ls
HelloWorld.class HelloWorld.java builder.py
[frank@pacman chapter8]$
```

Summary

This chapter has shown how to create scripts with Jython. We have gone from the most simple one- and two-line scripts to large scripts with lots of optional inputs. We hope this will help you create your own tools to help automate some of the repetition out of your days.

■ ■ ■

Jython and Java Integration

Java integration is the heart of Jython application development. Most Jython developers are either Python developers that are looking to make use of the vast library of tools that the JVM has to offer, or Java developers that would like to utilize the Python language semantics without migrating to a completely different platform. The fact is that most Jython developers are using it so that they can take advantage of the vast libraries available to the Java world, and in order to do so there needs to be a certain amount of Java integration in the application. Whether you plan to use some of the existing Java libraries in your application, or you're interested in mixing some great Python code into your Java application, this chapter is geared to help with the integration.

This chapter will focus on integrating Java and Python, but it will explore several different angles on the topic. You will learn several techniques to make use Jython code within your Java applications. Perhaps you'd like to simplify your code a bit; this chapter will show you how to write certain portions of your code in Jython and others in Java so that you can make code as simple as possible.

You'll also learn how to make use of the many Java libraries within your Jython applications while using Pythonic syntax! Forget about coding those programs in Java: why not use Jython so that the Java implementations in the libraries are behind the scenes? This chapter will show how to write Python code and use the libraries directly from it.

Using Java Within Jython Applications

Making use of Java from within Jython applications is about as seamless as using external Jython modules within a Jython script. As you learned in Chapter 8, you can simply import the required Java classes and use them directly. Java classes can be called in the same fashion as Jython classes, and the same goes for method calling. You simply call a class method and pass parameters the same way you'd do in Python.

Type coercion occurs much as it does when using Jython in Java in order to seamlessly integrate the two languages. In the following table, you will see the Java types that are coerced into Python types and how they match up. Table 10-1 was taken from the Jython user guide.

Table 10-1. Python and Java Types

Java Type	Python Type
char	String(length of 1)
boolean	Integer(True = not zero)

Table 10-1. Python and Java Types (continued)

Java Type	Python Type
byte, short, int, long	Integer
java.lang.String, byte[], char[]	String
java.lang.Class	JavaClass
Foo[]	Array(containing objects of class or subclass of Foo)
java.lang.Object	String
orb.python.core.PyObject	Unchanged
Foo	class Foo

Another thing to note about the utilization of Java within Jython is that there may be some naming conflicts. If a Java object conflicts with a Python object name, then you can simply fully qualify the Java object in order to ensure that the conflict is resolved. Another technique which was also discussed in Chapter 8 is making use of the "as" keyword when importing in order to rename an imported piece of code.

In the next couple of examples, you will see some Java objects being imported and used from within Jython.

Listing 10-1. Using Java in Jython

```
>>> from java.lang import Math
>>> Math.max(4, 7)
7L
>>> Math.pow(10,5)
100000.0
>>> Math.round(8.75)
9L
>>> Math.abs(9.765)
9.765
>>> Math.abs(-9.765)
9.765
>>> from java.lang import System as javasystem
>>> javasystem.out.println("Hello")
Hello
```

Now let's create a Java object and use it from within a Jython application.

Beach.java

```
public class Beach {

    private String name;
    private String city;
```

```java
    public Beach(String name, String city){
        this.name = name;
        this.city = city;
    }

    public String getName() {
        return name;
    }

    public void setName(String name) {
        this.name = name;
    }

    public String getCity() {
        return city;
    }

    public void setCity(String city) {
        this.city = city;
    }

}
```

Using Beach.java in Jython

```
>>> import Beach
>>> beach = Beach("Cocoa Beach","Cocoa Beach")
>>> beach.getName()
u'Cocoa Beach'
>>> print beach.getName()
Cocoa Beach
```

As we had learned in Chapter 8, one thing you'll need to do is ensure that the Java class you wish to use resides within your CLASSPATH. In the example above, I created a JAR file that contained the Beach class and then put that JAR on the CLASSPATH.

It is also possible to extend or subclass Java classes via Jython classes. This allows us to extend the functionality of a given Java class using Jython objects, which can be quite helpful at times. The next example shows a Jython class extending a Java class that includes some calculation functionality. The Jython class then adds another calculation method and makes use of the calculation methods from both the Java class and the Jython class.

Listing 10-2. Extending Java Classes

Calculator.java
```java
/**
 * Java calculator class that contains two simple methods
 */
public class Calculator {

    public Calculator(){

    }
```

```java
    public double calculateTip(double cost, double tipPercentage){
        return cost * tipPercentage;
    }

    public double calculateTax(double cost, double taxPercentage){
        return cost * taxPercentage;
    }

}
```

JythonCalc.py

```python
import Calculator
from java.lang import Math

class JythonCalc(Calculator):
    def __init__(self):
        pass

    def calculateTotal(self, cost, tip, tax):
        return cost + self.calculateTip(tip) + self.calculateTax(tax)


if __name__ == "__main__":
    calc = JythonCalc()
    cost = 23.75
    tip = .15
    tax = .07
    print "Starting Cost: ", cost
    print "Tip Percentage: ", tip
    print "Tax Percentage: ", tax
    print Math.round(calc.calculateTotal(cost, tip, tax))
```

Result
```
Starting Cost:  23.75
Tip Percentage:  0.15
Tax Percentage:  0.07
29
```

Using Jython Within Java Applications

Often, it is handy to have the ability to make use of Jython from within a Java application. Perhaps there is a class that would be better implemented in Python syntax, such as a Javabean. Or maybe there is a handy piece of Jython code that would be useful within some Java logic. Whatever the case may be, there are several approaches you can use in order to achieve this combination of technologies. In this section, we'll cover some of the older techniques for using Jython within Java, and then go into the current and future best practices for doing this. In the end, you should have a good understanding for how to use a module, script, or even just a few lines of Jython within your Java application. You will also have an overall understanding for the way that Jython has evolved in this area.

Object Factories

Perhaps the most widely used technique used today for incorporating Jython code within Java applications is the object factory design pattern. This idea basically enables seamless integration between Java and Jython via the use of object factories. There are different implementations of the logic, but all of them do have the same result in the end.

Implementations of the object factory paradigm allow one to include Jython modules within Java applications without the use of an extra compilation step. Moreover, this technique allows for a clean integration of Jython and Java code through usage of Java interfaces. In this section, I will explain the main concept of the object factory technique and then I will show you various implementations.

Let's take a look at an overview of the entire procedure from a high level. Say that you'd like to use one of your existing Jython modules as an object container within a Java application. Begin by coding a Java interface that contains definitions for those methods contained in the module that you'd like to expose to the Java application. Next, you would modify the Jython module to implement the newly coded Java interface. After this, code a Java factory class that would make the necessary conversions of the module from a PyObject into a Java object. Lastly, take the newly created Java object and use it as you wish. It may sound like a lot of steps in order to perform a simple task, but I think you'll agree that it is not very difficult once you've seen it in action.

Over the next few sections, I will take you through different examples of the implementation. The first example is a simple and elegant approach that involves a one-to-one Jython object and factory mapping. In the second example, we'll take a look at a very loosely coupled approach for working with object factories that basically allows one factory to be used for all Jython objects. Each of these methodologies has its own benefit and you can use the one that works best for you.

One-to-One Jython Object Factories

We will first discuss the notion of creating a separate object factory for each Jython object we wish to use. This one-to-one technique can prove to create lots of boilerplate code, but it has some advantages that we'll take a closer look at later on. In order to utilize a Jython module using this technique, you must either ensure that the .py module is contained within your sys.path, or hard code the path to the module within your Java code. Let's take a look at an example of this technique in use with a Java application that uses a Jython class representing a building.

Listing 10-3. Creating a One-To-One Object Factory

Building.py
```python
# A python module that implements a Java interface to
# create a building object
from org.jython.book.interfaces import BuildingType

class Building(BuildingType):
    def __init__(self, name, address, id):
        self.name = name
        self.address  =  address
        self.id = id

    def getBuildingName(self):
        return self.name

    def getBuildingAddress(self):
        return self.address

    def getBuldingId(self):
```

```
    return self.id
```

We begin with a Jython module named *Building.py* that is placed somewhere on our sys.path. Now, we must first ensure that there are no name conflicts before doing so or we could see some quite unexpected results. It is usually a safe bet to place this file at the source root for your application unless you explicitly place the file in your sys.path elsewhere. You can see that our *Building.py* object is a simple container for holding building information. We must explicitly implement a Java interface within our Jython class. This will allow the PythonInterpreter to coerce our object later. Our second piece of code is the Java interface that we implemented in *Building.py*. As you can see from the code, the returning Jython types are going to be coerced into Java types, so we define our interface methods using the eventual Java types. Let's take a look at the Java interface next.

BuildingType.java
```java
// Java interface for a building object
package org.jython.book.interfaces;

public interface BuildingType {

    public String getBuildingName();
    public String getBuildingAddress();
    public String getBuildingId();

}
```

Looking through the definitions contained within the Java interface, it is plain to see that the python module that subclasses it simply implements each of the definitions. If we wanted to change the python code a bit and add some code to one of the methods we could do so without touching the Java interface. The next piece of code that we need is a factory written in Java. This factory has the job of coercing the python module into a Java class.

BuildingFactory.java
```java
/**
 *
 * Object Factory that is used to coerce python module into a
 * Java class
 */
package org.jython.book.util;

import org.jython.book.interfaces.BuildingType;
import org.python.core.PyObject;
import org.python.core.PyString;
import org.python.util.PythonInterpreter;

public class BuildingFactory {

    private PyObject buildingClass;

    /**
     * Create a new PythonInterpreter object, then use it to
     * execute some python code.  In this case, we want to
     * import the python module that we will coerce.
     *
     * Once the module is imported than we obtain a reference to
     * it and assign the reference to a Java variable
```

```java
    */
    public BuildingFactory() {
        PythonInterpreter interpreter = new PythonInterpreter();
        interpreter.exec("from Building import Building");
        buildingClass = interpreter.get("Building");
    }

    /**
     * The create method is responsible for performing the actual
     * coercion of the referenced python module into Java bytecode
     */
    public BuildingType create (String name, String location, String id) {
        PyObject buildingObject = buildingClass.__call__(new PyString(name),
                                              new PyString(location),
                                              new PyString(id));
        return (BuildingType)buildingObject.__tojava__(BuildingType.class);
    }

}
```

The third piece of code in the example above plays a most important role, since this is the object factory that will coerce our Jython code into a resulting Java class. In the constructor, a new instance of the PythonInterpreter is created. We then utilize the interpreter to obtain a reference to our Jython object and store it into our PyObject. Next, there is a static method named *create* that will be called in order to coerce our Jython object into Java and return the resulting class. It does so by performing a *__call__* on the PyObject wrapper itself, and as you can see we have the ability to pass parameters to it if we like. The parameters must also be wrapped by PyObjects. The coercion takes place when the *__tojava__* method is called on the PyObject wrapper. In order to make object implement our Java interface, we must pass the interface *EmployeeType.class* to the *__tojava__* call.

Main.java

```java
package org.jython.book;

import org.jython.book.util.BuildingFactory;
import org.jython.book.interfaces.BuildingType;

public class Main {

    private static void print(BuildingType building) {
        System.out.println("Building Info: " +
                building.getBuildingId() + " " +
                building.getBuildingName() + " " +
                building.getBuildingAddress());

    }

    /**
     * Create three building objects by calling the create() method of
     * the factory.
     */
    public static void main(String[] args) {
        BuildingFactory factory = new BuildingFactory();
        print(factory.create("BUILDING-A", "100 WEST MAIN", "1"));
        print(factory.create("BUILDING-B", "110 WEST MAIN", "2"));
```

```
        print(factory.create("BUILDING-C", "120 WEST MAIN", "3"));
    }
}
```

The last bit of provided code, *Main.java*, shows how to make use of our factory. You can see that the factory takes care of all the heavy lifting and our implementation in *Main.java* is quite small. Simply call the *factory.create()* method to instantiate a new PyObject and coerce it into Java.

This procedure for using the object factory design has the benefit of maintaining complete awareness of the Jython object from within Java code. In other words, creating a separate factory for each Jython object allows for the use of passing arguments into the constructor of the Jython object. Since the factory is being designed for a specific Jython object, we can code the *__call__* on the PyObject with specific arguments that will be passed into the new constructor of the coerced Jython object. Not only does this allow for passing arguments into the constructor, but also increases the potential for good documentation of the object since the Java developer will know exactly what the new constructor will look like. The procedures performed in this subsection are probably the most frequently used throughout the Jython community. In the next section, we'll take a look at the same technique applied to a generic object factory that can be used by any Jython object.

Summary of One-to-One Object Factory

The key to this design pattern is the creation of a factory method that utilizes PythonInterpreter in order to load the desired Jython module. Once the factory has loaded the module via PythonInterpreter, it creates a PyObject instance of the module. Lastly, the factory coerces the PyObject into Java code using the PyObject __tojava__ method.

Overall, the idea is not very difficult to implement and relatively straightforward. However, the different implementations come into play when it comes to passing references for the Jython module and a corresponding Java interface. It is important to note that the factory takes care of instantiating the Jython object and translating it into Java. All work that is performed against the resulting Java object is coded against a corresponding Java interface. This is a great design because it allows us to change the Jython code implementation if we wish without altering the definition contained within the interface. The Java code can be compiled once and we can change the Jython code at will without breaking the application.

Making Use of a Loosely Coupled Object Factory

The object factory design does not have to be implemented using a one to one strategy such as that depicted in the example above. It is possible to design the factory in such a way that it is generic enough to be utilized for any Jython object. This technique allows for less boilerplate coding as you only require one Singleton factory that can be used for all Jython objects. It also allows for ease of use as you can separate the object factory logic into its own project and then apply it wherever you'd like. For instance, I've created a project named PlyJy (http://kenai.com/projects/plyjy) that basically contains a Jython object factory that can be used in any Java application in order to create Jython objects from Java without worrying about the factory. You can go to Kenai and download it now to begin learning about loosely coupled object factories. In this section we'll take a look at the design behind this project and how it works.

Let's take a look at the same example from above and apply the loosely coupled object factory design. You will notice that this technique forces the Java developer to do a bit more work when creating the object from the factory, but it has the advantage of saving the time that is spent to create a separate factory for each Jython object. You can also see that now we need to code setters into our Jython object and expose them via the Java interface as we can no longer make use of the constructor for passing arguments into the object since the loosely coupled factory makes a generic *__call__* on the PyObject.

Listing 10-4. Using a Loosely Coupled Object Factory

Building.py

```python
from org.jython.book.interfaces import BuildingType

#  Building object that subclasses a Java interface

class Building(BuildingType):
    def __init__(self):
        self.name = None
        self.address  =  None
        self.id = -1

    def getBuildingName(self):
        return self.name

    def setBuildingName(self, name):
        self.name = name;

    def getBuildingAddress(self):
        return self.address

    def setBuildingAddress(self, address):
        self.address = address

    def getBuildingId(self):
        return self.id

    def setBuildingId(self, id):
        self.id = id
```

If we follow this paradigm then you can see that our Jython module must be coded a bit differently than it was in our one-to-one example. The main differences are in the initializer as it no longer takes any arguments, and we therefore have coded setter methods into our object. The rest of the concept still holds true in that we must implement a Java interface that will expose those methods we wish to invoke from within our Java application. In this case, we coded the *BuildingType.java* interface and included the necessary setter definitions so that we have a way to load our class with values.

BuildingType.java

```java
package org.jython.book.interfaces;

/**
  * Java interface defining getters and setters
  */
public interface BuildingType {

    public String getBuildingName();
    public String getBuildingAddress();
    public int getBuildingId();
    public void setBuildingName(String name);
    public void setBuildingAddress(String address);
```

```
    public void setBuildingId(int id);

}
```

Our next step is to code a loosely coupled object. If you take a look at the code in the *JythonObjectFactory.java* class you will see that it is a singleton; that is it can only be instantiated one time. The important method to look at is *createObject()* as it does all of the work.

JythonObjectFactory.java

```java
import java.util.logging.Level;
import java.util.logging.Logger;
import org.python.core.PyObject;
import org.python.util.PythonInterpreter;

/**
 * Object factory implementation that is defined
 * in a generic fashion.
 *
 */

public class JythonObjectFactory {
    private static JythonObjectFactory instance = null;
    private static PyObject pyObject = null;

    protected JythonObjectFactory() {

    }
    /**
     * Create a singleton object.  Only allow one instance to be created
     */
    public static JythonObjectFactory getInstance(){
        if(instance == null){
            instance = new JythonObjectFactory();
        }

        return instance;

    }

    /**
     * The createObject() method is responsible for the actual creation of the
     * Jython object into Java bytecode.
     */
    public static Object createObject(Object interfaceType, String moduleName){
        Object javaInt = null;
        // Create a PythonInterpreter object and import our Jython module
        //   to obtain a reference.
        PythonInterpreter interpreter = new PythonInterpreter();
        interpreter.exec("from " + moduleName + " import " + moduleName);

        pyObject = interpreter.get(moduleName);

        try {
```

```
                // Create a new object reference of the Jython module and
                // store into PyObject.
                PyObject newObj = pyObject.__call__();
                // Call __tojava__ method on the new object along with the interface name
                // to create the java bytecode
                javaInt = newObj.__tojava__(Class.forName(interfaceType.toString().substring(
                        interfaceType.toString().indexOf(" ")+1,
interfaceType.toString().length())));
        } catch (ClassNotFoundException ex) {
                Logger.getLogger(JythonObjectFactory.class.getName()).log(Level.SEVERE, null,
ex);
        }

        return javaInt;
    }

}
```

As you can see from the code, the PythonInterpreter is responsible for obtaining a reference to the Jython object name that we pass as a String value into the method. Once the PythonInterpreter has obtained the object and stored it into a PyObject, its *__call__()* method is invoked without any parameters. This will retrieve an empty object that is then stored into another PyObject referenced by *newObj*. Lastly, our newly obtained object is coerced into Java code by calling the *__tojava__()* method which takes the fully qualified name of the Java interface we've implemented with our Jython object. The new Java object is then returned.

Main.java

```
import java.io.IOException;
import java.util.logging.Level;
import java.util.logging.Logger;
import org.jythonbook.interfaces.BuildingType;
import org.jybhonbook.factory.JythonObjectFactory;

public class Main {

    public static void main(String[] args) {

        // Obtain an instance of the object factory
        JythonObjectFactory factory = JythonObjectFactory.getInstance();

        // Call the createObject() method on the object factory by
        // passing the Java interface and the name of the Jython module
        // in String format.  The returning object is casted to the the same
        // type as the Java interface and stored into a variable.
        BuildingType building = (BuildingType) factory.createObject(
                BuildingType.class, "Building");
        // Populate the object with values using the setter methods
        building.setBuildingName("BUIDING-A");
        building.setBuildingAddress("100 MAIN ST.");
        building.setBuildingId(1);
        System.out.println(building.getBuildingId() + " " + building.getBuildingName() + " "
+
                building.getBuildingAddress());
```

```
    }

}
```

Taking a look at the *Main.java* code, you can see that the factory is instantiated or referenced via the use of the *JythonObjectFactory.getInstance()*. Once we have an instance of the factory, the *createObject(Interface, String)* is called passing the interface and a string representation of the module name we wish to use. The code must cast the coerced object using the interface as well. This example assumes that the object resides somewhere on your sys.path, otherwise you can use the *createObjectFromPath(Interface, String)* that accepts the string representation for the path to the module we'd like to coerce. This is of course not a preferred technique since it will now include hard-coded paths, but it can be useful to apply this technique for testing purposes. For example if you've got two Jython modules coded and one of them contains a different object implementation for testing purposes, then this technique will allow you to point to the test module.

More Efficient Version of Loosely Coupled Object Factory

Another similar, yet, more refined implementation omits the use of PythonInterpreter and instead makes use of PySystemState. Why would we want another implementation that produces the same results? Well, there are a couple of reasons. The loosely coupled object factory design I described in the beginning of this section instantiates the PythonInterpreter and then makes calls against it. This can cause a decrease in performance, as it is quite expensive to use the interpreter. On the other hand, we can make use of PySystemState and save ourselves the trouble of incurring extra overhead making calls to the interpreter. Not only does the next example show how to utilize this technique, but it also shows how we can make calls upon the coerced object and pass arguments at the same time.

Listing 10-5. Use PySystemState to Code a Loosely Coupled Factory

JythonObjectFactory.java

```java
package org.jython.book.util;

import org.python.core.Py;

import org.python.core.PyObject;
import org.python.core.PySystemState;

/**
 *  Jython Object Factory using PySystemState
 */
public class JythonObjectFactory {

    private final Class interfaceType;
    private final PyObject klass;


    // Constructor obtains a reference to the importer, module, and the class name
    public JythonObjectFactory(PySystemState state, Class interfaceType, String moduleName,
String className) {
        this.interfaceType = interfaceType;
        PyObject importer = state.getBuiltins().__getitem__(Py.newString("__import__"));
```

```
        PyObject module = importer.__call__(Py.newString(moduleName));
        klass = module.__getattr__(className);
        System.err.println("module=" + module + ",class=" + klass);
    }

    //  This constructor passes through to the other constructor
    public JythonObjectFactory(Class interfaceType, String moduleName, String className) {
        this(new PySystemState(), interfaceType, moduleName, className);
    }

    // All of the followng methods return
    // a coerced Jython object based upon the pieces of information
    // that were passed into the factory.  The differences are
    // between them are the number of arguments that can be passed
    // in as arguents to the object.
    public Object createObject() {
        return klass.__call__().__tojava__(interfaceType);
    }

    public Object createObject(Object arg1) {
        return klass.__call__(Py.java2py(arg1)).__tojava__(interfaceType);
    }

    public Object createObject(Object arg1, Object arg2) {
        return klass.__call__(Py.java2py(arg1),
Py.java2py(arg2)).__tojava__(interfaceType);
    }

    public Object createObject(Object arg1, Object arg2, Object arg3) {
        return klass.__call__(Py.java2py(arg1), Py.java2py(arg2),
Py.java2py(arg3)).__tojava__(interfaceType);
    }

    public Object createObject(Object args[], String keywords[]) {
        PyObject convertedArgs[] = new PyObject[args.length];
        for (int i = 0; i < args.length; i++) {
            convertedArgs[i] = Py.java2py(args[i]);
        }
        return klass.__call__(convertedArgs, keywords).__tojava__(interfaceType);
    }

    public Object createObject(Object... args) {
        return createObject(args, Py.NoKeywords);
    }

}
```

Main.java

```
import org.jython.book.interfaces.BuildingType;
import org.jython.book.util.JythonObjectFactory;

public class Main{
```

```java
public static void main(String args[]) {

        JythonObjectFactory factory = new JythonObjectFactory(
                BuildingType.class, "building", "Building");

        BuildingType building = (BuildingType) factory.createObject();

        building.setBuildingName("BUIDING-A");
        building.setBuildingAddress("100 MAIN ST.");
        building.setBuildingId(1);

        System.out.println(building.getBuildingId() + " " + building.getBuildingName() + " "
+
                building.getBuildingAddress());
    }

}
```

As you can see from the code, there are quite a few differences from the object factory implementation shown previously. First, you can see that the instantiation of the object factory requires different arguments. In this case, we pass in the interface, module, and class name. Next, you can see that the PySystemState obtains a reference to the importer PyObject. The importer then makes a __call__ to the module we've requested. The requested module must be contained somewhere on the sys.path. Lastly, we obtain a reference to our class by calling the __getattr__ method on the module. We can now use the returned class to perform the coercion of our Jython object into Java. As mentioned previously, you'll note that this particular implementation includes several createObject() variations allowing one to pass arguments to the module when it is being called. This, in effect, gives us the ability to pass arguments into the initializer of the Jython object.

Which object factory is best? Your choice, depending upon the situation you're application is encountering. Bottom line is that there are several ways to perform the object factory design and they all allow seamless use of Jython objects from within Java code.

Now that we have a coerced Jython object, we can go ahead and utilize the methods that have been defined in the Java interface. As you can see, the simple example above sets a few values and then prints out the object values. Hopefully you can see how easy it is to create a single object factory that we can be use for any Jython object rather than just one.

Returning __doc__ Strings

It is also very easy to obtain the __doc__ string from any of your Jython classes by coding an accessor method on the object itself. We'll add some code to the building object that was used in the previous examples. It doesn't matter what type of factory you decide to work with, this trick will work with both.

Listing 10-6. __doc__ Strings

Building.py

```python
from org.jython.book.interfaces import BuildingType
# Notice the doc string that has been added after the class definition below
class Building(BuildingType):
    ''' Class to hold building objects '''
```

```python
    def __init__(self):
        self.name = None
        self.address  =  None
        self.id = -1

 def getBuildingName(self):
        return self.name

    def setBuildingName(self, name):
        self.name = name;

    def getBuildingAddress(self):
        return self.address

    def setBuildingAddress(self, address):
        self.address = address

    def getBuildingId(self):
        return self.id

    def setBuildingId(self, id):
        self.id = id

    def getDoc(self):
        return self.__doc__...
```

BuildingType.java
```java
package org.jython.book.interfaces;

public interface BuildingType {

    public String getBuildingName();
    public String getBuildingAddress();
    public int getBuildingId();
    public void setBuildingName(String name);
    public void setBuildingAddress(String address);
    public void setBuildingId(int id);
    public String getDoc();

}
```

Main.java

```java
import java.io.IOException;
import java.util.logging.Level;
import java.util.logging.Logger;
```

```java
import org.jython.book.interfaces.BuildingType;
import org.plyjy.factory.JythonObjectFactory;

public class Main {

    public static void main(String[] args) {

        JythonObjectFactory factory = JythonObjectFactory.getInstance();
        BuildingType building = (BuildingType) factory.createObject(
                BuildingType.class, "Building");
        building.setBuildingName("BUIDING-A");
        building.setBuildingAddress("100 MAIN ST.");
        building.setBuildingId(1);
        System.out.println(building.getBuildingId() + " " + building.getBuildingName() + " "
+
                building.getBuildingAddress());

        //  It is easy to print out the documentation for our Jython object
        System.out.println(building.getDoc());

    }
}
```

Result:

```
1 BUIDING-A 100 MAIN ST.
 Class to hold building objects
```

Applying the Design to Different Object Types

This design will work with all object types, not just plain old Jython objects. In the following example, the Jython module is a class containing a simple calculator method. The factory coercion works the same way, and the result is a Jython class that is converted into Java.

Listing 10-7. Different Method Types

CostCalculator.py
```python
from org.jython.book.interfaces import CostCalculatorType

class CostCalculator(CostCalculatorType, object):
    ''' Cost Calculator Utility '''

    def __init__(self):
        print 'Initializing'
        pass

    #  The implementation for the definition contained in the Java interface
    def calculateCost(self, salePrice, tax):
        return salePrice + (salePrice * tax)
```

CostCalculatorType.java
```java
package org.jython.book.interfaces;
```

```java
public interface CostCalculatorType {

    public double calculateCost(double salePrice, double tax);

}
```

Main.java
```java
import java.io.IOException;
import java.util.logging.Level;
import java.util.logging.Logger;
import org.jython.book.interfaces.CostCalculatorType;
import org.plyjy.factory.JythonObjectFactory;

public class Main {

    public static void main(String[] args) {

        //  Create factory and coerce Jython calculator object
        JythonObjectFactory factory = JythonObjectFactory.getInstance();
        CostCalculatorType costCalc = (CostCalculatorType) factory.createObject(
                CostCalculatorType.class, "CostCalculator");
        System.out.println(costCalc.calculateCost(25.96, .07));

    }
}
```

Result
```
Initializing
27.7772
```

A BIT OF HISTORY

Prior to Jython 2.5, the standard distribution of Jython included a utility known as jythonc. Its main purpose was to provide the ability to convert Python modules into Java classes so that Java applications could seamlessly make use of Python code, albeit in a roundabout fashion. jythonc actually compiles the Jython code down into Java .class files and then the classes are utilized within the Java application. This utility could also be used to freeze code modules, create jar files, and to perform other tasks depending upon which options were used. This technique is no longer the recommended approach for utilizing Jython within Java applications. As a matter of fact, jythonc is no longer packaged with the Jython distribution beginning with the 2.5 release.

In order for jythonc to take a Jython class and turn it into a corresponding Java class, it had to adhere to a few standards. First, the Jython class had to subclass a Java object, either a class or interface. It also had to do one of the following: override a Java method, implement a Java method, or create a new method using a signature.

While this method worked well and did what it was meant to do, it caused a separation between the Jython code and the Java code. The step of using jythonc to compile Jython into Java is clean, yet, it creates a rift in the development process. Code should work seamlessly without the need for separate compilation procedure. One should have the ability to utilize Jython classes and modules from within a Java application by reference only, and without a special compiler in between. There have been some significant advances in this area, and many of the newer techniques have been discussed in this chapter.

JSR-223

With the release of Java SE 6 came a new advantage for dynamic languages on the JVM. JSR-223 enables dynamic languages to be callable via Java in a seamless manner. Although this method of accessing Jython code is not quite as flexible as using an object factory, it is quite useful for running short Jython scripts from within Java code. The scripting project (https://scripting.dev.java.net/) contains many engines that can be used to run different languages within Java. In order to run the Jython engine, you must obtain jython-engine.jar from the scripting project and place it into your classpath. You must also place jython.jar in the classpath, and it does not yet function with Jython 2.5 so Jython 2.5.1 must be used.

Below is a small example showing the utilization of the scripting engine.

Listing 10-8. Using JSR-223

```
import javax.script.ScriptEngine;
import javax.script.ScriptEngineManager;
import javax.script.ScriptException;

public class Main {

    /**
     * @param args the command line arguments
     */
    public static void main(String[] args) throws ScriptException {
        ScriptEngine engine = new ScriptEngineManager().getEngineByName("python");

        // Using the eval() method on the engine causes a direct
        // interpretataion and execution of the code string passed into it
        engine.eval("import sys");
        engine.eval("print sys");

        // Using the put() method allows one to place values into
        // specified variables within the engine
        engine.put("a", "42");

        //  As you can see, once the variable has been set with
        //  a value by using the put() method, we an issue eval statements
        //  to use it.
        engine.eval("print a");
        engine.eval("x = 2 + 2");

        //  Using the get() method allows one to obtain the value
        //  of a specified variable from the engine instance
        Object x = engine.get("x");
```

```
        System.out.println("x: " + x);
    }

}
```

Next, we see the result of running the application. The first two lines are automatically generated when the Jython interpreter is initiated; they display the JAR filescontained within the CLASSPATH. Following those lines, we see the actual program output.

Result
```
*sys-package-mgr*: processing new jar, '/jsr223-engines/jython/build/jython-engine.jar'
*sys-package-mgr*: processing modified jar, '/System/Library/Java/Extensions/QTJava.zip'
sys module
42
x: 4
```

Utilizing PythonInterpreter
A similar technique to JSR-223 for embedding Jython is making use of the PythonInterpreter directly. This style of embedding code is very similar to making use of a scripting engine, but it has the advantage of working with Jython 2.5. Another advantage is that the PythonInterpreter enables you to make use of PyObjects directly. In order to make use of the PythonInterpreter technique, you only need to have jython.jar in your classpath; there is no need to have an extra engine involved.

Listing 10-9. Using PythonInterpreter

```
import org.python.core.PyException;
import org.python.core.PyInteger;
import org.python.core.PyObject;
import org.python.util.PythonInterpreter;

public class Main {

    /**
     * @param args the command line arguments
     */
    public static void main(String[] args) throws PyException {

        // Create an instance of the PythonInterpreter
        PythonInterpreter interp = new PythonInterpreter();

        // The exec() method executes strings of code
        interp.exec("import sys");
        interp.exec("print sys");

        // Set variable values within the PythonInterpreter instance
        interp.set("a", new PyInteger(42));
        interp.exec("print a");
        interp.exec("x = 2+2");

        //  Obtain the value of an object from the PythonInterpreter and store it
        //  into a PyObject.
```

```
        PyObject x = interp.get("x");
        System.out.println("x: " + x);
    }

}
```

In the class above, we make use of the PythonInterpreter to execute Python code within the Java class. First, we create an instance of the PythonInterpreter object. Next, we make exec() calls against it to execute strings of code passed into it. Next we use the set() method in order to set variables within the interpreter instance. Lastly, we obtain a copy of the object that is stored in the variable x within the interpreter. We must store that object as a PyObject in our Java code.

Results
```
<module 'sys' (built-in)>
42
x: 4
```

The following is a list of methods available for use within a PythonInterpreter object along with a description of functionality.

Table 10-2. PythonInterpreter Methods

Method	Description
setIn(PyObject)	Set the Python object to use for the standard input stream
setIn(java.io.Reader)	Set a java.io.Reader to use for the standard input stream
setIn(java.io.InputStream)	Set a java.io.InputStream to use for the standard input stream
setOut(PyObject)	Set the Python object to use for the standard output stream
setOut(java.io.Writer)	Set the java.io.Writer to use for the standard output stream
setOut(java,io.OutputStream)	Set the java.io.OutputStream to use for the standard output stream
setErr(PyObject)	Set a Python error object to use for the standard error stream
setErr(java.io.Writer	Set a java.io.Writer to use for the standard error stream
setErr(java.io.OutputStream)	Set a java.io.OutputStream to use for the standard error stream
eval(String)	Evaluate a string as Python source and return the result
eval(PyObject)	Evaluate a Python code object and return the result
exec(String)	Execute a Python source string in the local namespace

Table 10-2. PythonInterpreter Methods (continued)

Method	Description
exec(PyObject)	Execute a Python code object in the local namespace
execfile(String filename)	Execute a file of Python source in the local namespace
execfile(java.io.InputStream)	Execute an input stream of Python source in the local namespace
compile(String)	Compile a Python source string as an expression or module
compile(script, filename)	Compile a script of Python source as an expression or module
set(String name, Object value)	Set a variable of Object type in the local namespace
set(String name, PyObject value)	Set a variable of PyObject type in the local namespace
get(String)	Get the value of a variable in the local namespace
get(String name, Class<T> javaclass	Get the value of a variable in the local namespace. The value will be returned as an instance of the given Java class.

Summary

Integrating Jython and Java is really at the heart of the Jython language. Using Java within Jython works just as we as adding other Jython modules; both integrate seamlessly. What makes this nice is that now we can use the full set of libraries and APIs available to Java from our Jython applications. Having the ability of using Java within Jython also provides the advantage of writing Java code in the Python syntax.

Utilizing design patterns such as the Jython object factory, we can also harness our Jython code from within Java applications. Although *jythonc* is no longer part of the Jython distribution, we can still effectively use Jython from within Java. There are object factory examples available, as well as projects such as PlyJy (http://kenai.com/projects/plyjy) that give the ability to use object factories by simply including a JAR in your Java application.

We learned that there are more ways to use Jython from within Java as well. The Java language added scripting language support with JSR-223 with the release of Java 6. Using a jython engine, we can make use of the JSR-223 dialect to sprinkle Jython code into our Java applications. Similarly, the PythonInterpreter can be used from within Java code to invoke Jython. Also keep an eye on projects such as Clamp (http://github.com/groves/clamp/tree/master): the Clamp project has the goal to make use of annotations in order to create Java classes from Jython classes. It will be exciting to see where this project goes, and it will be documented once the project has been completed.

In the next chapter, you will see how we can use Jython from within integrated development environments. Specifically, we will take a look at developing Jython with Eclipse and Netbeans. Utilizing an IDE can greatly increase developer productivity, and also assist in subtleties such as adding modules and JAR files to the classpath.

CHAPTER 11

■ ■ ■

Using Jython in an IDE

In this chapter, we will discuss developing Jython applications using two of the most popular integrated development environments, Eclipse and Netbeans. There are many other development environments available for Python and Jython today; however, these two are perhaps the most popular and contain the most Jython-specific tools. Eclipse has had a plug-in known as PyDev for a number of years, and this plug-in provides rich support for developing and maintaining Python and Jython applications alike. Netbeans began to include Python and Jython support with version 6.5 and later. The Netbeans IDE also provides rich support for development and maintenance of Python and Jython applications.

Please note that in this chapter we will refer to Python/Jython as Jython. All of the IDE options discussed are available for both Python and Jython unless otherwise noted. For readability and consistency sake, we'll not refer to both Python and Jython throughout this chapter unless there is some feature that is not available for Python or Jython specifically. Also note that we will call the plug-ins discussed by their names, so in the case of Netbeans the plug-in is called *Netbeans Python Plug-in*. This plug-in works with both Python and Jython in all cases.

Eclipse

Naturally, you will need to have Eclipse installed on your machine to use Jython with it. The latest available version when this book is being written is Eclipse 3.5 (also known as Eclipse Galileo), and it is the recommended version to use to follow this section. Versions 3.2, 3.3, and 3.4 will work, too, although there will be minor user interface differences which may confuse you while following this section.

If you don't have Eclipse installed on your machine, go to www.eclipse.org/downloads and download the version for Java developers.

Installing PyDev

Eclipse doesn't include built-in Jython support. Thus, we will use PyDev, an excellent plug-in which adds support for the Python language and includes specialized support for Jython. PyDev's home page is http://pydev.org, but you won't need to manually download and install it.

To install the plug-in, start Eclipse and go to Help>Install new Software..., and type http://pydev.org/updates into the "Work with" input box. Press Enter. After a short moment, you will see an entry for PyDev in the bigger box below. Just select it, clicking on the checkbox that appears at the left of PyDev (see Figure 11-1), and then click the Next button.

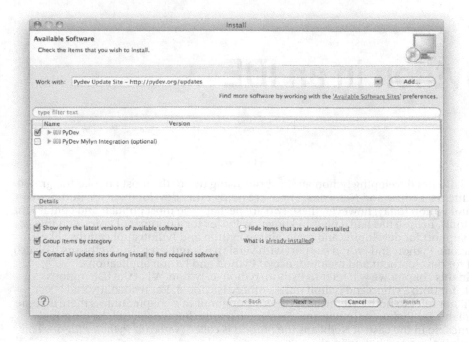

Figure 11-1. Installing PyDev

After this, just follow the wizard, read the license agreement, and, if you agree with the Eclipse Public License v1.0, accept it. Then click the Finish button.

Once the plug-in has been installed by Eclipse, you will be asked if you want to restart the IDE to enable the plug-in. As that is the recommended option, do so. Once Eclipse restarts itself, you will enjoy full Python support on the IDE.

Minimal Configuration

Before starting a PyDev project you must tell PyDev which Python interpreters are available. In this context, an interpreter is just a particular installation of some implementation of Python. When starting you will normally only need one interpreter, and for this chapter we will only use Jython 2.5.1. To configure it, open the Eclipse Preferences dialog (via Windows>Preferences in the main menu bar). On the text box located at the top of the left panel (called "Filter text"), type "Jython." This will filter the myriad of Eclipse (and PyDev!) options and will present us with a much simplified view, in which you will spot the "Interpreter – Jython" section on the left.

Once you have selected the "Interpreter – Jython" section, you will be presented with an empty list of Jython interpreters at the top of the right side. We clearly need to fix that! So, click the New button, enter "Jython 2.5.1" as the Interpreter Name, click Browse, and find jython.jar inside your Jython 2.5.1 installation.

■ **Note** Even if this is the only runtime we will use in this chapter, we recommend you use a naming schema like the one proposed here, including both the implementation name (Jython) and the full version (2.5.1) on the interpreter name. This will avoid confusion and name clashing when adding new interpreters in the future.

After selecting the jython.jar file, PyDev will automatically detect the default, *global* sys.path entries. PyDev always infer the right values, so unless you have very special needs, just accept the default selection and click OK.

If all has gone well, you will now see an entry on the list of Jython interpreters, representing the information you just entered. It will be similar to Figure 11-2 (of course, your filesystem paths will differ).

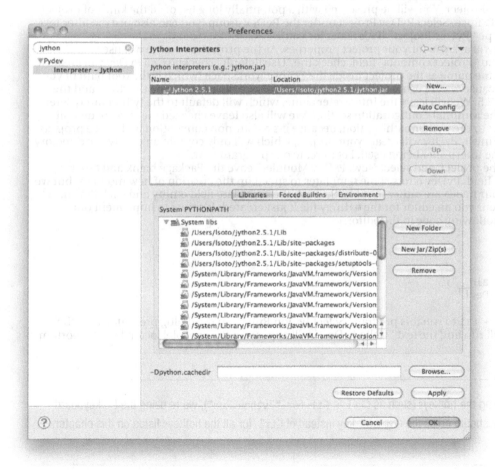

Figure 11-2. List of Jython interpreters

That's all. Click OK and you will be ready to develop with Jython while enjoying the support provided by a modern IDE.

If you are curious, you may want to explore the other options found on the Preferences window, below the PyDev section (after clearing the search filter we used to quickly go to the Jython interpreter configuration). But in our experience, it's rarely needed to change most of the other options available.

In the next sections we will take a look to the more important PyDev features to have a more pleasant learning experience and make you more productive.

Hello PyDev!: Creating Projects and Executing Modules

Once you see the first piece of example code on this chapter, it may seem overly simplistic. It is, indeed, a very dumb example. The point is to keep the focus on the basic steps you will perform for the lifecycle of any Python-based project inside the Eclipse IDE, which will apply to simple and complex projects. So, as you probably guessed, our first project will be a Hello World. Let's start it!

Go to File>New >Project. You will be presented with a potentially long list of all the kinds of projects you can create with Eclipse. Select PyDev Project under the PyDev group (you can also use the filter text box at the top and type "PyDev Project" if it's faster for you).

The next dialog will ask you for your project properties. As the project name, we will use LearningPyDev. In the "Project contents" field, check the "Use default" checkbox, so PyDev will create a directory with the same name as the project inside the Eclipse workspace (which is the root path of your eclipse projects). Because we are using Jython 2.5.1, we will change the project type to Jython and the grammar version to 2.5. We will leave the Interpreter alone, which will default to the Jython interpreter we just defined on the Minimal Configuration section. We will also leave checked the "Create default 'src' folder and add it to the pythonpath" option, because it's a common convention on Eclipse projects.

After you click Finish, PyDev will create your project, which will only contain an empty `src` directory and a reference to the interpreter being used. Let's create our program now.

Right-click on the project, and select New>PyDev Module. Leave the Package blank and enter "main" in the Name field. PyDev offers some templates to speed up the creation of new modules, but we won't use them, as our needs are rather humble. So leave the Template field empty and click Finish.

PyDev will present you an editor for the `main.py` file it just created. It's time to implement our program. Write the following code in the editor:

Listing 11-1.

```
if __name__ == "__main__":
    print "Hello PyDev!"
```

and then press `Ctrl + F11` to run this program. Select Jython Run from the dialog presented and click OK. The program will run and the text "Hello PyDev!" will appear on the console, located on the bottom area of the IDE.

■ **Note** When describing the hotkeys (such as `Ctrl + F11` for "Jython Run"), we're using the PC keyboard convention. Mac users should press the `Command` key instead of `Ctrl` for all the hotkeys listed on this chapter, unless otherwise noted.

If you manually typed the program, you probably noted that the IDE knows that in Python a line ending in ":" marks the start of a block and will automatically put your cursor at the appropriate level of indentation in the next line. See what happens if you manually override this decision and put the print statement at the same indentation level of the if statement and save the file. The IDE will highlight the line flagging the error. If you hover at the error mark, you will see the explanation of the error, as seen in Figure 11-3.

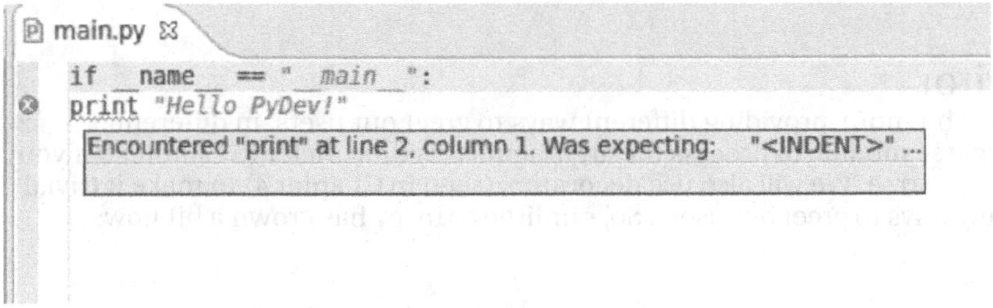

Figure 11-3. Error explanation appears when you hover over the error mark.

Expect the same kind of feedback for whatever syntax error you made. It helps to avoid the frustration of going on edit-run loops only to find further minor syntax errors.

Passing Command-line Arguments and Customizing Execution

Command line arguments may seem old fashioned, but they are actually a very simple and effective way to let programs interact with the outside. Because you have learned to use Jython as a scripting language, it won't be uncommon to write scripts that will take their input from the command line (note that for unattended execution, reading input from the command line is way more convenient that obtaining data from the standard input, let alone using a GUI).

As you have probably guessed, we will make our toy program to take a command line argument. The argument will represent the name of the user to greet, to build a more personalized solution. Here is how our main.py should look:

Listing 11-2.

```
import sys
if __name__ = "__main__":
    if len(sys.argv) < 2:
        print "Sorry, I can't greet you if you don't say your name"
    else:
        print "Hello %s!" % sys.argv[1]
```

If you hit Ctrl + F11 again, you will see the "Sorry I can't greet you…" message on the console. It makes sense, because you didn't pass the name. Not to say that it was your fault, as you didn't have a chance to say your name.

To specify command line arguments, go to the Run>Run Configurations menu, and you will find an entry named "LearningPyDev main.py" in the Jython Run section on the left. It will probably be already selected, but if it's not, select it manually. Then, on the main section of the dialog, you will find ways to customize the execution of our script. You can change aspects such as the current directory, pass special argument to the JVM, change the interpreter to use, set environment variables, and so on. We just need to specify an argument, so let's type "Bob" in the "Program arguments" box and click Run.

As you'd expect, the program now prints "Hello Bob!" on the console. Note that the value you entered is remembered; that is, if you press Ctrl + F11 now, the program will print "Hello Bob!" again. Some people may point out that this behavior makes testing this kind of program very awkward, because the Run Configurations dialog will have to be opened each time the arguments need to be changed. But if we really want to test our programs (which *is* a good idea), we should do it in the right way. We will look into that soon, but first let's finish our tour on basic IDE features.

Playing with the Editor

Let's extend our example code a bit more, providing different ways to greet our users, in different languages. We will use the optparse module to process the arguments this time. Refer to Chapter 9 if you want to remember how to use optparse. We will also use decorators (seen in Chapter 4) to make it trivial to extend our program with new ways to greet our users. So, our little main.py has grown a bit now.

Listing 11-3.

```
# -*- coding: utf-8 -*-
import sys
from optparse import OptionParser

greetings = dict(en=u'Hello %s!',
                 es=u'Hola %s!',
                 fr=u'Bonjour %s!',
                 pt=u'Alò %s!')

uis = {}
def register_ui(ui_name):
    def decorator(f):
        uis[ui_name] = f
        return f
    return decorator

def message(ui, msg):
    if ui in uis:
        uis[ui](msg)
    else:
        raise ValueError("No greeter named %s" % ui)

def list_uis():
    return uis.keys()

@register_ui('console')
def print_message(msg):
    print msg

@register_ui('window')
def show_message_as_window(msg):
    from javax.swing import JFrame, JLabel
    frame = JFrame(msg,
                   defaultCloseOperation=JFrame.EXIT_ON_CLOSE,
                   size=(100, 100),
                   visible=True)
```

```
        frame.contentPane.add(JLabel(msg))

if __name__ == "__main__":
    parser = OptionParser()
    parser.add_option('--ui', dest='ui', default='console',
                        help="Sets the UI to use to greet the user. One of: %s" %
                        ", ".join("'%s'" % ui for ui in list_uis()))
    parser.add_option('--lang', dest='lang', default='en',
                        help="Sets the language to use")
    options, args = parser.parse_args(sys.argv)
    if len(args) < 2:
        print "Sorry, I can't greet you if you don't say your name"
        sys.exit(1)

    if options.lang not in greetings:
        print "Sorry, I don't speak '%s'" % options.lang
        sys.exit(1)

    msg = greetings[options.lang] % args[1]

    try:
        message(options.ui, msg)
    except ValueError, e:
        print "Invalid UI name\n"
        print "Valid UIs:\n\n" + "\n".join(' * ' + ui for ui in list_uis())
        sys.exit(1)
```

Take a little time to play with this code in the editor. Try pressing Ctrl + Space (don't change Ctrl with Command if you are using Mac OS X; this hotkey is the same on every platform), which is the shortcut for automatic code completion (also known as Intellisense in Microsoft's parlance) on different locations. It will provide completion for import statements (try completing that line just after the import token, or in the middle of the OptionParser token) and attribute or method access (like on sys.exit or parser.add_option or even in JFrame.EXIT_ON_CLOSE which is accessing a Java class!) It also provides hints about the parameters in the case of methods.

In general, every time you type a dot, the automatic completion list will pop up, if the IDE knows enough about the symbol you just typed to provide help. But you can also call for help at any point. For example, go to the bottom of the code and type "message(." Suppose you just forgot the order of the parameters to that function. Solution: Press Ctrl + Space and PyDev will complete the statement, using the name of the formal parameters of the function.

Also try Ctrl + Space on keywords like "def." PyDev will provide you little templates that may save you some typing. You can customize the templates on the PyDev>Editor>Templates section of the Eclipse Preferences window (available on the Window>Preferences main menu).

The other thing you may have noted now that we have a more sizable program with some imports, functions, and global variables is that the Outline panel on the right side of the IDE window shows a tree-structure view of code being edited showing such features. It also displays classes, by the way.

And don't forget to run the code! Of course, it's not really spectacular to see that after pressing Ctrl + F11 we still get the same boring "Hello Bob!" text on the console. But if you edit the command line argument (via the Run Configurations dialog) to the following: "Bob --lang es --ui window," you will get a nice window greeting Bob in Spanish. Also see what happens if you specify a non supported UI (say, --ui speech) or an unsupported language. We even support the --help! So we have a generic, polyglot greeter which also happens to be reasonably robust and user friendly (for command line program standards that is).

At this point you are probably tired of manually testing the program editing the command line argument on that dialog. Just one more section and we will see a better way to test our program using the IDE. Actually, part of the next section will help us move toward the solution.

A Bit of Structure: Packages, Modules, and Navigation

If you like simplicity you may be asking (or swearing, depending on your character) why we over-engineered the last example. There are simpler (in the sense of a more concise and understandable code) solutions to the same problem statement. But we needed to grow the toy code to explore another aspect of IDEs, which for some people are a big reason to use them: organizing complex code bases. And you don't expect me to put a full-blown Pet Store example in this book to get to that point, do you?

So, let's suppose that the complications we introduced (mainly the registry of UIs exposed via decorators) are perfectly justified, because we are working on a slightly complicated problem. In other words: let's extrapolate.

The point is, we know that the great majority of our projects can't be confined to just one file (one Python module). Even our very dumb example is starting to get unpleasant to read. And, when we realize that we need more than one module, we also realize we need to group our modules under a common umbrella, to keep it clear that our modules form a coherent thing together and to lower the chances of name clashing with other projects. So, as seen in Chapter 8, the Python solution to this problem is modules and packages.

Our plan is to organize the code as follows: everything will go under the package "hello." The core logic, including the language support, will go into the package itself (into its __init__.py file) and each UI will go into its own module under the "hello" package. The main.py script will remain as the command line entry point.

Right-click on the project and select New>PyDev Package. Enter "hello" as the Name and click Finish. PyDev will create the package and open an editor for its __init.py__ file. As we said, we will move the core logic to this package, so this file will contain the following code, extracted from our previous version of the main code:

Listing 11-4.

```
# -*- coding: utf-8 -*-
greetings = dict(en=u'Hello %s!',
                 es=u'Hola %s!',
                 fr=u'Bonjour %s!',
                 pt=u'Alò %s!')

class LanguageNotSupportedException(ValueError):
    pass

class UINotSupportedExeption(ValueError):
    pass

uis = {}
def register_ui(ui_name):
    def decorator(f):
        uis[ui_name] = f
        return f
    return decorator

def message(ui, msg):
    '''
```

```
    Displays the message `msg` via the specified UI which has to be
    previously registered.
    '''
    if ui in uis:
        uis[ui](msg)
    else:
        raise UINotSupportedException(ui)

def list_uis():
    return uis.keys()

def greet(name, lang, ui):
    '''
    Greets the person called `name` using the language `lang` via the
    specified UI which has to be previously registered.
    '''
    if lang not in greetings:
        raise LanguageNotSupportedException(lang)
    message(ui, greetings[lang] % name)
```

Note that we embraced the idea of modularizing our code, providing exceptions to notify clients of problems when calling the greeter, instead of directly printing messages on the standard output.

Now we will create the hello.console module containing the console UI. Right-click on the project, select New>PyDev Module, Enter "hello" as the Package and "console" as the Name. You can avoid typing the package name if you right-click on the package instead of the project. Click Finish and copy the print_message function there:

Listing 11-5.

```
from hello import register_ui

@register_ui('console')
def print_message(msg):
    print msg
```

Likewise, create the window module inside the hello package, and put there the code for show_message_as_window:

Listing 11-6.

```
from javax.swing import JFrame, JLabel
from hello import register_ui

@register_ui('window')
def show_message_as_window(msg):
    frame = JFrame(msg,
                   defaultCloseOperation=JFrame.EXIT_ON_CLOSE,
                   size=(100, 100),
                   visible=True)
    frame.contentPane.add(JLabel(msg))
```

Finally, the code for our old main.py is slightly reshaped into the following:

Listing 11-7.

```
import sys
import hello, hello.console, hello.window
from optparse import OptionParser

def main(args):
    parser = OptionParser()
    parser.add_option('--ui', dest='ui', default='console',
                      help="Sets the UI to use to greet the user. One of: %s" %
                      ", ".join("'%s'" % ui for ui in list_uis()))
    parser.add_option('--lang', dest='lang', default='en',
                      help="Sets the language to use")
    options, args = parser.parse_args(args)
    if len(args) < 2:
        print "Sorry, I can't greet you if you don't say your name"
        return 1
    try:
        hello.greet(args[1], options.lang, options.ui)
    except hello.LanguageNotSupportedException:
        print "Sorry, I don't speak '%s'" % options.lang
        return 1
    except hello.UINotSupportedException:
        print "Invalid UI name\n"
        print "Valid UIs:\n\n" + "\n".join(' * ' + ui for ui in hello.list_uis())
        return 1
    return 0

if __name__ == "__main__":
    main(sys.argv)
```

■ **Tip** Until now, we have used PyDev's wizards to create new modules and packages. But, as you saw in Chapter 8, modules are just files with the .py extension located on the sys.path or inside packages, and packages are just directories that happen to contain a __init__.py file. So you may want to create modules using New>File and packages using New>Folder if you don't like the wizards.

Now we have our code split over many files. On a small project, navigating through it using the left-side project tree (called the PyDev Package Explorer) isn't difficult, but you can imagine that on a project with dozens of files it would be. So we will see some ways to ease the navigation of a code base.

First, let's suppose you are reading main.py and want to jump to the definition of the hello.greet function, called on line 17. Instead of manually changing to such a file and scanning until finding the function, just press Ctrl and click greet. PyDev will automatically move you into the definition. This also works on most variables and modules (try it on the import statements, for example).

Another good way to quickly jump between files without having to resort to the Package Explorer is to use Ctrl + Shift + R, which is the shortcut for "Open Resource". Just type (part of) the file name you want to jump to and PyDev will search on every package and directory of your open projects.

Now that you have many files, note that you don't need to necessarily have the file you want to run opened and active on the editor. For every script you run (using the procedure in which you need to be editing the program and then press Ctrl + F11) the IDE will remember that such script is something you are interested in running and will add it to the "Run History". You can access the "Run History" on the main menu under *Run -> Run History*, or in the dropdown button located in the main toolbar, along the green "play" icon. In both places you will find the latest programs you ran, and many times using this list and selecting the script you want to re-run will be more convenient than jumping to the script on the editor and then pressing Ctrl + F11.

Finally, the IDE internally records a history of your "jumps" between files, just like a web browser do for web pages you visit. And just like a web browser you can go back and forward. To do this, use the appropriate button on the toolbar or the default shortcuts which are Ctrl + Left and Ctrl + Right.

Testing

Okay, it's about time to explore our options to test our code, without resorting to the cumbersome manual black box testing we have been doing changing the command line argument and observing the output.

PyDev supports running PyUnit tests from the IDE, so we will write them. Let's create a module named tests on the hello package with the following code:

Listing 11-8.

```python
import unittest
import hello

class UIMock(object):
    def __init__(self):
        self.msgs = []
    def __call__(self, msg):
        self.msgs.append(msg)

class TestUIs(unittest.TestCase):
    def setUp(self):
        global hello
        hello = reload(hello)
        self.foo = UIMock()
        self.bar = UIMock()
        hello.register_ui('foo')(self.foo)
        hello.register_ui('bar')(self.bar)
        hello.message('foo', "message using the foo UI")
        hello.message('foo', "another message using foo")
        hello.message('bar', "message using the bar UI")

    def testBarMessages(self):
        self.assertEqual(["message using the bar UI"], self.bar.msgs)

    def testFooMessages(self):
        self.assertEqual(["message using the foo UI",
                          "another message using foo"],
                          self.foo.msgs)
    def testNonExistentUI(self):
        self.assertRaises(hello.UINotSupportedExeption,
```

```
                        hello.message, 'non-existent-ui', 'msg')
    def testListUIs(self):
        uis = hello.list_uis()
        self.assertEqual(2, len(uis))
        self.assert_('foo' in uis)
        self.assert_('bar' in uis)
```

As you can see, the test covers the functionality of the dispatching of messages to different UIs. A nice feature of PyDev is the automatic discovery of tests, so you don't need to code anything else to run the previous tests. Just right-click on the src folder on the Package Explorer and select Run As>Jython unit-test. You will see the output of the test almost immediately on the console:

Listing 11-9.

```
Finding files...
['/home/lsoto/eclipse3.5/workspace-jythonbook/LearningPyDev/src/'] ... done
Importing test modules ... done.

testBarMessages (hello.tests.TestUIs) ... ok
testFooMessages (hello.tests.TestUIs) ... ok
testListUIs (hello.tests.TestUIs) ... ok
testNonExistentUI (hello.tests.TestUIs) ... ok

----------------------------------------------------------------------
Ran 4 tests in 0.064s

OK
```

Python's unittest is not the only testing option on the Python world. A convenient way to do tests which are more black-box-like than unit test, though equally automated is doctest.

■ **Note** We will cover testing tools in much greater detail in Chapter 18, so take a look at that chapter if you feel too disoriented.

The nice thing about doctests is that they look like an interactive session with the interpreter, which makes them quite legible and easy to create. We will test our console module using a doctest.

First, click the right-most button on the console's toolbar (you will recognize it as the one with a plus sign on its upper left-hand corner, which has the Open Console tip when you pass the mouse over it). From the menu, select PyDev Console. To the next dialog, answer Jython Console. After doing this you will get an interactive interpreter embedded on the IDE.

Let's start exploring our own code using the interpreter:

Listing 11-10.

```
>>> from hello import console
>>> console.print_message("testing")
testing
```

We highly encourage you to type those two commands yourself. You will note how code completion also works on the interactive interpreter!

Back to the topic, we just interactively checked that our console module works as expected. The cool thing is that we can copy and paste this very snippet as a doctest that will serve to automatically check that the behavior we just tested will stay the same in the future.

Create a module named `doctests` inside the "hello" package and paste those three lines from the interactive console, surrounding them by triple quotes (because they are not syntactically correct Python code after all). After adding a little of boilerplate to make this file executable, it will look like this:

Listing 11-11.

```
"""
>>> from hello import console
>>> console.print_message("testing")
testing
"""

if __name__ == "__main__":
    import doctest
    doctest.testmod(verbose=True)
```

After doing this, you can run this test via the Run>Jython run *menu* while `doctests.py` is the currently active file on the editor. If all goes well, you will get the following output:

Listing 11-12.

```
Trying:
    from hello import console
Expecting nothing
ok
Trying:
    console.print_message("testing")
Expecting:
    testing
ok
1 items passed all tests:
   2 tests in __main__
2 tests in 1 items.
2 passed and 0 failed.
Test passed.
```

After running the doctest you will notice that your interactive console has gone away, replaced by the output console showing the test results. To go back to the interactive console, look for the console button in the console tab toolbar, exactly at the left of the button you used to spawn the console. Then on the drop-down menu select the PyDev Console, as shown in Figure 11-4.

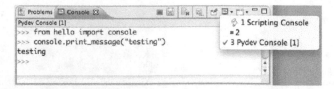

Figure 11-4. Selecting PyDev Console

As you can see, you can use the interactive console to play with your code, try ideas, and test them. And later a simple test can be made just by copying and pasting text from the same interactive console session. Of special interest is the fact that, because Jython code can access Java APIs quite easily, you can also test classes written with Java in this way.

Adding Java Libraries to the Project

Finally, we will show you how to integrate Java libraries into your project. We said some pages ago that we could add a "speech" interface for our greeter. It doesn't sound like a bad idea after all, because (like with almost any aspect) the Java world has good libraries to solve that problem.

We will use the FreeTTS library, which can be downloaded from http://freetts.sourceforge.net/docs/index.php. (You should download the binary version.)

After downloading FreeTTS, you will have to extract the archive on some place on your hard disk. Then, we will import a JAR file from FreeTTS into our PyDev project.

Right-click the project and select Import. Then choose General>File System and browse to the directory in which you expanded FreeTTS and select it. Finally, expand the directory on the left side panel and check the lib subdirectory. See Figure 11-5.

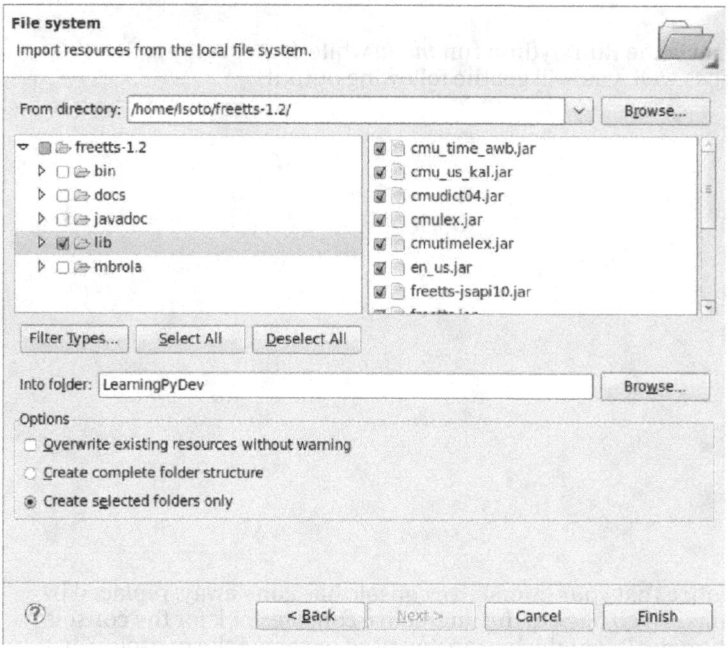

Figure 11-5. Adding Java libraries to the project

After clicking Finish, you will see that the files are now part of your project.

■ **Tip** Alternatively, and depending on your operating system, the same operation can be performed copying the files or folders from the file manager and pasting it into the project (either via menu, keyboard shortcuts, or drag and drop).

Now, the files are part of the project, but we need to tell PyDev that lib/freetts.jar is a JAR file and should be added to the sys.path of our project environment. To do this, right-click on the project and select Properties. Then, on the left panel of the dialog, select PyDev - PYTHONPATH. Then click the "Add zip/jar/egg" button and select the lib/freetts.jar file on the right side of the dialog that will appear. Click OK on both dialogs and you are ready to use this library from Python code.

The code for our new hello.speech module is as follows:

Listing 11-13.

```
from com.sun.speech.freetts import VoiceManager
from hello import register_ui

@register_ui('speech')
def speech_message(msg):
    voice = VoiceManager().getVoice("kevin16")
    voice.allocate()
    voice.speak(msg)
    voice.deallocate()
```

If you play with the code on the editor you will notice that PyDev also provides completion for imports statement referencing the Java library we are using.

Finally, we will change the second line of main.py from:

Listing 11-14.

```
import hello, hello.console, hello.window
to
import hello, hello.console, hello.window, hello.speech
```

in order to load the speech UI too. Feel free to power on the speakers and use the --ui speech option to let the computer greet yourself and your friends!

There you go, our humble greeter has finally evolved into a quite interesting, portable program with speech synthesis abilities. It's still a toy, but one which shows how quickly you can move with the power of Jython, the diversity of Java, and the help of an IDE.

Debugging

PyDev also offers full debugging capabilities for your Jython code. To try it just put some breakpoints in your code by double-clicking on the left margin of the editor, and then start your program using the F11 shortcut instead of Ctrl + F11.

Once the debugger hits your breakpoint, the IDE will ask you to change its perspective. This means it will change to a different layout, better suited for debugging activities. Answer Yes and you will find yourself on the debugging perspective, shown in Figure 11-6.

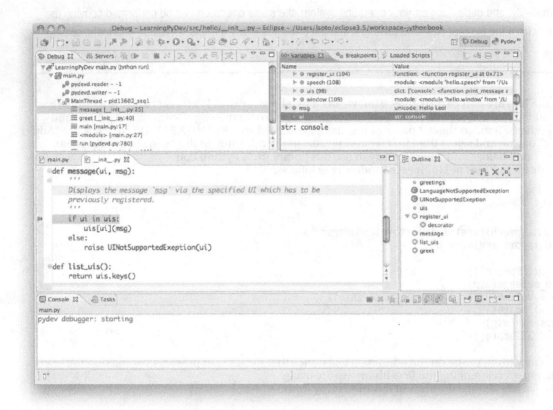

Figure 11-6. Debugging perspective

The perspective offers the typical elements of a debugger. In the upper left area in the contents of the "Debug" tab we have the call stack for each running thread. Click on an item of the call to navigate to the particular line of code which made the corresponding call. The call stack view also has influence over what is shown by the Variables panel on the upper right-hand area, which lists all the current local and global variables. You can "drill down" on every non-primitive value to see its components, as a tree. By default the variables shown are from the point of view of the code being currently executed. But if we select a different element on the call stack in the left area it will show the variables for the line of code associated with that particular stack frame.

Also in the same upper right-hand area there is the Breakpoints tab, which is quite useful for taking a global look at all the breakpoints defined. Clicking on the breakpoint entry will navigate the code editor to the associated line of code, of course. And you can disable, enable, and remove breakpoints by right-clicking on the entries.

The rest of the elements are already known: the central area is filled by the main editor (using less space this time to make room for the extra tools) and its outline, while the output console takes the lower area.

Once you reach a breakpoint you can control the execution, by using Step Into (F5) to go into the code of the next function call, Step Over (F6) to run the current line and stop again, Step Return (F7) to execute the remaining code of the current function, and Resume Execution (F8) to let the program continue running until the next breakpoint is reached (or the program finishes).

Once you finish your debugging session, you can go back to the normal editing perspective by selecting PyDev on the upper right-hand area of the main IDE Window (which will have the Debug button pushed while staying in the debugging perspective).

Conclusion about Eclipse

PyDev is a very mature plug-in for the Eclipse platform, which can be an important element in your toolbox. Automatic completion and suggestions help a lot when learning new APIs (both Python APIs and Java APIs!) especially if paired with the interactive console. It is also a good way to introduce a whole team into Jython or into a specific Jython project, because the project-level configuration can be shared via normal source control systems. Not to mention that programmers coming from the Java world will find themselves much more comfortable on a familiar environment.

To us, IDEs are a useful part of our toolbox, and tend to shine on big codebases and/or complex code which we may not completely understand yet. Powerful navigation and refactoring abilities are key to the process of understanding such projects and are features that should only improve in the future. Even if the refactoring capabilities are not still as complete as the state of the art on Java IDEs, we encourage you to try them on PyDev: "Extract local variable," "Inline local variable," and "Extract method" are quite useful. Even if the alternative of doing the refactor manually isn't as painful with Python as with Java (or any other statically typed language without type inference), when the IDE can do the right thing for you and avoid some mechanical work, you will be more productive.

Finally, the debugging capabilities of PyDev are superb and will end your days of using print as a poor man's debugger (seriously, we did that for a while!) Even more advanced Python users who master the art of import pdb; pdb.set_trace() should give it a try.

Now, PyDev isn't the only IDE available for Jython. If you are already using the Netbeans IDE or didn't like Eclipse or PyDev for some reason, take a look at the rest of this chapter, in which we will cover the Netbeans plug-in for Python development.

Netbeans

The Netbeans integrated development environment has been serving the Java community well for over ten years now. During that time, the tool has matured quite a bit from what began as an ordinary Java development tool into what is today an advanced development and testing environment for Java and other languages alike. As Java and JavaEE application development still remain an integral part of the tool, other languages such as JRuby, Python, Groovy, and Scala have earned themselves a niche in the tool as well. Most of these languages are supported as plug-ins to the core development environment, which is what makes Netbeans such an easy IDE to extend, as it is very easy to build additional features to distribute. The Python support within Netbeans began as a small plug-in known as nbPython, but it has grown into a fully featured Python development environment and it continues to grow.

The Netbeans Python support provides developers with all of the expected IDE features, such as code completion, color-coding, and easy runtime development. It also includes some nice advanced features for debugging applications and the like.

IDE Installation and Configuration

The first step for installing the Netbeans Python development environment is to download the current release of the Netbeans IDE. At the time of this writing, Netbeans 6.7.1 is the most recent release, but 6.8 is right around the corner. You can find the IDE download by going to the web site www.netbeans.org

and clicking on the download link. Once you do so, you'll be presented with plenty of different download options. These are variations of the IDE that are focused on providing different features for developers depending upon what they will use the most. Nobody wants a bulky, memory-hungry development tool that will overhaul a computer to the extreme. By providing several different configurations of the IDE, Netbeans gives you the option to leave off the extras and only install those pieces that are essential to your development. The different flavors for the IDE include Java SE, Java, Ruby, C/C++, PHP, and All. For those developers only interested in developing core Java applications, the Java SE download would suffice. Likewise, someone interested in any of the other languages could download the IDE configuration specific to that language. For the purposes of this book and in our everyday development, we use the All option, because as we enjoy having all of the options available. However, there are options available for adding features if you download only the Java SE or another low-profile build and wish to add more later.

At the time of this writing, there is also a link near the top of the downloads page for PythonEA distribution. If that link or a similar Python Netbeans distribution link is available, then you can use it to download and install just the Jython-specific features of the Netbeans IDE. We definitely do not recommend taking this approach unless you plan to purely code Python applications alone. It seems to us that a large population of the Jython developer community also codes some Java, and may even integrate Java and Jython within their applications. If this is the case, you will want to have the Java-specific features of Netbeans available as well. That is why we do not recommend the Python-only distribution for Jython developers, but the choice is there for you to make.

Now that you've obtained the IDE, it is important to take a look at the license. Python support for Netbeans is licensed under CDDL version 1.0, so it may be a good idea to take a look at that as well. It is easy to install in any environment using the intuitive Netbeans installer. Perhaps the most daunting task when using a new IDE is configuring it for your needs. This should not be the case with Netbeans though because the configuration for Java and Python alike are quite simple. For instance, if you working with the fully-featured installation, you will already have application servers available for use as Netbeans installs Glassfish by default. Note that it is a smart idea to change that admin password very soon after installation in order to avoid any potentially embarrassing security issues.

When the IDE initially opens up, you are presented with a main window that includes links to blogs and articles pertaining to Netbeans features. You also have the standard menu items available such as File, Edit, Tools, and so on. In this chapter we will specifically cover the configuration and use of the Jython features; however, there are very useful tutorials available online and in book format for covering other Netbeans features. One thing you should note at this point is that with the initial installation, Python/Jython development tools are not yet installed unless you chose to install the *PythonEA* distribution. Assuming that you have installed the full Netbeans distribution, you will need to add the Python plug-in via the Netbeans plug-in center. You will need to go to the *Tools* menu and then open the *Plug-ins submenu. From there, you should choose the Available Plug-ins* tab and sort by category. Select all of the plug-ins in the *Python* category and then install. This option will install the Python plug-in as well as a distribution of Jython. You will need to follow on-screen directions to complete the installation.

Once the plug-in has been successfully installed then it is time to configure your Python and Jython homes. To do so, go to the *Tools* menu and then open the *Python Platforms* menu as this will open the platform manager for Python/Jython. At the time of this writing, the default Jython version that was installed with the Python plug-in was 2.5+. You most likely have your own Jython installation by now that includes additional packages that you may wish to use. As this is the case, go ahead and add your Jython installation as a platform option and make it the default (see Figure 11-7).

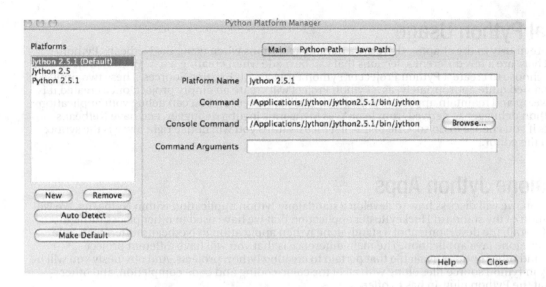

Figure 11-7. Adding your Jython installation as a platform option and making it the default

To do so, click on the New button underneath the platform listing. You can try to select the Auto Detect option, but we did not have luck with Netbeans finding our Jython installation using it. If you choose the New button, then you will be presented with a file chooser window. You should choose the Jython executable that resides in the area <JYTHON_HOME>/bin and all of the other necessary fields will auto-populate with the correct values. Once completed, choose the Close button near the bottom of the Python Platform Manager window. You are now ready to start programming with Python and Jython in Netbeans.

Advanced Python Options

If you enter the Netbeans preferences window you will find some more advanced options for customizing your Python plug-in. If you go to the Editor tab, you can set up Python specific options for formatting, code templates, and hints. In doing so, you can completely customize the way that Netbeans displays code and offers assistance when working with Jython. You can also choose to set up different fonts and coloring for Python code by selecting the Fonts and Colors tab. This is one example of just how customizable Netbeans really is because you can set up different fonts and colors for each language type.

If you choose the Miscellaneous tab you can add different file types to the Netbeans IDE and associate them with different IDE features. If you look through the pull-down menu of files, you can see that files with the extension of py or pyc are associated as Python files. This ensures that files with the associated extensions will make use of their designated Netbeans features. For instance, if we wanted to designate a different extension on some Jython-related files, we could easily do so and associate this extension with Python files in Netbeans. Of course, we do not recommend doing so, as Jython will not import files with unknown extensions! Once we've made this association then we can create files with an extension of that we've added and use them within Netbeans just as if they were Python files. Lastly, you can alter a few basic options such as enabling prompting for python program arguments, and changing debugger port and shell colors from the Python tab in Netbeans preferences.

General Python Usage

As stated previously in the chapter, there are a number of options when using the Netbeans Python solution. There are a few different selections that can be made when creating a new Python project. You can either choose to create a Python Project *or* Python Project with Existing Sources. These two project types are named quite appropriately, as a Python Project will create an empty project; once created it is easy to develop and maintain applications and scripts alike. Moreover, you can debug your application via the Python debugger as derived from Jean-Yves Mengant's jpydbg debugger, and have Netbeans create tests if you choose to do so. One of the first nice features you will notice right away is the syntax coloring in the editor.

Standalone Jython Apps

In this section, we will discuss how to develop a standalone Jython application within Netbeans. We will use a variation of the standard HockeyRoster application that we have used in other places throughout the book. Overall, the development of a stand-alone Jython application in Netbeans differs very little from a stand-alone Java application. The main difference is that you will have different project properties and other options available that pertain to creating Jython projects. And obviously you will be developing in Jython source files along with all of the color-coding and code completion, and other options that the Python plug-in has to offer.

To get started, go ahead and create a new Python Project by using the File menu or the shortcut in the Netbeans toolbar. For the purposes of this section, name the new project HockeyRoster. Uncheck the option to Create Main File, as we will do this manually. Once your project has been created, explore some of the options you have available by right-clicking (Ctrl-click) on the project name. The resulting menu should allow you the option to create new files, run, debug, or test your application, build eggs, work with code coverage, and more. At this point you can also change the view of your Python packages within Netbeans by choosing the "View Python Packages as" option. This will allow you the option to either see the application in list or tree mode, your preference. You can search through your code using the Find option, share it on Kenai with the integrated Netbeans Kenai support, look at the local file history, or use your code with a version control system.

■ **Note** In case you are not familiar with project Kenai, it is an online service started by Sun Microsystems for hosting open source projects and code. For more information, go to www.kenai.com and check it out.

Click on the Properties option and the Project Properties window should appear. From within the Project Properties window, there are options listed on the left-hand side including Source, Python, Run, and Formatting. The Source option provides the ability to change source location or add new source locations to your project. The Test Root Folders section within this option allows you to add a location where Python tests reside so that you can use them with your project. The Python option allows you to change your Python platform and add locations, JARs, and files to your Python path. Changing your Python platform provides a handy ability to test your program on Jython and Python alike, if you want to ensure that your code works on each platform. The Run option provides the ability to add or change the Main module, and add application arguments. Lastly, the Formatting option allows you to specify different formatting options in Netbeans for this particular project. This is great, because each different project can have different colored text, and so on, depending upon the options chosen.

At this point, create the Main module for the HockeyRoster application. Go to File>New and right-clicking (Cntrl-click) on the project, or use the toolbar icon. From here you can either create an

Executable Module, Module, Empty Module, Python Package, or Unit Test. Choose to create an Executable Module and name the main file HockeyRoster.py, and keep in mind that when we created the project we had the ability to have the IDE generate this file for us but we chose to decline. Personally, we like to organize our projects using the Python packaging system. Create some packages now using the same process that you used to create a file and name the package jythonbook. Once created, drag your HockeyRoster.py module into the jythonbook package to move it into place. Note that you can also create several packages at the same time by naming a package like jythonbook.features or something of the like, which will create both of the resulting packages.

The HockeyRoster main module will be the implementation module for our application, but we still need somewhere to store each of the player's information. For this, we will create a module named Player. Go ahead and create an Empty Module named Player within the same jythonbook package. Now we will code the Player class for our project. To do so, erase the code that was auto-generated by Netbeans in the Player.py module and type the following. Note that you can change the default code that is created when generating a new file by changing the template for Python applications.

Listing 11-15.

```
# Player.py
# Container to hold player information
class Player:

    def __init__(self, id, first, last, position):
        self.id = id
        self.first = first
        self.last = last
        self.position = position

    def add_assist(self):
        self.assists = assists + 1
```

The first thing to note is that Netbeans will maintain your indentation level. It is also easy to decrease the indentation level by using the SHIFT + TAB keyboard shortcut. Using the default environment settings, the keywords should be in a different color (blue by default) than the other code. Method names will be in bold, and references to *self* or variables will be in a different color as well. You should notice some code completion, mainly the automatic *self* placement after you type a method name and then the right parentheses. Other subtle code completion features also help to make our development lives easier. If you make an error, indentation or otherwise, you will see a red underline near the error, and a red error badge on the line number within the left-hand side of the editor. Netbeans will offer you some assistance in determining the cause of the error if you hover your mouse over the red error badge or underline.

Now that we have coded the first class in our stand-alone Jython application, it is time to take a look at the implementation code. The *HockeyRoster.py* module is the heart of our roster application, as it controls what is done with the team. We will use the *shelve* technique to store our *Player* objects to disk for the roster application. As you can see from the following code, this is a very basic application and is much the same as the implementation that will be found in the next chapter using Hibernate persistence.

Listing 11-16.

```
# HockeyRoster.py
#
# Implementation logic for the HockeyRoster application
```

217

```python
# Import Player class from the Player module
from Player import Player

# Import shelve for storage to disk
import shelve

class HockeyRoster:
    def __init__(self):
        self.player_data = shelve.open("players")

    def make_selection(self):
        '''
        Creates a selector for our application.  The function prints output to the
        command line.  It then takes a parameter as keyboard input at the command
        line in order to choose our application option.
        '''
        options_dict = {1:self.add_player,
                        2:self.print_roster,
                        3:self.search_roster,
                        4:self.remove_player}
        print "Please chose an option\n"

        selection = raw_input('''Press 1 to add a player, 2 to print the roster,
                            3 to search for a player on the team,
                            4 to remove player, 5 to quit: ''')
        if int(selection) not in options_dict:
            if int(selection) == 5:
                print "Thanks for using the HockeyRoster application."
            else:
                print "Not a valid option, please try again\n"
                self.make_selection()
        else:
            func = options_dict[int(selection)]
            if func:
                func()
            else:
                print "Thanks for using the HockeyRoster application."

    def add_player(self):
        '''
        Accepts keyboard input to add a player object to the roster list.
        This function creates a new player object each time it is invoked
        and appends it to the list.
        '''
        add_new = 'Y'
        print "Add a player to the roster by providing the following information\n"

        while add_new.upper() == 'Y':
            first = raw_input("First Name: ")
            last = raw_input("Last Name: ")
            position = raw_input("Position: ")

            id = self.return_player_count() + 1
```

```
            print id
            #set player and shelve
            player = Player(id, first, last, position)
            self.player_data[str(id)] = player


            print "Player successfully added to the roster\n"
            add_new = raw_input("Add another? (Y or N)")

        self.make_selection()

    def print_roster(self):
        '''
        Prints the contents of the list to the command line as a report
        '''
        print "====================\n"
        print "Complete Team Roster\n"
        print "====================\n\n"
        player_list = self.return_player_list()
        for player in player_list:
            print "%s %s - %s" % (player_list[player].first,
                    player_list[player].last, player_list[player].position)
        print "\n"
        print "=== End of Roster ===\n"
        self.make_selection()

    def search_roster(self):
        '''
        Takes input from the command line for a player's name to search within the
        roster list.  If the player is found in the list then an affirmative message
        is printed.  If not found, then a negative message is printed.
        '''
        index = 0
        found = False
        print "Enter a player name below to search the team\n"
        first = raw_input("First Name: ")
        last = raw_input("Last Name: ")
        position = None
        player_list = self.return_player_list()

        for player_key in player_list:
            player = player_list[player_key]
            if player.first.upper() == first.upper() and \
               player.last.upper() == last.upper():
                position = player.position

        if position:
            print '%s %s is in the roster as %s' % (first, last, position)
        else:
            print '%s %s is not in the roster.' % (first, last)
        self.make_selection()

    def remove_player(self):
        '''
```

```
            Removes a player from the list
            '''
            index = 0
            found = False
            print "Enter a player name below to remove them from the team roster\n"
            first = raw_input("First Name: ")
            last = raw_input("Last Name: ")
            position = None
            player_list = self.return_player_list()
            found_player = None

            for player_key in player_list:
                player = player_list[player_key]
                if player.first.upper() == first.upper() and \
                    player.last.upper() == last.upper():
                     found_player = player
                     break

            if found_player:
                print '''%s %s is in the roster as %s,
                        are you sure you wish to remove?''' % (found_player.first,
                                                               found_player.last,
                                                               found_player.position)
                yesno = raw_input("Y or N")
                if yesno.upper() == 'Y':
                    # remove player from shelve
                    print 'The player has been removed from the roster',
                    found_player.id
                    del(self.player_data[str(found_player.id)])
                else:
                    print 'The player will not be removed'
            else:
                print '%s %s is not in the roster.' % (first, last)
            self.make_selection()

    def return_player_list(self):
        return self.player_data

    def return_player_count(self):
        return len(self.player_data)

# main
#
# This is the application entry point.  It simply prints the applicaion title
# to the command line and then invokes the makeSelection() function.
if __name__ == "__main__":
    print "Hockey Roster Application\n\n"
    hockey = HockeyRoster()
    hockey.make_selection()
```

The code should be relatively easy to follow at this point in the book. The main function initiates the process as expected, and as you see it either creates or obtains a reference to the shelve or dictionary where the roster is stored. Once this occurs the processing is forwarded to the make_selection() function that drives the program. The important thing to note here is that, when using Netbeans, the code is laid out nicely, and that code completion will assist with imports and completion of various code blocks. To run your program, you can either right-click (Ctrl+click) on the project or set the project as the main project within Netbeans and use the toolbar or pull-down menus. If everything has been set up correctly, you should see the program output displaying in the Netbeans output window. You can interact with the output window just as you would with the terminal.

Jython and Java Integrated Apps

Rather than repeat the different ways in which Jython and Java can be intermixed within an application, this section will focus on how to do so from within the Netbeans IDE. There are various approaches that can be taken in order to perform integration, and this section will not cover all of them. However, the goal is to provide you with some guidelines and examples to use when developing integrated Jython and Java applications within Netbeans.

Using a JAR or Java Project in Your Jython App

Making use of Java from within a Jython application is all about importing and ensuring that you have the necessary Java class files and/or JAR files in your classpath. In order to achieve this technique successfully, you can easily ensure that all of the necessary files will be recognized by the Netbeans project. Therefore, the focus of this section is on using the Python project properties to set up the sys.path for your project. To follow along, go ahead and use your HockeyRoster Jython project that was created earlier in this section.

Let's say that we wish to add some features to the project that are implemented in a Java project named HockeyIntegration that we are coding in Netbeans. Furthermore, let's assume that the HockeyIntegration Java project compiles into a JAR file. Let's set up the HockeyIntegration project by choosing New>Project. When the New Project window appears, select Java as the category, and Java Application as the project and click Next. Now make sure you name your application HockeyIntegration and click Finish. See Figure 11-8.

Your java application is now created and you are ready to begin development. In order to use this project from within our HockeyRoster project, you'll need to open up the project properties by right-clicking on your Jython project and choosing the Properties option. Once the window is open, click on the Python menu item on the left-hand side of the window. This will give you access to the sys.path so you can add other Python modules, eggs, Java classes, JAR files, and so on. Click on the Add button and then traverse to the project directory for the Java application you are developing. Once there, go to the dist directory and select the resulting JAR file and click OK. You can now use any of the Java project's features from within your Jython application.

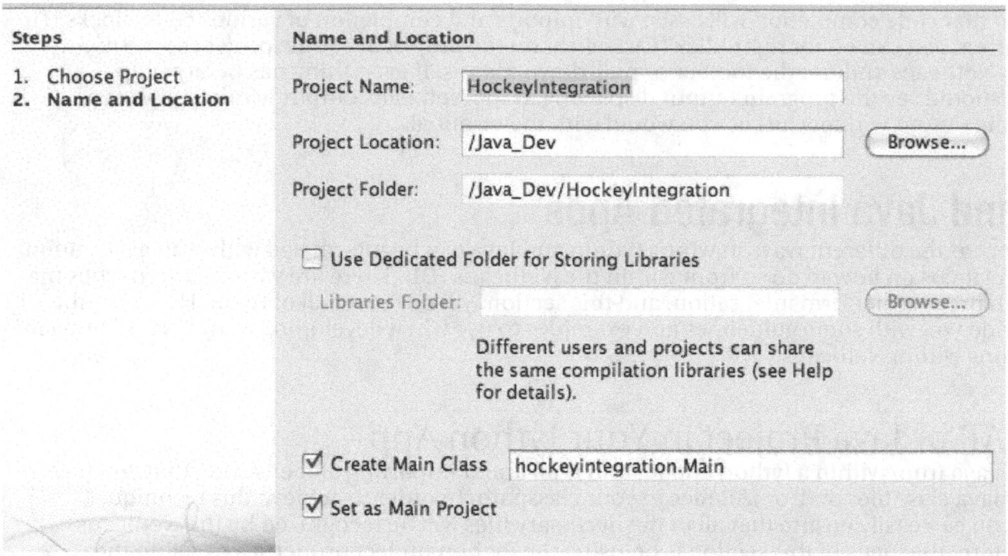

Steps	Name and Location
1. Choose Project	Project Name: HockeyIntegration
2. Name and Location	Project Location: /Java_Dev [Browse...]
	Project Folder: /Java_Dev/HockeyIntegration

☐ Use Dedicated Folder for Storing Libraries

Libraries Folder: [Browse...]

Different users and projects can share the same compilation libraries (see Help for details).

☑ Create Main Class hockeyintegration.Main

☑ Set as Main Project

Figure 11-8.

If you are interested in utilizing a Java API that exists within the standard Java library, then you are in great shape. As you should know by now, Jython automatically provides access to the entire Java standard library. You merely import the Java classes that you wish to use within your Jython application and begin using, nothing special to set up within Netbeans. At the time of this writing, the Netbeans Python EA did not support import completion for the standard Java library. However, we suspect that this feature will be added in a subsequent release.

Using Jython in Java

If you are interested in using Jython or Python modules from within your Java applications, Netbeans makes it easy to do. As mentioned in Chapter 10, the most common method of utilizing Jython from Java is to use the object factory pattern. However, there are other ways to do this, such as using the clamp project, which is not yet production-ready at the time of writing. For the purposes of this section, we'll discuss how to utilize another Netbeans Jython project as well as other Jython modules from within your Java application using the object factory pattern.

In order to effectively demonstrate the use of the object factory pattern from within Netbeans, we'll be making use of the PlyJy project, which provides object factory implementations that can be used out of the box. If you haven't done so already, go to the Project Kenai site find the PlyJy project and download the provided JAR. We will use the Netbeans project properties window in our Java project to add this JAR file to our project. Doing so will effectively diminish the requirement of coding any object factory implementations by hand and we'll be able to directly utilize Jython classes in our project.

Create a Java project named ObjectFactoryExample by selecting New>Project>Java Application. Once you've done so, right-click (Cntrl+click) on the project and choose Properties. Once the project properties window appears, click the Libraries option on the left-hand side. From there, add the PlyJy JAR file that you previously downloaded to your project classpath. You will also have to add the jython.jar file for the appropriate version of Jython that you wish to use. In our case, we will utilize the Jython 2.5.1 release. See Figure 11-9.

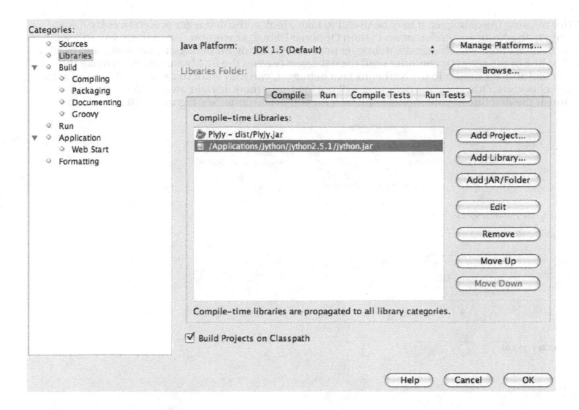

Figure 11-9. Adding the JAR file

The next step is to ensure that any and all Jython modules that you wish to use are in your CLASSPATH somewhere. This can be easily done by either adding them to your application as regular code modules somewhere and then going into the project properties window and including that directory in the Compile-Time Libraries list contained the Libraries section, or by clicking the Add JAR/Folder button. Although this step may seem unnecessary because the modules are already part of your project, it must be done in order to place them into your CLASSPATH. Once they've been added to the CLASSPATH successfully, you can begin to make use of them via the object factory pattern. Netbeans will seamlessly use the modules in your application as if all of the code was written in the same language. At this point your project should be set up and ready for using object factories. To learn more about using object factories, please refer to Chapter 10.

The Netbeans Python Debugger

As mentioned previously, the Netbeans IDE also includes a Python debugger that is derived from Jean-Yves Mengant's jpydbg debugger. This section will discuss how to make use of the Netbeans Python debugger along with some examples using our HockeyRoster code that was written in the previous section. If you have used a debugger in another IDE, or perhaps the Java debugger that is available for Netbeans, this debugger will feel quite familiar. The Python debugger includes many features such as breakpoints, run-time local variable values, code stepping, and more.

Prior to using the debugger, it may be useful to take a look at the debugger preferences by navigating to the Netbeans Preferences>Python Options>Debugger window. From there you will see that you have the ability to change the debugger port, code coloring for debugging sessions, and to stop at the first line of the script or continue until the debugger reaches the first breakpoint. To make the debugger feel and act similar to the Netbeans Java debugger, you may want to de-select the "Stop at the first line" checkbox. Otherwise the debugger will not load your module right away, but rather stop execution at the first line of your module and wait for you to continue. See Figure 11-10.

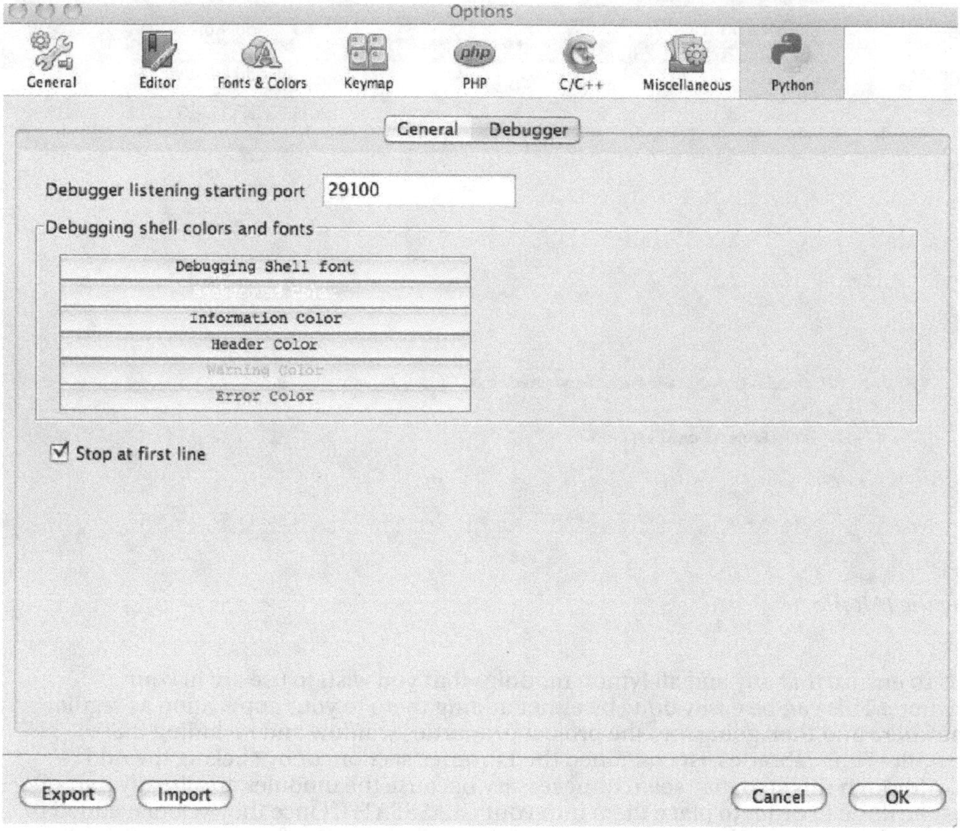

Figure 11-10. The Netbeans Python debugger

Making use of the Python debugger included with Netbeans is much like working from the Jython interactive interpreter from the command-line or terminal window. If you have selected the "Stop at first line" checkbox in the debugger preferences, the debugger will halt at the first line of code in your main module and you must use the debugger Continue button to move to the first line of code that is executed. However, if you have de-selected the checkbox, then the module will automatically run your program until it reaches the first breakpoint. For the purposes of this exercise, let's keep the checkbox selected. In order to set a breakpoint, click on the margin to the left of the line in your code where you would like the debugger to halt program execution. In our case, let's open the HockeyRoster.py module and set a breakpoint in the code as shown in Figure 11-11.

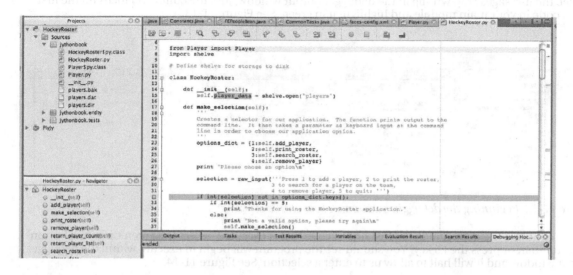

Figure 11-11. Setting a breakpoint in the code

Now that we've set a breakpoint, we need to start our debugger. However, prior to debugging it is important to make sure that Netbeans knows which module to use for starting the program. To do so, right-click on your project and select Properties. When the properties window opens, select Run in the left-hand side of the window. You should now type or browse to the module that you wish to use as a starting point for your program. See Figure 11-12.

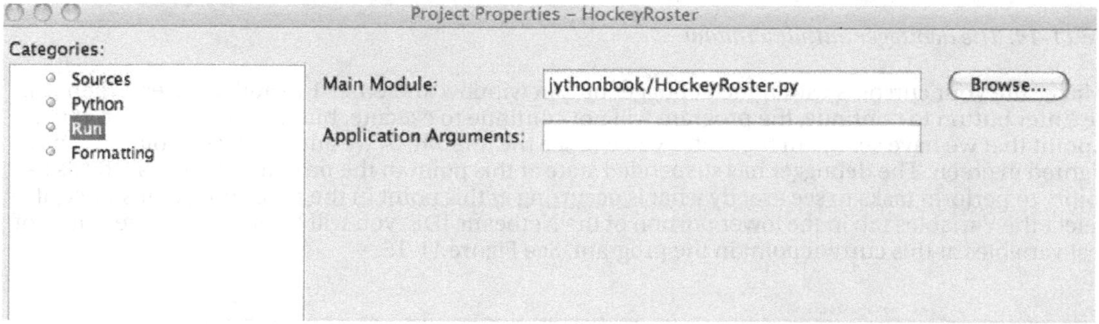

Figure 11-12. Click Browse to select the module you wish to use as a starting point.

Note that this may already be automatically filled in for you by Netbeans. Once you've ensured that you have set the main module, you can begin the debugging session. To do so, you can either select your program and use the Debug menu option, or you can right-click on the project and select Debug. Once you've started the debugger, you will see a series of messages appearing in the debugging window near the bottom of the IDE window to indicate that the debugger has been started. After a few seconds, you will see the messages stop writing in the debugger output window, and the editor will focus on the first line of code in your main module and highlight it in green. See Figure 11-13.

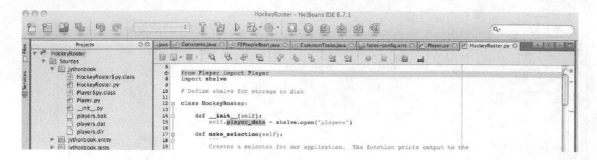

Figure 11-13. *Beginning the debugging session*

To continue the debugger to the first line of code that is executed, select the green Continue button in the toolbar, or press the F5 key. You should see the program will begin to execute within the debugger output window and it will halt to allow us to enter a selection. See Figure 11-14.

Output	Tasks	Test Results	Watches	Variables	Evaluation Re...	Call Stack	Breakpoints	Search Results	Debugg...

busy

```
localDebugger None
JPyDbg connecting  localhost  on in= 29100 /out= 29101
JPyDbg10001 : connected to  localhost
>>>>>>>>[stdout:]Hockey Roster Application
[stdout:]Please chose an option
[stdout:]Press 1 to add a player, 2 to print the roster,                3 to search for a player on the team,
            4 to remove player, 5 to quit: >>>
```

Figure 11-14. *The debugger output window*

Make sure your cursor is within the debugger output window and enter 1 to add a player. When you hit the Enter button to continue, the program will not continue to execute, but instead it will halt at the breakpoint that we have set up. In the editor you will see the line which we added a breakpoint to is now highlighted in green. The debugger has suspended state at this point in the program, and this affords us the ability to perform tasks to see exactly what is occurring at this point in the program. For instance, if you select the Variables tab in the lower portion of the Netbeans IDE, you will be able to see the values of all local variables at this current point in the program. See Figure 11-15.

Output	Tasks	Test Results	Watches	Variables	Evaluation Re...	Call Stack	Breakpoints	Search Results	Debugging H...
Name				Type			Value		
▶ options_dict				MAP			{1: <bound method HockeyRoster.add_pla...		
◆ selection				String			1		
▶ ◆ self				COMPOSITE			<__main__.HockeyRoster instance at 0x2>		

Figure 11-15. *The values of all local variables at this current point in the program*

You can also select the Call Stack tab to see the execution order of your program to this point. See Figure 11-16.

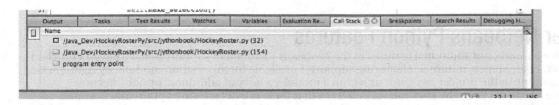

Figure 11-16. The execution order of your program

Once you've evaluated the program at the breakpoint, you can continue the program execution by stepping forward through the code using the buttons in the toolbar. You can also click the Continue button to run the program until it reaches the next breakpoint, or in this case because we have no more breakpoints, it will just continue the program execution as normal. The debugger is especially helpful if you are attempting to evaluate a specific line of code or portion of your program by stepping through the code and executing it line by line.

Another nice feature of the debugger is that you can set certain conditions on breakpoints. To do so, set a breakpoint in your code and then right-click on the breakpoint and select Breakpoint and then Properties from the resulting window. At this point you will see the additional breakpoint options. In this case, set up a condition that will cause the debugger to halt only if the *selection* variable is equal to 3, as shown in Figure 11-17.

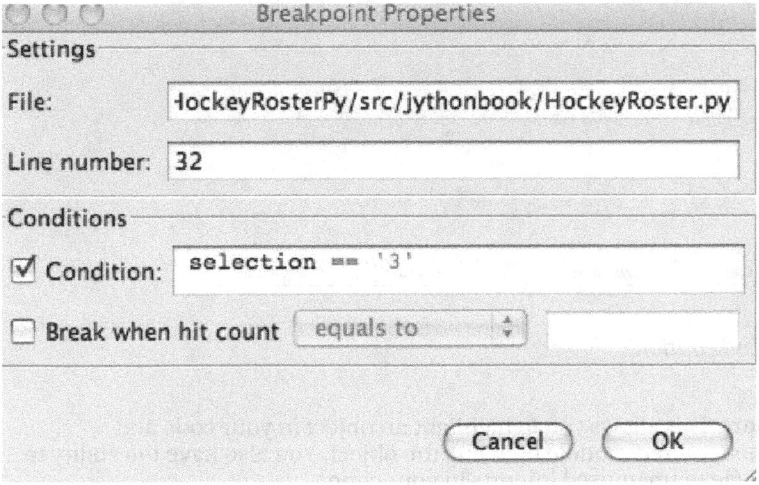

Figure 11-17. Setting a condition for halting the debugger

At this point you can run the debugger again, and if you select the option of 3 during your program execution you will notice that the debugger will halt.

The Netbeans Python debugger offers enough options to fill up an entire chapter worth of reading, but hopefully the content covered in this section will help you get started. Once you've mastered the use of the debugger, it can save you lots of time.

Other Netbeans Python Features

There are a number of additional features in the Netbeans Python IDE support that we haven't touched upon yet. For instance, minimal refactoring support is available for any Python module. By right-clicking on the module in the project navigator or within a module, a bevy of additional options become available to you via the right-click menu. You'll see that there is a Refactoring option that becomes available. However at the time of this writing the only available refactoring options were Rename, Move, Copy, and Safely Delete. There is a Navigate feature that allows for one to perform shortcuts such as highlighting a variable and finding its declaration. The Navigate feature also allows you to jump to any line in your code by simply providing a line number. If your Python class is inheriting from some other object, you can use the Navigate feature to quickly go to the super implementation. It is easy to find the usages of any Python module, method, function, or variable by using the Find Usages feature. If your code is not formatted correctly, you can quickly have the IDE format it for you by choosing the Format option, which is also available in the right-click menu.

Another nice feature that is available in the right-click menu is Insert Code. This feature allows you to choose from a number of different templates in order to have the IDE auto-generate code for you. Once you select the Insert Code option, another menu appears allowing you to choose from a code templates including Property, Constructor, Method, and Class. Once a template is chosen, the IDE auto-generates the code to create a generic Python property, constructor, method, or class. You can then refine the automatically generated code to your needs. This feature allows the developer to type less, and if used widely throughout a program it can ensure that code is written in a consistent manner. See Figure 11-18.

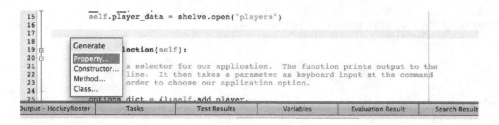

Figure 11-18. The very handy Insert Code option

Another nice feature is Fast Import. This allows you to highlight an object in your code and automatically have the IDE import the required module for using the object. You also have the ability to Fix Imports, which will automatically clean up unused imports in your code.

Along with all of the other features that are available with the Netbeans IDE, these additional features are like the icing on the cake! Keep in mind that you are not required to right-click each time that you wish to use one of these additional features, there are also keyboard shortcuts for each of them. The keyboard shortcuts will differ depending upon which operating system you are using.

Summary

As with most other programming languages, you have several options to use for an IDE when developing Jython. In this chapter we covered two of the most widely used IDE options for developing Jython applications, Netbeans and Eclipse. Eclipse offers a truly complete IDE solution for developing Jython applications, both stand alone and web-based. PyDev is under constant development and always getting better, adding new features and streamlining existing features.

Netbeans Jython support is in still in development at the time of this writing. Many of the main features such as code completion and syntax coloring are already in place. It is possible to develop Jython applications including Jython and Java integration as well as web-based applications. In the future, Netbeans Jython support will develop to include many more features and they will surely be covered in future releases of this book.

In the next chapter, we will take a look at developing some applications utilizing databases. The zxJDBC API will be covered and you'll learn how to develop Jython applications utilizing standard database transactions. Object relational mapping is also available for Jython in various forms, we'll discuss many of those options as well.

CHAPTER 12

■■■

Databases and Jython: Object Relational Mapping and Using JDBC

In this chapter, we will look at zxJDBC package, which is a standard part of Jython since version 2.1 and complies with the Python 2.0 DBI standard. zxJDBC can be an appropriate choice for simple one-off scripts where database portability is not a concern. In addition, it's (generally) necessary to use zxJDBC when writing a new dialect for SQLAlchemy or Django. (But that's not strictly true: you can use pg8000, a pure Python DBI driver, and of course write your own DBI drivers. But please don't do that.) So knowing how zxJDBC works can be useful when working with these packages. However, it's too low level for us to recommend for more general usage. Use SQLAlchemy or Django if at all possible. Finally, JDBC itself is also directly accessible, like any other Java package from Jython. Simply use the java.sql package. In practice this should be rarely necessary.

The second portion of this chapter will focus on using object relational mapping with Jython. The release of Jython 2.5 has presented many new options for object relational mapping. In this chapter we'll focus on using SQLAlchemy with Jython, as well as using Java technologies such as Hibernate. In the end you should have a couple of different choices for using object relational mapping in your Jython applications.

ZxJDBC—Using Python's DB API via JDBC

The zxJDBC package provides an easy-to-use Python wrapper around JDBC. zxJDBC bridges two standards:

- JDBC is the standard platform for database access in Java.

- DBI is the standard database API for Python apps.

ZxJDBC, part of Jython, provides a DBI 2.0 standard compliant interface to JDBC. Over 200 drivers are available for JDBC (http://developers.sun.com/product/jdbc/drivers), and they all work with zxJDBC. High performance drivers are available for all major relational databases, including DB2, Derby, MySQL, Oracle, PostgreSQL, SQLite, SQL Server, and Sybase. And drivers are also available for non-relational and specialized databases, too.

However, unlike JDBC, zxJDBC when used in the simplest way possible, blocks SQL injection attacks, minimizes overhead, and avoids resource exhaustion. In addition, zxJDBC defaults to using a transactional model (when available), instead of autocommit.

First we will look at connections and cursors, which are the key resources in working with zxJDBC, just like any other DBI package. Then we will look at what you can do them with them, in terms of typical queries and data manipulating transactions.

Getting Started

The first step in developing an application that utilizes a database back-end is to determine what database or databases the application will use. In the case of using zxJDBC or another JDBC implementation, the determination of what database the application will make use of is critical to the overall development process. Many application developers will choose to use an object relational mapper for this very reason. When an application is coded with a JDBC implementation, whereas SQL code is hand-coded, the specified database of choice will cause different dialects of SQL to be used. One of the benefits of object relation mapping (ORM) technology is that the SQL is transparent to the developer. The ORM technology takes care of the different dialects behind the scenes. This is one of the reasons why ORM technology may be slower at implementing support for many different databases. Take SQLAlchemy or Django for instance: each of these technologies must have a different dialect coded for each database. Using an ORM can make an application more portable over many different databases. However, as stated in the preface using zxJDBC would be a fine choice if your application is only going to target one or two databases.

While using JDBC for Java, one has to deal with the task of finding and registering a driver for the database. Most of the major databases make their JDBC drivers readily available for use. Others may make you register prior to downloading the driver, or in some cases purchase it. Because zxJDBC is an alternative implementation of JDBC, one must use a JDBC driver in order to use the API. Most JDBC drivers come in the format of a JAR file that can be installed to an application server container, and IDE. In order to make use of a particular database driver, it must reside within the CLASSPATH. As mentioned previously, to find a given JDBC driver for a particular database, take a look at the Sun Microsystems JDBC Driver search page (http://developers.sun.com/product/jdbc/drivers) as it contains a listing of different JDBC drivers for *most* of the databases available today.

■ **Note** Examples in this section are for Jython 2.5.1 and later. Jython 2.5.1 introduced some simplifications for working with connections and cursors. In addition, we assume PostgreSQL for most examples, using the world sample database (also available for MySQL). In order to follow along with the examples in the following sections, you should have a PostgreSQL database available with the *world* database example. Please go to the PostgreSQL homepage at http://www.postgresql.org to download the database. The world database sample is available with the source for this book. It can be installed into a PostgreSQL database by opening psql and initiating the following command:

postgres=# \i <path to world sql>/world.sql

As stated previously, once a driver has been obtained it must be placed into the classpath. What follows are a few examples for adding JDBC drivers to the CLASSPATH for a couple of the most popular databases.

Listing 12-1. Adding JDBC drivers for popular databases to the CLASSPATH

```
# Oracle

    # Windows
    set CLASSPATH=<PATH TO JDBC>\ojdbc14.jar;%CLASSPATH%

    # OS X
```

```
    export CLASSPATH=<PATH TO JDBC>/ojdbc14.jar:$CLASSPATH

# PostgreSQL

    # Windows
    set CLASSPATH=<PATH TO JDBC>\postgresql-x.x.jdbc4.jar;%CLASSPATH%

    # OS X
    export CLASSPATH=<PATH TO JDBC>/postgresql-x.x.jdbc4.jar:$CLASSPATH
```

After the appropriate JAR file for the target database has been added to the CLASSPATH, development can commence. It is important to note that zxJDBC (and all other JDBC implementations) use a similar procedure for working with the database. One must perform the following tasks to use a JDBC implementation:

- Create a connection.

- Create a query or statement.

- Obtain results of query or statement.

- If using a query, obtain results in a cursor and iterate over data to perform tasks.

- Close cursor.

- Close connection (If not using the with_statement syntax in versions of Jython prior to 2.5.1).

Over the next few sections, we'll take a look at each of these steps and how zxJDBC can make them easier than using JDBC directly.

Connections

A database connection is simply a resource object that manages access to the database system. Because database resources are generally expensive objects to allocate, and can be readily exhausted, it is important to close them as soon as you're finished using them. There are two ways to create database connections:

- *Direct creation.* Standalone code, such as a script, will directly create a connection.

- *JNDI.* Code managed by a container should use JNDI for connection creation. Such containers include GlassFish, JBoss, Tomcat, WebLogic, and WebSphere. Normally connections are pooled when run in this context and are also associated with a given security context.

The following is an example of the best way to create a database connection outside of a managed container using Jython 2.5.1. It is important to note that prior to 2.5.1, the *with_statement* syntax was not available. This is due to the underlying implementation of PyConnection in versions of Jython prior to 2.5.1. As a rule, any object that can be used via the *with_statement* must implement certain functionality, including the *__exit__* method. Please see the note that follows to find out how to implement this functionality in versions prior to 2.5.1. Another thing to notice is that in order to connect, we must use a JDBC url which conforms to the standards of a given database in this case, PostgreSQL.

Listing 12-2. py

```
from __future__ import with_statement
from com.ziclix.python.sql import zxJDBC
```

```
# for example
jdbc_url = "jdbc:postgresql:test"
username = "postgres"
password = "jython25"
driver = "org.postgresql.Driver"

# obtain a connection using the with-statment
with zxJDBC.connect(jdbc_url, username, password, driver) as conn:
    with conn:
        with conn.cursor() as c:
            c.execute("select name from country")
            c.fetchone()
```

Walking through the steps, you can see that the *with_statement* and zxJDBC are imported as we will use them to obtain our connection. The next step is to define a series of string values that will be used for the connection activity. Note that these only need to be defined once if set up as globals. Lastly, the connection is obtained and some work is done. Now let's take a look at this same procedure coded in Java for comparison.

Listing 12-3.

```
import java.sql.*;
import org.postgresql.Driver;

...
// In some method
Connection conn = null;
String jdbc_url = "jdbc:postgresql:test";
String username = "postgres";
String password = "jython25";
String driver = "org.postgresql.Driver";
try {
    DriverManager.registerDriver(new org.postgresql.Driver());
    conn = DriverManager.getConnection(jdbc_url,
                            username, password);
    // do something using statement and resultset
    conn.close();
}
catch(Exception e) {
    logWriter.error("getBeanConnection ERROR: ",e);

}
```

■ **Note** In versions of Jython prior to 2.5.1, the *with_statement* syntax is not available. For this reason, we must work directly with the connection (i.e. close it when finished). Take a look at the following code for an example of using zxJDBC connections without the with_statement functionality.

from __future__ import with_statement from com.ziclix.python.sql import zxJDBC

```
# for example jdbc_url = "jdbc:postgresql:test" username = "postgres" password = "jython25" driver =
"org.postgresql.Driver"

conn = zxJDBC.connect(jdbc_url, username, password, driver) do_something(conn) # Be sure to clean up by
closing the connection (and cursor) conn.close()
```

The *with* statement ensures that the connection is immediately closed following the work. The alternative is to use finally to perform the close. Using the latter technique allows for more tightly controlled exception handling technique, but also adds a considerable amount of code. As noted previously, the with statement is not available in versions of Jython prior to 2.5.1, so this is the recommended approach when using those versions:

Listing 12-4.

```
try:
    conn = zxJDBC.connect(jdbc_url, username, password, driver)
    do_something(conn)
finally:
    conn.close()
```

The connection (PyConnection) object in zxJDBC has a number of methods and attributes that can be used to perform various functions and obtain metadata information. For instance, the *close* method can be used to close the connection. Tables 12-1 and 12-2 are listings of all available methods and attributes for a connection and what they do.

Table 12-1. Connection Methods

Method	Functionality
close	Close the connection now (rather than whenever __del__ is called).
commit	Commits all work that has been performed against a connection.
cursor	Returns a new cursor object from the connection.
rollback	In case a database does provide transactions, this method causes the database to roll back to the start of any pending transaction.
nativesql	Converts the given SQL statement into the system's native SQL grammar.
autocommit	Enable or disable autocommit on a connection. Default is disabled.
dbname	Returns the name of the database.

Table 12-2. Connection Attributes (continued)

Method	Functionality
dbversion	Returns the version of database.
drivername	Returns the database driver name.
driverversion	Returns the database driver version.
closed	Returns a Boolean stating whether connection is closed.

Of course, we can always use the connection to obtain a listing of all methods and attributes using the syntax shown in Listing 12-5.

Listing 12-5.

```
>>> conn.__methods__
['close', 'commit', 'cursor', 'rollback', 'nativesql']
>>> conn.__members__
['autocommit', 'dbname', 'dbversion', 'drivername', 'driverversion', 'url',
'__connection__', '__cursors__', '__statements__', 'closed']
```

■ **Note** Connection pools help ensure for more robust operation, by providing for reuse of connections while ensuring the connections are in fact valid. Often naive code will hold a connection for a very long time, to avoid the overhead of creating a connection, and then go to the trouble of managing reconnecting in the event of a network or server failure. It's better to let that be managed by the connection pool infrastructure instead of reinventing it.

All transactions, if supported, are done within the context of a connection. We will be discussing transactions further in the subsection on data modification, but Listing 12-6 is the basic recipe.

Listing 12-6. Transaction Recipe

```
try:
    # Obtain a connection that is not using auto-commit (default for zxJDBC)
    conn = zxJDBC.connect(jdbc_url, username, password, driver)
    # Perform all work on connection
    do_something(conn)
    # After all work is complete, commit
    conn.commit()
except:
```

```
# If a failure occurs along the way, rollback all previous work
conn.rollback()
```

ZxJDBC.lookup

In a managed container, you would use zxJDBC.lookup instead of zxJDBC.connect. If you have code that needs to run both inside and outside containers, we recommend you use a factory to abstract this. Inside a container, like an app server, you should use JDNI to allocate the resource. Generally the connection will be managed by a connection pool (see Listing 12-7).

Listing 12-7.

```
factory = "com.sun.jndi.fscontext.RefFSContextFactory"
db = zxJDBC.lookup('jdbc/postgresDS',
    INITIAL_CONTEXT_FACTORY=factory)
```
This example assumes that the datasource defined in the container is named "jdbc/postgresDS," and it uses the Sun FileSystem JNDI reference implementation. This lookup process does not require knowing the JDBC URL or the driver factory class. These aspects, as well as possibly the user name and password, are configured by the administrator of the container using tools specific to that container. Most often by convention you will find that JNDI names typically resemble a *jdbc/NAME* format.

Cursors

Once you have a connection, you probably want to do something with it. Because you can do multiple things within a transaction, such as query one table, update another, you need one more resource, which is a cursor. A cursor in zxJDBC is a wrapper around the JDBC statement and resultSet objects that provides a very *Pythonic* syntax for working with the database. The result is an easy to use and extremely flexible API. Cursors are used to hold data that has been obtained via the database, and they can be used in a variety of fashions which we will discuss. There are two types of cursors available for use, static and dynamic. A static cursor is the default type, and it basically performs an iteration on an entire resultSet at once. The latter dynamic cursor is known as a lazy cursor and it only iterates through the resultSet on an as-needed basis. The following listings are examples of creating each type of cursor.

Listing 12-8. Creating all possible cursor types

```
# Assume that necessary imports have been performed
# and that a connection has been obtained and assigned
# to a variable 'conn'

cursor = conn.cursor() # static cursor creation

cursor = conn.cursor(True) # dynamic cursor creation with the Boolean argument
```

Dynamic cursors tend to perform better due to memory constraints; however, in some cases they are not as convenient as working with a static cursor. For example, if you'd like to query the database to find a row count it is very easy with a static cursor because all rows are obtained at once. This is not possible with a dynamic cursor and one must perform two queries in order to achieve the same result.

Listing 12-9.

```
# Using a static cursor to obtain rowcount
>>> cursor = conn.cursor()
>>> cursor.execute("select * from country")
>>> cursor.rowcount
239

# Using a dynamic cursor to obtain rowcount
>>> cursor = conn.cursor(1)
>>> cursor.execute("select * from country")
>>> cursor.rowcount
0

# Since rowcount does not work with dynamic, we must
# perform a separate count query to obtain information
>>> cursor.execute("select count(*) from country")
>>> cursor.fetchone()
(239L,)
```

Cursors are used to execute queries, inserts, updates, deletes, and/or issue database commands. Like connections, cursors have a number of methods and attributes that can be used to perform actions or obtain metadata information. See Tables 12-3 and 12-4.

Table 12-3. Cursor Methods

Method	Functionality
tables	Retrieves a list of tables (catalog, schema-pattern, table-pattern, types).
columns	Retrieves a list of columns (catalog, schema-pattern, table-name-pattern, column-name-pattern).
primarykeys	Retrieves a list of primary keys (catalog, schema, table).
foreignkeys	Retrieves a list of foreign keys (primary-catalog, primary-schema, primary-table, foreign-catalog, foreign-schema, foreign-table).
procedures	Retrieves a list of procedures (catalog, schema, tables).
procedurecolumns	Retrieves a list of procedure columns (catalog, schema-pattern, procedure-pattern, column-pattern).
statistics	Obtains statistics on the query (catalog, schema, table, unique, approximation).
bestrow	Optimal set of columns that uniquely identify a row.

Table 12-3. Cursor Methods (continued)

Method	Functionality
versioncolumns	Columns that are automatically updated when any value in a row is updated.
close	Closes the cursor.
execute	Executes code contained within the cursor.
executemany	Used to execute prepared statements or sql with a parameter list.
fetchone	Fetch the next row of a query result set, returning a single sequence, or None if no more data exists.
fetchall	Fetch all (remaining) rows of a query result, returning them as a sequence of sequences.
fetchmany	Fetch the next set of rows of a query result, returning a sequence of sequences.
callproc	Executes a stored procedure.
next	Moves to the next row in the cursor.
write	Execute the sql written to this file-like object.

Table 12-4. Cursor Attributes

Attribute	Functionality
arraysize	Number of rows *fetchmany()* should return without any arguments.
rowcount	Returns the number of resulting rows.
rownumber	Returns the current row number.
description	Returns information regarding each column in the query.
datahandler	Returns the specified datahandler.
warnings	Returns all warnings on the cursor.

Table 12-4. Cursor Attributes (continued)

Attribute	Functionality
lastrowid	Returns the rowid of the last row fetched.
updatecount	Returns the number of updates that the current cursor has performed.
closed	Returns a boolean representing whether the cursor has been closed.
connection	Returns the connection object that contains the cursor.

A number of the methods and attributes above cannot be used until a cursor has been executed with a query or statement of some kind. Most of the time, the particular method or attribute name will provide a good enough description of its functionality.

Creating and Executing Queries

As you've seen previously, it is quite easy to initiate a query against a given cursor. Simply provide a *select* statement in string format as a parameter to the cursor *execute()* or *executemany()* methods and then use one of the *fetch* methods to iterate over the returned results. In the following examples we query the world data and display some cursor data via the associated attributes and methods.

Listing 12-10.

```
>>> cursor = conn.cursor()
>>> cursor.execute("select country, region from country")

# Fetch next record
>>> cursor.fetchone()
((AFG,Afghanistan,Asia,"Southern and Central
Asia",652090,1919,22720000,45.9,5976.00,,Afganistan/Afqanestan,"Islamic Emirate","Mohammad
Omar",1,AF), u'Southern and Central Asia')

# Calling fetchmany() without any parameters returns next record
>>> cursor.fetchmany()
[((NLD,Netherlands,Europe,"Western
Europe",41526,1581,15864000,78.3,371362.00,360478.00,Nederland,"Constitutional
Monarchy",Beatrix,5,NL), u'Western Europe')]

# Fetch the next two records
>>> cursor.fetchmany(2)
[((ANT,"Netherlands Antilles","North
America",Caribbean,800,,217000,74.7,1941.00,,"Nederlandse Antillen","Nonmetropolitan
Territory of The Netherlands",Beatrix,33,AN), u'Caribbean'), ((ALB,Albania,Europe,"Southern
Europe",28748,1912,3401200,71.6,3205.00,2500.00,Shqip?ria,Republic,"Rexhep Mejdani",34,AL),
u'Southern Europe')]
```

```
# Calling fetchall() would retrieve the rest of the records
>>> cursor.fetchall()
...

# Using description provides data regarding the query in the cursor
>>> cursor.description
[('country', 1111, 2147483647, None, None, None, 2), ('region', 12, 2147483647, None, None,
None, 0)]
```

Creating a cursor using the with_statement syntax is easy, please take a look at the following example for use with Jython 2.5.1 and beyond.

Listing 12-11.

```
with conn.cursor() as c:
    do_some_work(c)
```

Like connections, you need to ensure the resource is appropriately closed. So you can just do this to follow the shorter examples we will look at:

Listing 12-12.

```
>>> c = conn.cursor()
>>> # work with cursor
```

As you can see, queries are easy to work with using cursors. In the previous example, we used the *fetchall()* method to retrieve all of the results of the query. However, there are other options available for cases where all results are not desired including the *fetchone()* and *fetchmany()* options. Sometimes it is best to iterate over results of a query in order to work with each record separately. Listing 12-13 iterates over the countries contained within the country table.

Listing 12-13.

```
>>> from com.ziclix.python.sql import zxJDBC
>>> conn =
zxJDBC.connect("jdbc:postgresql:test","postgres","jython25","org.postgresql.Driver")
>>> cursor = conn.cursor()
>>> cursor.execute("select name from country")
>>> while cursor.next():
...     print cursor.fetchone()
...
(u'Netherlands Antilles',)
(u'Algeria',)
(u'Andorra',)
...
```

Often, queries are not hard-coded, and we need the ability to substitute values in the query to select the data that our application requires. Developers also need a way to create dynamic SQL statements at times. Of course, there are multiple ways to perform these feats. The easiest way to substitute variables or create a dynamic query is to simply use string concatenation. After all, the *execute()* method takes a string-based query. Listing 12-14 shows how to use string concatenation for dynamically forming a query and also substituting variables.

Listing 12-14. String Concatenation for Dynamic Query Formation

```
# Assume that the user selected a pull-down menu choice determining
# what results to retrieve from the database, either continent or country name.
# The selected choice is stored in the selectedChoice variable.  Let's also assume
# that we are interested in all continents or countries beginning with the letter "A"

>>> qry = "select " + selectedChoice + " from country where " + selectedChoice + " like
'A%'"
>>> cursor.execute(qry)
>>> while cursor.next():
...     print cursor.fetchone()
...
(u'Albania',)
(u'American Samoa',)
...
```

This technique works very well for creating dynamic queries, but it also has its share of issues. For instance, reading through concatenated strings of code can become troublesome on the eyes. Maintaining such code is a tedious task. Above that, string concatenation is not the safest way to construct a query as it opens an application up for a SQL injection attack. SQL injection is a technique that is used to pass undesirable SQL code into an application in such a way that it alters a query to perform unwanted tasks. If the user has the ability to type free text into a textfield and have that text passed into a string concatenated query, it is best to perform some other means of filtering to ensure certain keywords or commenting symbols are not contained in the value. A better way of getting around these issues is to make use of prepared statements.

■ **Note** Ideally, never construct a query statement directly from user data. SQL injection attacks employ such construction as their attack vector. Even when not malicious, user data will often contain characters, such as quotation marks, that can cause the query to fail if not properly escaped. In all cases, it's important to scrub and then escape the user data before it's used in the query.

One other consideration is that such queries will generally consume more resources unless the database statement cache is able to match it (if at all).

But there are two important exceptions to our recommendation:

SQL statement requirements: Bind variables cannot be used everywhere. However, specifics will depend on the database.

Ad hoc or unrepresentative queries: In databases like Oracle, the statement cache will cache the execution plan, without taking in account lopsided distributions of values that are indexed, but are known to the database if presented literally. In those cases, a more efficient execution plan will result if the value is put in the statement directly.

However, even in these exceptional cases, it's imperative that any user data is fully scrubbed. A good solution is to use some sort of mapping table, either an internal dictionary or a mapping table driven from the database itself. In certain cases, a carefully constructed regular expression may also work. Be careful.

Prepared Statements

To get around using the string concatenation technique for substituting variables, we can use a technique known as *prepared statements*. Prepared statements allow one to use bind variables for data substitution, and they are generally safer to use because most security considerations are taken care of without developer interaction. However, it is always a good idea to filter input to help reduce the risk. Prepared statements in zxJDBC work the same as they do in JDBC, just a simpler syntax. In Listing 12-15, we will perform a query on the country table using a prepared statement. Note that the question marks are used as place holders for the substituted variables. It is also important to note that the *executemany()* method is invoked when using a prepared statement. Any substitution variables being passed into the prepared statement must be in the form of a tuple or list.

Listing 12-15. Using Prepared Statements

```
# Passing a string value into the query
qry = "select continent from country where name = ?"
>>> cursor.executemany(qry,['Austria'])
>>> cursor.fetchall()
[(u'Europe',)]

# Passing some variables into the query
>>> continent1 = 'Asia'
>>> continent2 = 'Africa'
>>> qry = "select name from country where continent in (?,?)"
>>> cursor.executemany(qry, [continent1, continent2])
>>> cursor.fetchall()
[(u'Afghanistan',), (u'Algeria',), (u'Angola',), (u'United Arab Emirates',), (u'Armenia',),
(u'Azerbaijan',),
...
```

Resource Management

You should always close connections and cursors. This is not only good practice but absolutely essential in a managed container so as to avoid exhausting the corresponding connection pool, which needs the connections returned as soon as they are no longer in use. The `with` statement makes it easy. See Listing 12-16.

Listing 12-16. Managing Connections Using With Statements

```
from __future__ import with_statement
from itertools import islice
from com.ziclix.python.sql import zxJDBC

# externalize
jdbc_url =  "jdbc:oracle:thin:@host:port:sid"
```

243

```
username = "world"
password = "world"
driver = "oracle.jdbc.driver.OracleDriver"

with zxJDBC.connect(jdbc_url, username, password, driver) as conn:
    with conn:
        with conn.cursor() as c:
            c.execute("select * from emp")
            for row in islice(c, 20):
                print row # let's redo this w/ namedtuple momentarily...
```

The older alternative is available. It's more verbose, and similar to the Java code that would normally have to be written to ensure that the resource is closed. See Listing 12-17.

Listing 12-17. Managing Connections Avoiding the With Statement

```
try:
    conn = zxJDBC.connect(jdbc_url, username, password, driver)
    cursor = conn.cursor()
    #do something with the cursor
# Be sure to clean up by closing the connection (and cursor)
finally:
    if cursor:
        cursor.close()
    if conn:
        conn.close()
```

Metadata

As mentioned previously in this chapter, it is possible to obtain metadata information via the use of certain attributes that are available to both connection and cursor objects. zxJDBC matches these attributes to the properties that are found in the JDBC *java.sql.DatabaseMetaData* object. Therefore, when one of these attributes is called, the JDBC *DatabaseMetaData* object is actually obtaining the information.

Listing 12-18 shows how to retrieve metadata about a connection, cursor, or even a specific query. Note that whenever obtaining metadata about a cursor, you must fetch the data after setting up the attributes.

Listing 12-18. Retrieving Metadata About a Connection, Cursor or Specific Query

```
# Obtain information about the connection using connection attributes
>>> conn.dbname
'PostgreSQL'
>>> conn.dbversion
'8.4.0'
>>> conn.drivername
'PostgreSQL Native Driver'
# Check for existing cursors
>>> conn.__cursors__
[<PyExtendedCursor object instance at 1>]
```

```
# Obtain information about the cursor and the query
>>> cursor = conn.cursor()
# List all tables
>>> cursor.tables(None, None, '%', ('TABLE',))
>>> cursor.fetchall()
[(None, u'public', u'city', u'TABLE', None), (None, u'public', u'country', u'TABLE', None),
(None, u'public', u'countrylanguage', u'TABLE', None), (None, u'public', u'test', u'TABLE',
None)]
```

Data Manipulation Language and Data Definition Language

Any application that will manipulate data contained in a RDBMS must be able to issue Data
Manipulation Language (DML). Of course, DML consists of issuing statements such as INSERT,
UPDATE, and DELETE. . .the basics of CRUD programming. zxJDBC makes it rather easy to use DML in a
standard cursor object. When doing so, the cursor will return a value to provide information about the
result. A standard DML transaction in JDBC uses a prepared statement with the cursor object, and
assigns the result to a variable that can be read afterwards to determine whether the statement
succeeded.

ZxJDBC also uses cursors to define new constructs in the database using Data Definition Language
(DDL). Examples of doing such are creating tables, altering tables, creating indexes, and the like.
Similarly to performing DML with zxJDBC, a resulting DDL statement returns a value to assist in
determining whether the statement succeeded or not.

In the next couple of examples, we'll create a table, insert some values, delete values, and finally
delete the table.

Listing 12-19. Using DML

```
# Create a table named PYTHON_IMPLEMENTATIONS
>>> stmt = "create table python_implementations (id integer, python_implementation varchar,
current_version varchar)"
>>> result = cursor.execute(stmt)
>>> print result
None
>>> cursor.tables(None, None, '%', ('TABLE',))
# Ensure table was created
>>> cursor.fetchall()
[(None, u'public', u'city', u'TABLE', None), (None, u'public', u'country', u'TABLE', None),
(None, u'public', u'countrylanguage', u'TABLE', None), (None, u'public',
u'python_implementations', u'TABLE',   None), (None, u'public', u'test', u'TABLE', None)]

# Insert some values into the table
>>> stmt = "insert into PYTHON_IMPLEMENTATIONS values (?, ?, ?)"
>>> result = cursor.executemany(stmt, [1,'Jython','2.5.1'])
>>> result = cursor.executemany(stmt, [2,'CPython','3.1.1'])
>>> result = cursor.executemany(stmt, [3,'IronPython','2.0.2'])
>>> result = cursor.executemany(stmt, [4,'PyPy','1.1'])
>>> conn.commit()

# Query the database
>>> cursor.execute("select python_implementation, current_version from
python_implementations")
>>> cursor.rowcount
```

```
4
>>> cursor.fetchall()
[(u'Jython', u'2.5.1'), (u'CPython', u'3.1.1'), (u'IronPython', u'2.0.2'), (u'PyPy',
u'1.1')]

# Update values and re-query
>>> stmt = "update python_implementations set python_implementation = 'CPython -Standard
Implementation' where id = 2"
>>> result = cursor.execute(stmt)
>>> print result
None
>>> conn.commit()
>>> cursor.execute("select python_implementation, current_version from
python_implementations")
>>> cursor.fetchall()
[(u'Jython', u'2.5.1'), (u'IronPython', u'2.0.2'), (u'PyPy', u'1.1'), (u'CPython -Standard
Implementation', u'3.1.1')]
```

It is a good practice to make use of bulk inserts and updates. Each time a commit is issued it incurs a performance penalty. If DML statements are grouped together and then followed by a commit, the resulting transaction will perform much better. Another good reason to use bulk DML statements is to ensure transactional safety. It is likely that if one statement in a transaction fails, all others should be rolled back. As mentioned previously in the chapter, using a try/except clause will maintain transactional dependencies. If one statement fails then all others will be rolled back. Likewise, if they all succeed then they will be committed to the database with one final commit.

Calling Procedures

Database applications often make use of procedures and functions that live inside the database. Most often these procedures are written in a SQL procedural language such as Oracle's PL/SQL or PostgreSQL's PL/pgSQL. Writing database procedures and using them with external applications such written in Python, Java, or the like makes lots of sense, because procedures are often the easiest way to work with data. Not only are they running close to the metal since they are in the database, but they also perform much faster than say a Jython application that needs to connect and close connections on the database. Since a procedure lives within the database, there is no performance penalty due to connections being made.

ZxJDBC can easily invoke a database procedure just as JDBC can do. This helps developers to create applications that have some of the more database-centric code residing within the database as procedures, and other application-specific code running on the application server and interacting seamlessly with the database. In order to make a call to a database procedure, zxJDBC offers the *callproc()* method which takes the name of the procedure to be invoked. In Listing 12-20, we create a relatively useless procedure and then call it using Jython (Listing 12-21).

Listing 12-20. PostgreSQL Procedure

```
CREATE OR REPLACE FUNCTION proc_test(
  OUT out_parameter CHAR VARYING(25) )
AS $$
DECLARE
BEGIN
  SELECT python_implementation
    INTO out_parameter
```

```
        FROM python_implementations
        WHERE id = 1;

    RETURN;
END;
$$ LANGUAGE plpgsql;
```

Listing 12-21. Jython Calling Code

```
>>> result = cursor.callproc('proc_test')
>>> cursor.fetchall()
[(u'Jython',)]
```

Although this example was relatively trivial, it is easily to see how the use of database procedures from zxJDBC could easily become important. Combining database procedures and functions with application code is a powerful technique, but it does tie an application to a specific database so it should be used wisely.

Customizing zxJDBC Calls

At times, it is convenient to have the ability to alter or manipulate a SQL statement automatically. This can be done before the statement is sent to the database, after it is sent to the database, or even just to obtain information about the statement that has been sent. To manipulate or customize data calls, it is possible to make use of the *DataHandler* interface that is available via zxJDBC. There are basically three different methods for handling type mappings when using DataHandler. They are called at different times in the process, one when fetching and the other when binding objects for use in a prepared statement. These datatype mapping callbacks are categorized into four different groups: life cycle, developer support, binding prepared statements, and building results.

At first mention, customizing and manipulating statements can seem overwhelming and perhaps even a bit daunting. However, the zxJDBC DataHandler makes this task fairly trivial. Simply create a handler class and implement the functionality that is required by overriding a given handler method. What follows is a listing of the various methods that can be overridden, and we'll look at a simple example afterward.

Life Cycle
public void preExecute(Statement stmt) throws SQLException;
A callback prior to each execution of the statement. If the statement is a PreparedStatement (created when parameters are sent to the execute method), all the parameters will have been set.
public void postExecute(Statement stmt) throws SQLException;
A callback after successfully executing the statement. This is particularly useful for cases such as auto-incrementing columns where the statement knows the inserted value.

Developer Support
public String getMetaDataName(String name);
A callback for determining the proper case of a name used in a DatabaseMetaData method, such as getTables(). This is particularly useful for Oracle which expects all names to be upper case.
public PyObject getRowId(Statement stmt) throws SQLException;
A callback for returning the row id of the last insert statement.

Binding Prepared Statements

public Object getJDBCObject(PyObject object, int type);
This method is called when a PreparedStatement is created through use of the execute method.
When the parameters are being bound to the statement, the DataHandler gets a callback to map the
type. *This is only called if type bindings are present.*
public Object getJDBCObject(PyObject object);
This method is called when no type bindings are present during the execution of a
PreparedStatement.

Building Results

public PyObject getPyObject(ResultSet set, int col, int type);
This method is called upon fetching data from the database. Given the JDBC type, return the
appropriate PyObject subclass from the Java object at column col in the ResultSet set.
Now we'll examine a simple example of utilizing this technique. The recipe basically follows these steps:

1. Create a handler class to implement a particular functionality (must
   implement the DataHandler interface).

2. Assign the created handler class to a given cursor object.

3. Use the cursor object to make database calls.

In Listing 12-22, we override the *preExecute* method to print a message stating that the functionality
has been altered. As you can see, it is quite easy to do and opens up numerous possibilities.

Listing 12-22. PyHandler.py

```
from com.ziclix.python.sql import DataHandler

class PyHandler(DataHandler):
    def __init__(self, handler):
        self.handler = handler
        print 'Inside DataHandler'
    def getPyObject(self, set, col, datatype):
        return self.handler.getPyObject(set, col, datatype)
    def getJDBCObject(self, object, datatype):
        print "handling prepared statement"
        return self.handler.getJDBCObject(object, datatype)
    def preExecute(self, stmt):
        print "calling pre-execute to alter behavior"
        return self.handler.preExecute(stmt)
```

Jython Interpreter Code

```
>>> cursor.datahandler = PyHandler(cursor.datahandler)
Inside DataHandler
>>> cursor.execute("insert into test values (?,?)", [1,2])
calling pre-execute
```

History

zxJDBC was contributed by Brian Zimmer, one-time lead committer for Jython. This API was written to enable Jython developers to have the capability of working with databases using techniques that more closely resembled the Python DB API. The package eventually became part of the Jython distribution and today it is one of the most important underlying APIs for working with higher level frameworks such as Django. The zxJDBC API is evolving at the time of this publication, and it is likely to become more useful in future releases.

Object Relational Mapping

Although zxJDBC certainly offers a viable option for database access via Jython, there are many other solutions available. Many developers today are choosing to use ORM (Object Relational Mapping) solutions to work with the database. This section is not an introduction to ORM, we assume that you are at least a bit familiar with the topic. Furthermore, the ORM solutions that are about to be discussed have an enormous amount of very good documentation already available either on the web or in book format. Therefore, this section will give insight on how to use these technologies with Jython, but it will not go into great detail on how each ORM solution works. With that said, there is no doubt in stating that these solutions are all very powerful and capable for standalone and enterprise applications alike.

In the next couple of sections, we'll cover how to use some of the most popular ORM solutions available today with Jython. You'll learn how to set up your environment and how to code Jython to work with each ORM. By the end of this chapter, you should have enough knowledge to begin working with these ORMs using Jython, and even start building Jython ORM applications.

SqlAlchemy

No doubt about it, SqlAlchemy is one of the most widely known and used ORM solutions for the Python programming language. It has been around long enough that its maturity and stability make it a great contender for use in your applications. It is simple to setup, and easy-to-use for both new databases and legacy databases alike. You can download and install SqlAlchemy and begin using it in a very short amount of time. The syntax for using this solution is very straight forward, and as with other ORM technologies, working with database entities occurs via the use of a mapper that links a special Jython class to a particular table in the database. The overall result is that the application persists through the use of entity classes as opposed to database SQL transactions.

In this section we will cover the installation and configuration of SqlAlchemy with Jython. The section will then show you how to get started using it through a few short examples; we will not get into great detail as there are plenty of excellent references on SqlAlchemy already. However, this section should fill in the gaps for making use of this great solution on Jython.

Installation

We'll begin by downloading SqlAlchemy from the web site (www.sqlalchemy.org), at the time of this writing the version that should be used is 0.6. This version has been installed and tested with the Jython 2.5.0 release. Once you've downloaded the package, unzip it to a directory on your workstation and then traverse to that directory in your terminal or command prompt. Once you are inside of your SqlAlchemy directory, issue the following command to install:

```
jython setup.py install
```

Once you've completed this process, SqlAlchemy should be successfully installed into your jython Lib site-packages directory. You can now access the SqlAlchemy modules from Jython, and you can open up your terminal and check to ensure that the install was a success by importing sqlalchemy and checking the version. See Listing 12-23.

Listing 12-23.

```
>>> import sqlalchemy
>>> sqlalchemy.__version__
'0.6beta1'
>>>
```

After we've ensured that the installation was a success, it is time to begin working with SqlAlchemy via the terminal. However, we have one step left before we can begin. Jython uses zxJDBC to implement the Python database API in Java. The end result is that most of the dialects that are available for use with SqlAlchemy will not work with Jython out of the box. This is because the dialects need to be rewritten to implement zxJDBC. At the time of this writing, we could only find one completed dialect, zxoracle, that was rewritten to use zxJDBC, and we'll be showing you some examples based upon zxoracle in the next sections. However, other dialects are in the works including SQL Server and MySQL. The bad news is that SqlAlchemy will not yet work with every database available, on the other hand, Oracle is a very good start and implementing a new dialect is not very difficult. You can find the zxoracle.py dialect included in the source for this book. Browse through it and you will find that it may not be too difficult to implement a similar dialect for the database of your choice. You can either place zxoracle somewhere on your Jython path, or place it into the Lib directory in your Jython installation.

Lastly, we will need to ensure that our database JDBC driver is somewhere on our path so that Jython can access it. Once you've performed the procedures included in this section, start up Jython and practice some basic SqlAlchemy using the information from the next couple of sections.

Using SqlAlchemy

We can work directly with SqlAlchemy via the terminal or command line. There is a relatively basic set of steps you'll need to follow in order to work with it. First, import the necessary modules for the tasks you plan to perform. Second, create an engine to use while accessing your database. Third, create your database tables if you have not yet done so, and map them to Python classes using a SqlAlchemy mapper. Lastly, begin to work with the database.

Now there are a couple of different ways to do things in this technology, just like any other. For instance, you can either follow a very granular process for table creation, class creation, and mapping that involves separate steps for each, or you can use what is known as a declarative procedure and perform all of these tasks at the same time. We will show you how to do each of these in this chapter, along with performing basic database activities using SqlAlchemy. If you are new to SqlAlchemy, we suggest reading through this section and then going to sqlalchemy.org and reading through some of the large library of documentation available there. However, if you're already familiar with SqlAlchemy, you can move on if you wish because the rest of this section is a basic tutorial of the ORM solution itself.

Our first step is to create an engine that can be used with our database. Once we've got an engine created then we can begin to perform database tasks making use of it. Type the following lines of code (Listing 12-24) in your terminal, replacing database specific information with the details of your development database.

Listing 12-24. Creating a Database Engine and Performing Database Tasks

```
>>> import zxoracle
>>> from sqlalchemy import create_engine
>>> db = create_engine('zxoracle://schema:password@hostname:port/database')
```

Next, we'll create the metadata that is necessary to create our database table using SqlAlchemy (Listing 12-25). You can create one or more tables via metadata, and they are not actually created until after the metadata is applied to your database engine using a create_all() call on the metadata. In this example, we are going to walk you through the creation of a table named Player that will be used in an application example in the next section.

Listing 12-25. Creating a Database Table

```
>>>player = Table('player', metadata,
...     Column('id', Integer, primary_key=True),
...     Column('first', String(50)),
...     Column('last', String(50)),
...     Column('position', String(30)))
>>> metadata.create_all(engine)
```

Our table should now exist in the database and the next step is to create a Python class to use for accessing this table. See Listing 12-26.

Listing 12-26. Creating a Python Class to Access a Database Table

```
class Player(object):
    def __init__(self, first, last, position):
        self.first = first
        self.last = last
        self.position = position

    def __repr__(self):
        return "<Player('%s', '%s', '%s')>" %(self.first, self.last, self.position)
```

The next step is to create a mapper to correlate the Player python object and the player database table. To do this, we use the mapper() function to create a new Mapper object binding the class and table together (Listing 12-27). The mapper function then stores the object away for future reference.

Listing 12-27. Create a Mapper to Correlate the Python Object and the Database Table

```
>>> from sqlalchemy.orm import mapper
>>> mapper(Player, player)
<Mapper at 0x4; Player>
```

Creating the mapper is the last step in the process of setting up the environment to work with our table. Now, let's go back and take a quick look at performing all of these steps in an easier way. If we want to create a table, class, and mapper all at once, then we can do this declaratively. Please note that with the Oracle dialect, we need to use a sequence to generate the auto-incremented id column for the table. To do so, import the sqlalchemy.schema.Sequence object and pass it to the id column when creating. You must ensure that you've manually created this sequence in your Oracle database or this will not work. See Listing 12-28.

Listing 12-28. Creating a Table, Class and Mapper at Once

```
SQL> create sequence id_seq
  2   start with 1
  3   increment by 1;

Sequence created.
```

```
# Delarative creation of the table, class, and mapper
>>> from sqlalchemy.ext.declarative import declarative_base
>>> from sqlalchemy.schema import Sequence
>>> Base = declarative_base()
>>> class Player(object):
...     __tablename__ = 'player'
...     id = Column(Integer, Sequence('id_seq'), primary_key=True)
...     first = Column(String(50))
...     last = Column(String(50))
...     position = Column(String(30))
...     def __init__(self, first, last, position):
...         self.first = first
...         self.last = last
...         self.position = position
...     def __repr__(self):
...         return "<Player('%s','%s','%s')>" % (self.first, self.last, self.position)
...
```

It is time to create a session and begin working with our database. We must create a session class and bind it to our database engine that was defined with create_engine earlier. Once created, the Session class will create new session object for our database. The Session class can also do other things that are out of scope for this section, but you can read more about them at sqlalchemy.org or other great references available on the web. See Listing 12-29.

Listing 12-29. Creating a Session Class

```
>>> from sqlalchemy.orm import sessionmaker
>>> Session = sessionmaker(bind=db)
```

We can start to create Player objects now and save them to our session. The objects will persist in the database once they are needed; this is also known as a flush(). If we create the object in the session and then query for it, SqlAlchemy will first persist the object to the database and then perform the query. See Listing 12-30.

Listing 12-30. Creating and Querying the Player Object

```
#Import sqlalchemy module and zxoracle
>>> import zxoracle
>>> from sqlalchemy import create_engine
>>> from sqlalchemy import Table, Column, String, Integer, MetaData, ForeignKey
>>> from sqlalchemy.schema import Sequence

# Create engine
>>> db = create_engine('zxoracle://schema:password@hostname:port/database')

# Create metadata and table
>>> metadata = MetaData()
>>> player = Table('player', metadata,
...     Column('id', Integer, Sequence('id_seq'), primary_key=True),
...     Column('first', String(50)),
...     Column('last', String(50)),
```

```
...       Column('position', String(30)))
>>> metadata.create_all(db)

# Create class to hold table object
>>> class Player(object):
...       def __init__(self, first, last, position):
...             self.first = first
...             self.last = last
...             self.position = position
...       def __repr__(self):
...             return "<Player('%s','%s','%s')>" % (self.first, self.last, self.position)

# Create mapper to map the table to the class
>>> from sqlalchemy.orm import mapper
>>> mapper(Player, player)
<Mapper at 0x4; Player>

# Create Session class and bind it to the database
>>> from sqlalchemy.orm import sessionmaker
>>> Session = sessionmaker(bind=db)
>>> session = Session()

# Create player objects, add them to the session
>>> player1 = Player('Josh', 'Juneau', 'forward')
>>> player2 = Player('Jim', 'Baker', 'forward')
>>> player3 = Player('Frank', 'Wierzbicki', 'defense')
>>> player4 = Player('Leo', 'Soto', 'defense')
>>> player5 = Player('Vic', 'Ng', 'center')
>>> session.add(player1)
>>> session.add(player2)
>>> session.add(player3)
>>> session.add(player4)
>>> session.add(player5)

# Query the objects
>>> forwards = session.query(Player).filter_by(position='forward').all()
>>> forwards
[<Player('Josh','Juneau','forward')>, <Player('Jim','Baker','forward')>]
>>> defensemen = session.query(Player).filter_by(position='defense').all()
>>> defensemen
[<Player('Frank','Wierzbicki','defense')>, <Player('Leo','Soto','defense')>]
>>> center = session.query(Player).filter_by(position='center').all()
>>> center
[<Player('Vic','Ng','center')>]
```

Well, hopefully from this example you can see the benefits of using SqlAlchemy. Of course, you can perform all of the necessary SQL actions such as insert, update, select, and delete against the objects. However, as said before, there are many very good tutorials where you can learn how to do these things. We've barely scratched the surface of what you can do with SqlAlchemy, it is a very powerful tool to add to any Jython or Python developer's arsenal.

Hibernate

Hibernate is a very popular object relational mapping solution used in the Java world. As a matter of fact, it is so popular that many other ORM solutions are either making use of Hibernate or extending it in various ways. As Jython developers, we can make use of Hibernate to create powerful hybrid applications. Because Hibernate works by mapping POJO (plain old Java object) classes to database tables, we cannot map our Jython objects to it directly. While we could always try to make use of an object factory to coerce our Jython objects into a format that Hibernate could use, this approach leaves a bit to be desired. Therefore, if you wish to create an application coded entirely using Jython, this would probably not be the best ORM solution. However, most Jython developers are used to doing a bit of work in Java and as such, they can harness the maturity and power of the Hibernate API to create first-class hybrid applications. This section will show you how to create database persistence objects using Hibernate and Java, and then use them directly from a Jython application. The end result, code the entity POJOs in Java, place them into a JAR file along with Hibernate and all required mapping documents, and then import the JAR into your Jython application and use.

We have found that the easiest way to create such an application is to make use of an IDE such as Eclipse or Netbeans. Then create two separate projects, one of the projects would be a pure Java application that will include the entity beans. The other project would be a pure Jython application that would include everything else. In this situation, you could simply add resulting JAR from your Java project into the sys.path of your Jython project and you'll be ready to go. However, this works just as well if you do not wish to use an IDE.

It is important to note that this section will provide you with one use case for using Jython, Java, and Hibernate together. There may be many other scenarios in which this combination of technologies would work out just as well, if not better. It is also good to note that this section will not cover Hibernate in any great depth; we'll just scratch the surface of what it is capable of doing. There are a plethora of great Hibernate tutorials available on the web if you find this solution to be useful.

Entity Classes and Hibernate Configuration

Because our Hibernate entity beans must be coded in Java, most of the Hibernate configuration will reside in your Java project. Hibernate works in a straightforward manner. You basically map a table to a POJO and use a configuration file to map the two together. It is also possible to use annotations as opposed to XML configuration files, but for the purposes of this use case we will show you how to use the configuration files.

The first configuration file we need to assemble is the hibernate.cfg.xml, which you can find in the root of your Java project directory tree. The purpose of this file is to define your database connection information as well as declare which entity configuration files will be used in your project. For the purposes of this example, we will be using the PostgreSql database, and we'll be using the classic examples of the hockey roster application. This makes for a very simple use-case as we only deal with one table here, the Player table. Hibernate makes it very possible to work with multiple tables and even associate them in various ways.

Listing 12-31.

```
<?xml version="1.0" encoding="UTF-8"?>
<!DOCTYPE hibernate-configuration PUBLIC "-//Hibernate/Hibernate Configuration DTD 3.0//EN"
"http://hibernate.sourceforge.net/hibernate-configuration-3.0.dtd">
<hibernate-configuration>
  <session-factory>
    <!-- Database connection settings -->
    <property name="connection.driver_class">org.postgresql.Driver</property>
    <property name="connection.url">jdbc:postgresql://localhost/database-name</property>
```

```
        <property name="connection.username">username</property>
        <property name="connection.password">password</property>
        <!-- JDBC connection pool (use the built-in) -->
        <property name="connection.pool_size">1</property>
        <!-- SQL dialect -->
        <property name="dialect">org.hibernate.dialect.PostgreSQLDialect</property>
        <mapping resource="org/jythonbook/entity/Player.hbm.xml"/>
    </session-factory>
</hibernate-configuration>
```

Our next step is to code the plain old Java object for our database table. In this case, we'll code an object named Player that contains only four database columns: id, first, last, and position. As you'll see, we use standard public accessor methods with private variables in this class.

Listing 12-32.

```
package org.jythonbook.entity;

public class Player {

    public Player(){}

    private long id;
    private String first;
    private String last;
    private String position;

    public long getId(){
        return this.id;
    }

    private void setId(long id){
        this.id = id;
    }

    public String getFirst(){
        return this.first;
    }

    public void setFirst(String first){
        this.first = first;
    }

    public String getLast(){
        return this.last;
    }

    public void setLast(String last){
        this.last = last;
    }

    public String getPosition(){
        return this.position;
```

```
    }

    public void setPosition(String position){
        this.position = position;
    }

}
```

Lastly, we will create a configuration file that will be used by Hibernate to map our POJO to the database table itself. We'll ensure that the primary key value is always populated by using a generator class type of increment. Hibernate also allows for the use of other generators, including sequences if desired. The player.hbm.xml file should go into the same package as our POJO, in this case, the org.jythonbook.entity package.

Listing 12-33. Creating a Hibernate Configuration File

```xml
<?xml version="1.0"?>
<!DOCTYPE hibernate-mapping PUBLIC
"-//Hibernate/Hibernate Mapping DTD 3.0//EN"
"http://hibernate.sourceforge.net/hibernate-mapping-3.0.dtd">
<hibernate-mapping
package="org.jythonbook.entity">

    <class name="Player" table="player" lazy="true">
        <comment>Player for Hockey Team</comment>

        <id name="id" column="id">
            <generator class="increment"/>
        </id>

        <property name="first" column="first"/>
        <property name="last" column="last"/>
        <property name="position" column="position"/>

    </class>

</hibernate-mapping>
```

That is all we have to do inside of the Java project for our simple example. Of course, you can add as many entity classes as you'd like to your own project. The main point to remember is that all of the entity classes are coded in Java, and we will code the rest of the application in Jython.

Jython Implementation Using the Java Entity Classes

The remainder of our use-case will be coded in Jython. Although all of the Hibernate configuration files and entity classes are coded and place within the Java project, we'll need to import that project into the Jython project, and also import the Hibernate JAR file so that we can make use of its database session and transactional utilities to work with the entities. In the case of Netbeans, you'd create a Python application then set the Python platform to Jython 2.5.0. After that, you should add all of the required Hibernate JAR files as well as the Java project JAR file to the Python path from within the project properties. Once you've set up the project and taken care of the dependencies, you're ready to code the implementation.

As said previously, for this example we are coding a hockey roster implementation. The application runs on the command line and basically allows one to add players to a roster, remove players, and check the current roster. All of the database transactions will make use of the Player entity we coded in our Java application, and we'll make use of Hibernate's transaction management from within our Jython code.

Listing 12-34. Hockey Roster Application Code

```
from org.hibernate.cfg import Environment
from org.hibernate.cfg import Configuration
from org.hibernate import Query
from org.hibernate import Session
from org.hibernate import SessionFactory
from org.hibernate import Transaction
from org.jythonbook.entity import Player


class HockeyRoster:

    def __init__(self):
        self.cfg = Configuration().configure()
        self.factory = self.cfg.buildSessionFactory()

    def make_selection(self):
        '''
        Creates a selector for our application.  The function prints output to the
        command line.  It then takes a parameter as keyboard input at the command
        line in order to choose our application option.
        '''

        options_dict = {1:self.add_player,
                        2:self.print_roster,
                        3:self.search_roster,
                        4:self.remove_player}
        print "Please chose an option\n"

        selection = raw_input('''Press 1 to add a player, 2 to print the roster,
                              3 to search for a player on the team,
                              4 to remove player, 5 to quit: ''')
        if int(selection) not in options_dict.keys():
                if int(selection) == 5:
                    print "Thanks for using the HockeyRoster application."
                else:
                    print "Not a valid option, please try again\n"
                    self.make_selection()
        else:
            func = options_dict[int(selection)]
            if func:
                func()
            else:
                print "Thanks for using the HockeyRoster application."

    def add_player(self):
        '''
        Accepts keyboard input to add a player object to the roster list.
```

257

```
    This function creates a new player object each time it is invoked
    and inserts a record into the corresponding database table.
    '''
    addNew = 'Y'
    print "Add a player to the roster by providing the following information\n"
    while addNew.upper() == 'Y':
        first = raw_input("First Name: ")
        last = raw_input("Last Name: ")
        position = raw_input("Position: ")
        id = len(self.return_player_list())
        session = self.factory.openSession()
        try:
            tx = session.beginTransaction()
            player = Player()
            player.first = first
            player.last = last
            player.position = position
            session.save(player)
            tx.commit()
        except Exception,e:
            if tx!=None:
                tx.rollback()
                print e
        finally:
            session.close()

        print "Player successfully added to the roster\n"
        addNew = raw_input("Add another? (Y or N)")
    self.make_selection()

def print_roster(self):
    '''
    Prints the contents of the Player database table
    '''
    print "=====================\n"
    print "Complete Team Roster\n"
    print "=======================\n\n"
    playerList = self.return_player_list()
    for player in playerList:
        print "%s %s - %s" % (player.first, player.last, player.position)
    print "\n"
    print "=== End of Roster ===\n"
    self.make_selection()

def search_roster(self):
    '''
    Takes input from the command line for a player's name to search within the
    database.  If the player is found in the list then an affirmative message
    is printed.  If not found, then a negative message is printed.
    '''
    index = 0
    found = False
    print "Enter a player name below to search the team\n"
    first = raw_input("First Name: ")
```

```
        last = raw_input("Last Name: ")
        position = None
        playerList = self.return_player_list()
        while index < len(playerList):
            player = playerList[index]
            if player.first.upper() == first.upper():
                if player.last.upper() == last.upper():
                    found = True
                    position = player.position
            index = index + 1
        if found:
            print '%s %s is in the roster as %s' % (first, last, position)
        else:
            print '%s %s is not in the roster.' % (first, last)
        self.make_selection()

    def remove_player(self):
        '''
            Removes a designated player from the database
        '''
        index = 0
        found = False
        print "Enter a player name below to remove them from the team roster\n"
        first = raw_input("First Name: ")
        last = raw_input("Last Name: ")
        position = None
        playerList = self.return_player_list()
        found_player = Player()
        while index < len(playerList):
            player = playerList[index]
            if player.first.upper() == first.upper():
                if player.last.upper() == last.upper():
                    found = True
                    found_player = player
            index = index + 1
        if found:
            print '''%s %s is in the roster as %s,
                    are you sure you wish to remove?''' % (found_player.first,
                                                            found_player.last,
                                                            found_player.position)
            yesno = raw_input("Y or N")
            if yesno.upper() == 'Y':
                session = self.factory.openSession()
                tx = None
                try:
                    delQuery = "delete from Player player where id = %s" % (found_player.id)

                    tx = session.beginTransaction()
                    q = session.createQuery(delQuery)
                    q.executeUpdate()
                    tx.commit()
                    print 'The player has been removed from the roster', found_player.id
                except Exception,e:
                    if tx!=None:
```

```
                        tx.rollback()
                    print e
                finally:
                    session.close
            else:
                print 'The player will not be removed'
        else:
            print '%s %s is not in the roster.' % (first, last)
        self.make_selection()

    def return_player_list(self):
        '''
        Connects to database and retrieves the contents of the
        player table
        '''
        session = self.factory.openSession()
        try:
            tx = session.beginTransaction()
            playerList = session.createQuery("from Player").list()
            tx.commit()
        except Exception,e:
            if tx!=None:
                tx.rollback()
            print e
        finally:
            session.close
        return playerList

# main
#
# This is the application entry point.  It simply prints the application title
# to the command line and then invokes the makeSelection() function.
if __name__ == "__main__":
    print "Hockey Roster Application\n\n"
    hockey = HockeyRoster()
    hockey.make_selection()
```

We begin our implementation in the main block, where the HockeyRoster class is instantiated. As you can see, the hibernate configuration is initialized and the session factory is built within the class initializer. Next, the make_selection() method is invoked which begins the actual execution of the program. The entire Hibernate configuration resides within the Java project, so we are not working with XML here, just making use of it. The code then begins to branch so that various tasks can be performed. In the case of adding a player to the roster, a user could enter the number 1 at the command prompt. You can see that the addPlayer() function simply creates a new Player object, populates it, and saves it into the database. Likewise, the searchRoster() function calls another function named returnPlayerList() which queries the player table using Hibernate query language and returns a list of Player objects.

In the end, we have a completely scalable solution. We can code our entities using a mature and widely used Java ORM solution, and then implement the rest of the application in Jython. This allows us to make use of the best features of the Python language, but at the same time, persist our data using Java.

Summary

You would be hard-pressed to find too many enterprise-level applications today that do not make use of a relational database in one form or another. The majority of applications in use today use databases to store information as they help to provide robust solutions. That being said, the topics covered in this chapter are very important to any developer. In this chapter, we learned that there are many different ways to implement database applications in Jython, specifically through the Java database connectivity API or an object relational mapping solution.

PART III

Developing Applications
with Jython

CHAPTER 13

■ ■ ■

Simple Web Applications

One of the major benefits of using Jython is the ability to make use of Java platform capabilities programming in the Python programming language instead of Java. In the Java world today, the most widely used web development technique is the Java servlet. Now in JavaEE, there are techniques and frameworks used so that we can essentially code HTML or other markup languages as opposed to writing pure Java servlets. However, sometimes writing a pure Java servlet still has its advantages. We can use Jython to write servlets and this adds many more advantages above and beyond what Java has to offer because now we can make use of Python language features as well. Similarly, we can code web start applications using Jython instead of pure Java to make our lives easier. Coding these applications in pure Java has proven sometimes to be a difficult and sometimes grueling task. We can use some of the techniques available in Jython to make our lives easier. We can even code WSGI applications with Jython making use of the *modjy* integration in the Jython project.

In this chapter, we will cover three techniques for coding simple web applications using Jython: servlets, web start, and WSGI. We'll get into details on using each of these different techniques here, but we will discuss deployment of such solutions in Chapter 17.

Servlets

Servlets are a Java platform technology for building web-based applications. They are a platform- and server-independent technology for serving content to the web. If you are unfamiliar with Java servlets, it would be worthwhile to learn more about them. An excellent resource is wikipedia (http://en.wikipedia.org/wiki/Java_Servlet); however, there are a number of other great places to find out more about Java servlets. Writing servlets in Jython is a very productive and easy way to make use of Jython within a web application. Java servlets are rarely written using straight Java anymore. Most Java developers make use of Java Server Pages (JSP), Java Server Faces (JSF), or some other framework so that they can use a markup language to work with web content as opposed to only working with Java code. However, in some cases it is still quite useful to use a pure Java servlet. For these cases we can make our lives easier by using Jython instead. There are also great use-cases for JSP; similarly, we can use Jython for implementing the logic in our JSP code. The latter technique allows us to apply a model-view-controller (MVC) paradigm to our programming model, where we separate our front-end markup from any implementation logic. Either technique is rather easy to implement, and you can even add this functionality to any existing Java web application without any trouble.

Another feature offered to us by Jython servlet usage is dynamic testing. Because Jython compiles at runtime, we can make code changes on the fly without recompiling and redeploying our web application. This can make it very easy to test web applications, because usually the most painful part of web application development is the wait time between deployment to the servlet container and testing.

Configuring Your Web Application for Jython Servlets

Very little needs to be done in any web application to make it compatible for use with Jython servlets. Jython contains a built-in class named *PyServlet* that facilitates the creation of Java servlets using Jython source files. We can make use of PyServlet quite easily in our application by adding the necessary XML configuration into the application's web.xml descriptor such that the *PyServlet* class gets loaded at runtime and any file that contains the *.py* suffix will be passed to it. Once this configuration has been added to a web application, and *jython.jar* has been added to the CLASSPATH then the web application is ready to use Jython servlets. See Listing 13-1.

Listing 13-1. Making a Web Application Compatible with Jython

```
<servlet>
    <servlet-name>PyServlet</servlet-name>
    <servlet-class>org.python.util.PyServlet</servlet-class>
    <load-on-startup>1</load-on-startup>
</servlet>

<servlet-mapping>
    <servlet-name>PyServlet</servlet-name>
    <url-pattern>*.py</url-pattern>
</servlet-mapping>
```

Any servlet that is going to be used by a Java servlet container also needs to be added to the *web.xml* file as well, since this allows for the correct mapping of the servlet via the URL. For the purposes of this book, we will code a servlet named *NewJythonServlet* in the next section, so the following XML configuration will need to be added to the web.xml file. See Listing 13-2.

Listing 13-2. Coding a Jython Servlet

```
<servlet>
    <servlet-name>NewJythonServlet</servlet-name>
    <servlet-class>NewJythonServlet</servlet-class>
</servlet>
<servlet-mapping>
    <servlet-name>NewJythonServlet</servlet-name>
    <url-pattern>/NewJythonServlet</url-pattern>
</servlet-mapping>
```

Writing a Simple Servlet

In order to write a servlet, we must have the *javax.servlet.http.HttpServlet* abstract Java class within our CLASSPATH so that it can be extended by our Jython servlet to help facilitate the code. This abstract class, along with the other servlet implementation classes, is part of the *servlet-api.jar* file. According to the abstract class, there are two methods that we should override in any Java servlet, those being *doGet* and *doPost*. The former performs the HTTP GET operation while the latter performs the HTTP POST operation for a servlet. Other commonly overridden methods include *doPut*, *doDelete*, and *getServletInfo*. The first performs the HTTP PUT operation, the second performs the HTTP DELETE operation, and the last provides a description for a servlet. In the following example, and in most use-cases, only the *doGet* and *doPost* are used.

Let's first show the code for an extremely simple Java servlet. This servlet contains no functionality other than printing its name along with its location in the web application to the screen. Following that code we will take a look at the same servlet coded in Jython for comparison (Listing 13-3).

Listing 13-3. NewJavaServlet.java

```java
import java.io.IOException;
import java.io.PrintWriter;
import javax.servlet.ServletException;
import javax.servlet.http.HttpServlet;
import javax.servlet.http.HttpServletRequest;
import javax.servlet.http.HttpServletResponse;

public class NewJavaServlet extends HttpServlet {

    protected void processRequest(HttpServletRequest request,
HttpServletResponse response)
    throws ServletException, IOException {
        response.setContentType("text/html;charset=UTF-8");
        PrintWriter out = response.getWriter();
        try {

            out.println("<html>");
            out.println("<head>");
            out.println("<title>Servlet NewJavaServlet Test</title>");
            out.println("</head>");
            out.println("<body>");
            out.println("<h1>Servlet NewJavaServlet at " + request.getContextPath () +
"</h1>");
            out.println("</body>");
            out.println("</html>");

        } finally {
            out.close();
        }
    }

    @Override
    protected void doGet(HttpServletRequest request, HttpServletResponse response)
    throws ServletException, IOException {
        processRequest(request, response);
    }

    @Override
     protected void doPost(HttpServletRequest request, HttpServletResponse response)
    throws ServletException, IOException {
        processRequest(request, response);
    }

    @Override
    public String getServletInfo() {
        return "Short description";
    }
```

267

```
}
```

All commenting has been removed from the code in an attempt to make the code a bit shorter. Now, Listing 13-4 is the equivalent servlet code written in Jython.

Listing 13-4.

```
from javax.servlet.http import HttpServlet

class NewJythonServlet (HttpServlet):
    def doGet(self,request,response):
            self.doPost (request,response)

    def doPost(self,request,response):
            toClient = response.getWriter()
            response.setContentType ("text/html")
            toClient.println ("<html><head><title>Jython Servlet Test</title>" +
                                    "<body><h1>Servlet Jython Servlet at" +
                                    request.getContextPath() +
"</h1></body></html>")

    def getServletInfo(self):
        return "Short Description"
```

Not only is the concise code an attractive feature, but also the easy development lifecycle for working with dynamic servlets. As stated previously, there is no need to redeploy each time you make a change because of the compile at runtime that Jython offers. Simply change the Jython servlet, save, and reload the webpage to see the update. If you begin to think about the possibilities you'll realize that the code above is just a basic example, you can do anything in a Jython servlet that you can with Java and even most of what can be done using the Python language as well.

To summarize the use of Jython servlets, you simply include *jython.jar* and *servlet-api.jar* in your CLASSPATH. Add necessary XML to the web.xml, and then finally code the servlet by extending the javax.servlet.http.HttpServlet abstract class.

Using JSP with Jython

Harnessing Jython servlets allows for a more productive development lifecycle, but in certain situations Jython code may not be the most convenient way to deal with front-facing web code. Sometimes using a markup language such as HTML works better for developing sophisticated front-ends. For instance, it is easy enough to include JavaScript code within a Jython servlet. However, all of the JavaScript code would be written within the context of a String. Not only does this eliminate the usefulness of an IDE for situations such as semantic code coloring and auto completion, but it also makes code harder to read and understand. Cleanly separating such code from Jython or Java makes code more clear to read, and easier to maintain in the long run. One possible solution would be to choose from one of the Python template languages such as Django, but using Java Server Pages (JSP) technology can also be a nice solution.

Using a JSP allows one to integrate Java code into HTML markup in order to generate dynamic page content. We are not fans of JSP. There, we said it: JSP can make code a living nightmare if the technology is not used correctly. Although JSP can make it very easy to mix JavaScript, HTML, and Java into one file, it can make maintenance very difficult. Mixing Java code with HTML or JavaScript is a bad idea. The same would also be true for mixing Jython and HTML or JavaScript.

The Model-View-Controller (MVC) paradigm allows for clean separation between logic code, such as Java or Jython, and markup code such as HTML. JavaScript is always gets grouped into the same arena as HTML because it is a client-side scripting language. In other words, JavaScript code should also be separated from the logic code. In thinking about MVC, the controller code would be the markup and JavaScript code used to capture data from the end-user. Model code would be the business logic that manipulates the data. Model code is contained within our Jython or Java. The view would be the markup and JavaScript displaying the result.

Clean separation using MVC can be achieved successfully by combining JSP with Jython servlets. In this section we will take a look at a simple example of how to do so. As with many of the other examples in this text it will only brush upon the surface of great features that are available. Once you learn how to make use of JSP and Jython servlets you can explore further into the technology.

Configuring for JSP

There is no real configuration above and beyond that of configuring a web application to make use of Jython servlets. Add the necessary XML to the web.xml deployment descriptor, include the correct JARs in your application, and begin coding. What is important to note is that the *.py* files that will be used for the Jython servlets must reside within your CLASSPATH. It is common for the Jython servlets to reside in the same directory as the JSP web pages themselves. This can make things easier, but it can also be frowned upon because this concept does not make use of packages for organizing code. For simplicity sake, we will place the servlet code into the same directory as the JSP, but you can do it differently.

Coding the Controller/View

The view portion of the application will be coded using markup and JavaScript code. Obviously, this technique utilizes JSP to contain the markup, and the JavaScript can either be embedded directly into the JSP or reside in separate *.js* files as needed. The latter is the preferred method in order to make things clean, but many web applications embed small amounts of JavaScript within the pages themselves.

The JSP in this example is rather simple, there is no JavaScript in the example and it only contains a couple of input text areas. This JSP will include two forms because we will have two separate submit buttons on the page. Each of these forms will redirect to a different Jython servlet, which will do something with the data that has been supplied within the input text. In our example, the first form contains a small textbox in which the user can type any text that will be redisplayed on the page once the corresponding submit button has been pressed. Very cool, eh? Not really, but it is of good value for learning the correlation between JSP and the servlet implementation. The second form contains two text boxes in which the user will place numbers; hitting the submit button in this form will cause the numbers to be passed to another servlet that will calculate and return the sum of the two numbers. Listing 13-5 is the code for this simple JSP.

Listing 13-5. JSP Code for a Simple Controller/Viewer Application

testJSP.jsp

```
<%@page contentType="text/html" pageEncoding="UTF-8"%>
<!DOCTYPE HTML PUBLIC "-//W3C//DTD HTML 4.01 Transitional//EN"
    "http://www.w3.org/TR/html4/loose.dtd">
<%@ taglib prefix="c" uri="http://java.sun.com/jstl/core" %>

<html>
    <head>
        <meta http-equiv="Content-Type" content="text/html; charset=UTF-8">
```

```
        <title>Jython JSP Test</title>
    </head>
    <body>
        <form method="GET" action="add_to_page.py">
            <input type="text" name="p">
            <input type="submit">
        </form>
        <br/>

            <p>${page_text}</p>

        <br/>

        <form method="GET" action="add_numbers.py">
            <input type="text" name="x">
            +
            <input type="text" name="y">
            =
            ${sum}
            <br/>
            <input type="submit" title="Add Numbers">

        </form>

    </body>
</html>
```

In this JSP example, you can see that the first form redirects to a Jython servlet named *add_to_page.py, which plays the role of the controller*. In this case, the text that is contained within the input textbox named *p* will be passed into the servlet, and redisplayed in on the page. The text to be redisplayed will be stored in an attribute named *page_text*, and you can see that it is referenced within the JSP page using the ${} notation. Listing 13-6 is the code for *add_to_page.py*.

Listing 13-6. A Simple Jython Controller Servlet

```
########################################################################
#  add_to_page.py
#
#  Simple servlet that takes some text from a web page and redisplays
#  it.
########################################################################

import java, javax, sys

class add_to_page(javax.servlet.http.HttpServlet):

    def doGet(self, request, response):
        self.doPost(request, response)

    def doPost(self, request, response):
        addtext = request.getParameter("p")
        if not addtext:
            addtext = ""
```

```
    request.setAttribute("page_text", addtext)

    dispatcher = request.getRequestDispatcher("testJython.jsp")
    dispatcher.forward(request, response)
```

Quick and simple, the servlet takes the request and obtains value contained within the parameter *p*. It then assigns that value to a variable named *addtext*. This variable is then assigned to an attribute in the request named *page_text* and forwarded back to the *testJython.jsp* page. The code could just as easily have forwarded to a different JSP, which is how we'd go about creating a more in-depth application.

The second form in our JSP takes two values and returns the resulting sum to the page. If someone were to enter text instead of numerical values into the text boxes then an error message would be displayed in place of the sum. While very simplistic, this servlet demonstrates that any business logic can be coded in the servlet, including database calls, and so on. See Listing 13-7.

Listing 13-7. Jython Servlet Business Logic

```
#########################################################################
#  add_numbers.py
#
#  Calculates the sum for two numbers and returns it.
#########################################################################

import javax

class add_numbers(javax.servlet.http.HttpServlet):

    def doGet(self, request, response):
        self.doPost(request, response)

    def doPost(self, request, response):
        x = request.getParameter("x")
        y = request.getParameter("y")

        if not x or not y:
            sum = "<font color='red'>You must place numbers in each value box</font>"
        else:
            try:
                sum = int(x) + int(y)
            except ValueError, e:
                sum = "<font color='red'>You must place numbers only in each value
box</font>"

        request.setAttribute("sum", sum)

        dispatcher = request.getRequestDispatcher("testJython.jsp")
        dispatcher.forward(request, response)
```

If we add the JSP and the servlets to the web application we created in the previous Jython Servlet section, then this example should work out-of-the-box.

It is also possible to embed code into Java Server Pages by using various template tags known as scriptlets to enclose the code. In such cases, the JSP must contain Java code unless a special framework such as the Bean Scripting Framework (http://jakarta.apache.org/bsf/) is used along with JSP. For more details on using Java Server Pages, please take a look at the Sun Microsystems JSP documentation (http://java.sun.com/products/jsp/docs.html) or pick up a book such as *Beginning JSP, JSF and Tomcat Web Development: From Novice to Professional* from Apress.

Applets and Java Web Start

At the time of this writing, applets in Jython 2.5.0 are not yet an available option. This is because applets must be statically compiled and available for embedding within a webpage using the *<applet>* or *<object>* tag. The static compiler known as *jythonc* has been removed in Jython 2.5.0 in order to make way for better techniques. Jythonc was good for performing certain tasks, such as static compilation of Jython applets, but it created a disconnect in the development lifecycle as it was a separate compilation step that should not be necessary in order to perform simple tasks such as Jython and Java integration. In a future release of Jython, namely 2.5.1 or another release in the near future, a better way to perform static compilation for applets will be included.

For now, in order to develop Jython applets you will need to use a previous distribution including *jythonc* and then associate them to the webpage with the *<applet>* or *<object>* tag. In Jython, applets are coded in much the same fashion as a standard Java applet. However, the resulting lines of code are significantly smaller in Jython because of its sophisticated syntax. GUI development in general with Jython is a big productivity boost compared to developing a Java Swing application for much the same reason. This is why coding applets in Jython is a viable solution and one that should not be overlooked.

Another option for distributing GUI-based applications on the web is to make use of the Java Web Start technology. The only disadvantage of creating a web start application is that it cannot be embedded directly into any web page. A web start application downloads content to the client's desktop and then runs on the client's local JVM. Development of a Java Web Start application is no different than development of a standalone desktop application. The user interface can be coded using Jython and the Java Swing API, much like the coding for an applet user interface. Once you're ready to deploy a web start application then you need to create a Java Network Launching Protocol (JNLP) file that is used for deployment and bundle it with the application. After that has been done, you need to copy the bundle to a web server and create a web page that can be used to launch the application.

In this section we will develop a small web start application to demonstrate how it can be done using the object factory design pattern and also using pure Jython along with the standalone Jython JAR file for distribution. Note that there are probably other ways to achieve the same result and that these are just a couple of possible implementations for such an application.

Coding a Simple GUI-Based Web Application

The web start application that we will develop in this demonstration is very simple, but they can be as advanced as you'd like in the end. The purpose of this section is not to show you how to develop a web-based GUI application, but rather, the process of developing such an application. You can actually take any of the Swing-based applications that were discussed in the GUI chapter and deploy them using web start technology quite easily. As stated in the previous section, there are many different ways to deploy a Jython web start application. We prefer to make use of the object factory design pattern to create simple Jython Swing applications. However, it can also be done using all .py files and then distributed using the Jython stand-alone JAR file. We will discuss each of those techniques in this section. We find that if you are mixing Java and Jython code then the object factory pattern works best. The JAR method may work best for you if developing a strictly Jython application.

Object Factory Application Design

The application we'll be developing in this section is a simple GUI that takes a line of text and redisplays it in JTextArea. We used Netbeans 6.7 to develop the application, so some of this section may reference particular features that are available in that IDE. To get started with creating an object factory web start application, we first need to create a project. We created a new Java application in Netbeans named *JythonSwingApp* and then added *jython.jar* and *plyjy.jar* to the classpath.

First, create the *Main.java* class which will really be the driver for the application. The goal for Main.java is to use the Jython object factory pattern to coerce a Jython-based Swing application into Java. This class will be the starting point for the application and then the Jython code will perform all of the work under the covers. Using this pattern, we also need a Java interface that can be implemented via the Jython code, so this example also uses a very simple interface that defines a *start()* method which will be used to make our GUI visible. Lastly, the Jython class named below is the code for our *Main.java* driver and the Java interface. The directory structure of this application is as shown in Listing 13-8.

Listing 13-8. Object Factory Application Code

JythonSwingApp
JythonSimpleSwing.py
jythonswingapp
   Main.java
   jythonswingapp.interfaces
   JySwingType.java
Main.java

```
package jythonswingapp;

import jythonswingapp.interfaces.JySwingType;
import org.plyjy.factory.JythonObjectFactory;


public class Main {

    JythonObjectFactory factory;

    public static void invokeJython(){

        JySwingType jySwing = (JySwingType) JythonObjectFactory
                .createObject(JySwingType.class, "JythonSimpleSwing");
        jySwing.start();
    }

    public static void main(String[] args) {
        invokeJython();
    }

}
```

As you can see, *Main.java* doesn't do much else except coercing the Jython module and invoking the *start()* method. In Listing 13-9, you will see the *JySwingType.java* interface along with the implementation class that is obviously coded in Jython.

Listing 13-9. JySwingType.java Interface and Implementation

```
*JySwingType.java*
package jythonswingapp.interfaces;

public interface JySwingType {
    public void start();
}


*JythonSimpleSwing.py*
import javax.swing as swing
import java.awt as awt
from jythonswingapp.interfaces import JySwingType
import add_player as add_player
import Player as Player

class JythonSimpleSwing(JySwingType, object):
    def __init__(self):
        self.frame=swing.JFrame(title="My Frame", size=(300,300))
        self.frame.defaultCloseOperation=swing.JFrame.EXIT_ON_CLOSE;
        self.frame.layout=awt.BorderLayout()
        self.panel1=swing.JPanel(awt.BorderLayout())
        self.panel2=swing.JPanel(awt.GridLayout(4,1))
        self.panel2.preferredSize = awt.Dimension(10,100)
        self.panel3=swing.JPanel(awt.BorderLayout())

        self.title=swing.JLabel("Text Rendering")
        self.button1=swing.JButton("Print Text", actionPerformed=self.printMessage)
        self.button2=swing.JButton("Clear Text", actionPerformed=self.clearMessage)
        self.textField=swing.JTextField(30)
        self.outputText=swing.JTextArea(4,15)


        self.panel1.add(self.title)
        self.panel2.add(self.textField)
        self.panel2.add(self.button1)
        self.panel2.add(self.button2)
        self.panel3.add(self.outputText)

        self.frame.contentPane.add(self.panel1, awt.BorderLayout.PAGE_START)
        self.frame.contentPane.add(self.panel2, awt.BorderLayout.CENTER)
        self.frame.contentPane.add(self.panel3, awt.BorderLayout.PAGE_END)

    def start(self):
        self.frame.visible=1

    def printMessage(self,event):
        print "Print Text!"
        self.text = self.textField.getText()
        self.outputText.append(self.text)
```

```
def clearMessage(self, event):
    self.outputText.text = ""
```

If you are using Netbeans, when you clean and build your project a JAR file is automatically generated for you. However, you can easily create a JAR file at the command-line or terminal by ensuring that the *JythonSimpleSwing.py* module resides within your classpath and using the *java -jar* option. Another nice feature of using an IDE such as Netbeans is that you can make this into a web-start application by going into the project properties and checking a couple of boxes. Specifically, if you go into the project properties and select *Application - Web Start* from the left-hand menu, then check the *Enable Web Start* option then the IDE will take care of generating the necessary files to make this happen. Netbeans also has the option to self sign the JAR file which is required to run most applications on another machine via web start. Go ahead and try it out, just ensure that you clean and build your project again after making the changes.

To manually create the necessary files for a web start application, you'll need to generate two additional files that will be placed outside of the application JAR. Create the JAR for your project as you would normally do, and then create a corresponding JNLP file which is used to launch the application, and an HTML page that will reference the JNLP. The HTML page obviously is where you'd open the application if running it from the web. Listing 13-10 is some example code for generating a JNLP as well as embedding in HTML.

Listing 13-10. JNLP Code for Web Start

```
*launch.jnlp*
<?xml version="1.0" encoding="UTF-8" standalone="no"?>
<jnlp codebase="file:/path-to-jar/" href="launch.jnlp" spec="1.0+">
    <information>
        <title>JythonSwingApp</title>
        <vendor>YourName</vendor>
        <homepage href=""/>
        <description>JythonSwingApp</description>
        <description kind="short">JythonSwingApp</description>
    </information>
<security>
<all-permissions/>
</security>
    <resources>
<j2se version="1.5+"/>
<jar eager="true" href="JythonSwingApp.jar" main="true"/>
    <jar href="lib/PlyJy.jar"/>
<jar href="lib/jython.jar"/>
</resources>
    <application-desc main-class="jythonswingapp.Main">
    </application-desc>
</jnlp>

*launch.html*
<html>
    <head>
        <title>Test page for launching the application via JNLP</title>
    </head>
    <body>
        <h3>Test page for launching the application via JNLP</h3>
        <a href="launch.jnlp">Launch the application</a>
```

```
    <!-- Or use the following script element to launch with the Deployment Toolkit -->
    <!-- Open the deployJava.js script to view its documentation -->
    <!--
    <script src="http://java.com/js/deployJava.js"></script>
    <script>
        var url="http://[fill in your URL]/launch.jnlp"
        deployJava.createWebStartLaunchButton(url, "1.6")
    </script>
    -->
</body>
</html>
```

In the end, Java web start is a very good way to distribute Jython applications via the web.

Distributing via Standalone JAR

It is possible to distribute a web start application using the Jython standalone JAR option. To do so, you must have a copy of the Jython standalone JAR file, explode it, and add your code into the file, then JAR it back up to deploy. The only drawback to using this method is that you may need to ensure files are in the correct locations in order to make it work correctly, which can sometimes be tedious.

In order to distribute your Jython applications via a JAR, first download the Jython standalone distribution. Once you have this, you can extract the files from the *jython.jar* using a tool to expand the JAR such as Stuffit or 7zip. Once the JAR has been exploded, you will need to add any of your *.py* scripts into the *Lib* directory, and any Java classes into the root. For instance, if you have a Java class named *org.jythonbook.Book*, you would place it into the appropriate directory according to the package structure. If you have any additional JAR files to include with your application then you will need to make sure that they are in your classpath. Once you've completed this setup, JAR your manipulated standalone Jython JAR back up into a ZIP format using a tool such as those noted before. You can then rename the ZIP to a JAR. The application can now be run using the java "-jar" option from the command line using an optional external *.py* file to invoke your application.

```
$ java -jar newStandaloneJar.jar {optional .py file}
```

This is only one such technique used to make a JAR file for containing your applications. There are other ways to perform such techniques, but this seems to be the most straight forward and easiest to do.

WSGI and Modjy

WSGI, also known as the *Web Server Gateway Interface*, is a low-level API that provides communication between a web server and a web application. Actually, WSGI is a lot more than that and you can actually write complete web applications using WSGI. However, WSGI is more of a standard interface to call python methods and functions. Python PEP 333 specifies the proposed standard interface between web servers and Python web applications or frameworks, to promote web application portability across a variety of web servers.

This section will show you how to utilize WSGI to create a very simple "Hello Jython" application by utilizing *modjy*. Modjy is an implementation of a WSGI compliant gateway/server for Jython, built on Java/J2EE servlets. Taken from the modjy website (http://opensource.xhaus.com/projects/modjy/wiki), modjy is characterized as follows:

> *Jython WSGI applications run inside a Java/J2EE container and incoming requests are handled by the servlet container. The container is configured to route requests to the modjy servlet. The*

modjy servlet then creates an embedded Jython interpreter inside the servlet container, and loads a configured Jython web application. For instance, a Django application can be loaded via modjy. The modjy servlet then delegates the requests to the configured WSGI application or framework. Lastly, the WSGI response is routed back to the client through the servlet container.

Running a Modjy Application in Glassfish

To run a modjy application in any Java servlet container, the first step is to create a Java web application that will be packaged up as a WAR file. You can create an application from scratch or use an IDE such as Netbeans 6.7 to assist. Once you've created your web application, ensure that *jython.jar* resides in the CLASSPATH as modjy is now part of Jython as of 2.5.0. Lastly, you will need to configure the modjy servlet within the application deployment descriptor (web.xml). In this example, we took the modjy sample application for Google App Engine and deployed it in my local Glassfish environment.

To configure the application deployment descriptor with modjy, we simply configure the modjy servlet, provide the necessary parameters, and then provide a servlet mapping. In the configuration file shown in Listing 13-11, note that the modjy servlet class is *com.xhaus.modjy.ModjyServlet*. The first parameter you will need to use with the servlet is named *python.home*. Set the value of this parameter equal to your Jython home. Next, set the parameter *python.cachedir.skip* equal to true. The *app_filename* parameter provides the name of the application callable. Other parameters will be set up the same for each modjy application you configure. The last piece of the web.xml that needs to be set up is the servlet mapping. In the example, we set up all URLs to map to the modjy servlet.

Listing 13-11. Configuring the Modjy Servlet

```
*web.xml*
<?xml version="1.0" encoding="ISO-8859-1"?>
<!DOCTYPE web-app
    PUBLIC "-//Sun Microsystems, Inc.//DTD Web Application 2.3//EN"
    "http://java.sun.com/dtd/web-app_2_3.dtd">
<web-app>

  <display-name>modjy demo application</display-name>
  <description>
    modjy WSGI demo application
  </description>

  <servlet>
    <servlet-name>modjy</servlet-name>
    <servlet-class>com.xhaus.modjy.ModjyJServlet</servlet-class>
    <init-param>
      <param-name>python.home</param-name>
      <param-value>/Applications/jython/jython2.5.0/</param-value>
    </init-param>
    <init-param>
      <param-name>python.cachedir.skip</param-name>
      <param-value>true</param-value>
    </init-param>
<!--
      There are two different ways you can specify an application to modjy
      1. Using the app_import_name mechanism
      2. Using a combination of app_directory/app_filename/app_callable_name
      Examples of both are given below
```

```
              See the documentation for more details.
              http://modjy.xhaus.com/locating.html#locating_callables
    -->
    <!--
              This is the app_import_name mechanism. If you specify a value
              for this variable, then it will take precedence over the other mechanism
        <init-param>
            <param-name>app_import_name</param-name>
            <param-value>my_wsgi_module.my_handler_class().handler_method</param-value>
        </init-param>
    -->
    <!--
              And this is the app_directory/app_filename/app_callable_name combo
              The defaults for these three variables are ""/application.py/handler
              So if you specify no values at all for any of app_* variables, then modjy
              will by default look for "handler" in "application.py" in the servlet
              context root.
        <init-param>
            <param-name>app_directory</param-name>
            <param-value>some_sub_directory</param-value>
        </init-param>
    -->
        <init-param>
            <param-name>app_filename</param-name>
            <param-value>demo_app.py</param-value>
        </init-param>
    <!--
              Supply a value for this parameter if you want your application
              callable to have a different name than the default.
        <init-param>
            <param-name>app_callable_name</param-name>
            <param-value>my_handler_func</param-value>
        </init-param>
    -->
            <!-- Do you want application callables to be cached? -->
        <init-param>
            <param-name>cache_callables</param-name>
            <param-value>1</param-value>
        </init-param>
        <!-- Should the application be reloaded if it's .py file changes? -->
        <!-- Does not work with the app_import_name mechanism -->
        <init-param>
            <param-name>reload_on_mod</param-name>
            <param-value>1</param-value>
        </init-param>
        <init-param>
            <param-name>log_level</param-name>
            <param-value>debug</param-value>
    <!--    <param-value>info</param-value>   -->
    <!--    <param-value>warn</param-value>   -->
    <!--    <param-value>error</param-value> -->
    <!--    <param-value>fatal</param-value> -->
        </init-param>
        <load-on-startup>1</load-on-startup>
```

```
    </servlet>

<servlet-mapping>
  <servlet-name>modjy</servlet-name>
  <url-pattern>/*</url-pattern>
</servlet-mapping>

</web-app>
```

The demo_app should be coded as shown in Listing 13-12. As part of the WSGI standard, the application provides a function that the server calls for each request. In this case, that function is named *handler*. The function must take two parameters, the first being a dictionary of CGI-defined environment variables. The second is a callback that returns the HTTP headers. The callback function should also be called as follows *start_response(status, response_headers, exx_info=None)*, where status is an HTTP status, response_headers is a list of HTTP headers, and exc_info is for exception handling. Let's take a look at the *demo_app.py* application and identify the features we've just discussed.

Listing 13-12.

```python
import sys
import string

def escape_html(s): return s.replace('&', '&amp;').replace('<', '&lt;').replace('>', '&gt;')

def cutoff(s, n=100):
    if len(s) > n: return s[:n]+ '.. cut ..'
    return s

def handler(environ, start_response):
    writer = start_response("200 OK", [ ('content-type', 'text/html') ])
    response_parts = '''<html><head>
                        <title>Modjy demo WSGI application running on Local Server!</title>
                        </head>
                        <body>
                        <p>Modjy servlet running correctly:
                            jython $version on $platform:
                        </p>
                        <h3>Hello jython WSGI on your local server!</h3>
                        <h4>Here are the contents of the WSGI environment</h4>'''
    environ_str = "<table border='1'>"
    keys = environ.keys()
    keys.sort()
    for ix, name in enumerate(keys):
        if ix % 2:
            background='#ffffff'
        else:
            background='#eeeeee'
        style = " style='background-color:%s;'" % background
        value = escape_html(cutoff(str(environ[name]))) or ' '
        environ_str = "%s\n<tr><td%s>%s</td><td%s>%s</td></tr>" % \
            (environ_str, style, name, style, value)
    environ_str = "%s\n</table>" % environ_str
    response_parts = response_parts + environ_str + '</body></html>\n'
```

```
response_text = string.Template(response_parts)
return [response_text.substitute(version=sys.version, platform=sys.platform)]
```

This application returns the environment configuration for the server on which you run the application. As you can see, the page is quite simple to code and really resembles a servlet.

Once the application has been set up and configured, simply compile the code into a WAR file and deploy it to the Java servlet container of your choice. In this case, we used Glassfish V2 and it worked nicely. However, this same application should be deployable to Tomcat, JBoss, or the like.

Summary

There are various ways that we can use Jython for creating simple web-based applications. Jython servlets are a good way to make content available on the web, and you can also utilize them along with a JSP page which allows for a Model-View-Controller situation. This is a good technique to use for developing sophisticated web applications, especially those mixing some JavaScript into the action because it really helps to organize things. Most Java web applications use frameworks or other techniques in order to help organize applications in such a way as to apply the MVC concept. It is great to have a way to do such work with Jython as well.

This chapter also discussed creation of WSGI applications in Jython making use of modjy. This is a good low-level way to generate web applications as well, although modjy and WSGI are usually used for implementing web frameworks and the like. Solutions such as Django use WSGI in order to follow the standard put forth for all Python web frameworks with PEP 333. You can see from the section in this chapter that WSGI is also a nice quick way to write web applications, much like writing a servlet in Jython.

In the next chapters, you will learn more about using web frameworks available to Jython, specifically Django and Pylons. These two frameworks can make any web developers life much easier, and now that they are available on the Java platform via Jython they are even more powerful. Using a templating technique such as Django can be really productive and it is a good way to design a full-blown web application. Techniques discussed in this chapter can also be used for developing large web applications, but using a standard framework such as those discussed in the following chapter should be considered. There are many great ways to code Jython web applications today, and the options continue to grow!

## CHAPTER 14

Web Applications With Django

Django is a modern Python web framework that redefined web development in the Python world. A full-stack approach, pragmatic design, and superb documentation are some of the reasons for its success.

If fast web development using the Python language sounds good to you, then fast web development using the Python language while being integrated with the whole Java world (which has a strong presence on the enterprise web space) sounds even better. Running Django on Jython allows you to do just that.

And for the Java world, having Django as an option to quickly build web applications while still having the chance to use the existing Java APIs and technologies is very attractive.

In this chapter we will start with a quick introduction to allow you to have Django running with your Jython installation in a few steps. Then we will build a simple web application so you can get a feeling of the framework. In the second half of the chapter, we will take a look at the many opportunities of integration between Django web applications and the JavaEE world.

Getting Django

Strictly speaking, to use Django with Jython you only need to have Django itself, and nothing more. But, without third-party libraries, you won't be able to connect to any database, because the built-in Django database backends depend on libraries written in C, which aren't available on Jython.

In practice, you will need at least two packages: Django itself and "django-jython," which, as you can imagine, is a collection of Django add-ons that can be quite useful if you happen to be running Django on top of Jython. In particular it includes database backends.

Because the process of getting these two libraries slightly varies depending on your platform, and because it's a manual, boring task, we will use a utility to automatically grab and install these libraries. The utility is called setuptools. The catch is that we need to manually install setuptools, of course, but this is quite straightforward. If you haven't installed setuptools before, please take a look at Appendix A for more details.

After you have setuptools installed, the easy_install command will be available. Note that if you are on a Windows platform you may need to type easy_install.py instead of just easy_install. Armed with this, we proceed to install Django.

```
$ easy_install Django
```

Note We're assuming that the bin directory of the Jython installation is on the front of your PATH. If it's not, you will have to explicitly type that path preceding each command like jython or easy_install with that path (so you will need to type something like /path/to/jython/bin/easy_install instead of just easy_install).

By reading the output of easy_install you can see how it is doing all the tedious work of locating the right package, downloading, and installing it. See Listing 14-1.

Listing 14-1. Output from Easy_install Command

```
Searching for Django
Reading http://pypi.python.org/simple/Django/
Reading http://www.djangoproject.com/
Reading http://www.djangoproject.com/download/1.1.1/tarball/
Best match: Django 1.1.1
Downloading http://media.djangoproject.com/releases/1.1.1/Django-1.1.1.tar.gz
Processing Django-1.1.1.tar.gz
Running Django-1.1.1/setup.py -q bdist_egg --dist-dir
/tmp/easy_install-nTnmlU/Django-1.1.1/egg-dist-tmp-L-pq4s
zip_safe flag not set; analyzing archive contents...
Unable to analyze compiled code on this platform.
Please ask the author to include a 'zip_safe' setting (either True or False)
in the package's setup.py
Adding Django 1.1.1 to easy-install.pth file
Installing django-admin.py script to /home/lsoto/jython2.5.0/bin

Installed /home/lsoto/jython2.5.0/Lib/site-packages/Django-1.1.1-py2.5.egg
Processing dependencies for Django==1.1.1
Finished processing dependencies for Django==1.1.1
```

Then we install django-jython:

```
$ easy_install django-jython
```

Again, you will get an output similar to what you've seen in the previous case. Once this is finished, you are ready.

If you want to look behind the scenes, take a look at the Lib/site-packages subdirectory inside your Jython installation and you will entries for the libraries we just installed. Those entries are also listed on the easy-install.pth file, making them part of sys.path by default.

Just to make sure that everything went fine, start jython and try the statements shown in Listing 14-2, which import the top-level packages of Django and django-jython.

Listing 14-2. Import Django Packages

```
>>> import django
>>> import doj
```

If you don't get any error printed out on the screen, then everything is okay. Let's start our first application.

A Quick Tour of Django

Django is a full-stack framework. That means that its features cover everything from communication to databases, and from URL processing and to web page templating. As you may know, there are complete books that cover Django in detail. We aren't going to go into much detail, but we *are* going to touch many of the features included in the framework, so you can get a good feeling of its strengths in case you haven't had the chance to know or try Django in the past. That way you will know when Django is the right tool for a job.

■ **Note** If you are already familiar with Django, you won't find anything especially new in the rest of this section. Feel free to jump to the section "J2EE Deployment and Integration" to look at what's really special if you run Django on Jython.

The only way to take a broad view of such a featureful framework like Django is to build something really simple, and then gradually augment it as we look into what the framework offers. So, we will start following roughly what the official Django tutorial uses (a simple site for polls) to extend it later to touch most of the framework features. In other words: most of the code you will see in this section comes directly from the great Django tutorial you can find on http://docs.djangoproject.com/en/1.0/intro/tutorial01/. However, we've extended the code to show more Django features and adapted the material to fit into this section.

Now, as we said on the previous paragraph, Django handles communications with the database. Right now, the most solid backend in existence for Django/Jython is the one for PostgreSQL. So we encourage you to install PostgreSQL on your machine and set up a user and an empty database to use it in the course of this tour.

Starting a Project (and an "App")

Django projects, which are usually meant to be web sites (or "sub-sites" on a bigger portal) are composed of a settings file, a URL mappings file, and a set of "apps" that provide the actual features of the web site. As you surely have realized, many web sites share a lot of features: administration interfaces, user authentication/registration, commenting systems, news feeds, contact forms, and the like. That's why Django decouples the actual site features in the "app" concept: apps are meant to be *reusable* between different projects (sites).

As we will start small, our project will consist of only one app at first. We will call our project "pollsite." So, let's create a clean new directory for what we will build in this section, move to that directory and run:

```
$ django-admin.py startproject pollsite
```

And a Python package named "pollsite" will be created under the directory you created previously. At this point, the most important change we *need* to make to the default settings of our shiny new project is to fill in information enabling Django to talk to the database we created for this tour. So, open the file pollsite/settings.py with your text editor of choice and change lines starting with DATABASE with something like Listing 14-3.

Listing 14-3. Django Database Settings

```
DATABASE_ENGINE = 'doj.backends.zxjdbc.postgresql'
DATABASE_NAME = '<the name of the empty database you created>'
DATABASE_USER = '<the name of the user with R/W access to that database>'
DATABASE_PASSWORD = '<the password of that user>'
```

With this, you are telling Django to use the PostgreSQL driver provided by the doj package (which, if you remember from the Getting Django section, was the package name of the django-jython project) and to connect with the given credentials. This backend requires the PostgreSQL JDBC driver, which you can download at http://jdbc.postgresql.org/download.html.

Once you download the JDBC driver, you need to add it to the Java CLASSPATH. Another way to do it in Linux/Unix/MacOSX for the current session is:

```
$ export CLASSPATH=$CLASSPATH:/path/to/postgresql-jdbc.jar
```

If you are on Windows, the command is different:

```
$ set CLASSPATH=%CLASSPATH%:\path\to\postgresql-jdbc.jar
```

After you have done that, you will create the single app which will be the core of our project. Make sure you are in the pollsite directory and run:

```
$ jython manage.py startapp polls
```

This will create the basic structure of a Django app. A Django app is a "slice" of features of a web site. For example, Django comes with a comments app that includes all the bits to let you attach comments to every object of your system. It also has the admin app for providing an administrative frontend to the web site database. We will cover those two specific apps soon, but right now the main idea is to know that your Django project (web site) will consist of many Django apps, one for each major feature. We are starting with the polls app that will handle all the logic around basic polls of our web site.

Note that the polls app was created inside the project package, so we have the pollsite project and the pollsite.polls app.

Now we will see what's inside a Django app.

Models

In Django, you define your data schema in Python code, using Python classes. This central schema is used to generate the needed SQL statements to create the database schema, and to dynamically generate SQL queries when you manipulate objects of these special Python classes.

Now, in Django you don't define the schema of the whole project in a single central place. Because apps are the real providers of features, it follows that the schema of the whole project isn't more than the combination of the schemas of each app. By the way, we will switch to Django terminology now, and instead of talking about data schemas, we will talk about models (which are actually a bit more than just schemas, but the distinction is not important at this point).

If you look into the pollsite/polls directory, you will see that there is a models.py file, which is where the app's models must be defined. Listing 14-4 contains the model for simple polls, each poll containing many choices:

Listing 14-4. Simple Model Code for Polls

```
from django.db import models

class Poll(models.Model):
    question = models.CharField(max_length=200)
    pub_date = models.DateTimeField('date published')

    def __unicode__(self):
        return self.question
```

```
class Choice(models.Model):
    poll = models.ForeignKey(Poll)
    choice = models.CharField(max_length=200)
    votes = models.IntegerField()

    def __unicode__(self):
        return self.choice
```

As you can see, the map between a class inheriting from models.Model and a database table is clear, and it's more or less obvious how each Django field would be translated to a SQL field. Actually, Django fields can carry more information than SQL fields can, as you can see on the pub_date field, which includes a description more suited for human consumption: "date published." Django also provides more specialized fields for rather common types seen on today web applications, like EmailField, URLField, or FileField. They free you from having to write the same code again and again to deal with concerns such as validation or storage management for the data these fields will contain.

Once the models are defined, we want to create the tables that will hold the data on the database. First, you will need to add the app to the project settings file (yes, the fact that the app "lives" under the project package isn't enough). Edit the file pollsite/settings.py and add 'pollsite.polls' to the INSTALLED_APPS list. It will look like Listing 14-5.

Listing 14-5. Adding a Line to the INSTALLED_APPS List

```
INSTALLED_APPS = (
    'django.contrib.auth',
    'django.contrib.contenttypes',
    'django.contrib.sessions',
    'django.contrib.sites',
    'pollsite.polls',
)
```

■ **Note** As you see, there were a couple of apps already included in your project. These apps are included on every Django project by default, providing some of the basic features of the framework, such as sessions.

After that, we make sure we are located on the project directory and run:

```
$ jython manage.py syncdb
```

If the database connection information was correctly specified, Django will create tables and indexes for our models *and* for the models of the other apps that were also included by default on INSTALLED_APPS. One of these extra apps is django.contrib.auth, which handles user authentication. That's why you will also be asked for the username and password for the initial admin user for your site. See Listing 14-6.

Listing 14-6. Django Authentication Data

```
Creating table auth_permission
Creating table auth_group
Creating table auth_user
Creating table auth_message
Creating table django_content_type
Creating table django_session
Creating table django_site
Creating table polls_poll
Creating table polls_choice

You just installed Django's auth system, which means you don't have any
superusers defined.
Would you like to create one now? (yes/no):
```

Answer yes to that question, and provide the requested information, as in Listing 14-7.

Listing 14-7. Replying to Authentication Questions

```
Username (Leave blank to use u'lsoto'): admin
E-mail address: admin@mailinator.com
Warning: Problem with getpass. Passwords may be echoed.
Password: admin
Warning: Problem with getpass. Passwords may be echoed.
Password (again): admin
Superuser created successfully.
```

After this, Django will continue mapping your models to RDBMS artifacts, creating some indexes for your tables. See Listing 14-8.

Listing 14-8. Automatic Index Creation from Django

```
Installing index for auth.Permission model
Installing index for auth.Message model
Installing index for polls.Choice model
```

If we want to know what Django is doing behind the scenes, we can ask using the `sqlall` management command (which is how the commands recognized by `manage.py` are called, like the recently used `syncdb`). This command requires an app *label* as argument, and prints the SQL statements corresponding to the models contained in the app. By the way, the emphasis on *label* was intentional, as it corresponds to the last part of the "full name" of an app and not to the full name itself. In our case, the label of "pollsite.polls" is simply "polls." So, we can run:

```
$ jython manage.py sqlall polls
```

And we get the output shown in Listing 14-9.

Listing 14-9. Manage.py Output

```
BEGIN;
CREATE TABLE "polls_poll" (
    "id" serial NOT NULL PRIMARY KEY,
    "question" varchar(200) NOT NULL,
    "pub_date" timestamp with time zone NOT NULL
)
;
CREATE TABLE "polls_choice" (
    "id" serial NOT NULL PRIMARY KEY,
    "poll_id" integer NOT NULL
        REFERENCES "polls_poll" ("id") DEFERRABLE INITIALLY DEFERRED,
    "choice" varchar(200) NOT NULL,
    "votes" integer NOT NULL
)
;
CREATE INDEX "polls_choice_poll_id" ON "polls_choice" ("poll_id");
COMMIT;
```

Two things to note here: first, each table contains an id field that wasn't explicitly specified in our model definition. That's automatic, and is a sensible default (which can be overridden if you really need a different type of primary key, but that's outside the scope of this quick tour). Second, you can see how the SQL commands are tailored to the particular RDBMS we are using (PostgreSQL in this case); naturally, it may change if you use a different database backend.

Let's move on. We have our model defined, and we are ready to store polls. The typical next step here would be to make a CRUD administrative interface so polls can be created, edited, removed, and so on. Oh, and of course we may envision some searching and filtering capabilities for this administrator, knowing in advance that once the number of polls grows too much, the polls will become really hard to manage.

Well, no. We won't write the administrative interface from scratch. We will use one of the most useful features of Django: the admin app.

Bonus: The Admin

This is an intermission during our tour through the main architectural points of a Django project (namely, models, views, and templates), but it is a very nice intermission. The code for the administrative interface we talked about a couple of paragraphs back will consist on less than 20 lines of code!

First, let's enable the admin app. To do this, edit pollsite/settings.py and add 'django.contrib.admin' to the INSTALLED_APPS. Then edit pollsite/urls.py, which looks like Listing 14-10.

Listing 14-10. The Original Unchanged Urls.py

```
from django.conf.urls.defaults import *

# Uncomment the next two lines to enable the admin:
# from django.contrib import admin
# admin.autodiscover()

urlpatterns = patterns('',
```

```
    # Example:
    # (r'^pollsite/', include('pollsite.foo.urls')),

    # Uncomment the admin/doc line below and add 'django.contrib.admindocs'
    # to INSTALLED_APPS to enable admin documentation:
    # (r'^admin/doc/', include('django.contrib.admindocs.urls')),

    # Uncomment the next line to enable the admin:
    # (r'^admin/(.*)', admin.site.root),
)
```

And uncomment the lines that enable the admin (but not the admin/doc line!), so the file will look like Listing 14-11.

Listing 14-11. Enabling the Admin App from Urls.py

```
from django.conf.urls.defaults import *

# Uncomment the next two lines to enable the admin:
from django.contrib import admin
admin.autodiscover()

urlpatterns = patterns('',
    # Example:
    # (r'^pollsite/', include('pollsite.foo.urls')),

    # Uncomment the admin/doc line below and add 'django.contrib.admindocs'
    # to INSTALLED_APPS to enable admin documentation:
    # (r'^admin/doc/', include('django.contrib.admindocs.urls')),

    # Uncomment the next line to enable the admin:
    (r'^admin/(.*)', admin.site.root),
)
```

Now you can remove all the remaining commented lines, so urls.py ends up with the contents shown in Listing 14-12.

Listing 14-12. Final State of Urls.py

```
from django.conf.urls.defaults import *

from django.contrib import admin
admin.autodiscover()

urlpatterns = patterns('',
    (r'^admin/(.*)', admin.site.root),
)
```

Although we haven't explained this urls.py file yet, we will go into some more depth in the next section.

Finally, let's create the database artifacts needed by the admin app:

```
$ jython manage.py syncdb
```

Now we will see what this admin looks like. Let's run our site in development mode by executing:

```
$ jython manage.py runserver
```

■ **Note** The development web server is an easy way to test your web project. It will run indefinitely until you abort it (for example, hitting Ctrl + C) and it will reload itself when you change a source file already loaded by the server, thus giving almost instant feedback. But, be advised that using this development server in production is a really, really bad idea, because it can't handle multiple simultaneous connections and just has poor performance in general.

Using a web browser, navigate to http://localhost:8000/admin/. You will be presented with a login screen. Enter the user credentials you created when we first ran syncdb in the previous section. Once you log in, you will see a page like the one shown in Figure 14-1.

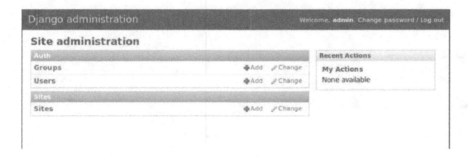

Figure 14-1. The Django admin

As you can see, the central area of the admin shows two boxes, titled "Auth" and "Sites." Those boxes correspond to the "auth" and "sites" apps that are built in in Django. The "Auth" box contains two entries: "Groups" and "Users," each corresponding to a model contained in the auth app. If you click the "Users" link you will be presented with the typical options to add, modify, and remove users. This is the kind of interface that the admin app can provide to any other Django app, so we will add our polls app to it.

Doing so is a matter of creating an admin.py file under your app (that is, pollsite/polls/admin.py). Then we declare to the admin app how we want to present our models. To administer polls, Listing 14-13 will do the trick.

Listing 14-13. Adding the Polls App to the Admin App

```
# polls admin.py
from pollsite.polls.models import Poll, Choice
```

```
from django.contrib import admin

class ChoiceInline(admin.StackedInline):
    model = Choice
    extra = 3

class PollAdmin(admin.ModelAdmin):
    fieldsets = [
        (None,               {'fields': ['question']}),
        ('Date information', {'fields': ['pub_date'],
                              'classes': ['collapse']}),
    ]
    inlines = [ChoiceInline]

admin.site.register(Poll, PollAdmin)
```

This may look like magic to you, but remember that we're moving quickly, as we want you to see what's possible with Django. Let's look first at what we get after writing this code. Start the development server, go to http://localhost:8000/admin/, and see how a new "Polls" box appears now. If you click the "Add" link in the "Polls" entry, you will see a page like the one in Figure 14-2.

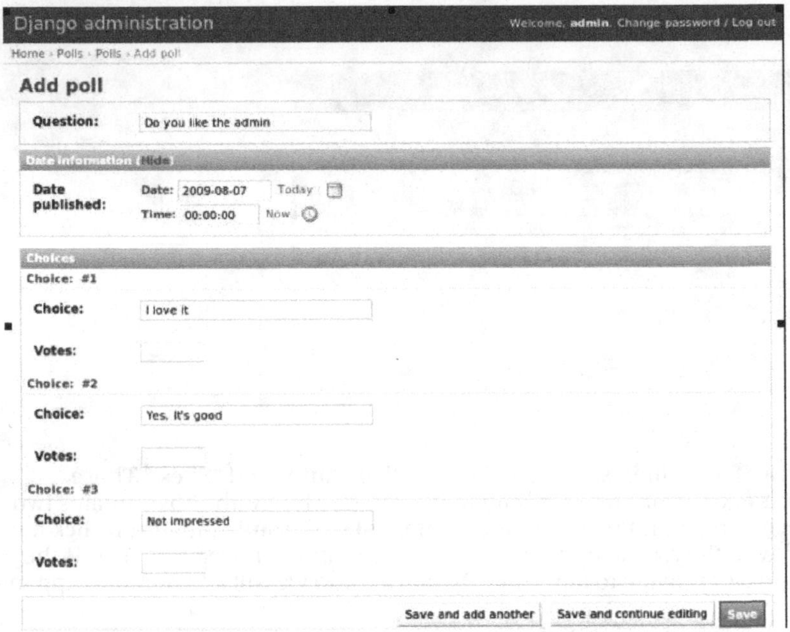

Figure 14-2. Adding a poll

Play a bit with the interface: create a couple of polls, remove one, modify the rest. Note that the user interface is divided into three parts, one for the question, another for the date (initially hidden) and the last part is dedicated to the choices. The first two were defined by the fieldsets of the PollAdmin class, which let you define the titles of each section (where None means no title), the fields contained (they can be more than one, of course), and additional CSS classes providing behaviors such as 'collapse'.

It's fairly obvious that we have "merged" the administration of our two models (Poll and Choice) into the same user interface, because choices ought to be edited "inline" with their corresponding poll. That was done via the ChoiceInline class, which declares what model will be inlined and how many empty slots will be shown. The inline is hooked into the PollAdmin later (because you can include many inlines on any ModelAdmin class).

Finally, PollAdmin is registered as the administrative interface for the Poll model using admin.site.register(). As you can see, everything is absolutely declarative and works like a charm.

You may be wondering what happened to the search/filter features we talked about a few paragraphs ago. We will implement those in the poll list interface that you can access when clicking the "Change" link for Polls in the main interface (or by clicking the link "Polls," or after adding a Poll).

So, add the following lines to the PollAdmin class:

```
search_fields = ['question']
list_filter = ['pub_date']
```

And play with the admin again (that's why it was a good idea to create a few polls in the last step). Figure 14-3 shows the search working, using "django" as the search string.

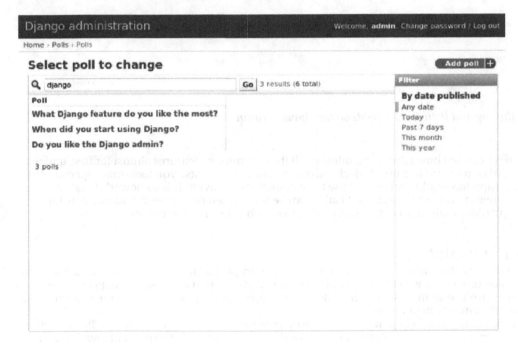

Figure 14-3. *Searching on the Django admin*

Now, if you try the filter by publishing date, it feels a bit awkward, because the list of polls only shows the name of the poll, so you can't see the publishing date of the polls being filtered, to check if the filter worked as advertised. That's easy to fix, by adding the following line to the PollAdmin class:

```
list_display = ['question', 'pub_date']
```

Figure 14-4 shows how the interface looks after all these additions.

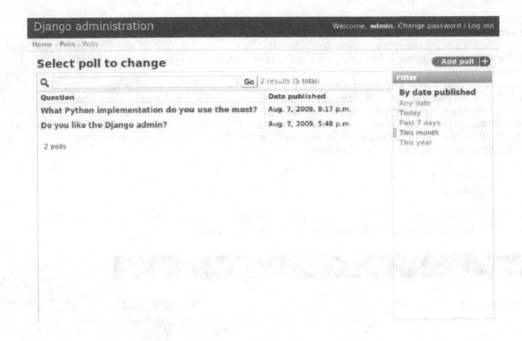

Figure 14-4. Filtering and listing more fields on the Django admin

Once again we can see how admin app offers us all these commons features almost for free, and we only have to say what we want in a purely declarative way. However, in case you have more special needs, the admin app has hooks that we can use to customize its behavior. It is so powerful that sometimes it happens that a whole web application can be built based purely on the admin. See the official docs http://docs.djangoproject.com/en/1.0/ref/contrib/admin/ for more information.

Views and Templates

Well, now that we know the admin, we won't be able to use a simple CRUD example to showcase the rest of the main architecture of the web framework. That's okay: CRUD is part of almost all data driven web applications, but it isn't what makes your site different. So, now that we have delegated the tedium to the admin app, we will concentrate on polls.

We already have our models in place, so it's time to write our views, which are the HTTP-oriented functions that will make our app talk to the outside world (which is, after all, the point of creating a *web* application).

■ **Note** Django developers half-jokingly say that Django follows the "MTV" pattern: Model, Template, and View. These three components map directly to what other modern frameworks call Model, View, and Controller. Django takes this apparently unorthodox naming schema because, strictly speaking, the controller is the framework itself.

What is called "controller" code in other frameworks is really tied to HTTP and output templates, so they can be considered part of the view layer. If you don't like this viewpoint, just remember to mentally map Django templates to "views" and Django views to "controllers."

By convention, code for views goes into the app views.py file. Views are simple functions that take an HTTP request, do some processing, and return an HTTP response. Because an HTTP response typically involves the construction of an HTML page, templates aid views with the job of creating HTML output (and other text-based outputs) in a more maintainable way than just by manually pasting strings together.

The polls app enables very simple navigation. First, the user will be presented with an "index" with access to the list of the latest polls. He will select one and we will show the poll "details," that is, a form with the available choices and a button so he can submit his choice. Once a choice is made, the user will be directed to a page showing the current results of the poll he just voted on.

Before writing the code for the views, a good way to start designing a Django app is to design its URLs. In Django you map URLs to view functions, using regular expressions. Modern web development takes URLs seriously, and nice URLs (not difficult to read URLs like "DoSomething.do" or "ThisIsNotNice.aspx") are the norm. Instead of patching ugly names with URL rewriting, Django offers a layer of indirection between the URL which triggers a view and the internal name you happen to give to such view. Also, as Django has an emphasis on apps that can be reused across multiple projects, there is a modular way to define URLs so an app can define the relative URLs for its views, and they can be later included on different projects.

Let's start by modifying the pollsite/urls.py file to the Listing 14-14.

Listing 14-14. Modifying Urls.py to Define Relative URLs for any App View Functions

```
from django.conf.urls.defaults import *

from django.contrib import admin
admin.autodiscover()

urlpatterns = patterns('',
    (r'^admin/(.*)', admin.site.root),
    (r'^polls/', include('pollsite.polls.urls')),
)
```

Note how we added the pattern that says: if the URL starts with polls/ continue matching it following the patterns defined on module pollsite.polls.urls. So let's create the file pollsite/polls/urls.py (note that it will live inside the app) and put the code shown in Listing 14-15 in it.

Listing 14-15. Matching Alternative URLs from Pollsite/polls/urls.py

```
from django.conf.urls.defaults import *

urlpatterns = patterns('pollsite.polls.views',
    (r'^$', 'index'),
    (r'^(\d+)/$', 'detail'),
    (r'^(\d+)/vote/$', 'vote'),
```

```
    (r'^(\d+)/results/$', 'results'),
)
```

The first pattern says: if there is nothing else to match (remember that polls/ was already matched by the previous pattern), use the index view. The other patterns include a placeholder for numbers, written in the regular expression as \d+, and it is captured (using the parenthesis) so it will be passed as argument to their respective views. The end result is that a URL such as polls/5/results/ will call the results view passing the string '5' as the second argument (the first view argument is always the request object). If you want to know more about Django URL dispatching, see http://docs.djangoproject.com/en/1.1/topics/http/urls/.

So, from the URL patterns we just created, it can be seen that we need to write the view functions named index, detail, vote and results. Listing 14-16 is code for pollsite/polls/views.py.

Listing 14-16. View Functions to Be Used from URL Patterns

```
from django.shortcuts import get_object_or_404, render_to_response
from django.http import HttpResponseRedirect
from django.core.urlresolvers import reverse
from pollsite.polls.models import Choice, Poll

def index(request):
    latest_poll_list = Poll.objects.all().order_by('-pub_date')[:5]
    return render_to_response('polls/index.html',
                              {'latest_poll_list': latest_poll_list})

def detail(request, poll_id):
    poll = get_object_or_404(Poll, pk=poll_id)
    return render_to_response('polls/detail.html', {'poll': poll})

def vote(request, poll_id):
    poll = get_object_or_404(Poll, pk=poll_id)
    try:
        selected_choice = poll.choice_set.get(pk=request.POST['choice'])
    except (KeyError, Choice.DoesNotExist):
        # Redisplay the poll voting form.
        return render_to_response('polls/detail.html', {
            'poll': poll,
            'error_message': "You didn't select a choice.",
        })
    else:
        selected_choice.votes += 1
        selected_choice.save()
        # Always return an HttpResponseRedirect after successfully dealing
        # with POST data. This prevents data from being posted twice if a
        # user hits the Back button.
        return HttpResponseRedirect(
            reverse('pollsite.polls.views.results', args=(poll.id,)))

def results(request, poll_id):
    poll = get_object_or_404(Poll, pk=poll_id)
    return render_to_response('polls/results.html', {'poll': poll})
```

We know this was a bit fast, but remember that we are taking a *quick* tour. The important thing here is to grasp the high-level concepts. Each function defined in this file is a view. You can identify the functions because they are defined inside the views.py file. You can also identify them because they receive a request as a first argument.

So, we defined the views named index, details, vote, and results that are going to be called when a URL matches the patterns defined previously. With the exception of vote, they are straightforward, and follow the same pattern: they search some data (using the Django ORM and helper functions such as get_object_or_404 which, even if you aren't familiar with them, it's easy to intuitively imagine what they do), and then end up calling render_to_response, passing the path of a template and a dictionary with the data passed to the template.

■ **Note** The three trivial views described here represent cases so common in web development that Django provides an abstraction to implement them with even less code. The abstraction is called "Generic Views," and you can learn about them on http://docs.djangoproject.com/en/1.1/ref/generic-views/, as well as in the Django tutorial at http://docs.djangoproject.com/en/1.1/intro/tutorial04/#use-generic-views-less-code-is-better.

The vote view is a bit more involved, and it ought to be, because it is the one doing interesting things, namely, registering a vote. It has two paths: one for the exceptional case, in which the user has not selected any choice, and one in which the user did select one. See how in the first case the view ends up rendering the same template which is rendered by the detail view: polls/detail.html; but we pass an extra variable to the template to display the error message so the user can know why he is still viewing the same page. In case the user selected a choice, we increment the votes and *redirect* the user to the results view.

We could have archived the redirection by just calling the view (something like return results(request, poll.id)) but, as the comments say, it is good practice to do an *actual* HTTP redirect after POST submissions to avoid problems with the browser back button (or the refresh button). Because the view code doesn't know to what URLs they are mapped (as this left to chance when you reuse the app), the reverse function gives you the URL for a given view and parameters.

Before taking a look at templates, we should quickly make a mental note about them. The Django template language is pretty simple and intentionally *not* as powerful as a programming language. You can't execute arbitrary Python code, nor call any function. It is designed this way to keep templates simple and web-designer-friendly. The main features of the template language are expressions, delimited by double braces ({{ and }}), and directives (called "template tags"), delimited by braces and the percent character ({% and %}). Expressions can contain dots that work for accessing Python attributes and also dictionary items (so you write {{ foo.bar }} even if in Python you would write foo['bar']), and also pipes (|) to apply filters to the expressions (like, for example, cut a paragraph on the first five words: {{ comment.text|truncatewords:5 }}). And that's pretty much it. You see how obvious they are on the following templates, but we'll give a bit of explanation when introducing some non obvious template tags.

Now it's time to see the templates for our views. You can infer by reading the views code we just wrote that we need three templates: polls/index.html, polls/detail.html, and polls/results.html. We will create the templates subdirectory inside the polls app, and then create the templates under it. Listing 14-17 shows is the content of pollsite/polls/templates/polls/index.html/.

Listing 14-17. Index File for Polls App Containing Template

```
{% if latest_poll_list %}
<ul>
  {% for poll in latest_poll_list %}
  <li><a href="{{ poll.id }}/">{{ poll.question }}</a></li>
  {% endfor %}
</ul>
{% else %}
<p>No polls are available.</p>
{% endif %}
```

Pretty simple, as you can see. Let's move to pollsite/polls/templates/polls/detail.html (Listing 14-18).

Listing 14-18. The Poll Template

```
<h1>{{ poll.question }}</h1>

{% if error_message %}<p><strong>{{ error_message }}</strong></p>{% endif %}

<form action="./vote/" method="post">
{% for choice in poll.choice_set.all %}
    <input type="radio" name="choice" id="choice{{ forloop.counter }}"
value="{    { choice.id }}" />
    <label for="choice{{ forloop.counter }}">{{ choice.choice }}</label><br />
{% endfor %}
<input type="submit" value="Vote" />
</form>
```

One perhaps surprising construct in this template is the {{ forloop.counter }} expression, which simply exposes the internal counter to the surrounding {% for %} loop.

Also note that the {% if %} template tag will evaluate an expression that is not defined to false, as will be the case with error_message when this template is called from the detail view.

Finally, Listing 14-19 is pollsite/polls/templates/polls/results.html.

Listing 14-19. The Results Template Code

```
<h1>{{ poll.question }}</h1>

<ul>
{% for choice in poll.choice_set.all %}
    <li>{{ choice.choice }} -- {{ choice.votes }}
    vote{{ choice.votes|pluralize }}</li>
{% endfor %}
</ul>
```

In this template you can see the use of a filter in the expression {{ choice.votes|pluralize }}. It will output an "s" if the number of votes is greater than 1, and nothing otherwise. To learn more about the template tags and filters available by default in Django, see http://docs.djangoproject.com/en/1.1/ref/templates/builtins/. And to find out how to create new filters and template tags, see http://docs.djangoproject.com/en/1.1/ref/templates/api/.

At this point we have a fully working poll site. It's not pretty, and can use a lot of polishing. But it works! Try it by navigating to http://localhost:8000/polls/.

Reusing Templates Without "include": Template Inheritance

Like many other template languages, Django also has an "include" directive. But its use is very rare, because there is a better solution for reusing templates: inheritance.

It works just like class inheritance. You define a base template, with many "blocks." Each block has a name. Then other templates can inherit from the base template and override or extend the blocks. You are free to build inheritance chains of any length you want, just like with class hierarchies.

You may have noted that our templates weren't producing valid HTML, but only fragments. It was convenient, to focus on the important parts of the templates, of course. But it also happens that with very minor modifications they will generate complete, pretty HTML pages. As you have probably guessed by now, they will extend from a site-wide base template.

Because we're not exactly good with web design, we will take a ready-made template from http://www.freecsstemplates.org/. In particular, we will modify this template: http://www.freecsstemplates.org/preview/exposure/.

Note that the base template is going to be site-wide, so it belongs to the project, not to an app. We will create a templates subdirectory under the *project* directory. Listing 14-20 is the content for pollsite/templates/base.html.

Listing 14-20. The Site-wide Template

```
<!DOCTYPE html PUBLIC "-//W3C//DTD XHTML 1.0 Strict//EN"
"http://www.w3.org/TR/    xhtml1/DTD/xhtml1-strict.dtd">
<html xmlns="http://www.w3.org/1999/xhtml">
  <head>
    <meta http-equiv="content-type" content="text/html; charset=utf-8" />
    <title>Polls</title>
    <link rel="alternate" type="application/rss+xml"
         title="RSS Feed"  href="/feeds/polls/" />
    <style>
      /* Irrelevant CSS code, see book sources if you are interested */
    </style>
  </head>
  <body>
    <!-- start header -->
    <div id="header">
      <div id="logo">
        <h1><a href="/polls/">Polls</a></h1>
        <p>an example for the Jython book</a></p>
      </div>
      <div id="menu">
        <ul>
          <li><a href="/polls/">Home</a></li>
          <li><a href="/contact/">Contact Us</a></li>
          <li><a href="/admin/">Admin</a></li>
        </ul>
      </div>
    </div>
```

```
<!-- end header -->
<!-- start page -->
    <div id="page">
    <!-- start content -->
      <div id="content">
        {% block content %} {% endblock %}
      </div>
    <!-- end content -->
        <br style="clear: both;" />
    </div>
<!-- end page -->
<!-- start footer -->
    <div id="footer">
        <p> <a href="/feeds/polls/">Subscribe to RSS Feed</a> </p>
        <p class="legal">
          &copy;2009 Apress. All Rights Reserved.
            &bull;  
          Design by
          <a href="http://www.freecsstemplates.org/">Free CSS Templates</a>
            &bull;  
          Icons by <a href="http://famfamfam.com/">FAMFAMFAM</a>. </p>
    </div>
<!-- end footer -->
  </body>
</html>
```

As you can see, the template declares only one block, named "content" (near the end of the template before the footer). You can define as many blocks as you want, but to keep things simple we will do only one.

Now, to let Django find this template we need to tweak the settings. Edit pollsite/settings.py and locate the TEMPLATE_DIRS section. Replace it with the Listing 14-21.

Listing 14-21. Editing Setting.py

```
import os
TEMPLATE_DIRS = (
    os.path.dirname(__file__) + '/templates',
    # Put strings here, like "/home/html/django_templates" or
    # "C:/www/django/templates".
    # Always use forward slashes, even on Windows.
    # Don't forget to use absolute paths, not relative paths.
)
```

That's a trick to avoid hardcoding the project root directory. The trick may not work in all situations, but it will work for us. Now that we have the base.html template in place, we will inherit from it in pollsite/polls/templates/polls/index.html. See Listing 14-22.

Listing 14-22. Inheriting from Base.html

```
{% extends 'base.html' %}
{% block content %}
```

```
{% if latest_poll_list %}
<ul>
  {% for poll in latest_poll_list %}
  <li><a href="{{ poll.id }}/">{{ poll.question }}</a></li>
  {% endfor %}
</ul>
{% else %}
<p>No polls are available.</p>
{% endif %}
{% endblock %}
```

As you can see, the changes are limited to the addition of the two first lines and the last one. The practical implication is that the template is overriding the "content" block and inheriting all the rest. Do the same with the other two templates of the poll app and test the application again, visiting http://localhost:8000/polls/. It will look as shown on Figure 14-5.

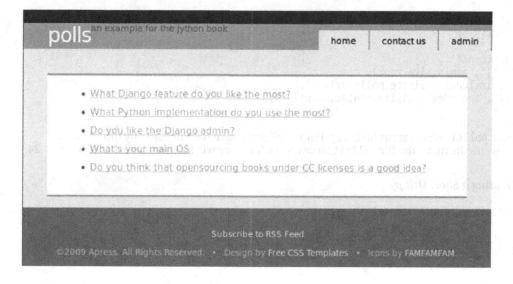

Figure 14-5. The poll site after applying a template

At this point we could consider our sample web application to be complete. But we want to highlight some other features included in Django that can help you to develop your web apps (just like the admin). To showcase them we will add the following features to our site:

1. A contact form (note that the link is already included in our common base template)

2. A RSS feed for the latest polls (also note the link was already added on the footer)

3. User Comments on polls

Forms

Django features some help to deal with HTML forms, which are always a bit tiresome. We will use this help to implement the "contact us" feature. Because it sounds like a common feature that could be reused on in the future, we will create a new app for it. Move to the project directory and run:

```
$ jython manage.py startapp contactus
```

Remember to add an entry for this app on pollsite/settings.py under the INSTALLED_APPS list as 'pollsite.contactus'.

Then we will delegate URL matching the /contact/ pattern to the app, by modifying pollsite/urls.py and adding one line for it (see Listing 14-23).

Listing 14-23. Modifying Urls.py Again

```
from django.conf.urls.defaults import *

from django.contrib import admin
admin.autodiscover()

urlpatterns = patterns('',
    (r'^admin/(.*)', admin.site.root),
    (r'^polls/', include('pollsite.polls.urls')),
    (r'^contact/', include('pollsite.contactus.urls')),
)
```

We now create pollsite/contactus/urls.py. For simplicity's sake we will use only one view to display and process the form. So the file pollsite/contactus/urls.py will simply consist of Listing 14-24.

Listing 14-24. Creating a Short Urls.py

```
from django.conf.urls.defaults import *

urlpatterns = patterns('pollsite.contactus.views',
    (r'^$', 'index'),
)
```

And the content of pollsite/contactus/views.py is shown in Listing 14-25.

Listing 14-25. Adding to Views.py

```
from django.shortcuts import render_to_response
from django.core.mail import mail_admins
from django import forms

class ContactForm(forms.Form):
    name = forms.CharField(max_length=200)
    email = forms.EmailField()
    title = forms.CharField(max_length=200)
    text = forms.CharField(widget=forms.Textarea)
```

```
def index(request):
    if request.method == 'POST':
        form = ContactForm(request.POST)
        if form.is_valid():
            mail_admins(
                "Contact Form: %s" % form.title,
                "%s <%s> Said: %s" % (form.name, form.email, form.text))
            return render_to_response("contactus/success.html")
    else:
        form = ContactForm()
    return render_to_response("contactus/form.html", {'form': form})
```

The important bit here is the ContactForm class in which the form is declaratively defined and which encapsulates the validation logic. We just call the is_valid() method on our view to invoke that logic and act accordingly. See http://docs.djangoproject.com/en/1.1/topics/email/#mail-admins to learn about the main_admins function included on Django and how to adjust the project settings to make it work.

Forms also provide quick ways to render them in templates. We will try that now. Listing 14-26 is the code for pollsite/contactus/templates/contactus/form.html, which is the template used inside the view we just wrote.

Listing 14-26. A Form Rendered in a Template

```
{% extends "base.html" %}
{% block content %}
<form action="." method="POST">
<table>
{{ form.as_table }}
</table>
<input type="submit" value="Send Message" >
</form>
{% endblock %}
```

Here we take advantage of the as_table() method of Django forms, which also takes care of rendering validation errors. Django forms also provide other convenience functions to render forms, but if none of them suits your need, you can always render the form in custom ways. See http://docs.djangoproject.com/en/1.1/topics/forms/ for details on form handling.

Before testing this contact form, we need to write the template pollsite/contactus/templates/contactus/success.html, which is also used from pollsite.contactus.views.index. This template is quite simple (see Listing 14-27).

Listing 14-27. Contact Form Template

```
{% extends "base.html" %}
{% block content %}
<h1> Send us a message </h1>
<p><b>Message received, thanks for your feedback!</p>
{% endblock %}
```

And we are done. Test it by navigation to http://localhost:8000/contact/. Try submitting the form without data, or with erroneous data (for example with an invalid email address). You will get something like what's shown in Figure 14-6. Without needing to write much code you get a lot of validation data basically for free. Of course the forms framework is extensible, so you can create custom form field types with their own validation or rendering code. Again, we refer you to http://docs.djangoproject.com/en/1.1/topics/forms/ for detailed information.

Figure 14-6. Django form validation in action

Feeds

It's time to implement the feed we are offering on the link right before the footer. It surely won't surprise you to know that Django includes ways to state your feeds declaratively and write them very quickly. Let's start by modifying pollsite/urls.py to leave it as shown in Listing 14-28.

Listing 14-28. Modifying Urls.py

```
from django.conf.urls.defaults import *
from pollsite.polls.feeds import PollFeed

from django.contrib import admin
admin.autodiscover()

urlpatterns = patterns('',
    (r'^admin/(.*)', admin.site.root),
    (r'^polls/', include('pollsite.polls.urls')),
    (r'^contact/', include('pollsite.contactus.urls')),
    (r'^feeds/(?P<url>.*)/$', 'django.contrib.syndication.views.feed',
     {'feed_dict': {'polls': PollFeed}}),
)
```

We are changing the import of the PollFeed class (which we haven't written yet) and we also need to change the last pattern for URLs starting with /feeds/, because it will map to a built-in view, which takes a dictionary with feeds as arguments. In our case, PollFeed is the only one. Writing this class, which will describe the feed, is very easy. Let's create the file pollsite/polls/feeds.py and put the following code on it. See Listing 14-29.

Listing 14-29. Creating Feeds.py

```python
from django.contrib.syndication.feeds import Feed
from django.core.urlresolvers import reverse
from pollsite.polls.models import Poll

class PollFeed(Feed):
    title = "Polls"
    link = "/polls"
    description = "Latest Polls"

    def items(self):
        return Poll.objects.all().order_by('-pub_date')

    def item_link(self, poll):
        return reverse('pollsite.polls.views.detail', args=(poll.id,))

    def item_pubdate(self, poll):
        return poll.pub_date
```

And we are almost ready. When a request for the URL /feeds/polls/ is received by Django, it will use this feed description to build all the XML data. The missing part is how the content of polls will be displayed in the feeds. To do this, we need to create another template. By convention, it has to be named feeds/<feed_name>_description.html, where <feed_name> is what we specified as the key on the feed_dict in pollsite/urls.py. Thus we create the file pollsite/polls/templates/feeds/polls_description.html with the very simple content shown in Listing 14-30.

Listing 14-30. Polls Display Description

```html
<ul>
    {% for choice in obj.choice_set.all %}
    <li>{{ choice.choice }}</li>
    {% endfor %}
</ul>
```

The idea is simple: Django passes each object returned by PollFeed.items() to this template, in which it takes the name obj. You then generate an HTML fragment which will be embedded on the feed result.

And that's all. Test it by pointing your browser to http://localhost:8000/feeds/polls/, or by subscribing to that URL with your preferred feed reader. Opera, for example, displays the feed as shown by Figure 14-7.

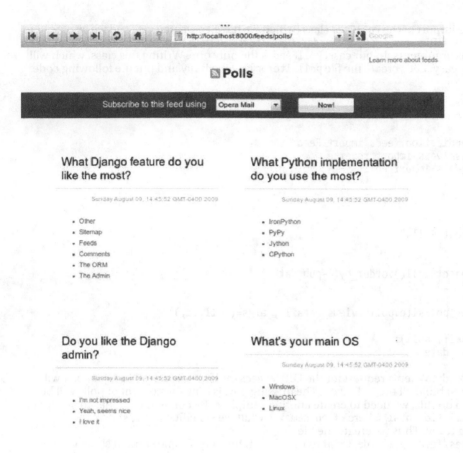

Figure 14-7. Poll feed in opera browser

Comments

Because comments are a common feature of current web sites, Django includes a mini-framework to make the incorporation of comments in any project or app fairly simple. We will show you how to use it in our project. First, add a new URL pattern for the Django comments app, so the pollsite/urls.py file will look like Listing 14-31.

Listing 14-31. Adding a New URL Pattern to Urls.py

```
from django.conf.urls.defaults import *
from pollsite.polls.feeds import PollFeed

from django.contrib import admin
admin.autodiscover()

urlpatterns = patterns('',
    (r'^admin/(.*)', admin.site.root),
```

```
    (r'^polls/', include('pollsite.polls.urls')),
    (r'^contact/', include('pollsite.contactus.urls')),
    (r'^feeds/(?P<url>.*)/$', 'django.contrib.syndication.views.feed',
     {'feed_dict': {'polls': PollFeed}}),
    (r'^comments/', include('django.contrib.comments.urls')),
)
```

Then add `'django.contrib.comments'` to the `INSTALLED_APPS` on `pollsite/settings.py`. After that, we will let Django create the necessary tables by running:

```
$ jython manage.py syncdb
```

The comments will be added to the poll page, so we must edit `pollsite/polls/templates/polls/detail.html`. We will add the following code just before the `{% endblock %}` line, which currently is the last line of the file (see Listing 14-32).

Listing 14-32. Adding Comments to Details.html

```
{% load comments %}
{% get_comment_list for poll as comments %}
{% get_comment_count for poll as comments_count %}

{% if comments %}
<p>{{ comments_count }} comments:</p>
{% for comment in comments %}
<div class="comment">
  <div class="title">
    <p><small>
    Posted by <a href="{{ comment.user_url }}">{{ comment.user_name }}</a>,
        {{ comment.submit_date|timesince }} ago:
    </small></p>
  </div>
  <div class="entry">
    <p>
    {{ comment.comment }}
    </p>
  </div>
</div>

{% endfor %}

{% else %}
<p>No comments yet.</p>
{% endif %}

<h2>Left your comment:</h2>
{% render_comment_form for poll %}
```

Basically, we are importing the "comments" template tag library (by doing `{% load comments %}`) and then we just use it. It supports binding comments to *any database object,* so we don't need to do anything special to make it work. Figure 14-8 shows what we get in exchange for that short snippet of code.

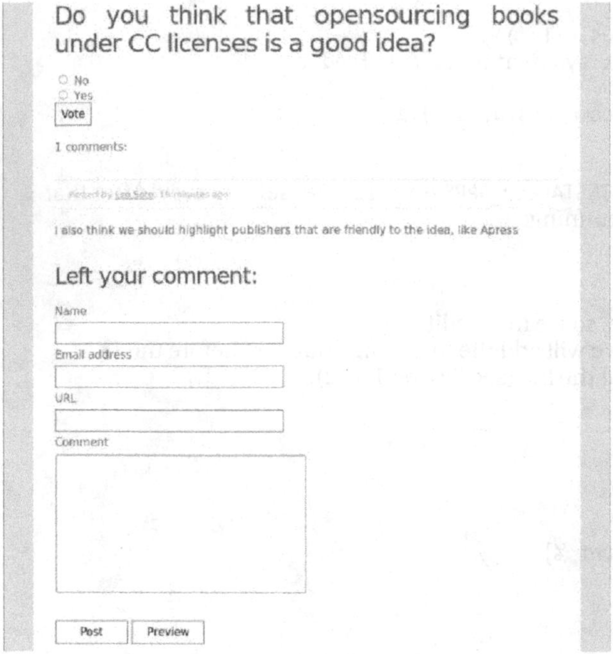

Figure 14-8. Comments powered poll

If you try the application by yourself you will note that after submitting a comment you get an ugly page showing the success message. Or if you don't enter all the data, you get an ugly error form. That's because we are using the comments templates. A quick and effective fix for that is creating the file `pollsite/templates/comments/base.html` with the following content:

```
{% extends 'base.html' %}
```

Yeah, it's only one line! It shows the power of template inheritance: all we needed to do was to change the base template of the comments framework to inherit from our global base template.

And More...

At this point we hope you have learned to appreciate Django's strengths. It's a very good web framework in itself, but it also takes the "batteries included" philosophy, and comes with solutions for many common problems in web development. This usually speeds up a lot the process of creating a new web site. And we didn't touch other features Django provides out of the box like user authentication or generic views.

But this book is about *Jython,* and we will use the rest of this chapter to show the interesting possibilities that appear when you run Django *on Jython.* If you want to learn more about Django itself, we recommend (again) the excellent official documentation available on http://docs.djangoproject.com/.

J2EE Deployment and Integration

Although you *could* deploy your application using Django's built in development server, it's a terrible idea. The development server isn't designed to operate under heavy load and this is really a job that is more suited to a proper application server. We're going to install Glassfish v2.1—an opensource highly performant JavaEE 5 application server from Sun Microsystems—and show deployment onto it.

Let's install Glassfish now; obtain the release from:

```
https://glassfish.dev.java.net/public/downloadsindex.html
```

At the time of this writing, Glassfish v3.0 is being prepared for release and it will support Django and Jython out of the box, but we'll stick to the stable release as its documentation is complete and its stability has been well established. Download the v2.1 release (currently v2.1-b60e). We strongly suggest you use JDK6 to do your deployment.

Once you have the installation JAR file, you can install it by issuing:

```
% java -Xmx256m -jar glassfish-installer-v2.1-b60e-windows.jar
```

If your glassfish installer file has a different name, just use that instead of the filename listed in the above example. Be careful where you invoke this command though—Glassfish will unpack the application server into a subdirectory "glassfish" in the directory that you start the installer.

One step that tripped us up during our impatient installation of Glassfish is that you actually need to invoke ant to complete the installation. On Unix and its derivatives you need to invoke:

```
% chmod -R +x lib/ant/bin
% lib/ant/bin/ant -f setup.xml
```

or for Windows:

```
% lib\ant\bin\ant -f setup.xml
```

This will complete the setup .You'll find a bin directory with "asadmin" or "asadmin.bat," which will indicate that the application server has been installed. You can start the server up by invoking:

```
% bin/asadmin start-domain -v
```

On Windows, this will start the server in the foreground. The process will not turn into daemon and run in the background. On Unix operating systems, the process will automatically become a daemon and run in the background. In either case, once the server is up and running, you will be able to reach the web administration screen through a browser by going to http://localhost:5000/. The default login is "admin" and the password is "adminadmin."

Currently, Django on Jython only supports the PostgreSQL, Oracle, and MySQL databases officially, but there is also a SQLite3 backend. Let's get the PostgreSQL backend working—you will need to obtain the PostgreSQL JDBC driver from http://jdbc.postgresql.org.

At the time of this writing, the latest version was in postgresql-8.4-701.jdbc4.jar. Copy that jar file into your GLASSFISH_HOME/domains/domain/domain1/lib directory. This will enable all your applications hosted in your appserver to use the same JDBC driver.

You should now have a GLASSFISH_HOME/domains/domain1/lib directory with the contents shown in Listing 14-33.

Listing 14-33. Lib Directory Contents

```
applibs/
classes/
databases/
ext/
postgresql-8.3-604.jdbc4.jar
```

You will need to stop and start the application server to let those libraries load up.

```
% bin/asadmin stop-domain
% bin/asadmin start-domain -v
```

Deploying Your First Application

Django on Jython includes a built-in command to support the creation of WAR files, but first, you will need to do a little bit of configuration to make everything run smoothly. First we'll set up a simple Django application that has the administration application enabled so that we have some models to play with. Create a project called "hello" and make sure you add "django.contrib.admin" and "doj" applications to the INSTALLED_APPS.

Now enable the user admin by editing urls.py and uncomment the admin lines. Your urls.py should now look something like Listing 14-34.

Listing 14-34. Enabling User Admin in Urls.py

```
from django.conf.urls.defaults import *
from django.contrib import admin
admin.autodiscover()
urlpatterns = patterns('',
    (r'^admin/(.*)', admin.site.root),
)
```

Disabling PostgreSQL Logins

The first thing we inevitably do on a development machine with PostgreSQL is disable authentication checks to the database. The fastest way to do this is to enable only local connections to the database by editing the pg_hba.conf file. For PostgreSQL 8.3, this file is typically located in c:\PostgreSQL8.3\data\pg_hba.conf and on UNIXes it is typically located in /etc/PostgreSQL/8.3/data/pg_hba.conf

At the bottom of the file, you'll find connection configuration information. Comment out all the lines and enable trusted connections from localhost. Your edited configuration should look something like Listing 14-35.

Listing 14-35. PostgreSQL Authentication Configuration

```
# TYPE  DATABASE    USER      CIDR-ADDRESS        METHOD
host    all         all       127.0.0.1/32        trust
```

This will let any username recognized by PostgreSQL connect to the database. You may need to create a PostgreSQL user with the "createuser" command. Consult your PostgreSQL documentation for more details. You do not want to do this for a public facing production server. You should consult the

PostgreSQL documentation for instructions for more suitable settings. After you've edited the connection configuration, you will need to restart the PostgreSQL server.

Create your PostgreSQL database using the createdb command now.

```
> createdb demodb
```

Setting up the database is straightforward; you just enable the pgsql backend from Django on Jython. Note that the backend will expect a username and password pair even though we've disabled them in PostgreSQL. You can populate anything you want for the DATABASE_NAME and DATABASE_USER settings. The database section of your settings module should now look something like Listing 14-36.

Listing 14-36. Database Section of Settings Module for PostgreSQL

```
DATABASE_ENGINE = 'doj.backends.zxjdbc.postgresql'
DATABASE_NAME = 'demodb'
DATABASE_USER = 'ngvictor'
DATABASE_PASSWORD = 'nosecrets'
```

Initialize your database now.

```
> jython manage.py syncdb
Creating table django_admin_log
Creating table auth_permission
Creating table auth_group
Creating table auth_user
Creating table auth_message
Creating table django_content_type
Creating table django_session
Creating table django_site
You just installed Django's auth system, which means you don't have any superusers defined.
Would you like to create one now? (yes/no): yes
Username: admin
E-mail address: admin@abc.com
Warning: Problem with getpass. Passwords may be echoed.
Password: admin
Warning: Problem with getpass. Passwords may be echoed.
Password (again): admin
Superuser created successfully.
Installing index for admin.
LogEntry model
Installing index for auth.Permission model
Installing index for auth.Message model
```

All of this should be review so far, now we're going to take the application and deploy it into the running Glassfish server. This is actually the easy part. Django on Jython comes with a custom "war" command that builds a self-contained file, which you can use to deploy into any Java servlet container.

A Note About WAR Files

For JavaEE servers, a common way to deploy your applications is to deploy a "WAR" file. This is just a fancy name for a zip file that contains your application and any dependencies it requires that the application server has not made available as a shared resource. This is a robust way of making sure that you minimize the impact of versioning changes of libraries if you want to deploy multiple applications in your app server.

Consider your Django applications over time. You will undoubtedly upgrade your version of Django, and you may upgrade the version of your database drivers. You may even decide to upgrade the version of the Jython language you wish to deploy on. These choices are ultimately up to you if you bundle all your dependencies in your WAR file. By bundling up all your dependencies into your WAR file, you can ensure that your app will "just work" when you go to deploy it. The server will automatically partition each application into its own space with concurrently running versions of the same code.

To enable the war command, add the "doj" application to your settings in the INSTALLED_APPS list. Next, you will need to enable your site's media directory and a context relative root for your media. Edit your settings.py module so that that your media files are properly configured to be served. The war command will automatically configure your media files so that they are served using a static file servlet and the URLs will be remapped to be after the context root.

Edit your settings module and configure the MEDIA_ROOT and MEDIA_URL lines.

```
MEDIA_ROOT = 'c:\dev\hello\media_root' MEDIA_URL = '/site_media/'
```

Now you will need to create the media_root subdirectory under your "hello" project and drop in a sample file so you can verify that static content serving is working. Place a file "sample.html" into your media_root directory. Put whatever contents you want into it: we're just using this to ensure that static files are properly served.

In English, that means when the previous configuration is used, "hello" will deployed into your servlet container and the container will assign some URL path to be the "context root" in Glassfish's case. This means your app will live in "http://localhost:8000/hello/". The site_media directory will be visible at "http://localhost:8000/hello/site_media". DOJ will automatically set the static content to be served by Glassfish's fileservlet, which is already highly performant. There is no need to setup a separate static file server for most deployments.

Build your WAR file now using the standard manage.py script, and deploy using the asadmin tool. See Listing 14-37.

Listing 14-37. Deploying a WAR File on Windows

```
c:\dev\hello>jython manage.py war

Assembling WAR on c:\docume~1\ngvictor\locals~1\temp\tmp1-_snn\hello

Copying WAR skeleton...
Copying jython.jar...
Copying Lib...
Copying django...
Copying media...
Copying hello...
Copying site_media...
Copying doj...
Building WAR on C:\dev\hello.war...
Cleaning c:\docume~1\ngvictor\locals~1\temp\tmp1-_snn...

Finished.

Now you can copy C:\dev\hello.war to whatever location your application server wants it.

C:\dev\hello>cd \glassfish
```

```
C:\glassfish>bin\asadmin.bat deploy hello.war
Command deploy executed successfully.

C:\glassfish>
```

That's it. You should now be able to see your application running on:

`http://localhost:8080/hello/`

The administration screen should also be visible at:

`http://localhost:8080/hello/admin/`

You can verify that your static media is being served correctly by going to:

`http://localhost:8080/hello/site_media/sample.html`

That's it. Your basic deployment to a servlet container is now working.

Extended Installation

The war command in doj provides extra options for you to specify extra JAR files to include with your application, and which can bring down the size of your WAR file. By default, the "war" command will bundle the following items:

- Jython
- Django and its administration media files
- your project and media files
- all of your libraries in site-packages

You can specialize your WAR file to include specific JAR files and you can instruct doj to assemble a WAR file with just the python packages that you require. The options for "manage.py war" are "--include-py-packages" and "--include-jar-libs." The basic usage is straightforward: simply pass in the location of your custom python packages and the JAR files to these two arguments and distutils will automatically decompress the contents of those compressed volumes and then recompress them into your WAR file.

To bundle up JAR files, you will need to specify a list of files to "--include-java-libs."

The following example bundles the jTDS JAR file and a regular python module called urllib3 with our WAR file.:

```
$ jython manage.py war --include-java-libs=$HOME/downloads/jtds-1.2.2.jar \
       --include-py-package=$HOME/PYTHON_ENV/lib/python2.5/site-packages/urllib3
```

You can have multiple JAR files or Python packages listed, but you must delimit them with your operating system's path separator. For Unix systems, this means ":" and for Windows it is ";".

Eggs can also be installed using "--include-py-path-entries" using the egg filename. For example

```
$ jython manage.py war --include-py-path-entries=$HOME/PYTHON_ENV/lib/python2.5/site-
packages/urllib3
```

311

Connection Pooling With JavaEE

Whenever your web application goes to fetch data from the database, the data has to come back over a database connection. Some databases, such as MySQL, have "cheap" database connections, but for many databases creating and releasing connections is quite expensive. Under high-load conditions, opening and closing database connections on every request can quickly consume too many file handles, and your application will crash.

The general solution to this is to employ database connection pooling. While your application will continue to create new connections and close them off, a connection pool will manage your database connections from a reusable set. When you go to close your connection, the connection pool will simply reclaim your connection for use at a later time. Using a pool means you can put an enforced upper limit restriction on the number of concurrent connections to the database. Having that upper limit means you can reason about how your application will perform when the upper limit of database connections is hit.

Although Django does not natively support database connection pools with CPython, you can enable them in the PostgreSQL driver for Django on Jython. Creating a connection pool that is visible to Django/Jython is a two-step process in Glassfish. First, we'll need to create a JDBC connection pool, and then we'll need to bind a JNDI name to that pool. In a JavaEE container, JNDI, the Java Naming and Directory Interface, is a registry of names bound to objects. It's really best thought of as a hashtable that typically abstracts a factory that emits objects.

In the case of database connections, JNDI abstracts a ConnectionFactory, which provides proxy objects that behave like database connections. These proxies automatically manage all the pooling behavior for us. Let's see this in practice now.

First we'll need to create a JDBC ConnectionFactory. Go to the administration screen of Glassfish and go down to Resources/JDBC/JDBC Resources/Connection Pools. From there you can click on the "New" button and start to configure your pool.

Set the name to "pgpool-demo", the resource type should be "javax.sql.ConnectionPoolDataSource" and the Database Vendor should be PostgreSQL. Your completed form should resemble that which is shown in Figure 14-9. Click "Next."

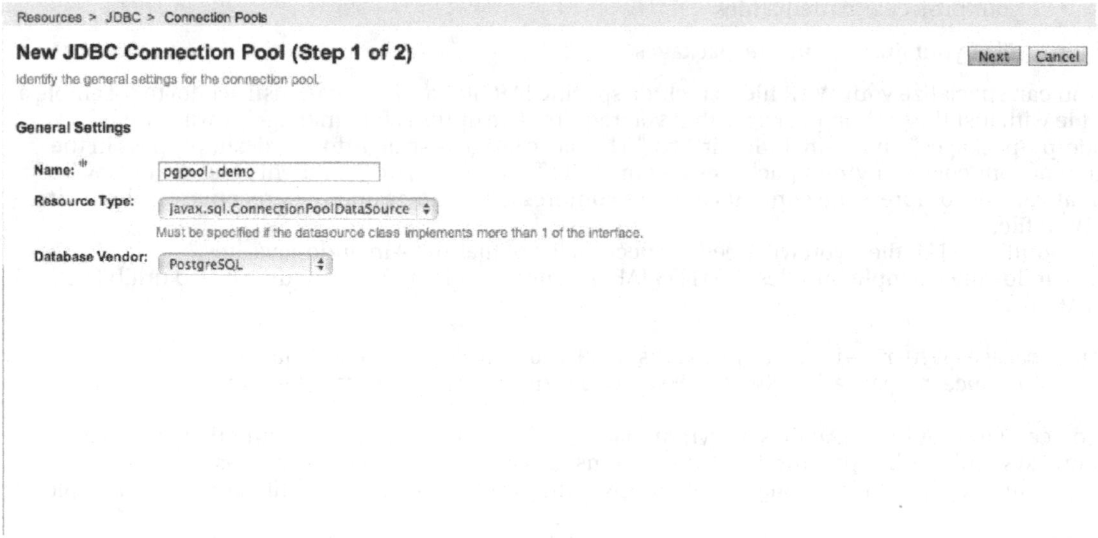

Figure 14-9. Adding a Glassfish JDBC Connection Pool

Later, you'll see a section with "Additional Properties." You'll need to set four parameters to make sure the connection is working, assuming that the database is configured for a username/password of ngvictor/nosecrets. Table 14-1 shows what you need to connect to your database.

Table 14-1. Database Connection Pool Properties

Name	Value
databaseName	demodb
serverName	localhost
Password	nosecrets
User	ngvictor

You can safely delete all the other properties—they're not needed. After your properties resemble those shown in Figure 14-10, click "Finish."

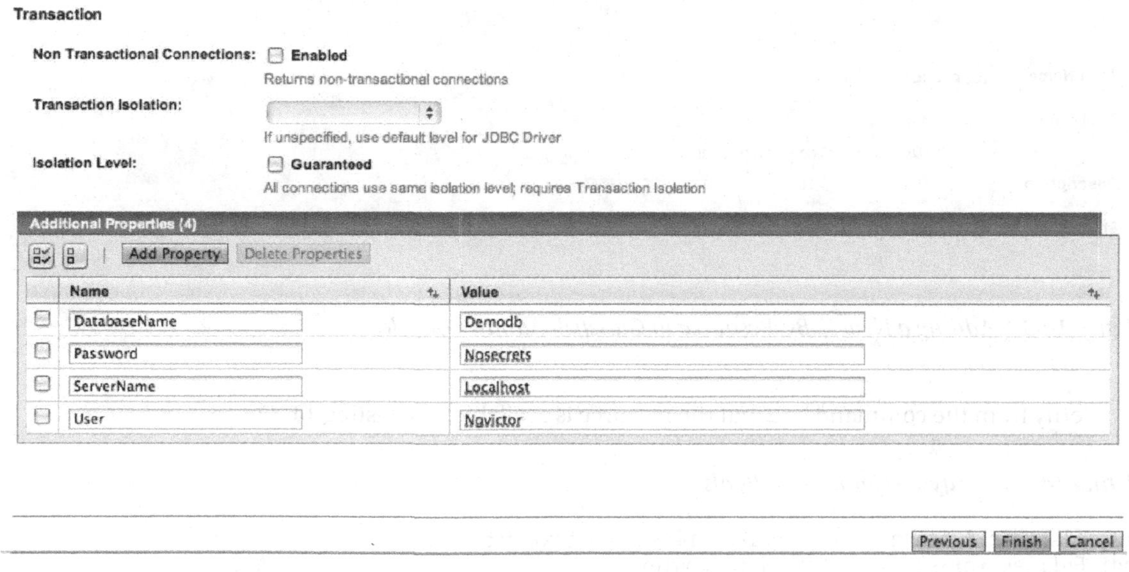

Figure 14-10. Connection Pool Properties in Glassfish Admin Console

Your pool will now be visible on the left-hand tree control in the Connection Pools list. Select it and try pinging it to make sure it's working. If all is well, Glassfish will show you a successful Ping message as seen in Figure 14-11.

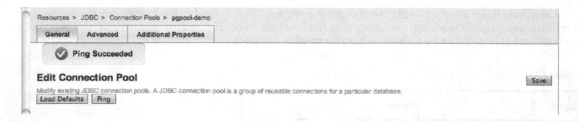

Figure 14-11. Successful Connection Pool Test

We now need to bind a JNDI name to the connection factory to provide a mechanism for Jython to see the pool. Go to the JDBC Resources and click "New." Use the JNDI name: "jdbc/pgpool-demo," and select the "pgpool-demo" as your pool name. Your form should now resemble that shown in Figure 14-12, and you can now hit "OK."

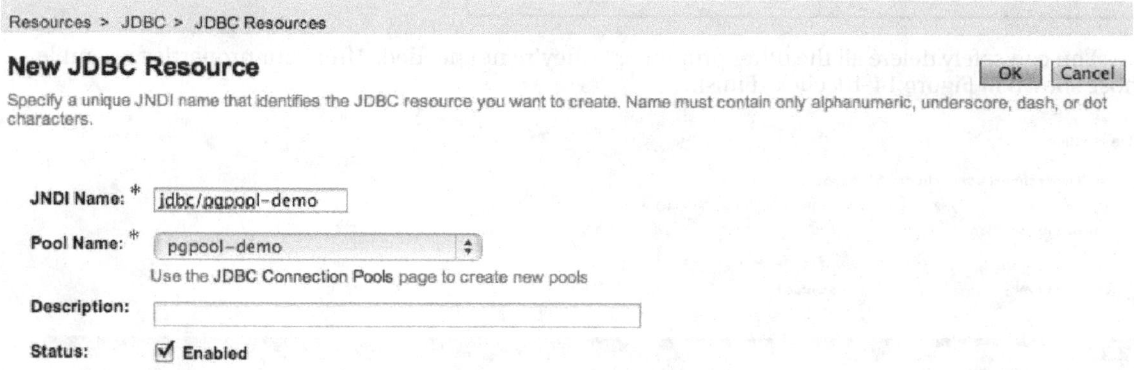

Figure 14-12. Adding a New JDBC Resource in Glassfish Admin Console

Verify from the command line that the resource is available. See Listing 14-38.

Listing 14-38. Verifying Connection Pools

```
glassfish\bin $ asadmin list-jndi-entries --context jdbc
Jndi Entries for server within jdbc context:
pgpool-demo__pm: javax.naming.Reference
__TimerPool: javax.naming.Reference
__TimerPool__pm: javax.naming.Reference
pgpool-demo: javax.naming.Reference
Command list-jndi-entries executed successfully.
```

Now, we need to enable the Django application to use the JNDI name based lookup if we are running in an application server, and fail back to regular database connection binding if JNDI can't be found. Edit your settings.py module and add an extra configuration to enable JNDI. See Listing 14-39.

Listing 14-39. Enabling JNDI in Settings.py

```
DATABASE_ENGINE = 'doj.backends.zxjdbc.postgresql'
DATABASE_NAME = 'demodb'
DATABASE_USER = 'ngvictor'
DATABASE_PASSWORD = 'nosecrets'
DATABASE_OPTIONS  = {'RAW_CONNECTION_FALLBACK': True, \
                     'JNDI_NAME': 'jdbc/pgpool-demo' }
```

Note that we're duplicating the configuration to connect to the database. This is because we want to be able to fall back to regular connection binding in the event that JNDI lookups fail. This makes our life easier when we're running in a testing or development environment.

That's it, you're finished configuring database connection pooling. That wasn't that bad now, was it?

Dealing With Long-running Tasks

When you're building a complex web application, you will inevitably end up having to deal with processes that need to be processed in the background. If you're building on top of CPython and Apache, you're out of luck here—there's no standard infrastructure available for you to handle these tasks. Luckily these services have had years of engineering work already done for you in the Java world. We'll take a look at two different strategies for dealing with long running tasks.

Thread Pools

The first strategy is to leverage managed thread pools in the JavaEE container. When your web application is running within Glassfish, each HTTP request is processed by the HTTP Service, which contains a threadpool. You can change the number of threads to affect the performance of the webserver. Glassfish will also let you create your own threadpools to execute arbitrary work units for you.

The basic API for threadpools is simple:

- WorkManager, which provides an abstracted interface to the thread pool.

- Work is an interface, which encapsulates your unit of work.

- WorkListener, which is an interface that lets you monitor the progress of your Work tasks.

First, we need to tell Glassfish to provision a threadpool for our use. In the Administration screen, go down to Configuration/Thread Pools. Click on "New" to create a new thread pool. Give your threadpool the name "backend-workers." Leave all the other settings as the default values and click "OK."

You've now got a thread pool that you can use. The threadpool exposes an interface where you can submit jobs to the pool and the pool will either execute the job synchronously within a thread, or you can schedule the job to run asynchronously. As long as your unit of work implements the javax.resource.spi.work.Work interface, the threadpool will happily run your code. A WorkUnit class may be as simple as Listing 14-40.

Listing 14-40. Implementing a WorkUnit Class

```
from javax.resource.spi.work import Work
```

```
class WorkUnit(Work):
    """
    This is an implementation of the Work interface.
    """
    def __init__(self, job_id):
        self.job_id = job_id

    def release(self):
        """
        This method is invoked by the threadpool to tell threads
        to abort the execution of a unit of work.
        """
        logger.warn("[%d] Glassfish asked the job to stop quickly" % self.job_id)

    def run(self):
        """
        This method is invoked by the threadpool when work is
        'running'
        """
        for i in range(20):
            logger.info("[%d] just doing some work" % self.job_id)
```

This WorkUnit class doesn't do anything very interesting, but it does illustrate the basic structure of what unit of work requires. We're just logging message to disk so that we can visually see the thread execute.

WorkManager implements several methods that can run your job and block until the threadpool completes your work, or it can run the job asynchronously. Generally, we prefer to run things asynchronously and simply check the status of the work over time. This lets me submit multiple jobs to the threadpool at once and check the status of each of the jobs.

To monitor the progress of work, we need to implement the WorkListener interface. This interface gives us notifications as a task progresses through the three phases of execution within the thread pool. Those states are:

- Accepted
- Started
- Completed

All jobs must go to either Completed or Rejected states. The simplest thing to do then is to simply build up lists capturing the events. When the length of the completed and the rejected lists together are the same as the number of jobs we submitted, we know that we are done. By using lists instead of simple counters, we can inspect the work objects in much more detail.

Listing 14-41 shows the code for our SimpleWorkListener.

Listing 14-41. Writing SimpleWorkListener Code

```
from javax.resource.spi.work import WorkListener
class SimpleWorkListener(WorkListener):
    """
    Just keep track of all work events as they come in
    """
```

```
def __init__(self):
    self.accepted = []
    self.completed = []
    self.rejected = []
    self.started = []

def workAccepted(self, work_event):
    self.accepted.append(work_event.getWork())
    logger.info("Work accepted %s" % str(work_event.getWork()))

def workCompleted(self, work_event):
    self.completed.append(work_event.getWork())
    logger.info("Work completed %s" % str(work_event.getWork()))

def workRejected(self, work_event):
    self.rejected.append(work_event.getWork())
    logger.info("Work rejected %s" % str(work_event.getWork()))

def workStarted(self, work_event):
    self.started.append(work_event.getWork())
    logger.info("Work started %s" % str(work_event.getWork()))
```

To access the threadpool, you simply need to know the name of the pool we want to access and schedule our jobs. Each time we schedule a unit of work, we need to tell the pool how long to wait until we timeout the job. We also need to provide a reference to the WorkListener object so that we can monitor the status of the jobs.

The code to do this is shown in Listing 14-42.

Listing 14-42. Dealing with the Threadpool

```
from com.sun.enterprise.connectors.work import CommonWorkManager
from javax.resource.spi.work import Work, WorkManager, WorkListener
wm = CommonWorkManager('backend-workers')
listener = SimpleWorkListener()
for i in range(5):
    work = WorkUnit(i)
    wm.scheduleWork(work, -1, None, listener)
```

You may notice that the scheduleWork method takes in a None constant in the third argument. This is the execution context—for our purposes, it's best to just ignore it and set it to None. The scheduleWork method will return immediately and the listener will get callback notifications as our work objects pass through. To verify that all our jobs have completed (or rejected), we simply need to check the listener's internal lists. See Listing 14-43.

Listing 14-43. Checking the Listener's Internal Lists

```
while len(listener.completed) + len(listener.rejected) < num_jobs:
    logger.info("Found %d jobs completed" % len(listener.completed))
    time.sleep(0.1)
```

That covers all the code you need to access thread pools and monitor the status of each unit of work. Ignoring the actual WorkUnit class, the actual code to manage the threadpool is about a dozen lines long.

■ **Note** Unfortunately, this API is not standard in the JavaEE 5 specification yet so the code listed here will only work in Glassfish. The API for parallel processing is being standardized for JavaEE 6, and until then you will need to know a little bit of the internals of your particular application server to get threadpools working. If you're working with Weblogic or Websphere, you will need to use the CommonJ APIs to access the threadpools, but the logic is largely the same.

Passing Messages Across Process Boundaries

While threadpools provide access to background job processing, sometimes it may be beneficial to have messages pass across process boundaries. Every week there seems to be a new Python package that tries to solve this problem, for Jython we are lucky enough to leverage Java's JMS. JMS specifies a message brokering technology where you may define publish/subscribe or point to point delivery of messages between different services. Messages are asynchronously sent to provide loose coupling and the broker deals with all manner of boring engineering details like delivery guarantees, security, durability of messages between server crashes and clustering.

Although you could use a hand rolled RESTful messaging implementation, using OpenMQ and JMS has many advantages.

- It's mature. Do you really think your messaging implementation handles all the corner cases? Server crashes? Network connectivity errors? Reliability guarantees? Clustering? Security? OpenMQ has almost 10 years of engineering behind it.

- The JMS standard is just that: standard. You gain the ability to send and receive messages between any JavaEE code.

- Interoperability. JMS isn't the only messaging broker in town. The Streaming Text Orientated Messaging Protocol (STOMP) is another standard that is popular amongst non-Java developers. You can turn a JMS broker into a STOMP broker using stompconnect. This means you can effectively pass messages between any messaging client and any messaging broker using any of a dozen different languages.

In JMS there are two types of message delivery mechanisms:

- Publish/Subscribe: This is for the times when we want to message one or more subscribers about events currently occurring. This is done through JMS "topics."

- Point to point messaging: These are single sender, single receiver message queues. Appropriately, JMS calls these "queues."

We need to provision a couple of objects in Glassfish to get JMS going. In a nutshell, we need to create a connection factory which clients will use to connect to the JMS broker. We'll create a publish/subscribe resource and a point to point messaging queue. In JMS terms, these are called "destinations". They can be thought of as postboxes that you send your mail to.

Go to the Glassfish administration screen and go to Resources/JMS Resources/Connection Factories. Create a new connection factory with the JNDI name "jms/MyConnectionFactory." Set the resource type to javax.jms.ConnectionFactory. Delete the username and password properties at the bottom of the screen and add a single property "imqDisableSetClientID" with a value of "false" as shown in Figure 14-13. Click "OK."

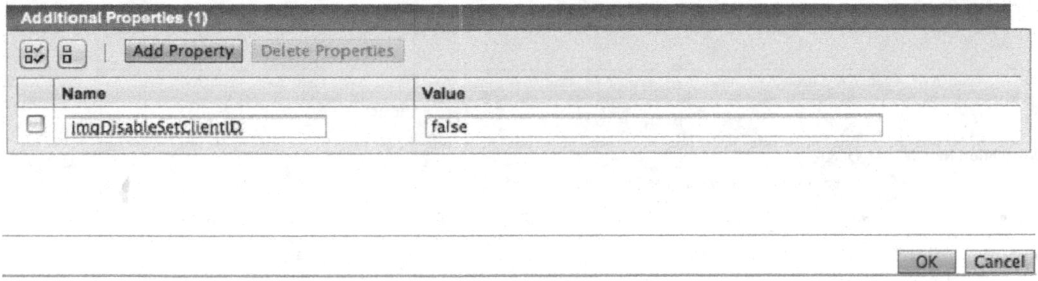

Figure 14-13. Connection Factory Properties in Glassfish Admin Console

By setting the imqDisableSetClientID to false, we are forcing clients to declare a username and password when they use the ConnectionFactory. OpenMQ uses the login to uniquely identify the clients of the JMS service so that it can properly enforce the delivery guarantees of the destination.

We now need to create the actual destinations—a topic for publish/subscribe and a queue for point to point messaging. Go to Resources/JMS Resources/Destination Resources and click "New". Set the JNDI name to "jms/MyTopic", the destination name to "MyTopic" and the Resource type to be "javax.jms.Topic" as shown in Figure 14-14. Click "OK" to save the topic.

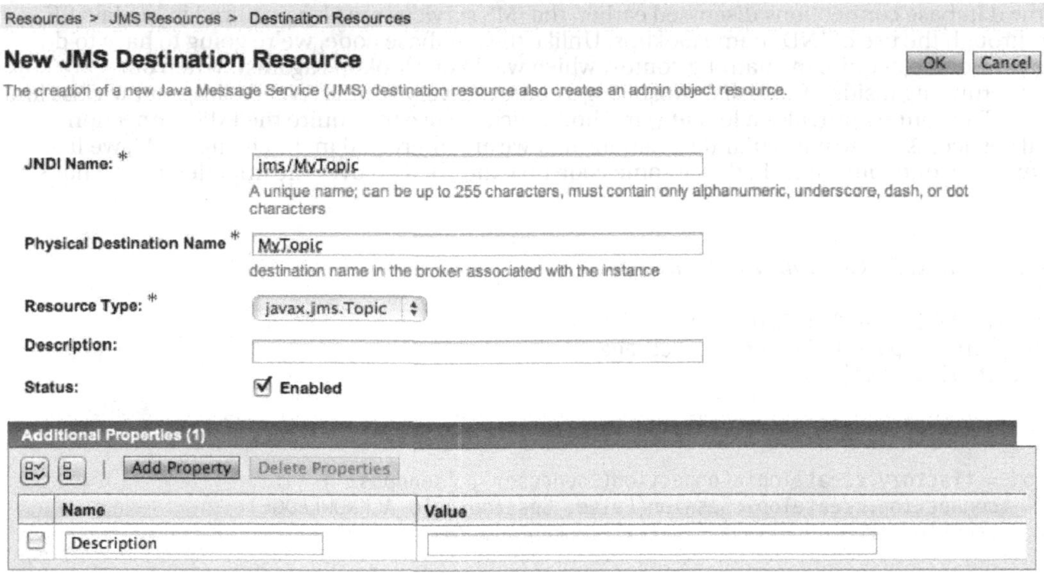

Figure 14-14. Adding a New JMS Topic Resource

319

Now we need to create the JMS queue for point to point messages. Create a new resource, set the JNDI name to "jms/MyQueue." the destination name to "MyQueue," and the resource type to "javax.jms.Queue," as shown in Figure 14-15. Click "OK" to save.

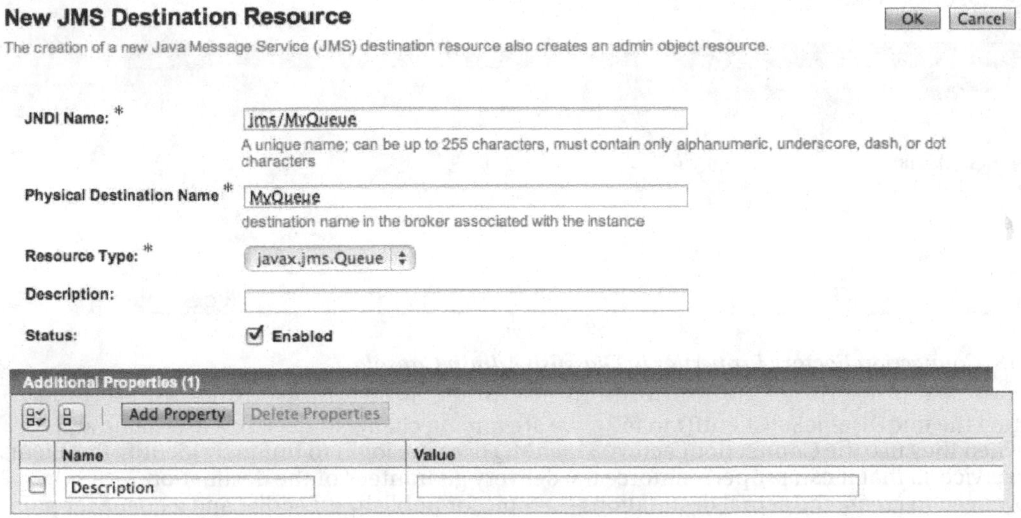

New JMS Destination Resource

OK   Cancel

The creation of a new Java Message Service (JMS) destination resource also creates an admin object resource.

JNDI Name: *   jms/MyQueue

A unique name; can be up to 255 characters, must contain only alphanumeric, underscore, dash, or dot characters

Physical Destination Name *   MyQueue

destination name in the broker associated with the instance

Resource Type: *   javax.jms.Queue ⬍

Description:

Status: ☑ Enabled

Additional Properties (1)

Add Property   Delete Properties

	Name	Value
☐	Description	

Figure 14-15. Adding a New JMS Queue Resource

Like the database connections discussed earlier, the JMS services are also acquired in the JavaEE container through the use of JNDI name lookups. Unlike the database code, we're going to have to do some manual work to acquire the naming context which we do our lookups against. When our application is running inside of Glassfish, acquiring a context is very simple. We just import the class and instantiate it. The context provides a lookup() method which we use to acquire the JMS connection factory and get access to the particular destinations that we are interested in. In Listing 14-44, we'll publish a message onto our topic. Let's see some code first and we'll go over the finer details of what's going on.

Listing 14-44. Context for Creating a Text Message

```
from javax.naming import InitialContext, Session
from javax.naming import DeliverMode, Message
context = InitialContext()

tfactory = context.lookup("jms/MyConnectionFactory")

tconnection = tfactory.createTopicConnection('senduser', 'sendpass')
tsession = tconnection.createTopicSession(False, Session.AUTO_ACKNOWLEDGE)
publisher = tsession.createPublisher(context.lookup("jms/MyTopic"))

message = tsession.createTextMessage()
msg = "Hello there : %s" % datetime.datetime.now()
message.setText(msg)
```

```
publisher.publish(message, DeliveryMode.PERSISTENT,
        Message.DEFAULT_PRIORITY, 100)
tconnection.close()
context.close()
```

In this code snippet, we acquire a topic connection through the connection factory. To reiterate, topics are for publish/subscribe scenarios. Next, we create a topic session, a context where we can send and receive messages. The two arguments passed when creating the topic session specify a transactional flag and how our client will acknowledge receipt of messages. We're going to just disable transactions and get the session to automatically send acknowledgements back to the broker on message receipt.

The last step to getting our publisher is creating the publisher itself. From there we can start publishing messages up to the broker.

At this point, it is important to distinguish between persistent messages and durable messages. JMS calls a message "persistent" if the messages received by the *broker* are persisted. This guarantees that senders know that the broker has received a message. It makes no guarantee that messages will actually be delivered to a final recipient.

Durable subscribers are guaranteed to receive messages in the case that they temporarily drop their connection to the broker and reconnect at a later time. The JMS broker will uniquely identify subscriber clients with a combination of the client ID, username and password to uniquely identify clients and manage message queues for each client.

Now we need to create the subscriber client. We're going to write a standalone client to show that your code doesn't have to live in the application server to receive messages. The only trick we're going to apply here is that while we can simply create an InitialContext with an empty constructor for code in the app server, code that exists outside of the application server must know where to find the JNDI naming service. Glassfish exposes the naming service via CORBA, the Common Object Request Broker Architecture. In short, we need to know a factory class name to create the context and we need to know the URL of where the object request broker is located.

The listener client shown in Listing 14-45 can be run on the same host as the Glassfish server.

Listing 14-45. Creating a Subscriber Client for JMS

```
"""
This is a standalone client that listens for messages from JMS
"""
from javax.jms import TopicConnectionFactory, MessageListener, Session
from javax.naming import InitialContext, Context
import time

def get_context():
    props = {}
    props[Context.INITIAL_CONTEXT_FACTORY]="com.sun.appserv.naming.S1ASCtxFactory"
    props[Context.PROVIDER_URL]="iiop://127.0.0.1:3700"
    context = InitialContext(props)
    return context

class TopicListener(MessageListener):
    def go(self):
        context = get_context()
        tfactory = context.lookup("jms/MyConnectionFactory")
        tconnection = tfactory.createTopicConnection('recvuser', 'recvpass')
        tsession = tconnection.createTopicSession(False, Session.AUTO_ACKNOWLEDGE)
        subscriber = tsession.createDurableSubscriber(context.lookup("jms/MyTopic"),
'mysub')
```

```
        subscriber.setMessageListener(self)
        tconnection.start()
        while True:
            time.sleep(1)
        context.close()
        tconnection.close()

    def onMessage(self, message):
        print message.getText()

if __name__ == '__main__':
    TopicListener().go()
```

There are only a few key differences between the subscriber and publisher side of a JMS topic. First, the subscriber is created with a unique client id—in this case, it's "mysub." This is used by JMS to determine what pending messages to send to the client in the case that the client drops the JMS connections and rebinds at a later time. If we don't care to receive missed messages, we could have created a non-durable subscriber with "createSubscriber" instead of "createDurableSubscriber" and we would not have to pass in a client ID.

Second, the listener employs a callback pattern for incoming messages. When a message is received, the onMessage will be called automatically by the subscriber object and the message object will be passed in.

Now we need to create our sending user and receiving user on the broker. Drop to the command line and go to GLASSFISH_HOME/imq/bin. We are going to create two users: one sender and one receiver. See Listing 14-46.

Listing 14-46. Creating Two JMS Users

```
GLASSFISH_HOME/imq/bin $ imqusermgr add -u senduser -p sendpass
User repository for broker instance: imqbroker
User senduser successfully added.

GLASSFISH_HOME/imq/bin $ imqusermgr add -u recvuser -p recvpass
User repository for broker instance: imqbroker
User recvuser successfully added.
```

We now have two new users with username/password pairs of senduser/sendpass and recvuser/recvpass.

You have enough code now to enable publish/subscribe messaging patterns in your code to signal applications that live outside of your application server. We can potentially have multiple listeners attached to the JMS broker and JMS will make sure that all subscribers get messages in a reliable way.

Let's take a look now at sending message through a queue: this provides reliable point to point messaging and it adds guarantees that messages are persisted in a safe manner to safeguard against server crashes. This time, we'll build our send and receive clients as individual standalone clients that communicate with the JMS broker. See Listing 14-47.

Listing 14-47. Sending Messages Through a Queue

```
from javax.jms import Session
from javax.naming import InitialContext, Context
import time
```

```
def get_context():
    props = {}
    props[Context.INITIAL_CONTEXT_FACTORY]="com.sun.appserv.naming.S1ASCtxFactory"
    props[Context.PROVIDER_URL]="iiop://127.0.0.1:3700"
    context = InitialContext(props)
    return context

def send():
    context = get_context()
    qfactory = context.lookup("jms/MyConnectionFactory")
    # This assumes a user has been provisioned on the broker with
    # username/password of 'senduser/sendpass'
    qconnection = qfactory.createQueueConnection('senduser', 'sendpass')
    qsession = qconnection.createQueueSession(False, Session.AUTO_ACKNOWLEDGE)
    qsender = qsession.createSender(context.lookup("jms/MyQueue"))
    msg = qsession.createTextMessage()
    for i in range(20):
        msg.setText('this is msg [%d]' % i)
        qsender.send(msg)

def recv():
    context = get_context()
    qfactory = context.lookup("jms/MyConnectionFactory")
    # This assumes a user has been provisioned on the broker with
    # username/password of 'recvuser/recvpass'
    qconnection = qfactory.createQueueConnection('recvuser', 'recvpass')
    qsession = qconnection.createQueueSession(False, Session.AUTO_ACKNOWLEDGE)
    qreceiver = qsession.createReceiver(context.lookup("jms/MyQueue"))
    qconnection.start()  # start the receiver

    print "Starting to receive messages now:"
    while True:
        msg = qreceiver.receive(1)
        if msg is not None and isinstance(msg, TextMessage):
            print msg.getText()
```

The send() and recv() functions are almost identical to the publish/subscriber code used to manage topics. A minor difference is that the JMS queue APIs don't use a callback object for message receipt. It is assumed that client applications will actively dequeue objects from the JMS queue instead of acting as a passive subscriber.

The beauty of this JMS code is that you can send messages to the broker and be assured that even in case the server goes down, your messages are not lost. When the server comes back up and your endpoint client reconnects: it will still receive all of its pending messages.

We can extend this example even further. As mentioned earlier in the chapter, Codehaus.org has a messaging project called STOMP, the Streaming Text Orientated Messaging Protocol. STOMP is simpler, but less performant than raw JMS messages, but the tradeoff is that clients exist in a dozen different languages. STOMP also provides an adapter called "stomp-connect," which allows us to turn a JMS broker into a STOMP messaging broker.

This will enable us to have applications written in just about *any* language communicate with our applications over JMS. There are times when we have existing CPython code that leverages various C libraries like Imagemagick or NumPy to do computations that are simply not supported with Jython or Java.

By using stompconnect, we can send work messages over JMS, bridge those messages over STOMP and have CPython clients process our requests. The completed work is then sent back over STOMP, bridged to JMS and received by our Jython code.

First, you'll need to obtain latest version of stomp-connect from codehaus.org. Download stompconnect-1.0.zip from here:

```
http://stomp.codehaus.org/Download
```

After you've unpacked the zip file, you'll need to configure a JNDI property file so that STOMP can act as a JMS client. The configuration is identical to our Jython client. Create a file called "jndi.properties" and place it in your stompconnect directory. The contents should have the two lines shown in Listing 14-48.

Listing 14-48. Jndi.properties Lines

```
java.naming.factory.initial=com.sun.appserv.naming.S1ASCtxFactory
java.naming.provider.url=iiop://127.0.0.1:3700
```

You now need to pull in some JAR files from Glassfish to gain access to JNDI, JMS and some logging classes that STOMP requires. Copy the following JAR files from GLASSFISH_HOME/lib into STOMPCONNECT_HOME/lib:

- appserv-admin.jar
- appserv-deployment-client.jar
- appserv-ext.jar
- appserv-rt.jar
- j2ee.jar
- javaee.jar

Copy the imqjmsra.jar file from GLASSFISH_HOME/imq/lib/imqjmsra.jar to STOMPCONNECT_HOME/lib.

You should be able to now start the connector with the following command line:

```
java -cp "lib\*;stompconnect-1.0.jar" \
    org.codehaus.stomp.jms.Main tcp://0.0.0.0:6666 \
    "jms/MyConnectionFactory"
```

If it works, you should see a bunch of output that ends with a message that the server is listening for connection on tcp://0.0.0.0:6666. Congratulations, you now have a STOMP broker acting as a bidirectional proxy for the OpenMQ JMS broker.

Receiving messages in CPython that originate from Jython+JMS is as simple as Listing 14-49.

Listing 14-49. Receiving Messages via a STOMP Broker

```
import stomp
serv = stomp.Stomp('localhost', 6666)
serv.connect({'client-id': 'reader_client', \
```

```
                'login': 'recvuser', \
            'passcode': 'recvpass'})
serv.subscribe({'destination': '/queue/MyQueue', 'ack': 'client'})
frame = self.serv.receive_frame()
if frame.command == 'MESSAGE':
    # The message content will arrive in the STOMP frame's
    # body section
    print frame.body
    serv.ack(frame)
```

Sending messages is just as straightforward. From our CPython code, we just need to import the stomp client and we can send messages back to our Jython code. See Listing 14-50.

Listing 14-50. Sending Messages via a STOMP Broker

```
import stomp
serv = stomp.Stomp('localhost', 6666)
serv.connect({'client-id': 'sending_client', \
                  'login': 'senduser', \
              'passcode': 'sendpass'})
serv.send({'destination': '/queue/MyQueue', 'body': 'Hello world!'})
```

Summary

We've covered a lot of ground here. We've shown you how to get Django on Jython to use database connection pooling to enforce limits on the database resources an application can consume. We've looked at setting up JMS queues and topic to provide both point to point and publish/subscribe messages between Jython processes. We then took those messaging services and provided interoperability between Jython code and non-Java code.

In our experience, the ability to remix a hand-picked collection of technologies is what gives Jython so much power. You can use both the technology in JavaEE, leveraging years of hard-won experience and get the benefit of using a lighter weight, more modern web application stack like Django.

The future of Jython and Django support in application server is very promising. Websphere now uses Jython for its official scripting language and the version 3 release of Glassfish will offer first class support of Django applications. You'll be able to deploy your web applications without building WAR files up. Just deploy straight from your source directory and you're off to the races.

CHAPTER 15

Introduction to Pylons

Although Django is currently the most popular webframework for Python, it is by no means your only choice. Where Django grew out of the needs of newsrooms to implement content management solutions rapidly, Pylons grew out of a need to build web applications in environments that may have existing databases to integrate with, and the applications don't fit neatly into the class of applications that are loosely defined in the "content management" space.

Pylons greatest strength is that it takes a best-of-breed approach to constructing its technology stack. Where everything is "built in" with Django and the entire application stack is specifically designed with a single worldview of how applications should be done, Pylons takes precisely the opposite approach. Pylons, the core codebase that lives in the pylons namespace, is remarkably small. With the 0.9.7 release, it's hovering around 5,500 lines of code. Django, by comparison, weighs in at about 125,000 lines of code.

Pylons manages to do this magic by leveraging existing libraries extensively, and the Pylons community works with many other Python projects to develop standard APIs to promote interoperability.

Ultimately, picking Django or Pylons is about deciding which tradeoffs you're willing to make. Although Django is extremely easy to learn because all the documentation is in one place and all the documentation relating to any particular component is always discussed in the context of building a web application, you lose some flexibility when you need to start doing things that are at the margins of what Django was designed for.

For example, in a project we've worked on recently, we needed to interact with a nontrivial database that was implemented in SQL Server 2000. For Django, implementing the SQL Server back-end was quite difficult. There aren't that many web developers using Django on Windows, never mind SQL Server. While the Django ORM is a part of Django, it is also not the core focus of Django. Supporting arbitrary databases is simply not a goal for Django, and rightly so.

Pylons uses SQLAlchemy, which is probably the most powerful database toolkit available in Python. It *only* focuses on database access. The SQL Server back-end was already built in a robust way for CPython, and implementing the extra code for a Jython backend took two days—and this was without seeing any of the code in SQLAlchemy's internals.

That experience alone sold us on Pylons. We don't have to rely on the webframework people being experts in databases. Similarly, we don't have to rely on the database experts to know anything about web templating.

In short, when you have to deal with the non-standard things, Pylons makes a fabulous choice, and, let's be honest, there's almost always non-standard things you're going to have to do.

A Guide for the Impatient

The best way to install Pylons is inside of a virtualenv. Create a new virtualenv for Jython and run easy_install:

Listing 15-1.

```
> easy_install "Pylons==0.9.7"
```

Create your application:

```
> paster create --template=pylons RosterTool
```

After initiating this command, you'll be prompted to enter information about your application. Let's accept the defaults for everything by just hitting Enter at each prompt. After you've entered the default information, your application will be created. You will see a directory named the same as your application created within your current directory. Go into that directory and you will see a series of .py files along with a couple of other files. To configure your development environment, open up the development.ini file in a text editor. You will see that there are several parameters in the file that can be changed, including email_to for the site administrator's email address, smtp_server if you wish to configure mail for application, and many more. For the purposes of this example, we'll leave the default values in the configuration file and continue.

Next, launch the development server using the following command from within the application (*RosterTool*) directory:

```
> paster serve --reload development.ini
```

Open a browser and connect to http://127.0.0.1:5000/, and you should see something that looks similar to Figure 15-1.

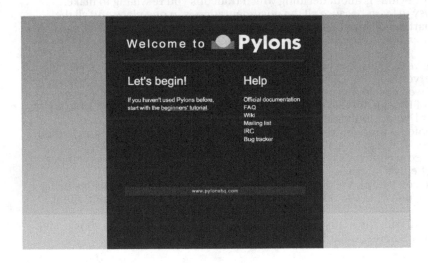

Figure 15-1. Pylons server

Now that we have the development server running, it is good to note that we can stop the server at any time by pressing Ctrl+C on the keyboard.

Now we have the base application created, and it is time to add some content. It is easy to create static HTML files for your Pylons application. Let's create a static file named welcome.html and drop it into RosterTool/rostertool/public/ directory.

Listing 15-2.

```
<html>
    <body>Just a static file</body>
</html>
```

You should now be able to load the static content by taking your browser to http://localhost:5000/welcome.html.

To create web content that handles requests, we need to create a controller for our application. A controller is a Python module that we map to a URL so that when the URL is visited, the controller is invoked. To add a controller, let's start by initiating the following command:

RosterTool/rostertool > paster controller roster

Paste will install a directory named "controllers" inside the rostertool directory and install some files in there including a module named roster.py. You can open it up and you'll see a class named "RosterController" and it will have a single method "index." Pylons is smart enough to automatically map a URL to a controller classname and invoke a method. We'll learn more about mapping URLs later in the chapter. To invoke the RosterController's index method, you just need to start the development server again and invoke the following:

http://localhost:5000/roster/index

Congratulations, you've got your most basic possible web application running now. It handles basic HTTP GET requests and calls a method on a controller and a response comes out. Let's cover each of these pieces in detail now.

A Note about Paste

While you were setting up your toy Pylons application, you probably wondered why Pylons seems to use a command line tool called "paster" instead of something obvious like "pylons." Paster is actually a part of the Paste set of tools that Pylons uses.

Paste is used to build web applications and frameworks, but most commonly it is used to build web application frameworks like Pylons. Every time you use "paster," that's Paste being called. Every time you access the HTTP request and response objects, that's WebOb, a descendant of Paste's HTTP wrapper code. Pylons uses Paste extensively for configuration management, testing, basic HTTP handling with WebOb. You would do well to at least skim over the Paste documentation to see what is available in paste, it is available at http://pythonpaste.org/.

Pylons MVC

Pylons, like Django and any reasonably sane webframework (or GUI toolkit for that matter) uses the model-view-controller design pattern.

Table 15-1 shows what this maps to in Pylons.

Table 15-1. Pylon MVC Design Pattern Mapping

Component	Implementation
Model	SQLAlchemy (or any other database toolkit you prefer)
View	Mako (or any templating language you prefer)
Controller	Plain Python code

To reiterate, Pylons is about letting you, the application developer, decide on the particular tradeoffs you're willing to make. If using a template language more similar to the one in Django is better for your web designers, then switch go Jinja2. If you don't really want to deal with SQLAlchemy, you can use SQLObject, files, a non-relational database, or raw SQL, if you prefer.

Pylons provides tools to help you hook these pieces together in a rational way.

Routes is a library that maps URLs to classes. This is your basic mechanism for dispatching methods whenever your webserver is hit. Routes provides similar functionality to what Django's URL dispatcher provides.

Webhelpers is the defacto standard library for Pylons. It contains commonly used functions for the web, such as flashing status messages to users, date conversion functions, HTML tag generation, pagination functions, text processing, and the list goes on.

Pylons also provides infrastructure so that you can manipulate things that are particular to web applications including:

- WSGI middleware to add cross-cutting functionality to your application with minimal intrusion into your existing codebase.

- A robust testing framework, including a shockingly good debugger you can use through the web.

- Helpers to enable REST-ful API development so you can expose your application as a programmatic interface.

Later in this chapter, we'll wrap up the hockey roster up in a web application. We'll target a few features:

- Form handling and validation to add new players through the web

- Login and authentication to make sure not anybody can edit our lists

- Add a JSON/REST api so that we can modify data from other tools

In the process, we'll use the interactive debugger from both command line and through the web to directly observe and interact with the state of the running application.

An Interlude into Java's Memory Model

A note about reloading: sometimes if you're doing development with Pylons on Jython, Java will throw an OutOfMemory error like this:

Listing 15-3.

```
java.lang.OutOfMemoryError: PermGen space
        at java.lang.ClassLoader.defineClass1(Native Method)
        at java.lang.ClassLoader.defineClass(ClassLoader.java:620)
```

Java keeps track of class definitions in something called the Permanent Generation heap space. This is a problem for Pylons when the HTTP threads are restarted and your classes are reloaded. The old class definitions don't go away; they never get garbage collected. Because Jython is dynamically creating Java classes behind the scenes, each time your development server restarts, you're potentially getting hundreds of new classes loaded into the JVM.

Repeat this several times and it doesn't take long until your JVM has run out of permgen space and it keels over and dies

To modify the permgen heap size, you'll need to instruct Java using some extended command line options. To set the heap to 128M, you'll need to use "-XX:MaxPermSize=128M."

To get this behavior by default for Jython, you'll want to edit your Jython startup script in JYTHON_HOME/bin/jython (or jython.bat) by editing the line that reads:

Listing 15-4.

```
set _JAVA_OPTS=
```

to be

```
set _JAVA_OPTS=-XX:MaxPermSize=128M
```

This shouldn't be a problem in production environments where you're not generating new class definitions during runtime, but it can be quite frustrating during development.

Invoking the Pylons Shell

Yes, we're going to start with testing right away because it will provide you with a way to explore the Pylons application in an interactive way.

Pylons gives you an interactive shell much like Django's. You can start it up with the following commands:

Listing 15-5.

```
RosterTool > jython setup.py egg_info
RosterTool > paster shell test.ini
```

This will yield a nice interactive shell you can start playing with right away. Now let's take a look at those request and response objects in our toy application.

Listing 15-6.

```
RosterTool > paster shell test.ini

Pylons Interactive Shell
Jython 2.5.0 (Release_2_5_0:6476, Jun 16 2009, 13:33:26)
```

```
[OpenJDK Server VM (Sun Microsystems Inc.)]

All objects from rostertool.lib.base are available
Additional Objects:
mapper    -  Routes mapper object
wsgiapp   -  This project's WSGI App instance
app       -  paste.fixture wrapped around wsgiapp

>>> resp = app.get('/roster/index')
>>> resp
<Response 200 OK 'Hello World'>
>>> resp.req
<Request at 0x43 GET http://localhost/roster/index>
```

Pylons lets you actually run requests against the application and play with the resulting response. Even for something as "simple" as the HTTP request and response, Pylons uses a library to provide convenience methods and attributes to make your development life easier. In this case, it's WebOb.

The request and the response objects both have literally dozens of attributes and methods that are provided by the framework. You will almost certainly benefit if you take time to browse through WebOb's documentation, which is available at http://pythonpaste.org/webob/.

Here's four attributes you really have to know to make sense of the request object. The best thing to do is to try playing with the request object in the shell.

request.GET

GET is a special dictionary of the variables that were passed in the URL. Pylons automatically converts URL arguments that appear multiple times into discrete key value pairs.

Listing 15-7.

```
>>> resp = app.get('/roster/index?foo=bar&x=42&x=50')
>>> resp.req.GET
UnicodeMultiDict([('foo', u'bar'), ('x', u'42'), ('x', u'50')])
>>> resp.req.GET['x']
u'50'
>>> resp.req.GET.getall('x')
[u'42', u'50']
```

Note how you can get either the last value or the list of values depending on how you choose to fetch values from the dictionary. This can cause subtle bugs if you're not paying attention.

request.POST

POST is similar to GET, but appropriately: it only returns the variables that were sent up during an HTTP POST submission.

request.params

Pylons merges all the GET and POST data into a single MultiValueDict. In almost all cases, this is the one attribute that you really want to use to get the data that the user sent to the server.

request.headers

This dictionary provides all the HTTP headers that the client sent to the server.

Context Variables and Application Globals

Most web frameworks provide a request scoped variable to act as a bag of values. Pylons is no exception: whenever you create a new controller with paste, it will automatically import an attribute 'c' which is the context variable.

This is one aspect of Pylons that we've found to be frustrating. The 'c' attribute is code generated as an import when you instruct paste to build you a new controller. The 'c' value is *not* an attribute of your controller—Pylons has special global threadsafe variables, this is just one of them. You can store variables that you want to exist for the duration of the request in the context. These values won't persist after the request/response cycle has completed, so don't confuse this with the session variable.

The other global variable you'll end up using a lot is pylons.session. This is where you'll store variables that need to persist over the course of several request/response cycles. You can treat this variable as a special dictionary: just use standard Jython dictionary syntax and Pylons will handle the rest.

Routes

Routes is much like Django's URL dispatcher. It provides a mechanism for you to map URLs to controllers classes and methods to invoke.

Generally, we find that Routes makes a tradeoff of less URL matching expressiveness in exchange for simpler reasoning about which URLs are directed to a particular controller and method. Routes doesn't support regular expressions, just simple variable substitution.

A typical route will look something like this:

```
map.connect('/{mycontroller}/{someaction}/{var1}/{var2}')
```

This route would find the controller called "mycontroller" (note the casing of the class) and invoke the "someaction" method on that object. Variables var1 and var2 would be passed in as arguments.

The connect() method of the map object will also take in optional arguments to fill in default values for URLs that do not have enough URL-encoded data in them to properly invoke a method with the minimum required number of arguments. The front page is an example of this; let's try connecting the frontpage to the Roster.index method.

Edit RosterTool/rostertool/config/routing.py so that there are 3 lines after #CUSTOM_ROUTES_HERE that should read like the following:

Listing 15-8.

```
map.connect('/', controller='roster', action='index')
map.connect('/{action}/{id}/', controller='roster')
map.connect('/add_player/', controller='roster', action='add_player')
```

While this *looks* like it should work, you can try running paster server: it won't.

By default, Pylons always tries to serve static content before searching for controllers and methods to invoke. You'll need to go to RosterTool/rostertool/public and delete the "index.html" file that paster installed when you first created your application. If you wanted to change the default implementation, you could tweak the middleware.py module to your liking.

Load http://localhost:5000/ again in your browser—the default index.html should be gone and you should now get your response from the controller method that is mapped to index, in this case, you should see "Hello World."

Controllers and Templates

Leveraging off of the Table model we defined in Chapter 12, let's create the hockey roster, but this time using the PostgreSQL database. We'll assume that you have a PostgreSQL installation running that allows you to create new databases. You can also use a different database if you choose by simply creating a different engine with SQLAlchemy. For more details, please visit the documentation about creating database engines at http://www.sqlalchemy.org/docs/05/dbengine.html.

Begin by opening up a Pylons interactive shell and typing the following commands:

Listing 15-9.

```
>>> from sqlalchemy import *
>>> from sqlalchemy.schema import Sequence
>>> db = create_engine('postgresql+zxjdbc://myuser:mypass@localhost:5432/mydb')
>>> connection = db.connect()
>>> metadata = MetaData()
>>> player = Table('player', metadata,
...     Column('id', Integer, primary_key=True),
...     Column('first', String(50)),
...     Column('last', String(50)),
...     Column('position', String(30)))
>>> metadata.create_all(engine)
```

Now let's wire the data up to the controllers, display some data, and get basic form handling working. We're going to create a basic CRUD (create, read, update, delete) interface to the sqlalchemy model. Because of space constraints, this HTML is going to be very basic; but you'll get a taste of how things fit together.

Paste doesn't just generate a stub for your controller—it will also code generate an empty functional test case in rostertool/tests/functional/ as test_roster.py. We'll visit testing shortly.

Controllers are really where the action occurs in Pylons. This is where your application will take data from the database and prepare it for a template to render it as HTML. Let's put the list of all players on the front page of the site. We'll implement a template to render the list of all players. Then, we'll implement a method in the controller to override the index() method of Roster to use SQLAlchemy to load the records from disk and send them to the template.

Along the way, we'll touch on template inheritance so that you can see how you can save keystrokes by subclassing your templates in Mako.

First, let's create two templates, base.html and list_players.html in the rostertool/templates directory.

Listing 15-10. base.html

```
<html>
    <body>
        <div class="header">
            ${self.header()}
        </div>
```

```
        ${self.body()}
    </body>
</html>

<%def name="header()">
    <h1>${c.page_title}</h1>
    <% messages = h.flash.pop_messages() %>
    % if messages:
    <ul id="flash-messages">
        % for message in messages:
        <li>${message}</li>
        % endfor
    </ul>
    % endif
</%def>
```

Listing 15-11. list_players.html

```
<%inherit file="base.html" />
<table border="1">
    <tr>
        <th>Position</th><th>Last name</th><th>First name</th><th>Edit</th>
    </tr>
    % for player in c.players:
        ${makerow(player)}
    % endfor
</table>

<h2>Add a new player</h2>
${h.form(h.url_for(controller='roster', action='add_player'), method='POST')}
    ${h.text('first', 'First Name')} <br />
    ${h.text('last', 'Last Name')} <br />
    ${h.text('position', 'Position')} <br />
    ${h.submit('add_player', "Add Player")}
${h.end_form()}

<%def name="makerow(row)">
<tr>
    <td>${row.position}</td>\
    <td>${row.last}</td>\
    <td>${row.first}</td>\
    <td><a href="${h.url_for(controller='roster', action='edit_player',
id=row.id)}">Edit</a></td>\
</tr>
</%def>
```

There's quite a bit going on here. The base template lets Mako define a boilerplate set of HTML that all pages can reuse. Each section is defined with a <%def name="block()"> section, and the blocks are overloaded in the subclassed templates. In effect, Mako lets your page templates look like objects with methods that can render subsections of your pages.

The list_players.html template has content that is immediately substituted into the self.body() method of the base template. The first part of our body uses our magic context variable 'c'. Here, we're iterating over each of the players in the database and rendering them into a table as a row. Note here that we can use the Mako method syntax to create a method called "makerow" and invoke it directly within our template.

■ **Note** Mako provides a rich set of functions for templating. We're only going to use the most basic parts of Mako: inheritance, variable substitution, and loop iteration to get the toy application working. I strongly suggest you dive into the Mako documentation to discover features and get a better understanding of how to use the template library.

Next, we add in a small form to create new players. The trick here is to see that the form is being generated programmatically by helper functions. Pylons automatically imports YOURPROJECT/lib/helpers (in our case, rostertool.lib.helpers) as the 'h' variable in your template. The helpers module typically imports functions from parts of Pylons or a dependent library to allow access to those features from anywhere in the application. Although this seems like a violation of "separation of concerns," look at the template and see what it buys us: we get fully decoupled URLs from the particular controller and method that need to be invoked. The template uses a special routes function "url_for" to compute the URL that would have been mapped for a particular controller and method. The last part of our base.html file contains code to display alert messages.

Let's take a look at our rostertool.lib.helpers module now.

Listing 15-12.

```
from routes import url_for
from webhelpers.html.tags import *
from webhelpers.pylonslib import Flash as _Flash

# Send alert messages back to the user
flash = _Flash()
```

Here, we're importing the url_for function from routes to do our URL reversal computations. We import HTML tag generators from the main html.tags helper modules and we import Flash to provide alert messages for our pages. We'll show you how flash messages are used when we cover the controller code in more detail in the next couple of pages.

Now, create a controller with paste (you've already done this if you were impatient at the beginning of the chapter).

■ **Note** If you have already created the controller using the quickstart at the beginning of the chapter, you will need to add the SQLAlchemy configuration to the development.ini file by adding the following line to the file:

sqlalchemy.url = postgresql+zxjdbc://dbuser:dbpassword@dbhost:port/dbname

---

Listing 15-13.

```
$ cd ROSTERTOOL/rostertool
$ paster controller roster
```

Next, we need to add the metadata for our database table to the RosterTool/rostertool/model/__init__.py module. To do so, change the file so that it reads as follows:

Listing 15-14.

```
"""The application's model objects"""
import sqlalchemy as sa
from sqlalchemy import orm, schema, types

from rostertool.model import meta

def init_model(engine):
    """Call me before using any of the tables or classes in the model"""
    ## Reflected tables must be defined and mapped here
    #global reflected_table
    #reflected_table = sa.Table("Reflected", meta.metadata, autoload=True,
    #                           autoload_with=engine)
    #orm.mapper(Reflected, reflected_table)
    #
    meta.Session.configure(bind=engine)
    meta.engine = engine

metadata = schema.MetaData()

# Create the metadata for the player table, and assign it to player_table
player_table = schema.Table('player', metadata,
    schema.Column('id', types.Integer, primary_key=True),
    schema.Column('first', types.Text(), nullable=False),
    schema.Column('last', types.Text(), nullable=False),
    schema.Column('position', types.Text(), nullable=False),
)

# Create a class to be used for mapping the player_table object
class Player(object):
    pass

# Map the Player class to the player_table object, we can now refer to the
# player_table using Player
orm.mapper(Player, player_table)
```

Note that we are creating the proper metadata for mapping to the player database table. We then create an empty Player class object and later use the orm.mapper to map the metadata to the empty Player object. We can now use the Player object to work with our database table.

Next, we should alter the index method that is created inside the RosterContoller class. We will add an import to bring in the meta and Player objects, and change the index function so that it queries the list of players in the database. In the end, the index function should read as follows:

Listing 15-15.

```
from rostertool.model import meta, Player
...
def index(self):
    session = meta.Session()
    c.page_title = 'Player List'
    c.players = session.query(Player).all()
    return render('list_players.html')
```

This code is fairly straightforward; we are simply using a SQLAlchemy session to load all the Player objects from disk and assigning to the special context variable 'c.' Pylons is then instructed to render the list_player.html file.

The context should be your default place to place values you want to pass to other parts of the application. Note that Pylons will automatically bind in URL values to the context so while you can grab the form values from self.form_result, you can also grab raw URL values from the context.

You should be able run the debug webserver now and you can get to the front page to load an empty list of players. Start up your debug webserver as you did at the beginning of this chapter and go to http://localhost:5000/ to see the page load with your list of players (currently an empty list).

Now we need to get to the meaty part where we can start create, edit, and delete players. We'll make sure that the inputs are at least minimally validated, errors are displayed to the user, and that alert messages are properly populated.

First, we need a page that shows just a single player and provides buttons for edit and delete.

Listing 15-16.

```
<%inherit file="base.html" />

<h2>Edit player</h2>
${h.form(h.url_for(controller='roster', action='save_player', id=c.player.id),
method='POST')}
    ${h.hidden('id', c.player.id)} <br />
    ${h.text('first', c.player.first)} <br />
    ${h.text('last', c.player.last)} <br />
    ${h.text('position', c.player.position)} <br />
    ${h.submit('save_player', "Save Player")}
${h.end_form()}

${h.form(h.url_for(controller='roster', action='delete_player', id=c.player.id),
method='POST')}
    ${h.hidden('id', c.player.id)} <br />
    ${h.hidden('first', c.player.first)} <br />
    ${h.hidden('last', c.player.last)} <br />
    ${h.hidden('position', c.player.position)} <br />
    ${h.submit('delete_player', "Delete Player")}
${h.end_form()}
```

This template assumes that there is a "player" value assigned to the context and, not surprisingly, it's going to be a full blown instance of the Player object that we first saw in Chapter 12. The helper functions let us define our HTML form using webhelper tag generation functions. This means you won't have to worry about escaping characters or remembering the particular details of the HTML attributes.

The helper.tag functions will do sensible things by default. The *h* is a default template variable that refers to the repository of helper functions.

We've set up the edit and delete forms to point to different URLs. You might want to "conserve" URLs, but having discrete URLs for each action has advantages, especially for debugging. You can trivially view which URLs are being hit on a webserver by reading log files. Seeing the same kind of behavior if the URLs are the same, but the behavior is dictated by some form value—well, that's a whole lot harder to debug. It's also a lot harder to setup in your controllers because you need to dispatch the behavior on a per method level. Why not just have separate methods for separate behavior? Everybody will thank you for it when they need to debug your code in the future.

Before we create our controller methods for create, edit and delete, we'll create a formencode schema to provide basic validation. Again, Pylons doesn't provide validation behavior—it just leverages another library to do so. Add the following class to rostertool/controllers/roster.py:

Listing 15-17.

```python
class PlayerForm(formencode.Schema):
    # You need the next line to drop the submit button values
    allow_extra_fields=True

    first = formencode.validators.String(not_empty=True)
    last = formencode.validators.String(not_empty=True)
    position = formencode.validators.String(not_empty=True)
```

This simply provides basic string verification on our inputs. Note how this doesn't provide any hint as to what the HTML form looks like—or that it's HTML at all. FormEncode can validate arbitrary Python dictionaries and return errors about them.

We're just going to show you the add method, and the edit_player methods. You should try to implement the save_player and delete_player methods to make sure you understand what's going on here. First, add the import for the validate decorator. Next, add the add_player and edit_player functions to the RosterConroller class.

Listing 15-18.

```python
from pylons.decorators import validate


@validate(schema=PlayerForm(), form='index', post_only=False, on_get=True)
def add_player(self):
    first = self.form_result['first']
    last = self.form_result['last']
    position = self.form_result['position']
    session = meta.Session()
    if session.query(Player).filter_by(first=first, last=last).count() > 0:
        h.flash("Player already exists!")
        return h.redirect_to(controller='roster')
    player = Player(first, last, position)
    session.add(player)
    session.commit()
    return h.redirect_to(controller='roster', action='index')

def edit_player(self, id):
    session = meta.Session()
```

```
player = session.query(Player).filter_by(id=id).one()
c.player = player
return render('edit_player.html')
```

A couple of notes here. The edit_player function is passed the 'id' attribute directly by Routes. In the edit_player method, 'player' is assigned to the context, but the context is never explicitly passed into the template renderer. Pylons is going to automatically take the attributes bound to the context and write them into the template and render the HTML output. The *c* variable is automatically available in the template namespace much like the *h* variable as discussed previously.

With the add_player method, we're using the validate decorator to enforce the inputs against the PlayerForm. In the case of error, the form attribute of the decorator is used to load an action against the current controller. In this case, 'index,' so the front page loads.

The SQLAlchemy code should be familiar to you if you have already gone through Chapter 12. The last line of the add_player method is a redirect to prevent problems with hitting reload in the browser. Once all data manipulation has occurred, the server redirects the client to a results page. In the case that a user hits reload on the result page, no data will be mutated.

Here's the signatures of the remaining methods you'll need to implement to make things work:

- save_player(self):

- delete_player(self):

If you get stuck, you can always consult the working sample code on the book's web site.

Adding a JSON API

JSON integration into Pylons is very straight forward. The steps are roughly the same as adding controller methods for plain HTML views. You invoke paste, paste then generates your controller stubs and test stubs, you add in some routes to wire controllers to URLs and then you just fill in the controller code.

Listing 15-19.

```
$ cd ROSTERTOOL_HOME/rostertool
$ paster controller api
```

Pylons provides a special @jsonify decorator which will automatically convert Python primitive types into JSON objects. It will *not* convert the POST data into an object though; that's your responsibility. Adding a simple read interface into the player list requires only adding a single method to your ApiController:

Listing 15-20.

```
@jsonify
def players(self):
    session = Session()
    players = [{'first': p.first,
                'last': p.last,
                'position': p.position,
                'id': p.id} for p in session.query(Player).all()]
    return players
```

Adding a hook so that people can POST data to your server in JSON format to create new player is almost as easy.

Listing 15-21.

```
import simplejson as json

@jsonify
def add_player(self):
    obj = json.loads(request.body)
    schema = PlayerForm()
    try:
        form_result = schema.to_python(obj)
    except formencode.Invalid, error:
        response.content_type = 'text/plain'
        return 'Invalid: '+unicode(error)
    else:
        session = Session()
        first, last, position = obj['first'], obj['last'], obj['position']
        if session.query(Player).filter_by(last=last, first=first,
                position=position).count() == 0:
            session.add(Player(first, last, position))
            session.commit()
            return {'result': 'OK'}
        else:
            return {'result':'fail', 'msg': 'Player already exists'}
```

Unit Testing, Functional Testing, and Logging

One of our favorite features in Pylons is its rich set of tools for testing and debugging. It even manages to take social networking, turn it upside-down, and make it into a debugger feature. We'll get to that shortly.

The first step to knowing how to test code in Pylons is to familiarize yourself with the nose testing framework. Nose makes testing simple by getting out of your way. There are no classes to subclass, just start writing functions that start with the word "test" and nose will run them. Write a class that has "test" prefixed in the name and nose will treat it as a suite of tests running each method that starts with "test." For each test method, nose will execute the setup() method just prior to executing your test and nose will execute the teardown() method after your test case.

Best of all, nose will automatically hunt down anything that looks like a test and will run it for you. There is no complicated chain of test cases you need to organize in a tree. The computer will do that for you.

Let's take a look at your first test case: we'll just instrument the model, in this case—SQLAlchemy. Because the model layer has no dependency on Pylons, this effectively tests only your SQLAlchemy model code.

In ROSTERTOOL_HOME/rostertool/tests, create a module called "test_models.py" with the following content

Listing 15-22.

```
from rostertool.model import Player, Session, engine

class TestModels(object):

    def setup(self):
        self.cleanup()

    def teardown(self):
        self.cleanup()

    def cleanup(self):
        session = Session()
        for player in session.query(Player):
            session.delete(player)
        session.commit()

    def test_create_player(self):
        session = Session()
        player1 = Player('Josh', 'Juneau', 'forward')
        player2 = Player('Jim', 'Baker', 'forward')
        session.add(player1)
        session.add(player2)

        # But 2 are in the session, but not in the database
        assert 2 == session.query(Player).count()
        assert 0 == engine.execute("select count(id) from player").fetchone()[0]
        session.commit()

        # Check that 2 records are all in the database
        assert 2 == session.query(Player).count()
        assert 2 == engine.execute("select count(id) from player").fetchone()[0]
```

Before we can run the tests, we'll need to edit the model module a little so that the models know to lookup the connection URL from Pylon's configuration file. In your test.ini, add a line setting the sqlalchemy.url setting to point to your database in the [app:main] section.

You should have a line that looks something like this:

Listing 15-23.

```
[app:main]
use = config:development.ini
sqlalchemy.url = postgresql+zxjdbc://username:password@localhost:5432/mydb
```

Now edit the model file so that the create_engine call uses that configuration. This is as simple as importing config from pylons and doing a dictionary lookup. The two lines you want are

Listing 15-24.

```
from pylons import config
engine = create_engine(config['sqlalchemy.url'])
```

and that's it. Your model will now lookup your database connection string from Pylons. Even better, nose will know how to use that configuration as well.

From the command line, you can run the tests from ROSTERTOOL_HOME like this now:

Listing 15-25.

```
ROSTERTOOL_HOME $ nosetests rostertool/tests/test_models.py
.
----------------------------------------------------------------------
Ran 1 test in 0.502s
```

Perfect! To capture stdout and get verbose output, you can choose to use the -sv option. Another nice option is -pdb-failures, which will drop you into the debugger on failures. Nose has its own active community of developers. You can get plug-ins to do coverage analysis and performance profiling with some of the plugins. Use "nosetests --help" for a list of the options available for a complete list.

Due to the nature of Pylons and its decoupled design, writing small unit tests to test each little piece of code is very easy. Feel free to assemble your tests any which way you want. Just want to have a bunch of test functions? Great! If you need to have setup and teardown and writing a test class makes sense, then do so.

Testing with nose is a joy—you aren't forced to fit into any particular structure with respect to where you tests must go so that they will be executed. You can organize your tests in a way that makes the most sense to *you*.

That covers basic unit testing, but suppose we want to test the JSON interface to our hockey roster. We really want to be able to invoke GET and POST on the URLs to make sure that URL routing is working as we expect. We want to make sure that the content-type is properly set to 'application/x-json.' In other words, we want to have a proper functional test, a test that's not as fine grained as a unit test.

The prior exposure to the 'app' object when we ran the paste shell should give you a rough idea of what is required. In Pylons, you can instrument your application code by using a TestController. Lucky for you, Pylons has already created one for you in your <app>/tests directory. Just import it, subclass it and you can start using the 'app' object just like you did inside of the shell.

Let's take a look at a functional test in detail now. Here's a sample you can save into rostertool/tests/functional/test_api.py:

Listing 15-26.

```
from rostertool.tests import *
import simplejson as json
from rostertool.model.models import Session, Player

class TestApiController(TestController):
    # Note that we're using subclasses of unittest.TestCase so we need
    # to be careful with setup/teardown camelcasing unlike nose's
    # default behavior

    def setUp(self):
```

```
        session = Session()
        for player in session.query(Player):
            session.delete(player)
        session.commit()

    def test_add_player(self):
        data = json.dumps({'first': 'Victor',
            'last': 'Ng',
            'position': 'Goalie'})
        # Note that the content-type is set in the headers to make
        # sure that paste.test doesn't URL encode our data
        response = self.app.post(url(controller='api', action='add_player'),
            params=data,
            headers={'content-type': 'application/x-json'})
        obj = json.loads(response.body)
        assert obj['result'] == 'OK'

        # Do it again and fail
        response = self.app.post(url(controller='api', action='add_player'),
            params=data,
            headers={'content-type': 'application/x-json'})
        obj = json.loads(response.body)
        assert obj['result'] <> 'OK'
```

There's a minor detail which you can easily miss when you're using the TestController as your superclass. First off, TestController is a descendant of unittest.TestCase from the standard python unit test library. Nose will not run 'setup' and 'teardown' methods on TestCase subclasses. Instead, you'll have to use the camel case names that TestCase uses.

Reading through the testcase should show you how much detail you can be exposed. All your headers are exposed, the response content is exposed; indeed, the HTTP response is completely exposed as an object for you to inspect and verify.

So great, now we can run small unit tests, bigger functional tests; let's take a look at the debugging facilities provided through the web.

Consider what happens with most web application stacks when an error occurs. Maybe you get a stack trace, maybe you don't. If you're lucky, you can see the local variables at each stack frame like Django does. Usually though, you're out of luck if you want to interact with the live application as the error is occurring.

Eventually, you may locate the part of the stack trace that triggered the error, but the only way of sharing that information is through either the mailing lists or by doing a formal patch against source control. Let's take a look at an example of that.

We're going to startup our application in development mode. We're also going to intentionally break some code in the controller to see the stack trace. But first, we'll need to put some data into our app.

Add a sqlalchemy.url configuration line to the development.ini file as you did in the test.ini configuration, and let's startup the application in development mode. We're going to have the server run so that any code changes on the file system are automatically detected and the code is reloaded
`$ paster serve development.ini --reload`

We'll add a single player "John Doe" as a center, and save the record. Next, let's intentionally break some code to trigger the debugger. Modify the RosterController's index method and edit the call that loads the list of players. We'll use the web session instead of the database session to try loading the Player objects.

Listing 15-27.

```
def index(self):
    db_session = meta.Session()
    c.page_title = 'Player List'
    c.players = session.query(Player).all()
    return render('list_players.html')
Load http://localhost:5000/ to see the error page.
```

There's a lot of information that Pylons throws back at you. Along the top of the screen, you'll see four tabs: Traceback, Extra Data, Template, and Source. Pylons will have put you in the Traceback tab by default to start with. If you look at the error, you'll see the exact line number in the source file that the error occurred in. What's special about Pylons traceback tab is that this is actually a fully interactive session.

You can select the "+" signs to expand each stackframe and a text input along with some local variables on that frame will be revealed. That text input is an interface into your server process. You can type virtually any Python command into it, hit Enter, and you will get back live results. From here, we can see that we should have used the 'db_session' and not the 'session' variable. See Figure 15-2.

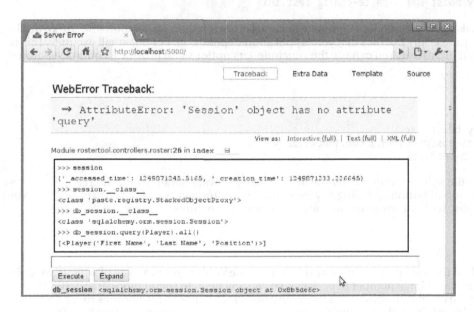

Figure 15-2. Error message caused by use of Session

This is pretty fantastic. If you click on the View link, you can even jump to the full source listing of the Jython module that caused the error. One bug in Pylons at the time of writing is that sometimes the hyperlink is malformed. So, although the traceback will correctly list the line number that the error occurred at, the source listing may go to the wrong line.

The Pylons developers have also embedded an interface into search engines to see if your error has been previously reported. If you scroll down to the bottom of your traceback page, you'll see another tab control with a Search Mail Lists option. Here, Pylons will automatically extract the exception message and provide you an interface so you can literally search all the mailing lists that are relevant to your particular Pylons installation.

If you can't find your error on the mailing lists, you can go to the next tab, Post Traceback, and submit your stacktrace to a webservice on PylonsHQ.com so that you can try to debug your problems online with other collaborators. Combining unit tests, functional tests, and the myriad of debugging options afforded to you in the web debugger, Pylons makes the debugging experience as painless as possible.

Deployment into a Servlet Container

Deploying your pylons application into a servlet container is very straight forward. Just install snakefight from PyPI using easy_install and you can start building WAR files.

Listing 15-28.

```
$ easy_install snakefight
...snakefight will download and install here ...
$ jython setup.py bdist_war --paste-config test.ini
```

By default, snakefight will bundle a complete instance of your Jython installation into the WAR file. What it doesn't include is any JAR files that your application depends on. For our small example, this is just the postgresql JDBC driver. You can use the --include-jars options and provide a comma separated list of JAR files.

Listing 15-29.

```
$ jython setup.py bdist_war \
    --include-jars=postgresql-8.3-604.jdbc4.jar \
    --paste-config=test.ini
```

The final WAR file will be located under the dist directory. It will contain your postgreql JDBC driver, a complete installation of Jython including anything located in site-packages and your application. Your war file should deploy without any issues into any standards compliant servlet container.

Summary

We've only scratched the surface of what's possible, but I hope you've gotten a taste of what is possible with Pylons. Pylons uses a large number of packages so you will need to spend more time getting over the initial learning curve, but the dividend is the ability to pick and choose the libraries that best solve your particular problems. It would be helpful to take a look at some other resources such as *The Definitive Guide to Pylons* from Apress, which is also available online at http://pylonsbook.com.

CHAPTER 16

■ ■ ■

GUI Applications

The C implementation of Python comes with Tkinter for writing Graphical User Interfaces (GUIs). The GUI toolkit that you get automatically with Jython is Swing, which is included with the Java Platform by default. Similar to CPython, there are other toolkits available for writing GUIs in Jython. Because Swing is available on any modern Java installation, we will focus on the use of Swing GUIs in this chapter.

Swing is a large subject, and can't be fully covered in a single chapter. In fact, there are entire books devoted to Swing. We will provide an introduction to Swing, but only enough to describe the use of Swing from Jython. For in-depth coverage of Swing, one of the many books or web tutorials, like the Swing tutorial at java.sun.com/docs/books/tutorial/uiswing provided by Sun Microsystems, should be used.

Using Swing from Jython has a number of advantages over the use of Swing in Java. For example, bean properties are less verbose in Jython, and binding actions in Jython is much less verbose (in Java you have to use anonymous classes, and in Jython you can pass a function).

Let's start with a simple Swing application in Java, and then we will look at the same application in Jython. See Listing 16-1.

Listing 16-1.

```java
import java.awt.event.ActionEvent;
import java.awt.event.ActionListener;
import javax.swing.JButton;
import javax.swing.JFrame;

public class HelloWorld {

    public static void main(String[] args) {
        JFrame frame = new JFrame("Hello Java!");
        frame.setDefaultCloseOperation(JFrame.EXIT_ON_CLOSE);
        frame.setSize(300, 300);
        JButton button = new JButton("Click Me!");
        button.addActionListener(
            new ActionListener() {
                public void actionPerformed(ActionEvent event) {
                    System.out.println("Clicked!");
                }
            }
        );
        frame.add(button);
        frame.setVisible(true);
    }
}
```

This simple application draws a JFrame that is completely filled with a JButton. When the button is pressed, "Click Me!" prints to the command line. See Figure 16-1.

Figure 16-1. *"Click Me" printed to the command line*

Now let's see what this program looks like in Jython (see Listing 16-2).

Listing 16-2.

```
from javax.swing import JButton, JFrame

frame = JFrame('Hello, Jython!',
          defaultCloseOperation = JFrame.EXIT_ON_CLOSE,
          size = (300, 300)
       )

def change_text(event):
    print 'Clicked!'

button = JButton('Click Me!', actionPerformed=change_text)
frame.add(button)
frame.visible = True
```

Except for the title, the application produces the same JFrame with JButton, printing "Click Me!" to the screen when the button is clicked. See Figure 16-2.

Figure 16-2. Results of the application created in Listing 16-2

Let's go through the Java and the Jython examples line by line to get a feel for the differences between writing Swing apps in Jython and Java. First the import statements:

Listing 16-3. In Java

```
import java.awt.event.ActionEvent;
import java.awt.event.ActionListener;
import javax.swing.JButton;
import javax.swing.JFrame;
```

Listing 16-4. In Jython

```
from javax.swing import JButton, JFrame
```

In Jython, it is always best to make imports explicit by using names, instead of from javax.swing import *. Note that we did not need to import ActionEvent or ActionListener, since Jython's dynamic typing allowed us to avoid mentioning these classes in our code.

Next, we have some code that creates a JFrame, and then sets a couple of bean properties.

Listing 16-5. In Java

```
JFrame frame = new JFrame("Hello Java!");
frame.setDefaultCloseOperation(JFrame.EXIT_ON_CLOSE);
frame.setSize(300, 300);
```

Listing 16-6. In Jython

```
frame = JFrame('Hello, Jython!',
            defaultCloseOperation = JFrame.EXIT_ON_CLOSE,
            size = (300, 300)
        )
```

In Java a new JFrame is created, and then the bean properties defaultCloseOperation and size are set. In Jython, we are able to add the bean property setters right inside the call to the constructor. This shortcut is covered in detail in Chapter 6. Still, it will bear some repeating here, because bean properties are so important in Swing libraries. In short, if you have bean getters and setters of the form getFoo/setFoo, you can treat them as properties of the object with the name "foo." So instead of x.getFoo() you can use x.foo. Instead of x.setFoo(bar) you can use x.foo = bar. If you take a look at any Swing app above a reasonable size, you are likely to see large blocks of setters like:

Listing 16-7.

```
JTextArea t = JTextArea();
t.setText(message)
t.setEditable(false)
t.setWrapStyleWord(true)
t.setLineWrap(true)
t.setAlignmentX(Component.LEFT_ALIGNMENT)
t.setSize(300, 1)
```

which, in our opinion, look better in the idiomatic Jython property setting style because they are so easy to read:

Listing 16-8.

```
t = JTextArea()
t.text = message
t.editable = False
t.wrapStyleWord = True
t.lineWrap = True
t.alignmentX = Component.LEFT_ALIGNMENT
t.size = (300, 1)
```

You can also roll the setters into the constructor:

```
t = JTextArea(text = message,
            editable = False,
            wrapStyleWord = True,
            lineWrap = True,
            alignmentX = Component.LEFT_ALIGNMENT,
```

```
                size = (300, 1)
        )
```

When you use properties rolled into the constructor, you need to watch out for the order in which the setters will be called. Generally this is not a problem, as the bean properties are not usually order dependent. The big exception is setVisible(): you probably have to set the visible property outside of the constructor after all properties have been set to avoid any strangeness while the properties are being set. Going back to our short example, the next block of code creates a JButton and binds the button to an action that prints out "Click Me!"

Listing 16-9. In Java

```java
JButton button = new JButton("Click Me!");
button.addActionListener(
    new ActionListener() {
        public void actionPerformed(ActionEvent event) {
            System.out.println("Clicked!");
        }
    }
);
frame.add(button);
```

Listing 16-10. In Jython

```python
def change_text(event):
    print 'Clicked!'

button = JButton('Click Me!', actionPerformed=change_text)
frame.add(button)
```

We think Jython's method is particularly nice here when compared to Java. Here we can pass a first class function "change_text" directly to the JButton in its constructor. This plays better than the more cumbersome Java "addActionListener," method where we need to create an anonymous ActionListener class and define its actionPerformed method with all the ceremony necessary for static type declarations. This is one case where Jython's readability really stands out. This works because Jython is able to automatically recognize events in Java code if they have corresponding *addEvent()* and *removeEvent()* methods. Jython takes the name of the event and makes it accessible using the nice Python syntax as long as the event methods are public. Finally, in both examples we set the visible property to True. Again, although we could have set this property in the frame constructor, the visible property is one of those rare order-dependent properties that we want to set at the right time (and in this case, last).

Listing 16-11. In Java

```java
frame.setVisible(true);
```

Listing 16-12. In Jython

```python
frame.visible = True
```

Now that we have looked at a simple example, it makes sense to see what a medium sized app might look like in Jython. Because Twitter apps have become the "Hello World" of GUI applications these days, we will go with the trend. The following application gives the user a login prompt. When the user successfully logs in, the most recent tweets in their timeline are displayed. See Listing 16-13.

Listing 16-13. Jython Twitter Client

```
import twitter
import re

from javax.swing import (BoxLayout, ImageIcon, JButton, JFrame, JPanel,
        JPasswordField, JLabel, JTextArea, JTextField, JScrollPane,
        SwingConstants, WindowConstants)
from java.awt import Component, GridLayout
from java.net import URL
from java.lang import Runnable

class JyTwitter(object):
    def __init__(self):
        self.frame = JFrame("Jython Twitter",
                            defaultCloseOperation = WindowConstants.EXIT_ON_CLOSE)


        self.loginPanel = JPanel(GridLayout(0,2))
        self.frame.add(self.loginPanel)

        self.usernameField = JTextField('',15)
        self.loginPanel.add(JLabel("username:", SwingConstants.RIGHT))
        self.loginPanel.add(self.usernameField)

        self.passwordField = JPasswordField('', 15)
        self.loginPanel.add(JLabel("password:", SwingConstants.RIGHT))
        self.loginPanel.add(self.passwordField)

        self.loginButton = JButton('Log in',actionPerformed=self.login)
        self.loginPanel.add(self.loginButton)

        self.message = JLabel("Please Log in")
        self.loginPanel.add(self.message)

        self.frame.pack()
        self.show()

    def login(self,event):
        self.message.text = "Attempting to Log in..."
        username = self.usernameField.text
        try:
            self.api = twitter.Api(username, self.passwordField.text)
            self.timeline(username)
            self.loginPanel.visible = False
            self.message.text = "Logged in"
        except:
            self.message.text = "Log in failed."
```

```
            raise
        self.frame.size = 400,800


    def timeline(self, username):
        timeline = self.api.GetFriendsTimeline(username)
        self.resultPanel = JPanel()
        self.resultPanel.layout = BoxLayout(self.resultPanel, BoxLayout.Y_AXIS)
        for s in timeline:
            self.showTweet(s)

        scrollpane = JScrollPane(JScrollPane.VERTICAL_SCROLLBAR_AS_NEEDED,
                                 JScrollPane.HORIZONTAL_SCROLLBAR_NEVER)
        scrollpane.preferredSize = 400, 800
        scrollpane.viewport.view = self.resultPanel

        self.frame.add(scrollpane)

    def showTweet(self, status):
        user = status.user
        p = JPanel()

        p.add(JLabel(ImageIcon(URL(user.profile_image_url))))

        p.add(JTextArea(text = status.text,
                        editable = False,
                        wrapStyleWord = True,
                        lineWrap = True,
                        alignmentX = Component.LEFT_ALIGNMENT,
                        size = (300, 1)
            ))
        self.resultPanel.add(p)

    def show(self):
        self.frame.visible = True

if __name__ == '__main__':
    JyTwitter()
```

This code depends on the python-twitter package. This package can be found on the Python package index (PyPi). If you have easy_install (see Appendix A for instructions on easy_install) then you can install python-twitter like this:

Listing 16-14.

```
jython easy_install python-twitter
```

This will automatically install python-twitter's dependency: simplejson. Now you should be able to run the application. You should see the login prompt shown in Figure 16-3.

Figure 16-3. Password prompt

If you put in the wrong password, you should get the message shown in Figure 16-4.

Figure 16-4. Failed login

And finally, once you have successfully logged in, you should see something that looks similar to Figure 16-5.

Figure 16-5. Login successful!

The constructor creates the outer frame, imaginatively called self.frame. We set defaultCloseOperation so that the app will terminate if the user closes the main window. We then create a loginPanel that holds the text fields for the user to enter username and password, and create a login button that will call the self.login method when clicked. We then add a "Please log in" label and make the frame visible.

Listing 16-15.

```
def __init__(self):
        self.frame = JFrame("Jython Twitter",
                            defaultCloseOperation = WindowConstants.EXIT_ON_CLOSE)

    self.loginPanel = JPanel(GridLayout(0,2))
    self.frame.add(self.loginPanel)

    self.usernameField = JTextField('',15)
    self.loginPanel.add(JLabel("username:", SwingConstants.RIGHT))
    self.loginPanel.add(self.usernameField)

    self.passwordField = JPasswordField('', 15)
    self.loginPanel.add(JLabel("password:", SwingConstants.RIGHT))
    self.loginPanel.add(self.passwordField)

    self.loginButton = JButton('Log in',actionPerformed=self.login)
    self.loginPanel.add(self.loginButton)

    self.message = JLabel("Please Log in")
    self.loginPanel.add(self.message)

    self.frame.pack()

    self.show()
```

The login method changes the label text and calls into python-twitter to attempt a login. It's in a try/except block that will display "Log in failed" if something goes wrong. A real application would check different types of exceptions to see what went wrong and change the display message accordingly.

Listing 16-16.

```
def login(self,event):
    self.message.text = "Attempting to Log in..."

    username = self.usernameField.text
    try:
        self.api = twitter.Api(username, self.passwordField.text)
        self.timeline(username)
        self.loginPanel.visible = False
        self.message.text = "Logged in"
    except:
        self.message.text = "Log in failed."
        raise
    self.frame.size = 400,800
```

If the login succeeds, we call the timeline method, which populates the frame with the latest tweets that the user is following. In the timeline method, we call GetFriendsTimeline from the python-twitter API; then we iterate through the status objects and call showTweet on each. All of this gets dropped into a JScrollPane and set to a reasonable size, and then it is added to the main frame.

Listing 16-17.

```
def timeline(self, username):
    timeline = self.api.GetFriendsTimeline(username)
    self.resultPanel = JPanel()
    self.resultPanel.layout = BoxLayout(self.resultPanel, BoxLayout.Y_AXIS)
    for s in timeline:
        self.showTweet(s)

    scrollpane = JScrollPane(JScrollPane.VERTICAL_SCROLLBAR_AS_NEEDED,
                             JScrollPane.HORIZONTAL_SCROLLBAR_NEVER)
    scrollpane.preferredSize = 400, 800
    scrollpane.viewport.view = self.resultPanel

    self.frame.add(scrollpane)
```

In the showTweet method, we go through the tweets and add a JLabel with the user's icon (fetched via URL from user.profile_image_url) and a JTextArea to contain the text of the tweet. Note all of the bean properties that we had to set to get the JTextArea to display correctly.

Listing 16-18.

```
def showTweet(self, status):
    user = status.user
    p = JPanel()

    p.add(JLabel(ImageIcon(URL(user.profile_image_url))))

    p.add(JTextArea(text = status.text,
                    editable = False,
                    wrapStyleWord = True,
                    lineWrap = True,
                    alignmentX = Component.LEFT_ALIGNMENT,
                    size = (300, 1)
    ))
    self.resultPanel.add(p)
```

Summary

And that concludes our quick tour of Swing GUIs built via Jython. Again, Swing is a very large subject, so you'll want to look into dedicated Swing resources to really get a handle on it. After this chapter, it should be reasonably straightforward to translate the Java Swing examples you find into Jython Swing examples.

CHAPTER 17

■ ■ ■

Deployment Targets

Deployment of Jython applications varies from container to container. However, they are all very similar and usually allow deployment of WAR file or exploded directory web applications. Deploying to "the cloud" is a different scenario all together. Some cloud environments have typical Java application servers available for hosting, while others such as the Google App Engine run a bit differently. In this chapter, we'll discuss how to deploy web-based Jython applications to a few of the more widely used Java application servers. We will also cover deployment of Jython web applications to the Google App Engine and mobile devices. Although many of the deployment scenarios are quite similar, this chapter will walk through some of the differences from container to container.

In the end, one of the most important things to remember is that we need to make Jython available to our application. There are different ways to do this: either by ensuring that the *jython.jar* file is included with the application server, or by packaging the JAR directly into each web application. This chapter assumes that you are using the latter technique. Placing the *jython.jar* directly into each web application is a good idea because it allows the web application to follow the Java paradigm of "deploy anywhere." You do not need to worry whether you are deploying to Tomcat or Glassfish because the Jython runtime is embedded in your application.

Lastly, this section will briefly cover some of the reasons why mobile deployment is not yet a viable option for Jython. While a couple of targets exist in the mobile world, namely Android and JavaFX, both environments are still very new and Jython has not yet been optimized to run on either.

Application Servers

As with any Java web application, the standard web archive (WAR) files are universal throughout the Java application servers available today. This is good because it makes things a bit easier when it comes to the "write once run everywhere" philosophy that has been brought forth with the Java name. The great part of using Jython for deployment to application servers is just that, we can harness the technologies of the JVM to make our lives easier and deploy a Jython web application to any application server in the WAR format with very little tweaking.

If you have not yet used Django or Pylons on Jython, then you may not be aware that the resulting application to be deployed is in the WAR format. This is great because it leaves no assumption as to how the application should be deployed. All WAR files are deployed in the same manner according to each application server. This section will discuss how to deploy a WAR file on each of the three most widely used Java application servers. Now, all application servers are not covered in this section mainly due to the number of servers available today. Such a document would take more than one section of a book, no doubt. However, you should be able to follow similar deployment instructions as those discussed here for any of the application servers available today for deploying Jython web applications in the WAR file format.

Tomcat

Arguably the most widely used of all Java application servers, Tomcat offers easy management and a small footprint compared to some of the other options available. Tomcat will plug into most IDEs that are in use today, so you can manage the web container from within your development environment. This makes it handy to deploy and undeploy applications on-the-fly. For the purposes of this section, we've used Netbeans 6.7, so there may be some references to it.

To get started, download the Apache Tomcat server from the site at http://tomcat.apache.org/. Tomcat is constantly evolving, so we'll note that when writing this book the deployment procedures were targeted for the 6.0.20 release. Once you have downloaded the server and placed it into a location on your hard drive, you may have to change permissions. We had to use the *chmod +x* command on the entire apache-tomcat-6.0.20 directory before we were able to run the server. You will also need to configure an administrative account by going into the */conf/tomcat-users.xml* file and adding one. Be sure to grant the administrative account the "manager" role. This should look something like the following once completed.

Listing 17-1. tomcat-users.xml

```
<tomcat-users>
   <user username="admin" password="myadminpassword" roles="manager"/>
</tomcat-users>
```

After this has been done, you can add the installation to an IDE environment of your choice if you'd like. For instance, if you wish to add to Netbeans 6.7 you will need to go to the "Services" tab in the navigator, right-click on servers, choose "Tomcat 6.x" option, and then fill in the appropriate information pertaining to your environment. Once complete, you will be able to start, stop, and manage the Tomcat installation from the IDE.

Deploying Web Start

Deploying a web start application is as easy as copying the necessary files to a location on the web server that is accessible via the web. In the case of Tomcat, you will need to copy the contents of your web start application to a single directory contained within the "<tomcat-root>/webapps/ROOT" directory. For instance, if you have a web-start application entitled *JythonWebStart*, then you would package the JAR file along with the JNLP and HTML file for the application into a directory entitled *JythonWebStart* and then place that directory into the "<tomcat-root>/webapps/ROOT" directory.

Once the application has been copied to the appropriate locations, you should be able to access it via the web if Tomcat is started. The URL should look something like the following: *http://your-server:8080/JythonWebStart/launch.jnlp*. Of course, you will need to use the server name and the port that you are using along with the appropriate JNLP name for your application.

Deploying a WAR or Exploded Directory Application

To deploy a web application to Tomcat, you have two options. You can either use a WAR file including all content for your entire web application, or you can deploy an exploded directory application which is basically copy-and-paste for your entire web application directory structure into the "<tomcat-root>/webapps/ROOT" directory. Either way will work the same, and we will discuss each technique in this section.

For manual deployment of a web application, you can copy either your exploded directory web application or your WAR file into the "<tomcat-root>/webapps" directory. By default, Tomcat is setup to "autodeploy" applications. This means that you can have Tomcat started when you copy your WAR or exploded directory into the "webapps" location. Once you've done this, you should see some feedback from the Tomcat server if you have a terminal open (or from within the IDE). After a few seconds the application should be deployed successfully and available via the URL. The bonus to deploying exploded directory applications is that you can take any file within the application and change it at will. Once you are done with the changes, that file will be redeployed when you save it. . .this really saves on development time!

If you do not wish to have autodeploy enabled (perhaps in a production environment), then you can deploy applications on startup of the server. This process is basically the same as "autodeploy," except any new applications that are copied into the "webapps" directory are not deployed until the server is restarted. Lastly, you can always make use of the Tomcat manager to deploy web applications as well. To do this, open your web browser to the index of Tomcat, usually http://localhost:8080/index.html, and then click on the "Manager" link in the left-hand menu. You will need to authenticate at that point using your administrator password, but once you are in the console deployment is quite easy. In an effort to avoid redundancy, we will once again redirect you to the Tomcat documentation for more information on deploying a web application via the Tomcat manager console.

Glassfish

At the time of writing, the Glassfish V2 application server was mainstream and widely used. The Glassfish V3 server was still in preview mode, but showed a lot of potential for Jython application deployment. In this section, we will cover WAR and web start deployment to Glassfish V2, because it is the most widely used version. We will also discuss deployment for Django on Glassfish V3, because this version has added support for Django (and more Python web frameworks soon). Glassfish is very similar to Tomcat in terms of deployment, but there are a couple of minor differences which will be covered in this section.

To start out, you will need to download a glassfish distribution from the site at https://glassfish.dev.java.net/. Again, we recommend downloading V2, because it is the most widely used at the time of this writing. Installation is quite easy, but a little more involved than that of Tomcat. The installation of Glassfish will not be covered in this text, because it varies depending upon which version you are using. There are detailed instructions for each version located on the Glassfish website, so we will redirect you there for more information.

Once you have Glassfish installed, you can utilize the server via the command-line or terminal, or you can use an IDE just like Tomcat. To register a Glassfish V2 or V3 installation with Netbeans 6.7, just go to the "Services" tab in the Netbeans navigator and right-click on "Servers" and then add the version you are planning to register. Once the "Add Server Instance" window appears, simply fill in the information depending upon your environment.

There is an administrative user named "admin" that is set up by default with a Glassfish installation. In order to change the default password, it is best to startup Glassfish and log into the administrative console. The default administrative console port is 4848.

Deploying Web Start

Deploying a web start application is basically the same as any other web server, you simply make the web start JAR, JNLP, and HTML file accessible via the web. On Glassfish, you need to traverse into your "domain" directory and you will find a "docroot" inside. The path should be similar to "<glassfish-install-loc>/domains/domain1/docroot". Anything placed within the docroot area is visible to the web, so of course this is where you will place any web-start application directories. Again, a typical web start application will consist of your application JAR file, a JNLP file, and an HTML page used to open the JNLP. All of these files should typically be placed inside a directory appropriately named per your application, and then you can copy this directory into docroot.

WAR File and Exploded Directory Deployment

Again, there are a variety of ways to deploy an application using Glassfish. Let's assume that you are using V2, you have the option to "hot deploy" or use the Glassfish Admin Console to deploy your application. Glassfish will work with either an exploded directory or WAR file deployment scenario. By default, the Glassfish "autodeploy" option is turned on, so it is quite easy to either copy your WAR or exploded directory application into the autodeploy location to deploy. If the application server is started, it will automatically start your application (if it runs without issues). The autodeploy directory for Glassfish V2 resides in the location "<glassfish-install-loc>/domains/domain1/autodeploy."

Glassfish v3 Django Deployment

The Glassfish V3 server has some capabilities built into it to help facilitate the process of deploying a Django application. In the future, there will also be support for other Jython web frameworks such as Pylons.

Other Java Application Servers

If you have read through the information contained in the previous sections, then you have a fairly good idea of what it is like to deploy a Jython web application to a Java application server. There is no difference between deploying Jython web applications and Java web applications for the most part. You must be sure that you include *jython.jar* as mentioned in the introduction, but for the most part deployment is the same. However, we have run into cases with some application servers such as JBoss where it wasn't so cut-and-dry to run a Jython application. For instance, we have tried to deploy a Jython servlet application on JBoss application server 5.1.0 GA and had lots of issues. For one, we had to manually add *servlet-api.jar* to the application because we were unable to compile the application in Netbeans without doing so...this was not the case with Tomcat or Glassfish. Similarly, we had issues trying to deploy a Jython web application to JBoss as there were several errors that had incurred when the container was scanning *jython.jar* for some reason.

All in all, with a bit of tweaking and perhaps an additional XML configuration file in the application, Jython web applications will deploy to *most* Java application servers. The bonus to deploying your application on a Java application server is that you are in complete control of the environment. For instance, you could embed the *jython.jar* file into the application server lib directory so that it was loaded at startup and available for all applications running in the environment. Likewise, you are in control of other necessary components such as database connection pools and so forth. If you deploy to another service that lives in "the cloud," you have very little control over the environment. In the next section, we'll study one such environment by Google which is known as the Google App Engine. While this "cloud" service is an entirely different environment than your basic Java web application server, it contains some nice features that allow one to test applications prior to deployment in the cloud.

Google App Engine

The new kid on the block, at least for the time of this writing, is the Google App Engine. Fresh to the likes of the Java platform, the Google App Engine can be used for deploying applications written in just about any language that runs on the JVM, Jython included. The App Engine went live in April of 2008, allowing Python developers to begin using its services to host Python applications and libraries. In the spring of 2009, the App Engine added support for the Java platform. Along with support of the Java language, most other languages that run on the JVM will also deploy and run on the Google App Engine, including Jython. It has been mentioned that more programming languages will be supported at some point in the future, but at the time of this writing Python and Java were the only supported languages.

The App Engine actually runs a slightly slimmed-down version of the standard Java library. You must download and develop using the Google App Engine SDK for Java in order to ensure that your application will run in the environment. You can download the SDK by visiting this link: http://code.google.com/appengine/downloads.html along with viewing the extensive documentation available on the Google App Engine site. The SDK comes complete with a development web server that can be used for testing your code before deploying, and several demo applications ranging from easy JSP programs to sophisticated demos that use Google authentication. No doubt about it, Google has done a good job at creating an easy learning environment for the App Engine so that developers can get up and running quickly.

In this section you will learn how to get started using the Google App Engine SDK, and how to deploy some Jython web applications. You will learn how to deploy a Jython servlet application as well as a WSGI application utilizing modjy. Once you've learned how to develop and use a Jython Google App Engine program using the development environment, you will learn a few specifics about deploying to the cloud. If you have not done so already, be sure to visit the link mentioned in the previous paragraph and download the SDK so that you can follow along in the sections to come.

■ **Note** The Google App Engine is a very large topic. Entire books could be written on the subject of developing Jython applications to run on the App Engine. With that said, we will cover the basics to get you up and running with developing Jython applications for the App Engine. Once you've read through this section, we suggest going to the Google App Engine documentation for further details.

Starting With an SDK Demo

We will start by running the demo application known as "guestbook" that comes with the Google App Engine SDK. This is a very simple Java application that allows one to sign in using an email address and post messages to the screen. In order to start the SDK web server and run the "guestbook" application, open up a terminal and traverse into the directory where you expanded the Google App Engine .zip file and run the following command:

`<app-engine-base-directory>/bin/dev_appserver.sh demos/guestbook/war`

Of course, if you are running on windows there is a corresponding .bat script for you to run that will start the web server. Once you've issued the preceding command it will only take a second or two before the web server starts. You can then open a browser and traverse to *http://localhost:8080* to invoke the "guestbook" application. This is a basic JSP-based Java web application, but we can deploy a Jython application and use it in the same manner as we will see in a few moments. You can stop the web server by pressing "CTRL+C".

Deploying to the Cloud

Prior to deploying your application to the cloud, you must of course set up an account with the Google App Engine. If you have another account with Google such as GMail, then you can easily activate your App Engine account using that same username. To do so, go to the Google App Engine link: http://code.google.com/appengine/ and click "Sign Up." Enter your existing account information or create a new account to get started.

After your account has been activated you will need to create an application by clicking on the "Create Application" button. You have a total of 10 available application slots to use if you are making use of the free App Engine account. Once you've created an application then you are ready to begin deploying to the cloud. In this section of the book, we create an application known as *jythongae*. This is the name of the application that you must create on the App Engine. You must also ensure that this name is supplied within the *appengine-web.xml* file.

Working With a Project

The Google App Engine provides project templates to get you started developing using the correct directory structure. Eclipse has a plug-in that makes it easy to generate Google App Engine projects and deploy them to the App Engine. If interested in making use of the plug-in, please visit http://code.google.com/appengine/docs/java/tools/eclipse.html to read more information and download the plug-in. Similarly, Netbeans has an App Engine plug-in that is available on the Kenai site appropriately named *nbappengine* (http://kenai.com/projects/nbappengine). In this text we will cover the use of Netbeans 6.7 to develop a simple Jython servlet application to deploy on the App Engine. You can either download and use the template available with one of these IDE plug-ins, or simply create a new Netbeans project and make use of the template provided with the App Engine SDK (<app-engine-base-directory/demos/new_project_template>) to create your project directory structure.

For the purposes of this tutorial, we will make use of the *nbappengine* plug-in. If you are using Eclipse you will find a section following this tutorial that provides some Eclipse plug-in specifics.

In order to install the nbappengine plug-in, you add the 'App Engine' update center to the Netbeans plug-in center by choosing the Settings tab and adding the update center using http://deadlock.netbeans.org/hudson/job/nbappengine/lastSuccessfulBuild/artifact/build/updates/updates.xml.gz as the URL. Once you've added the new update center you can select the Available Plugins tab and add all of the plug-ins in the "Google App Engine" category, then choose Install. After doing so, you can add the "App Engine" as a server in your Netbeans environment using the "Services" tab. To add the server, point to the base directory of your Google App Engine SDK. Once you have added the App Engine server to Netbeans, it will become an available deployment option for your web applications.

Create a new Java web project and name it JythonGAE. For the deployment server, choose "Google App Engine," and you will notice that when your web application is created an additional file will be created within the WEB-INF directory named appengine-web.xml. This is the Google App Engine configuration file for the JythonGAE application. Any of the .py files that we wish to use in our application must be mapped in this file so that they will not be treated as static files by the Google App Engine. By default, Google App Engine treats all files outside of the WEB-INF directory as static unless they are JSP files. Our application is going to make use of three Jython servlets, namely NewJythonServlet.py, AddNumbers.py and AddToPage.py. In our appengine-web.xml file we can exclude all .py files from being treated as static by adding the suffix to the exclusion list as follows.

Listing 17-2. appengine-web.xml

```xml
<?xml version="1.0" encoding="UTF-8"?>
<appengine-web-app xmlns="http://appengine.google.com/ns/1.0">
    <application>jythongae</application>
    <version>1</version>
    <static-files>
        <exclude path="/**.py"/>
    </static-files>
    <resource-files/>
    <ssl-enabled>false</ssl-enabled>
    <sessions-enabled>true</sessions-enabled>
</appengine-web-app>
```

At this point we will need to create a couple of additional directories within our WEB-INF project directory. We should create a *lib* directory and place *jython.jar* and *appengine-api-1.0-sdk-1.2.2.jar* into the directory. Note that the App Engine JAR may be named differently according to the version that you are using. We should now have a directory structure that resembles the following:

Listing 17-3.

```
JythonGAE
    WEB-INF
        lib
            jython.jar
            appengine-api-1.0-sdk-1.2.2.jar
        appengine-web.xml
        web.xml
    src
    web
```

Now that we have the application structure set up, it is time to begin building the actual logic. In a traditional Jython servlet application we need to ensure that the *PyServlet* class is initialized at startup and that all files ending in *.py* are passed to it. As we've seen in Chapter 13, this is done in the *web.xml* deployment descriptor. However, we have found that this alone does not work when deploying to the cloud. We found some inconsistencies while deploying against the Google App Engine development server and deploying to the cloud. For this reason, we will show you the way that we were able to get the application to function as expected in both the production and development Google App Engine environments. In Chapter 12, the object factory pattern for coercing Jython classes into Java was discussed. If this same pattern is applied to Jython servlet applications, then we can use the factories to coerce our Jython servlet into Java byte code at runtime. We then map the resulting coerced class to a servlet mapping in the application's web.xml deployment descriptor. We can also deploy our Jython applets and make use of *PyServlet* mapping to the *.py* extension in the *web.xml*. We will comment in the source where the code for the two implementations differs.

Object Factories with App Engine

In order to use object factories to coerce our code, we must use an object factory along with a Java interface, and once again we will use the PlyJy project to make this happen. Please note that if you choose to not use the object factory pattern and instead use PyServlet you can safely skip forward to the next subsection. The first step is to add *PlyJy.jar* to the *lib* directory that we created previously to ensure it is bundled with our application. There is a Java servlet contained within the PlyJy project named *JythonServletFacade*, and what this Java servlet does is essentially use the *JythonObjectFactory* class to coerce a named Jython servlet and then invoke its resulting *doGet* and *doPost* methods. There is also a simple Java interface named *JythonServletInterface* in the project, and it must be implemented by our Jython servlet in order for the coercion to work as expected.

Using PyServlet Mapping

When we use the PyServlet mapping implementation, there is no need to coerce objects using factories. You simply set up a servlet mapping within *web.xml* and use your Jython servlets directly with the .py extension in the URL. However, we've seen issues while using PyServlet on the App Engine in that this implementation will deploy to the development App Engine server environment, but when deployed to the cloud you will receive an error when trying to invoke the servlet. It is because of these inconsistencies that we chose to implement the object factory solution for Jython servlet to App Engine deployment.

Example Jython Servlet Application for App Engine

The next piece of the puzzle is the code for our application. In this example, we'll make use of a simple servlet that displays some text as well as the same example that was used in Chapter 13 with JSP and Jython. The following code sets up three Jython servlets. The first servlet simply displays some output, the next two perform some mathematical logic, and then there is a JSP to display the results for the mathematical servlets.

Listing 17-4. NewJythonServlet.py

```
from javax.servlet.http import HttpServlet
from org.plyjy.interfaces import JythonServletInterface

class NewJythonServlet (JythonServletInterface, HttpServlet):
        def doGet(self,request,response):
                self.doPost (request,response)

        def doPost(self,request,response):
                toClient = response.getWriter()
                response.setContentType ("text/html")
                toClient.println ("<html><head><title>Jython Servlet Test Using Object
Factory</title>" +
                                        "<body><h1>Jython Servlet Test for
GAE</h1></body></html>")

        def getServletInfo(self):
            return "Short Description"
```

Listing 17-5. AddNumbers.py

```
import javax
class add_numbers(javax.servlet.http.HttpServlet):
    def doGet(self, request, response):
        self.doPost(request, response)
    def doPost(self, request, response):
        x = request.getParameter("x")
        y = request.getParameter("y")
        if not x or not y:
            sum = "<font color='red'>You must place numbers in each value box</font>"
        else:
            try:
                sum = int(x) + int(y)
            except ValueError, e:
                sum = "<font color='red'>You must place numbers only in each value
box</font>"
        request.setAttribute("sum", sum)
        dispatcher = request.getRequestDispatcher("testJython.jsp")
        dispatcher.forward(request, response)
```

Listing 17-6. AddToPage.py

```python
import java, javax, sys

class add_to_page(javax.servlet.http.HttpServlet):
    def doGet(self, request, response):
        self.doPost(request, response)

    def doPost(self, request, response):
        addtext = request.getParameter("p")
        if not addtext:
            addtext = ""

        request.setAttribute("page_text", addtext)
        dispatcher = request.getRequestDispatcher("testJython.jsp")
        dispatcher.forward(request, response)
```

Listing 17-7. testjython.jsp

Note that this implementation differs if you plan to make use of the object factory technique. Instead of using *add_to_page.py* and *add_numbers.py* as your actions, you would utilize the servlet instead, namely */add_to_page* and */add_numbers*

```html
<html>
    <head>
        <meta http-equiv="Content-Type" content="text/html; charset=UTF-8">
        <title>Jython JSP Test</title>
    </head>
    <body>
        <form method="GET" action="add_to_page.py">
            <input type="text" name="p">
            <input type="submit">
        </form>
        <% Object page_text = request.getAttribute("page_text");
           Object sum = request.getAttribute("sum");
           if(page_text == null){
               page_text = "";
           }
           if(sum == null){
               sum = "";
           }
        %>
        <br/>
            <p><%= page_text %></p>
        <br/>
        <form method="GET" action="add_numbers.py">
            <input type="text" name="x">
            +
            <input type="text" name="y">
            =
            <%= sum %>
            <br/>
```

```
            <input type="submit" title="Add Numbers">
        </form>

    </body>
</html>
```

As mentioned previously, it is important that all of the Jython servlets reside within your classpath somewhere. If using Netbeans, you can either place the servlets into the source root of your project (not inside a package), or you can place them in the web folder that contains your JSP files. If doing the latter, we have found that you may have to tweak your CLASSPATH a bit by adding the web folder to your list of libraries from within the project properties. Next, we need to ensure that the deployment descriptor includes the necessary servlet definitions and mappings for the application. Now, if you are using the object factory implementation and the *JythonServletFacade* servlet, you would have noticed that there is a variable named *PyServletName* which the JythonObjectFactory is using as the name of our Jython servlet. Well, within the *web.xml* we must pass an *<init-param>* using *PyServletName* as the *<param-name>* and the name of our Jython servlet as the *<param-value>*. This will basically pass the name of the Jython servlet to the *JythonServletFacade* servlet so that it can be used by the object factory.

Listing 17-8. web.xml

```
<web-app>
    <display-name>Jython Google App Engine</display-name>

    <!-- Used for the PyServlet Implementation -->
    <servlet>
        <servlet-name>PyServlet</servlet-name>
        <servlet-class>org.python.util.PyServlet</servlet-class>
    </servlet>

    <!-- The next three servlets are used for the object factory implementation only.
         They can be excluded in the PyServlet implementation -->
    <servlet>
        <servlet-name>NewJythonServlet</servlet-name>
        <servlet-class>org.plyjy.servlets.JythonServletFacade</servlet-class>
        <init-param>
            <param-name>PyServletName</param-name>
            <param-value>NewJythonServlet</param-value>
        </init-param>
    </servlet>
    <servlet>
        <servlet-name>AddNumbers</servlet-name>
        <servlet-class>org.plyjy.servlets.JythonServletFacade</servlet-class>
        <init-param>
            <param-name>PyServletName</param-name>
            <param-value>AddNumbers</param-value>
        </init-param>
    </servlet>
    <servlet>
        <servlet-name>AddToPage</servlet-name>
        <servlet-class>org.plyjy.servlets.JythonServletFacade</servlet-class>
        <init-param>
            <param-name>PyServletName</param-name>
            <param-value>AddToPage</param-value>
```

```
        </init-param>
    </servlet>

    <!-- The following mapping should be used for the PyServlet implementation -->
    <servlet-mapping>
        <servlet-name>PyServlet</servlet-name>
        <url-pattern>*.py</url-pattern>
    </servlet-mapping>

    <!-- The following three mappings are used in the object factory implementation -->

    <servlet-mapping>
        <servlet-name>NewJythonServlet</servlet-name>
        <url-pattern>/NewJythonServlet</url-pattern>
    </servlet-mapping>
    <servlet-mapping>
        <servlet-name>AddNumbers</servlet-name>
        <url-pattern>/AddNumbers</url-pattern>
    </servlet-mapping>
    <servlet-mapping>
        <servlet-name>AddToPage</servlet-name>
        <url-pattern>/AddToPage</url-pattern>
    </servlet-mapping>
</web-app>
```

Note that when using the PyServlet implementation you should exclude those portions in the *web.xml* above that are used for the object factory implementation. The PyServlet mapping can be contained within the *web.xml* in both implementations without issue. That's it, now you can deploy the application to your Google App Engine development environment, and it should run without any issues. You can also choose to deploy to another web server to test for compatibility if you wish. You can deploy directly to the cloud by right-clicking the application and choosing the "Deploy to App Engine" option.

Using Eclipse

If you wish to use the Eclipse IDE for development, you should definitely download the Google App Engine plug-in using the link provided earlier in the chapter. You should also use the PyDev plug-in which is available at http://pydev.sourceforge.net/. For the purposes of this section, we used Eclipse Galileo and started a new project named "JythonGAE" as a Google Web Application. When creating the project, make sure you check the box for using Google App Engine and uncheck the Google Web Toolkit option. You will find that Eclipse creates a directory structure for your application that is much the same as the project template that is included with the Google App Engine SDK.

If you follow through the code example from the previous section, you can create the same code and set up the *web.xml* and *appengine-web.xml* the same way. The key is to ensure that you create a *lib* directory within the *WEB-INF* and you place the files in the appropriate location. You will need to ensure that your Jython servlets are contained in your CLASSPATH by either adding them to the source root for your project, or by going into the project properties and adding the *war* directory to your *Java Build Path*. When doing so, make sure you do *not* include the *WEB-INF* directory or you will receive errors.

When you are ready to deploy the application, you can choose to use the Google App Engine development environment or deploy to the cloud. You can run the application by right-clicking on the project and choosing *Run As* option and then choose the Google Web Application option. The first time you run the application you may need to set up the runtime. If you are ready to deploy to the cloud, you can right-click on the project and choose the *Google -> Deploy to App Engine* option. After entering your Google username and password then your application will be deployed.

Deploy Modjy to GAE

We can easily deploy WSGI applications using Jython's modjy API as well. To do so, you need to add an archive of the Jython *Lib* directory to your WEB-INF project directory. According to the modjy web site, you need to obtain the source for Jython, then zip the *Lib* directory and place it into another directory along with a file that will act as a pointer to the zip archive. The modjy site names the directory *python-lib* and names the pointer file *all.pth*. This pointer file can be named anything as long as the suffix is *.pth*. Inside the pointer file you need to explicitly name the zip archive that you had created for the *Lib* directory contents. Let's assume you named it lib.zip, in this case we will put the text "lib.zip" without the quotes into the *.pth* file. Now if we add the modjy *demo_app.py* demonstration application to the project then our directory structure should look as follows:

Listing 17-9.

```
modjy_app
    demo_app.py
    WEB-INF
        lib
            jython.jar
            appengine-api-1.0-sdk-1.2.2.jar
        python-lib
            lib.zip
            all.pth
```

Now if we run the application using Tomcat it should run as expected. Likewise, we can run it using the Google App Engine SDK web server and it should provide the expected results.

The Google App Engine is certainly an important deployment target for Jython. Google offers free hosting for smaller applications, and they also base account pricing on bandwidth. No doubt that it is a good way to put up a small site, and possibly build on it later. Most importantly, you can deploy Django, Pylons, and other applications via Jython to the App Engine by setting up your App Engine applications like the examples we had shown in this chapter.

Java Store

Another deployment target that is hot off the presses at the time of this book is the Java Store or Java Warehouse. This is a new concept brought to market by Sun Microsystems in order to help Java software developers market their applications via a single shop that is available online via a web start application. Similar to other application venues, The Java Store is a storefront application where people can go to search for applications that have been submitted by developers. The Java Warehouse is the repository of applications that are contained within the Java Store. This looks to be a very promising target for Java and Jython developers alike. It *should* be as easy as generating a JAR file that contains a Jython application and deploying it to the Java Store. Unfortunately, because the program is still in alpha mode at this time, we are unable to provide any specific details on distributing Jython applications via the Java Store. However, there are future plans to make alternative VM language applications easily deployable to the Java Warehouse. At this time, it is certainly possible to deploy a Jython application to the warehouse, but it can only deploy as a Java application. As of the time of this writing, only Java and JavaFX applications are directly deployable to the Java Warehouse. Please note that because this product is still in alpha mode, this book will not discuss such aspects of the program as memberships or fees that may be incurred for hosing your applications on the Java Store.

The requirements for publishing an application to the warehouse are as follows:

- Your application packed in a single jar file

- Descriptive text to document your application

- Graphic image files used for icons and to give the consumer an idea of your application's look.

In Chapter 13, we took a look at packaging and distributing Jython GUI applications in a JAR file. When a Jython application is packaged in a JAR file then it is certainly possible to use Java Web Start to host the application via the web. On the other hand, if one wishes to make a Jython GUI application available for purchase or for free, the Java Store would be another way of doing so. One likely way to deploy applications in a single JAR is to use the method discussed in Chapter 13, but there are other solutions as well. For instance, one could use the *One-Jar* product to create a single JAR file containing all of the necessary Jython code as well as other JAR files essential to the application. In the following section, we will discuss deployment of a Jython application using One-JAR so that you can see some similarities and differences to using the Jython standalone JAR technique.

Deploying a Single JAR

In order to deploy an application to the Java Warehouse, it must be packaged as a single JAR file. We've already discussed packaging Jython applications into a JAR file using the Jython standalone method in Chapter 13. In this section, you will learn how to make use of the One-JAR (http://one-jar.sourceforge.net/) product to distribute client-based Jython applications. In order to get started, you will need to grab a copy of One-JAR. There are a few options available on the download site, but for our purposes we will package an application using the source files for One-JAR. Once downloaded, the source for the project should look as follows.

Listing 17-10.

```
src
    com
        simontuffs
            onejar
                Boot.java
                Handler.java
                IProperties.java
                JarClassLoader.java
```

This source code for the One-Jar project must reside within the JAR file that we will build. Next, we need to create separate source directories for both our Jython source and our Java source. Likewise, we will create a separate source directory for the One-Jar source. Lastly, we'll create a *lib* directory into which we will place all of the required JAR files for the application. In order to run a Jython application, we'll need to package the Jython project source into a JAR file for our application. We will not need to use the entire *jython.jar*, but rather only a standalone version of it. The easiest way to obtain a standalone Jython JAR is to run the installer and choose the standalone option. After this is done, simply add the resulting jython.jar to the lib directory of application. In the end, the directory structure should resemble the following.

Listing 17-11.

```
one-jar-jython-example
    java
    lib
        jython.jar
    LICENSE.txt
```

```
onejar
    src
        com

            simontuffs
                onejar
                    Boot.java
                    Handler.java
                    IProperties.java
                    JarClassLoader.java
        one-jar-license.txt
    src
```

As you can see from the depiction of the file structure in this example, the *src* directory will contain our Jython source files. The LICENSE.txt included in this example was written by Ryan McGuire (http://www.enigmacurry.com). He has a detailed explanation of using One-Jar on his blog, and we've replicated some of his work in this example. . .including a version of the build.xml that we will put together in order to build the application. Let's take a look at the build file that we will use to build the application JAR. In this example we are using Apache Ant for the build system, but you could choose something different if you'd like.

Listing 17-12. build.xml

```xml
<project name="JythonSwingApp" default="dist" basedir=".">

  <!-- ##################################################
       These two properties are the only ones you are
       likely to want to change for your own projects:    -->
  <property name="jar.name" value="JythonSwingApp.jar" />
  <property name="java-main-class" value="Main" />
  <!-- ##################################################  -->

  <!-- Below here you don't need to change for simple projects -->
  <property name="src.dir" location="src"/>
  <property name="java.dir" location="java"/>
  <property name="onejar.dir" location="onejar"/>
  <property name="java-build.dir" location="java-build"/>
  <property name="build.dir" location="build"/>
  <property name="lib.dir" location="lib"/>

  <path id="classpath">
    <fileset dir="${lib.dir}" includes="**/*.jar"/>
  </path>

  <target name="clean">
    <delete dir="${java-build.dir}"/>
    <delete dir="${build.dir}"/>
    <delete file="${jar.name}"/>
  </target>

  <target name="dist" depends="clean">
    <!-- prepare the build directory -->
    <mkdir dir="${build.dir}/lib"/>
```

```
    <mkdir dir="${build.dir}/main"/>
    <!-- Build java code -->
    <mkdir dir="${java-build.dir}"/>
    <javac srcdir="${java.dir}" destdir="${java-build.dir}" classpathref="classpath"/>
    <!-- Build main.jar -->
    <jar destfile="${build.dir}/main/main.jar" basedir="${java-build.dir}">
      <manifest>
            <attribute name="Main-Class" value="Main" />
      </manifest>
    </jar>
    <delete file="${java-build.dir}"/>
    <!-- Add the python source -->
    <copy todir="${build.dir}">
      <fileset dir="${src.dir}"/>
    </copy>
    <!-- Add the libs -->
    <copy todir="${build.dir}/lib">
      <fileset dir="${lib.dir}"/>
    </copy>
    <!-- Compile OneJar -->
    <javac srcdir="${onejar.dir}" destdir="${build.dir}" classpathref="classpath"/>
    <!-- Copy the OneJar license file -->
    <copy file="${onejar.dir}/one-jar-license.txt" tofile="${build.dir}/one-jar-license.txt"
/>
    <!-- Build the jar -->
    <jar destfile="${jar.name}" basedir="${build.dir}">
      <manifest>
            <attribute name="Main-Class" value="com.simontuffs.onejar.Boot" />
            <attribute name="Class-Path" value="lib/jython-full.jar" />
      </manifest>
    </jar>
    <!-- clean up -->
    <delete dir="${java-build.dir}" />
    <delete dir="${build.dir}" />
  </target>

</project>
```

Because this is a Jython application, we can use as much Java source as we'd like. In this example, we will only use one Java source file *Main.java* to "drive" our application. In this case, we'll use the *PythonInterpreter* inside of our *Main.java* to invoke our simple Jython Swing application. Now let's take a look at the *Main.java* source.

Listing 17-13. Main.java

```java
import org.python.core.PyException;
import org.python.util.PythonInterpreter;

public class Main {
    public static void main(String[] args) throws PyException{
        PythonInterpreter intrp = new PythonInterpreter();
        intrp.exec("import JythonSimpleSwing as jy");
        intrp.exec("jy.JythonSimpleSwing().start()");
```

373

```
        }
}
```

Now that we've written the driver class, we'll place it into our *java* source directory. As stated previously, we'll place our Jython code into the *src* directory. In this example we are using the same simple Jython Swing application that we wrote for Chapter 13.

Listing 17-14. JythonSimpleSwing.py

```python
import sys

import javax.swing as swing
import java.awt as awt

class JythonSimpleSwing(object):
    def __init__(self):
        self.frame=swing.JFrame(title="My Frame", size=(300,300))
        self.frame.defaultCloseOperation=swing.JFrame.EXIT_ON_CLOSE;
        self.frame.layout=awt.BorderLayout()
        self.panel1=swing.JPanel(awt.BorderLayout())
        self.panel2=swing.JPanel(awt.GridLayout(4,1))
        self.panel2.preferredSize = awt.Dimension(10,100)
        self.panel3=swing.JPanel(awt.BorderLayout())

        self.title=swing.JLabel("Text Rendering")
        self.button1=swing.JButton("Print Text", actionPerformed=self.printMessage)
        self.button2=swing.JButton("Clear Text", actionPerformed=self.clearMessage)
        self.textField=swing.JTextField(30)
        self.outputText=swing.JTextArea(4,15)


        self.panel1.add(self.title)
        self.panel2.add(self.textField)
        self.panel2.add(self.button1)
        self.panel2.add(self.button2)
        self.panel3.add(self.outputText)

        self.frame.contentPane.add(self.panel1, awt.BorderLayout.PAGE_START)
        self.frame.contentPane.add(self.panel2, awt.BorderLayout.CENTER)
        self.frame.contentPane.add(self.panel3, awt.BorderLayout.PAGE_END)

    def start(self):
        self.frame.visible=1

    def printMessage(self,event):
        print "Print Text!"
        self.text = self.textField.getText()
        self.outputText.append(self.text)

    def clearMessage(self, event):
        self.outputText.text = ""
```

At this time, the application is ready to build using Ant. In order to run the build, simply traverse into the directory that contains *build.xml* and initiate the *ant* command. The resulting JAR can be run using the following syntax:

```
java -jar JythonSwingApp.jar
```

In some situations, such as deploying via web start, this JAR file will also need to be signed. There are many resources online that explain the signing of JAR files that topic will not be covered in this text. The JAR is now ready to be deployed and used on other machines. This method will be a good way to package an application for distribution via the Java Store.

Mobile

Mobile applications are the way of the future. At this time, there are a couple of different options for developing mobile applications using Jython. One way to develop mobile applications using Jython is to make use of the JavaFX API from Jython. Since JavaFX is all Java behind the scenes, it would be fairly simple to make use of the JavaFX API using Jython code. However, this technique is not really a production-quality result in my opinion for a couple of reasons. First, the JavaFX scripting language makes GUI development quite easy. While it is possible (see http://wiki.python.org/jython/JythonMonthly/Articles/December2007/2 for more details), the translation of JavaFX API using Jython would not be as easy as making use of the JavaFX script language. The second reason this is not feasible at the time of this writing is that JavaFX is simply not available on all mobile devices at this time. It is really just becoming available to the mobile world at this time and will take some time to become acclimated.

Another way to develop mobile applications using Jython is to make use of the Android operating system which is available via Google. Android is actively being used on mobile devices today, and its use is continuing to grow. Although in early stages, there is a project known as *Jythonroid* that is an implementation of Jython for the Android Dalvik Virtual Machine. Unfortunately, it was not under active development at the time of this writing, although some potential does exist for getting the project on track.

If you are interested in mobile development using Jython, please pay close attention to the two technologies discussed in this section. They are the primary deployment targets for Jython in the mobile world. As for the *Jythonroid* project, it is open source and available to developers. Interested parties may begin working on it again to make it functional and bring it up to date with the latest Android SDK.

Summary

Deploying Jython applications is very much like Java application deployment. For those of you who are familiar with Java application servers, deploying a Jython application should be a piece of cake. On the contrary, for those of you who are not familiar with Java application deployment this topic may take a bit of getting used to. In the end, it is easy to deploy a Jython web or client application using just about any of the available Java application servers that are available today.

Deploying Jython web applications is universally easy to do using the WAR file format. As long as *jython.jar* is either in the application server classpath or packaged along with the web application, Jython servlets should function without issue. We also learned that it is possible to deploy a JAR file containing a Jython GUI application via Java web start technology. Using a JNLP deployment file is quite easy to do; the trick to deploying Jython via a JAR file is to set the file up correctly. Once completed, an HTML page can be used to reference the JNLP and initiate the download of the JAR to the client machine.

Lastly, this section discussed use of the Google App Engine for deploying Jython servlet applications. While the Google App Engine environment is still relatively new at the time of this writing, it is an exceptional deployment target for any Python or Java application developer. Using a few tricks with the object factory technique, it is possible to deploy Jython servlets and use them directly or via a

JSP file on the App Engine. Stay tuned for more deployment targets to become available for Jython in the coming months and years. As cloud computing and mobile devices are becoming more popular, the number of deployment targets will continue to grow and Jython will be more useful with each one.

PART IV

■■■

Strategy and Technique

■ ■ ■

## CHAPTER 18

Testing and Continuous Integration

Nowadays, automated testing is a fundamental activity in software development. In this chapter, you will see a survey of the tools available for Jython in this field. These tools range from common tools used in the Python world to aid with unit testing, to more complex tools available in the Java world that can be extended or driven using Jython.

Python Testing Tools

Let's start the chapter with a discussion of the most common Python testing tools. We will start with UnitTest to get a feel for the process.

UnitTest

First we will take a look at the most classic test tool available in Python: UnitTest. It follows the conventions of most "xUnit" incarnations (such as JUnit); you subclass from TestCase class, write test methods (which must have a name starting with "test"), and optionally override the methods setUp() and tearDown(), which are executed around the test methods. And you can use the multiple assert*() methods provided by TestCase. The following is a very simple test case for functions of the built-in math module.

Listing 18-1.

```
import math
import unittest

class TestMath(unittest.TestCase):
    def testFloor(self):
        self.assertEqual(1, math.floor(1.01))
        self.assertEqual(0, math.floor(0.5))
        self.assertEqual(-1, math.floor(-0.5))
        self.assertEqual(-2, math.floor(-1.1))

    def testCeil(self):
        self.assertEqual(2, math.ceil(1.01))
        self.assertEqual(1, math.ceil(0.5))
        self.assertEqual(0, math.ceil(-0.5))
        self.assertEqual(-1, math.ceil(-1.1))
```

There are many other assertion methods besides assertEqual(), of course. The following lists the rest of the available assertion methods:

- assertNotEqual(a, b): The opposite of assertEqual().

- assertAlmostEqual(a, b): Only used for numeric comparison. It adds a sort of tolerance for insignificant differences by subtracting its first two arguments after rounding them to the seventh decimal place, and later comparing the result to zero. You can specify a different number of decimal places in the third argument. This is useful for comparing floating point numbers.

- assertNotAlmostEqual(a, b): The opposite of assertAlmostEqual().

- assert_(x): Accepts a Boolean argument, expecting it to be True. You can use it to write other checks, such as "greater than," or to check Boolean functions/attributes. (The trailing underscore is needed because assert is a keyword.)

- assertFalse(x). The opposite of assert_().

- assertRaises(exception, callable). Used to assert that an exception passed as the first argument is thrown when invoking the callable specified as the second argument. The rest of the arguments passed to assertRaises are passed on to the callable.

As an example, let's extend our test of mathematical functions using some of these other assertion functions:

Listing 18-2.

```
import math
import unittest
import operator

class TestMath(unittest.TestCase):

    # ...

    def testMultiplication(self):
        self.assertAlmostEqual(0.3, 0.1 * 3)

    def testDivision(self):
        self.assertRaises(ZeroDivisionError, operator.div, 1, 0)
        # The same assertion using a different idiom:
        self.assertRaises(ZeroDivisionError, lambda: 1 / 0)
```

Now, you may be wondering how to run this test case. The simple answer is to add the following to the file in which we defined it:

```
if __name__ == '__main__':
    unittest.main()
```

Finally, just run the module. Say, if you wrote all this code on a file named test_math.py, then run:

```
$ jython test_math.py
```

And you will see this output:

```
....
----------------------------------------------------------------------
Ran 4 tests in 0.005s

OK
```

Each dot before the dash line represents a successfully run test. Let's see what happens if we add a test that fails. Change the invocation assertAlmostEqual() method in testMultiplication() to use assertEqual() instead. If you run the module again, you will see the following output:

Listing 18-3.

```
...F
======================================================================
FAIL: testMultiplication (__main__.TestMath)
----------------------------------------------------------------------
Traceback (most recent call last):
  File "test_math.py", line 22, in testMultiplication
    self.assertEqual(0.3, 0.1 * 3)
AssertionError: 0.3 != 0.30000000000000004


----------------------------------------------------------------------
Ran 4 tests in 0.030s

FAILED (failures=1)
```

As you can see, the last dot is now an "F," and an explanation of the failure is printed, pointing out that 0.3 and 0.30000000000000004 are not equal. The last line also shows the grand total of 1 failure.

By the way, now you can imagine why using assertEquals(x, y) is better than assert_(x == y): if the test fails, assertEquals() provides helpful information, which assert_() can't possibly provide by itself. To see this in action, let's change testMultiplication() to use assert_():

```
class TestMath(unittest.TestCase):

    #...

    def testMultiplication(self):
        self.assert_(0.3 == 0.1 * 3)
```

If you run the test again, the output will be:

```
...F
======================================================================
FAIL: testMultiplication (__main__.TestMath)
----------------------------------------------------------------------
Traceback (most recent call last):
  File "test_math.py", line 24, in testMultiplication
    self.assert_(0.3 == 0.1 * 3)
AssertionError


----------------------------------------------------------------------
```

```
Ran 4 tests in 0.054s

FAILED (failures=1)
```

Now all that we have is the `traceback` and the `AssertionError` message. No extra information is provided to help us diagnose the failure, as was the case when we used `assertEqual()`. That's why all the specialized `assert*()` methods are so helpful. Actually, with the exception of `assertRaises()`, all assertion methods accept an extra parameter meant to be the debugging message, which will be shown in case the test fails. That lets you write helper methods such as:

Listing 18-4.

```python
class SomeTestCase(unittest.TestCase):
    def assertGreaterThan(a, b):
        self.assert_(a > b, '%d isn't greater than %d')

    def testSomething(self):
        self.assertGreaterThan(10, 4)
```

As your application gets bigger, the number of test cases will grow, too. Eventually, you may not want to keep all the tests in one Python module, for maintainability reasons. Let's create a new module named `test_lists.py` with the following test code:

Listing 18-5.

```python
import unittest

class TestLists(unittest.TestCase):
    def setUp(self):
        self.list = ['foo', 'bar', 'baz']

    def testLen(self):
        self.assertEqual(3, len(self.list))

    def testContains(self):
        self.assert_('foo' in self.list)
        self.assert_('bar' in self.list)
        self.assert_('baz' in self.list)

    def testSort(self):
        self.assertNotEqual(['bar', 'baz', 'foo'], self.list)
        self.list.sort()
        self.assertEqual(['bar', 'baz', 'foo'], self.list)
```

■ **Note** In the previous code, you can see an example of a `setUp()` method, which allows us to avoid repeating the same initialization code on each `test*()` method. The `setUp()` method is executed once before every test. Similarly, the `tearDown()` method is executed once after each test to perform cleanup activities.

And, restoring our math tests to a good state, the test_math.py will contain the following:

Listing 18-6.

```python
import math
import unittest
import operator

class TestMath(unittest.TestCase):
    def testFloor(self):
        self.assertEqual(1, math.floor(1.01))
        self.assertEqual(0, math.floor(0.5))
        self.assertEqual(-1, math.floor(-0.5))
        self.assertEqual(-2, math.floor(-1.1))

    def testCeil(self):
        self.assertEqual(2, math.ceil(1.01))
        self.assertEqual(1, math.ceil(0.5))
        self.assertEqual(0, math.ceil(-0.5))
        self.assertEqual(-1, math.ceil(-1.1))

    def testDivision(self):
        self.assertRaises(ZeroDivisionError, operator.div, 1, 0)
        # The same assertion using a different idiom:
        self.assertRaises(ZeroDivisionError, lambda: 1 / 0)

    def testMultiplication(self):
        self.assertAlmostEqual(0.3, 0.1 * 3)
```

Now, how do we run, in one pass, tests defined in different modules? One option is to manually build a *test suite*. A test suite is simply a collection of test cases (and/or other test suites) which, when run, will run all the test cases (and/or test suites) contained by it. Note that a new test case instance is built for each test method, so suites have already been built under the hood every time you have run a test module. Our work, then, is to "paste" the suites together.

Let's build suites using the interactive interpreter. First, import the involved modules:

Listing 18-7.

```python
>>> import unittest, test_math, test_lists
```

Then, obtain the test suites for each one of our test modules (which were implicitly created when running them using the unittest.main() shortcut), using the unittest.TestLoader class:

Listing 18-8.

```python
>>> loader = unittest.TestLoader()
>>> math_suite = loader.loadTestsFromModule(test_math)
>>> lists_suite = loader.loadTestsFromModule(test_lists)
```
Now we build a new suite, which combines these suites:
```python
>>> global_suite = unittest.TestSuite([math_suite, lists_suite])
```
And finally, we run the suite:

```
>>> unittest.TextTestRunner().run(global_suite)
.......
----------------------------------------------------------------------
Ran 7 tests in 0.010s

OK
<unittest._TextTestResult run=7 errors=0 failures=0>
```
   Or, if you want a more verbose output:
```
>>> unittest.TextTestRunner(verbosity=2).run(global_suite)
testCeil (test_math.TestMath) ... ok
testDivision (test_math.TestMath) ... ok
testFloor (test_math.TestMath) ... ok
testMultiplication (test_math.TestMath) ... ok
testContains (test_lists.TestLists) ... ok
testLen (test_lists.TestLists) ... ok
testSort (test_lists.TestLists) ... ok

----------------------------------------------------------------------
Ran 7 tests in 0.020s

OK
<unittest._TextTestResult run=7 errors=0 failures=0>
```

   Using this low-level knowledge about loaders, suites, and runners, you can easily write a script to run the tests of any project. Obviously, the details of the script will vary from project to project, depending on the way in which you decide to organize your tests. There are a number of other features that are included with the unittest framework. For more detailed information, please refer to the Python documentation.
   On the other hand, you won't typically write custom scripts to run all your tests. Using test tools that do automatic test discovery is a much more convenient approach. We will look at one of them shortly. But first, we must show you another testing tool that is very popular in the Python world: doctests.

Doctests

Doctests are an ingenious combination of, well, documentation and tests. A doctest is, in essence, no more than a snapshot of an interactive interpreter session, mixed with paragraphs of documentation, typically inside of a docstring. Here is a simple example:

Listing 18-9.

```
def is_even(number):
    """
    Checks if an integer number is even.

    >>> is_even(0)
    True

    >>> is_even(2)
    True

    >>> is_even(3)
    False
```

It works with very long numbers:

```
>>> is_even(100000000000000000000000000000)
True
```

And also with negatives:

```
>>> is_even(-100000000000000000000000000000001)
False
```

But not with floats:

```
>>> is_even(4.1)
Traceback (most recent call last):
...
ValueError: 4.1 isn't an integer
```

However, a value of type float will work as long as is an integer:

```
>>> is_even(4.0)
True
"""
remainder = number % 2
if 0 < remainder < 1:
    raise ValueError("%f isn't an integer" % number)
return remainder == 0
```

Note that, if we weren't talking about testing, we may have thought that the docstring of is_even() is just normal documentation, in which the convention of using the interpreter prompt to mark example expressions and their outputs was adopted. After all, in many cases we use examples as part of the documentation. Take a look at Java's SimpleDateFormat documentation, located in java.sun.com/javase/6/docs/api/java/text/SimpleDateFormat.html, and you will spot fragments like:

- "...using a pattern of mm/dd/yy and a SimpleDateFormat instance created on Jan 1, 1997, the string 01/11/12 would be interpreted as Jan 11, 2012...."

- "...01/02/3 or 01/02/003 are parsed, using the same pattern, as Jan 2, 3 AD...."

- "..."01/02/-3" is parsed as Jan 2, 4 BC...."

The magic of doctests is that it encourages the inclusion of these examples by doubling them as tests. Let's save our example code as even.py and add the following snippet at the end:

Listing 18-10.

```
if __name__ == "__main__":
    import doctest
    doctest.testmod()
    Then, run it:
$ jython even.py
```

Doctests are a bit shy and don't show any output on success. But to convince you that it is indeed testing our code, run it with the -v option:

```
$ jython even.py -v

Trying:
    is_even(0)
Expecting:
    True
ok
Trying:
    is_even(2)
Expecting:
    True
ok
Trying:
    is_even(3)
Expecting:
    False
ok
Trying:
    is_even(1000000000000000000000000000000)
Expecting:
    True
ok
Trying:
    is_even(-1000000000000000000000000000001)
Expecting:
    False
ok
Trying:
    is_even(4.1)
Expecting:
    Traceback (most recent call last):
    ...
    ValueError: 4.1 isn't an integer
ok
Trying:
    is_even(4.0)
Expecting:
    True
ok
1 items had no tests:
    __main__
1 items passed all tests:
    7 tests in __main__.is_even
7 tests in 2 items.
7 passed and 0 failed.
Test passed.
```

Doctests are a very, very convenient way to do testing, because the interactive examples can be directly copied and pasted from the interactive shell, transforming the manual testing in documentation examples and automated tests in one shot.

You don't really *need* to include doctests as part of the documentation of the feature they test. Nothing stops you from writing the following code in, say, the test_math_using_doctest.py module:

Listing 18-11.

```
"""
Doctests equivalent to test_math unittests seen in the previous section.

>>> import math

Tests for floor():

>>> math.floor(1.01)
1
>>> math.floor(0.5)
0
>>> math.floor(-0.5)
-1
>>> math.floor(-1.1)
-2

Tests for ceil():

>>> math.ceil(1.01)
2
>>> math.ceil(0.5)
1
>>> math.ceil(-0.5)
0
>>> math.ceil(-1.1)
-1

Test for division:

>>> 1 / 0
Traceback (most recent call last):
...
ZeroDivisionError: integer division or modulo by zero

Test for floating point multiplication:

>>> (0.3 - 0.1 * 3) < 0.0000001
True

"""
if __name__ == "__main__":
    import doctest
    doctest.testmod()
```

Something to note about the last test in the previous example is that, in some cases, doctests are not the cleanest way to express a test. Also note that, if that test fails, you will *not* get useful information about the failure. It will tell you that the output was False when True was expected, without the extra details that `assertAlmostEquals()` would give you. The moral of the story is to realize that doctest is just another tool in the toolbox, which can fit very well in some cases, but not in others.

■ **Note** Speaking of doctests gotchas: the use of dictionary outputs in doctests is a very common error that breaks the portability of your doctests across Python implementations (for example, Jython, CPython, and IronPython). The trap here is that the order of dict keys is implementation-dependent, so the test may pass when working on some implementation and fail horribly on others. The workaround is to convert the dict to a sequence of tuples and sort them, using sorted(mydict.items()).That shows the big downfall of doctests: it always does a textual comparison of the expression, converting the result to string. It isn't aware of the objects structure.

To take advantage of doctests, we have to follow some simple rules, like using the >>> prompt and leaving a blank line between sample output and the next paragraph. But if you think about it, it's the same kind of sane rules that makes the documentation readable by people.

The only common rule not illustrated by the examples in this section is the way to write expressions that are written on more than one line. As you may expect, you have to follow the same convention used by the interactive interpreter: start the continuation lines with an ellipsis (...). For example:

Listing 18-12.

```
"""
Addition is commutative:

>>> ((1 + 2) ==
...  (2 + 1))
True
"""
```

A Complete Example

Having seen the two test frameworks used in the Python world, let's see them applied to a more meaningful program. We will write code to check for solutions of the eight-queens chess puzzle. The idea of the puzzle is to place eight queens in a chessboard, with no queen attacking each other. Queens can attack any piece placed in the same row, column or diagonals. Figure 18-1 shows one of the solutions of the puzzle.

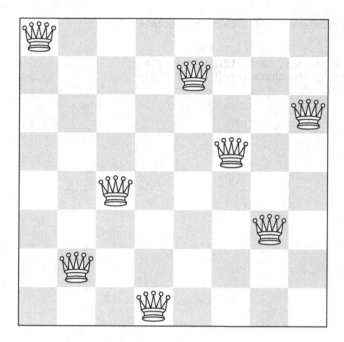

Figure 18-1. Eight queens chess

We like to use doctests to check the contract of the program with the outside, and unittest for what we could see as the internal tests. We do that because external interfaces tend to be clearly documented, and automated testing of the examples in the documentation is always a great thing. On the other hand, unittests shine on pointing us to the very specific source of a bug, or at the very least on providing more useful debugging information than doctests.

■ **Note** In practice, both types of tests have strengths and weaknesses, and you may find some cases in which you will prefer the readability and simplicity of doctests and only use them on your project. Or you will favor the granularity and isolation of unittests and only use them on your project. As with many things in life, it's a trade-off.

We'll develop this program in a test-driven development fashion. The tests will be written first, as a sort of specification for our program, and code will be written later to fulfill the tests' requirements.

Let's start by specifying the public interface of our puzzle checker, which will live on the eightqueen package. This is the start of the main module, eightqueen.checker:

Listing 18-13.

```
"""
eightqueen.checker: Validates solutions for the eight queens puzzle.
```

Provides the function is_solution(board) to determine if a board represents a valid solution of the puzzle.

The chess board is represented by list of 8 strings, each string of length 8. Positions occupied by a Queen are marked by the character 'Q', and empty spaces are represented by an space character.

Here is a valid board:

```
>>> board = [
...          'Q       ',
...          ' Q      ',
...          '  Q     ',
...          '   Q    ',
...          '    Q   ',
...          '     Q  ',
...          '      Q ',
...          '       Q']
```

Naturally, it is not a correct solution:

```
>>> is_solution(board)
False
```

Here is a correct solution:

```
>>> is_solution([
...          'Q       ',
...          '    Q   ',
...          '       Q',
...          '     Q  ',
...          '  Q     ',
...          '      Q ',
...          ' Q      ',
...          '   Q    '])
True
```

Malformed boards are rejected and a ValueError is thrown:

```
>>> is_solution([])
Traceback (most recent call last):
...
ValueError: Malformed board
```

Only 8 x 8 boards are supported.

```
>>> is_solution([
...             'Q   ',
...             ' Q  ',
...             '  Q ',
...             '   Q'])
Traceback (most recent call last):
...
```

```
ValueError: Malformed board

And they must only contains Qs and spaces:

>>> is_solution([
...                'X        ',
...                '    X   ',
...                '      X',
...                '     X  ',
...                '  X    ',
...                '       X ',
...                ' X      ',
...                '   X    '])
Traceback (most recent call last):
...
ValueError: Malformed board

And the total number of Qs must be eight:

>>> is_solution([
...                'QQQQQQQQ',
...                'Q       ',
...                '        ',
...                '        ',
...                '        ',
...                '        ',
...                '        ',
...                '        '])
Traceback (most recent call last):
...
ValueError: There must be exactly 8 queens in the board

>>> is_solution([
...                'QQQQQQQ ',
...                '        ',
...                '        ',
...                '        ',
...                '        ',
...                '        ',
...                '        ',
...                '        '])
Traceback (most recent call last):
...
ValueError: There must be exactly 8 queens in the board

"""
```

That's a good start; we know what we have to build. The doctests play the role of a more precise problem statement. Actually, it's an executable problem statement that can be used to verify our solution to the problem.

Now we will specify the "internal" interface that shows how we can solve the problem of writing the solution checker. It's common practice to write the unittests on a separate module. So here is the code for eightqueens.test_checker:

Listing 18-14.

```python
import unittest
from eightqueens import checker

BOARD_TOO_SMALL = ['Q' * 3 for i in range(3)]
BOARD_TOO_BIG = ['Q' * 10 for i in range(10)]
BOARD_WITH_TOO_MANY_COLS = ['Q' * 9 for i in range(8)]
BOARD_WITH_TOO_MANY_ROWS = ['Q' * 8 for i in range(9)]
BOARD_FULL_OF_QS = ['Q' * 8 for i in range(8)]
BOARD_FULL_OF_CRAP = [chr(65 + i) * 8 for i in range(8)]
BOARD_EMPTY = [' ' * 8 for i in range(8)]

BOARD_WITH_QS_IN_THE_SAME_ROW = [
                                 'Q   Q   ',
                                 '        ',
                                 '       Q',
                                 '     Q  ',
                                 '   Q    ',
                                 '      Q ',
                                 ' Q      ',
                                 '    Q   ']
BOARD_WITH_WRONG_SOLUTION = BOARD_WITH_QS_IN_THE_SAME_ROW

BOARD_WITH_QS_IN_THE_SAME_COL = [
                                 'Q       ',
                                 '    Q   ',
                                 '       Q',
                                 'Q       ',
                                 '  Q     ',
                                 '      Q ',
                                 ' Q      ',
                                 '   Q    ']

BOARD_WITH_QS_IN_THE_SAME_DIAG_1 = [
                                 '        ',
                                 '        ',
                                 '        ',
                                 '        ',
                                 '        ',
                                 '        ',
                                 'Q       ',
                                 ' Q      ']

BOARD_WITH_QS_IN_THE_SAME_DIAG_2 = [
                                 '        ',
                                 '    Q   ',
                                 '     Q  ',
                                 '        ',
                                 '        ',
```

```
                                      ']
BOARD_WITH_QS_IN_THE_SAME_DIAG_3 = [
                              '        ',
                              '    Q   ',
                              '        ',
                              '        ',
                              '  Q     ',
                              '        ']


BOARD_WITH_QS_IN_THE_SAME_DIAG_4 = [
                              '        ',
                              '     Q  ',
                              '        ',
                              '        ',
                              'Q       ',
                              '        ',
                              '        ']


BOARD_WITH_QS_IN_THE_SAME_DIAG_5 = [
                              '       Q',
                              '      Q ',
                              '     Q  ',
                              '    Q   ',
                              '   Q    ',
                              '  Q     ',
                              ' Q      ',
                              'Q       ']


BOARD_WITH_SOLUTION = [
                       'Q      ',
                       '    Q  ',
                       '      Q',
                       '     Q ',
                       '  Q    ',
                       '     Q ',
                       ' Q     ',
                       '   Q   ']


class ValidationTest(unittest.TestCase):
    def testValidateShape(self):
        def assertNotValidShape(board):
            self.assertFalse(checker._validate_shape(board))

        # Some invalid shapes:
        assertNotValidShape([])
```

```python
        assertNotValidShape(BOARD_TOO_SMALL)
        assertNotValidShape(BOARD_TOO_BIG)
        assertNotValidShape(BOARD_WITH_TOO_MANY_COLS)
        assertNotValidShape(BOARD_WITH_TOO_MANY_ROWS)

        def assertValidShape(board):
            self.assert_(checker._validate_shape(board))

        assertValidShape(BOARD_WITH_SOLUTION)
        # Shape validation doesn't care about board contents:
        assertValidShape(BOARD_FULL_OF_QS)
        assertValidShape(BOARD_FULL_OF_CRAP)

    def testValidateContents(self):
        # Valid content => only 'Q' and ' ' in the board
        self.assertFalse(checker._validate_contents(BOARD_FULL_OF_CRAP))
        self.assert_(checker._validate_contents(BOARD_WITH_SOLUTION))
        # Content validation doesn't care about the number of queens:
        self.assert_(checker._validate_contents(BOARD_FULL_OF_QS))


    def testValidateQueens(self):
        self.assertFalse(checker._validate_queens(BOARD_FULL_OF_QS))
        self.assertFalse(checker._validate_queens(BOARD_EMPTY))
        self.assert_(checker._validate_queens(BOARD_WITH_SOLUTION))
        self.assert_(checker._validate_queens(BOARD_WITH_WRONG_SOLUTION))


class PartialSolutionTest(unittest.TestCase):
    def testRowsOK(self):
        self.assert_(checker._rows_ok(BOARD_WITH_SOLUTION))
        self.assertFalse(checker._rows_ok(BOARD_WITH_QS_IN_THE_SAME_ROW))

    def testColsOK(self):
        self.assert_(checker._cols_ok(BOARD_WITH_SOLUTION))
        self.assertFalse(checker._cols_ok(BOARD_WITH_QS_IN_THE_SAME_COL))

    def testDiagonalsOK(self):
        self.assert_(checker._diagonals_ok(BOARD_WITH_SOLUTION))
        self.assertFalse(
            checker._diagonals_ok(BOARD_WITH_QS_IN_THE_SAME_DIAG_1))
        self.assertFalse(
            checker._diagonals_ok(BOARD_WITH_QS_IN_THE_SAME_DIAG_2))
        self.assertFalse(
            checker._diagonals_ok(BOARD_WITH_QS_IN_THE_SAME_DIAG_3))
        self.assertFalse(
            checker._diagonals_ok(BOARD_WITH_QS_IN_THE_SAME_DIAG_4))
        self.assertFalse(
            checker._diagonals_ok(BOARD_WITH_QS_IN_THE_SAME_DIAG_5))

class SolutionTest(unittest.TestCase):
    def testIsSolution(self):
        self.assert_(checker.is_solution(BOARD_WITH_SOLUTION))
```

```
    self.assertFalse(checker.is_solution(BOARD_WITH_QS_IN_THE_SAME_COL))
    self.assertFalse(checker.is_solution(BOARD_WITH_QS_IN_THE_SAME_ROW))
    self.assertFalse(checker.is_solution(BOARD_WITH_QS_IN_THE_SAME_DIAG_5))

    self.assertRaises(ValueError, checker.is_solution, BOARD_TOO_SMALL)
    self.assertRaises(ValueError, checker.is_solution, BOARD_FULL_OF_CRAP)
    self.assertRaises(ValueError, checker.is_solution, BOARD_EMPTY)
```

These unittests propose a way to solve the problem, decomposing it in two big tasks (input validation and the actual verification of solutions), and each task is decomposed on a smaller portion that is meant to be implemented by a function. In some way, they are an executable design of the solution.

So we have a mix of doctests and unittests. How do we run all of them in one shot? Previously we showed you how to manually compose a test suite for unit tests belonging to different modules, so that may be an answer. And indeed, there is a way to add doctests to test suites: doctest.DocTestSuite(module_with_doctests). But, because we are working on a more "real" testing example, we will use a real-world solution to this problem (as you can imagine, people got tired of the tedious work and more automated solutions appeared).

Nose

Nose is a tool for test discovery and execution. By default, Nose tries to run tests on any module whose name starts with "test." You can override that, of course. In our case, the example code of the previous section follows the convention (the test module is named eightqueens.test_checker).

An easy way to install Nose is via setuptools. If you have not yet installed setuptools, please see Appendix A for details on doing so. Once you have setuptools installed, you can proceed to install Nose:

Listing 18-15.

```
$ easy_install nose
```

Once Nose is installed, an executable named nosetests will appear on the bin/ directory of your Jython installation. Let's try it, locating ourselves on the parent directory of eightqueens and running:

Listing 18-16.

```
$ nosetests --with-doctest
```

By default, Nose does *not* run doctests, so we have to explicitly enable the doctest plug-in that comes built in with Nose.

Back to our example, here is the shortened output after running Nose:

Listing 18-17.

```
FEEEEEE

[Snipped output]

----------------------------------------------------------------------
Ran 8 tests in 1.133s
FAILED (errors=7, failures=1)
```

Of course, all of our tests (7 unittests and 1 doctest) failed. It's time to fix that. But first, let's run Nose again, *without* the doctests, because we will follow the unittests to construct the solution. And we know that as long as our unittests fail, the doctest will also likely fail. Once all unittests pass, we can check our whole program against the high level doctest and see if we missed something or did it right. Here is the Nose output for the unittests:

Listing 18-18.

```
$ nosetests
EEEEEEE
======================================================================
ERROR: testIsSolution (eightqueens.test_checker.SolutionTest)
----------------------------------------------------------------------
Traceback (most recent call last):
  File "/path/to/eightqueens/test_checker.py", line 149, in testIsSolution
    self.assert_(checker.is_solution(BOARD_WITH_SOLUTION))
AttributeError: 'module' object has no attribute 'is_solution'


======================================================================
ERROR: testColsOK (eightqueens.test_checker.PartialSolutionTest)
----------------------------------------------------------------------
Traceback (most recent call last):
  File "/path/to/eightqueens/test_checker.py", line 100, in testColsOK
    self.assert_(checker._cols_ok(BOARD_WITH_SOLUTION))
AttributeError: 'module' object has no attribute '_cols_ok'


======================================================================
ERROR: testDiagonalsOK (eightqueens.test_checker.PartialSolutionTest)
----------------------------------------------------------------------
Traceback (most recent call last):
  File "/path/to/eightqueens/test_checker.py", line 104, in testDiagonalsOK
    self.assert_(checker._diagonals_ok(BOARD_WITH_SOLUTION))
AttributeError: 'module' object has no attribute '_diagonals_ok'


======================================================================
ERROR: testRowsOK (eightqueens.test_checker.PartialSolutionTest)
----------------------------------------------------------------------
Traceback (most recent call last):
  File "/path/to/eightqueens/test_checker.py", line 96, in testRowsOK
    self.assert_(checker._rows_ok(BOARD_WITH_SOLUTION))
AttributeError: 'module' object has no attribute '_rows_ok'


======================================================================
ERROR: testValidateContents (eightqueens.test_checker.ValidationTest)
----------------------------------------------------------------------
Traceback (most recent call last):
  File "/path/to/eightqueens/test_checker.py", line 81, in testValidateContents
    self.assertFalse(checker._validate_contents(BOARD_FULL_OF_CRAP))
AttributeError: 'module' object has no attribute '_validate_contents'


======================================================================
ERROR: testValidateQueens (eightqueens.test_checker.ValidationTest)
```

```
-------------------------------------------------------------------------
Traceback (most recent call last):
  File "/path/to/eightqueens/test_checker.py", line 88, in testValidateQueens
    self.assertFalse(checker._validate_queens(BOARD_FULL_OF_QS))
AttributeError: 'module' object has no attribute '_validate_queens'

=========================================================================
ERROR: testValidateShape (eightqueens.test_checker.ValidationTest)
-------------------------------------------------------------------------
Traceback (most recent call last):
  File "/path/to/eightqueens/test_checker.py", line 65, in testValidateShape
    assertNotValidShape([])
  File "/path/to/eightqueens/test_checker.py", line 62, in assertNotValidShape
    self.assertFalse(checker._validate_shape(board))
AttributeError: 'module' object has no attribute '_validate_shape'


-------------------------------------------------------------------------
Ran 7 tests in 0.493s

FAILED (errors=7)
```

Let's start clearing the failures by coding the validation functions specified by the ValidationTest. That is, the _validate_shape(), _validate_contents(), and _validate_queens() functions, in the eightqueens.checker module:

```python
def _validate_shape(board):
    return (board and
            len(board) == 8 and
            all(len(row) == 8 for row in board))

def _validate_contents(board):
    for row in board:
        for square in row:
            if square not in ('Q', ' '):
                return False
    return True

def _count_queens(row):
    n = 0
    for square in row:
        if square == 'Q':
            n += 1
    return n

def _validate_queens(board):
    n = 0
    for row in board:
        n += _count_queens(row)
    return n == 8
```

And now run Nose again:

```
$ nosetests

EEEE...
=========================================================================
ERROR: testIsSolution (eightqueens.test_checker.SolutionTest)
-------------------------------------------------------------------------
```

```
Traceback (most recent call last):
  File "/path/to/eightqueens/test_checker.py", line 149, in testIsSolution
    self.assert_(checker.is_solution(BOARD_WITH_SOLUTION))
AttributeError: 'module' object has no attribute 'is_solution'

======================================================================
ERROR: testColsOK (eightqueens.test_checker.PartialSolutionTest)
----------------------------------------------------------------------
Traceback (most recent call last):
  File "/path/to/eightqueens/test_checker.py", line 100, in testColsOK
    self.assert_(checker._cols_ok(BOARD_WITH_SOLUTION))
AttributeError: 'module' object has no attribute '_cols_ok'

======================================================================
ERROR: testDiagonalsOK (eightqueens.test_checker.PartialSolutionTest)
----------------------------------------------------------------------
Traceback (most recent call last):
  File "/path/to/eightqueens/test_checker.py", line 104, in testDiagonalsOK
    self.assert_(checker._diagonals_ok(BOARD_WITH_SOLUTION))
AttributeError: 'module' object has no attribute '_diagonals_ok'

======================================================================
ERROR: testRowsOK (eightqueens.test_checker.PartialSolutionTest)
----------------------------------------------------------------------
Traceback (most recent call last):
  File "/path/to/eightqueens/test_checker.py", line 96, in testRowsOK
    self.assert_(checker._rows_ok(BOARD_WITH_SOLUTION))
AttributeError: 'module' object has no attribute '_rows_ok'

----------------------------------------------------------------------
Ran 7 tests in 0.534s

FAILED (errors=4)
```

We passed all the validation tests! Now we should implement the functions _rows_ok(), _cols_ok(), and _diagonals_ok(), to pass PartialSolutionTest:

```
def _scan_ok(board, coordinates):
    queen_already_found = False
    for i, j in coordinates:
        if board[i][j] == 'Q':
            if queen_already_found:
                return False
            else:
                queen_already_found = True
    return True


def _rows_ok(board):
    for i in range(8):
        if not _scan_ok(board, [(i, j) for j in range(8)]):
            return False
    return True

def _cols_ok(board):
    for j in range(8):
```

```
        if not _scan_ok(board, [(i, j) for i in range(8)]):
            return False
    return True

def _diagonals_ok(board):
    for k in range(8):
        # Diagonal: (0, k), (1, k + 1), ..., (7 - k, 7)...
        if not _scan_ok(board, [(i, k + i) for i in range(8 - k)]):
            return False
        # Diagonal: (k, 0), (k + 1, 1), ..., (7, 7 - k)
        if not _scan_ok(board, [(k + j, j) for j in range(8 - k)]):
            return False

        # Diagonal: (0, k), (1, k - 1), ..., (k, 0)
        if not _scan_ok(board, [(i, k - i) for i in range(k + 1)]):
            return False

        # Diagonal: (7, k), (6, k - 1), ..., (k, 7)
        if not _scan_ok(board, [(7 - j, k + j) for j in range(8 - k)]):
            return False
    return True
```

Let's try Nose again:

Listing 18-19.

```
$ nosetests

...E...
======================================================================
ERROR: testIsSolution (eightqueens.test_checker.SolutionTest)
----------------------------------------------------------------------
Traceback (most recent call last):
  File "/path/to/eightqueens/test_checker.py", line 149, in testIsSolution
    self.assert_(checker.is_solution(BOARD_WITH_SOLUTION))
AttributeError: 'module' object has no attribute 'is_solution'

----------------------------------------------------------------------
Ran 7 tests in 0.938s

FAILED (errors=1)
```

Finally, we have to assemble the pieces together to pass the test for is_solution():

```
def is_solution(board):
    if not _validate_shape(board) or not _validate_contents(board):
        raise ValueError("Malformed board")
    if not _validate_queens(board):
        raise ValueError("There must be exactly 8 queens in the board")
    return _rows_ok(board) and _cols_ok(board) and _diagonals_ok(board)
```

And we can hope that all test pass now:

```
$ nosetests

.......
----------------------------------------------------------------------
```

```
Ran 7 tests in 0.592s
```

OK

Indeed, they all pass. Moreover, we probably also pass the "problem statement," test, expressed in our doctest:

```
$ nosetests --with-doctest

........
----------------------------------------------------------------------
Ran 8 tests in 1.523s
```

OK

Objective accomplished! We have come up with a nicely documented and tested module, using the two testing tools shipped with the Python language, and Nose to run all our tests without manually building suites. For more information on Nose, please see the documentation available at the project web site: code.google.com/p/python-nose/.

Integration with Java?

You may be wondering how to integrate the testing frameworks of Python and Java. It is possible to write JUnit tests in Jython, but it's not really interesting, considering that you can test Java classes using unittest and doctest. The following is a perfectly valid doctest:

Listing 18-20.

```
"""
Tests for Java's DecimalFormat

>>> from java.text import DecimalFormat

A format for money:

>>> dolarFormat = DecimalFormat("$ ###,###.##")

The decimal part is only printed if needed:

>>> dolarFormat.format(1000)
u'$ 1.000'

Rounding is used when there are more decimal numbers than those defined by the
format:

>>> dolarFormat.format(123456.789)
u'$ 123.456,79'

The format can be used as a parser:

>>> dolarFormat.parse('$ 123')
123L
```

The parser ignores the unparseable text after the number:

```
>>> dolarFormat.parse("$ 123abcd")
123L
```

However, if it can't parse a number, it throws a ParseException:

```
>>> dolarFormat.parse("abcd")
Traceback (most recent call last):
...
ParseException: java.text.ParseException: Unparseable number: "abcd"
"""
```

So you can use all that you learned in this chapter to test code written in Java. We find this a very powerful tool for Java development: easy, flexible, and unceremonious testing using Jython and Python testing tools!

Continuous Integration

Martin Fowler defines continuous integration as "a software development practice where members of a team integrate their work frequently [...]. Each integration is verified by an automated build (including test) to detect integration errors as quickly as possible." Some software development teams report to have used this practice as early as the 1960s; however, it only became mainstream when advocated as part of the extreme programming practices. Nowadays, it is a widely applied practice, and in the Java world there is a wealth of tools to help with the technical challenge involved by it.

Hudson

One tool that currently has a lot of momentum and is growing an important user base is Hudson. Among its prominent features are the ease of installation and configuration, and the ability to deploy it in a distributed, master/slaves environment for cross-platform testing.

But we think Hudson's main strength is its highly modular, plug-in-based architecture, which has resulted in the creation of plug-ins to support most of the version control, build and reporting tools, and many languages. One of them is the Jython plug-in, which allows you to use the Python language to drive your builds.

You can find more details about the Hudson project at its homepage at hudson.dev.java.net.

Getting Hudson

Grab the latest version of Hudson from hudson-ci.org/latest/hudson.war. You can deploy it to any servlet container, such as Tomcat or Glassfish. But one of the cool features of Hudson is that you can test it by simply running:

Listing 18-21.

```
$ java -jar hudson.war
```

After a few seconds, you will see some logging output on the console, and Hudson will be up and running. If you visit the site localhost:8080 you will get a welcome page inviting you to start using Hudson creating new jobs.

■ **WARNING** The default mode of operation of Hudson fully trusts its users, letting them execute any command they want on the server, with the privileges of the user running Hudson. You can set stricter access control policies on the Configure System section of the Manage Hudson page.

Installing the Jython Plug-in

Before creating jobs, we will install the Jython plug-in. Click on the Manage Hudson link on the left-hand menu. Then click Manage Plug-ins. Now go to the Available tab. You will see a very long list of plug-ins (we told you this was the greatest Hudson strength!) Find the Jython Plug-in, click on the checkbox at its left (as shown in Figure 18-2), then scroll to the end of the page and click the Install button.

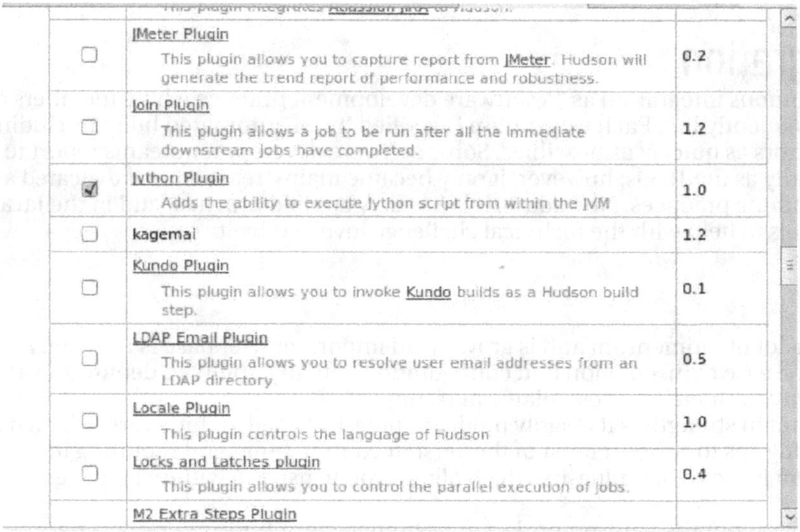

☐	**JMeter Plugin** This plugin allows you to capture report from JMeter. Hudson will generate the trend report of performance and robustness.	0.2
☐	**Join Plugin** This plugin allows a job to be run after all the immediate downstream jobs have completed.	1.2
☑	**Jython Plugin** Adds the ability to execute Jython script from within the JVM	1.0
☐	**kagemai**	1.2
☐	**Kundo Plugin** This plugin allows you to invoke Kundo builds as a Hudson build step.	0.1
☐	**LDAP Email Plugin** This plugin allows you to resolve user email addresses from an LDAP directory	0.5
☐	**Locale Plugin** This plugin controls the language of Hudson	1.0
☐	**Locks and Latches plugin** This plugin allows you to control the parallel execution of jobs.	0.4
	M2 Extra Steps Plugin	

Figure 18-2. Selecting the Jython Plug-in

You will see a bar showing the progress of the download and installation, and after little while you will be presented with a screen like that shown in Figure 18-3, notifying you that the process has finished. Press the Restart button, wait a little bit, and you will see the welcome screen again. Congratulations, you now have a Jython-powered Hudson!

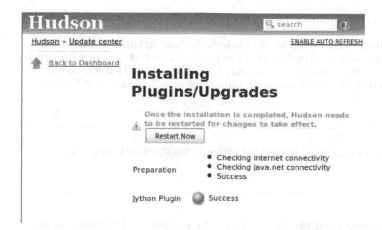

Figure 18-3. *The Jython Plug-in is successfully installed.*

Creating a Hudson Job for a Jython Project

Let's now follow the suggestion of the welcome screen and click the Create New Job link. A job roughly corresponds to the instructions needed by Hudson to build a project. It includes:

- The location from where the source code of the project should be obtained, and how often.

- How to start the build process for the project.

- How to collect information after the build process has finished.

After clicking the Create New Job link (the equivalent to the New Job entry on the left-hand menu), you will be asked for a name and type for the job. We will use the eightqueens project built on the previous section, so name the project "eightqueens", select the "Build a free-style software project" option, and press the OK button.

In the next screen, we need to set up an option on the Source Code Management section. You may want to experiment with your own repositories here (by default only CVS and Subversion are supported, but there are plug-ins for all the other VCSs used out there). For our example, we've hosted the code on a Subversion repository at: kenai.com/svn/jythonbook~eightqueens. So select Subversion and enter kenai.com/svn/jythonbook~eightqueens/trunk/eightqueens/ as the Repository URL.

■ **Note** Using the public repository will be enough to get a feeling of Hudson and its support of Jython. However, we encourage you to create your own repository so you can play freely with continuous integration, for example, committing bad code to see how failures are handled.

In the Build Triggers section, we have to specify when automated builds will happen. We will poll the repository so that a new build will be started after any change. Select Poll SCM and enter @hourly in the Schedule box. (If you want to know all the options for the schedule, click the help icon at the right of the box.)

In the Build section, we must tell Hudson how to build our project. By default, Hudson supports Shell scripts, Windows Batch files, and Ant scripts as build steps. For projects in which you mix Java and Python code and drive the build process with an ant file, the default Ant build step will suffice. In our case, we wrote our app in pure Python code, so we will use the Jython plug-in, which adds the Execute Jython Script build step.

■ **Note** At the time of writing, the Jython plug-in (version 1.0) does not ship with the standard library. This is expected to change in the next version.

So, click on Add Build Step and then select Execute Jython Script. We will use our knowledge of test suites gained in the UnitTest section. The following script will be enough to run our tests:

Listing 18-22.

```
import os, sys, unittest, doctest
from eightqueens import checker, test_checker

loader = unittest.TestLoader()
suite = unittest.TestSuite([loader.loadTestsFromModule(test_checker),
                            doctest.DocTestSuite(checker)])
result = unittest.TextTestRunner().run(suite)
print result
if not result.wasSuccessful():
    sys.exit(1)
```

Figure 18-4 shows how the page looks so far for the Source Code Management, Build Triggers, and Build sections.

Source Code Management

○ None

○ CVS

◉ Subversion

Modules   Repository URL   `http://kenai.com/svn/jythonbook~eightqueens/trunk/eightqueens/`

Local module directory (optional)

Add more locations...

Use update   ☑

If checked, Hudson will use 'svn update' whenever possible, making the build faster. But this causes the artifacts from the previous build to remain when a new build starts.

Repository browser   (Auto)

Advanced...

Build Triggers

☐ Build after other projects are built

☐ Build periodically

☑ Poll SCM

Schedule   @hourly

Build

▦ **Execute Jython script**

Script
```
loader = unittest.TestLoader()
suite = unittest.TestSuite([loader.loadTestsFromModule(test_checker),
                    doctest.DocTestSuite(checker)])
result = unittest.TextTestRunner().run(suite)
if not result.wasSuccessful():
    sys.exit(1)
```

See the list of available environment variables

Delete

Add build step ▼

Figure 18-4. Hudson Job Configuration

The next section explains how to specify an action to carry once the build has finished, ranging from collecting results from reports generated by static-analysis tools to testing runners to sending emails notifying someone of build breakage. We have left these options blank so far. Click the Save button at the bottom of the page.

At this point Hudson will show the job's main page. But it won't contain anything useful, because Hudson is waiting for the hourly trigger to poll the repository and kick the build. But we don't need to wait if we don't want to: just click the Build Now link on the left-hand menu. Shortly, a new entry will be shown in the Build History box (also on the left side, below the menu), as shown in Figure 18-5.

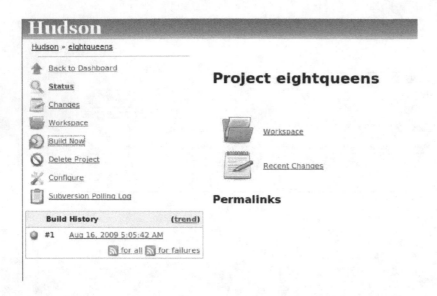

Figure 18-5. The first build of our first job

If you click on the link that just appeared, you will be directed to the page for the build we just made. If you click on the Console Output link on the left-hand menu, you will see what's shown in Figure 18-6.

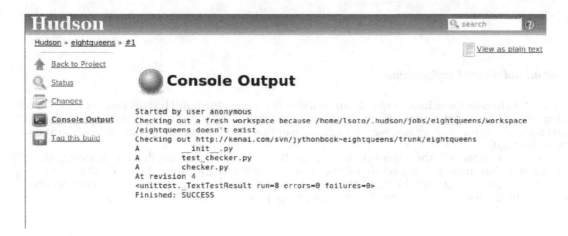

Figure 18-6. Console output for the build

As you would expect, it shows that our eight tests (remember that we had seven unittests and the module doctest) all passed.

Using Nose on Hudson

You may be wondering why we crafted a custom-built script instead of using Nose, because we stated that using Nose was much better than manually creating suites.

The problem is that the Jython runtime provided by the Jython Hudson plug-in comes without any extra library, so we can't assume the existence of Nose. One option would be to include Nose with the source tree on the repository, but it is not convenient.

One way to overcome the problem is to script the installation of Nose on the build script. Go back to the Job (also called Project by the Hudson user interface), select Configure on the left-hand menu, go to the Build section of the configuration, and change the Jython script for our job to:

Listing 18-23.

```
# Setup the environment
import os, sys, site, urllib2, tempfile
print "Base dir", os.getcwdu()
site_dir = os.path.join(os.getcwd(), 'site-packages')
if not os.path.exists(site_dir): os.mkdir(site_dir)
site.addsitedir(site_dir)
sys.executable = ''
os.environ['PYTHONPATH'] = ':'.join(sys.path)

# Get ez_setup:
ez_setup_path = os.path.join(site_dir, 'ez_setup.py')
if not os.path.exists(ez_setup_path):
    f = file(ez_setup_path, 'w')
    f.write(urllib2.urlopen('http://peak.telecommunity.com/dist/ez_setup.py').read())
    f.close()

# Install nose if not present
try:
    import nose
except ImportError:
    import ez_setup
    ez_setup.main(['--install-dir', site_dir, 'nose'])
    for mod in sys.modules.keys():
        if mod.startswith('nose'):
            del sys.modules[mod]
    for path in sys.path:
        if path.startswith(site_dir):
            sys.path.remove(site_dir)
    site.addsitedir(site_dir)
    import nose

# Run Tests!
nose.run(argv=['nosetests', '-v', '--with-doctest', '--with-xunit'])
```

The first half of the script is plumbing to download setuptools (ez_setup) and set an environment in which it will work. Then, we check for the availability of Nose, and if it's not present we install it using setuptools.

The interesting part is the last line:

Listing 18-24.

```
nose.run(argv=['nosetests', '-v', '--with-doctest', '--with-xunit'])
```

Here we are invoking Nose from python code, but using the command line syntax. Note the usage of the --with-xunit option. It generates JUnit-compatible XML reports for our tests, which can be read by Hudson to generate very useful test reports. By default, Nose will generate a file called nosetests.xml on the current directory.

To let Hudson know where the report can be found, scroll to the Post Build Actions section in the configuration, check "Publish JUnit test result reports," and enter "nosetests.xml" in the Test Report XMLs input box. Press Save. If Hudson points you that nosetests.xml "doesn't match anything," don't worry: just press Save again. Of course it doesn't match anything *yet*, because we haven't run the build again.

Trigger the build again, and after the build is finished, click on the link for it on the Build History box, or go to the job page and following the Last build [...] permalink). Figure 18-7 shows what you see if you look at the Console Output, and Figure 18-8 shows what you see on the Test Results page.

Console Output

```
Started by user anonymous
Updating http://kenai.com/svn/jythonbook~eightqueens/trunk/eightqueens
At revision 8
no change for http://kenai.com/svn/jythonbook~eightqueens/trunk/eightqueens since the previous build
Base dir /home/lsoto/.hudson/jobs/eightqueens/workspace
Downloading http://pypi.python.org/packages/2.5/s/setuptools/setuptools-0.6c9-py2.5.egg
Creating /home/lsoto/.hudson/jobs/eightqueens/workspace/site-packages/site.py
Searching for nose
Reading http://pypi.python.org/simple/nose/
Reading http://somethingaboutorange.com/mrl/projects/nose/
Best match: nose 0.11.1
Downloading http://somethingaboutorange.com/mrl/projects/nose/nose-0.11.1.tar.gz
Processing nose-0.11.1.tar.gz
Running nose-0.11.1/setup.py -q bdist_egg --dist-dir /tmp/easy_install-Og1DOO/nose-0.11.1/egg-dist-tmp-kYpY2p
no previously-included directories found matching 'doc/.build'
Adding nose 0.11.1 to easy-install.pth file
Installing nosetests-2.5 script to /home/lsoto/.hudson/jobs/eightqueens/workspace/site-packages
Installing nosetests script to /home/lsoto/.hudson/jobs/eightqueens/workspace/site-packages

Installed /home/lsoto/.hudson/jobs/eightqueens/workspace/site-packages/nose-0.11.1-py2.5.egg
Processing dependencies for nose
Finished processing dependencies for nose
Processing setuptools-0.6c9-py2.5.egg
Copying setuptools-0.6c9-py2.5.egg to /home/lsoto/.hudson/jobs/eightqueens/workspace/site-packages
Adding setuptools 0.6c9 to easy-install.pth file
Installing easy_install script to /home/lsoto/.hudson/jobs/eightqueens/workspace/site-packages
Installing easy_install-2.5 script to /home/lsoto/.hudson/jobs/eightqueens/workspace/site-packages

Installed /home/lsoto/.hudson/jobs/eightqueens/workspace/site-packages/setuptools-0.6c9-py2.5.egg
Processing dependencies for setuptools==0.6c9
Finished processing dependencies for setuptools==0.6c9
Doctest: eightqueens.checker ... ok
testColsOK (eightqueens.test_checker.PartialSolutionTest) ... ok
testDiagonalsOK (eightqueens.test_checker.PartialSolutionTest) ... ok
testRowsOK (eightqueens.test_checker.PartialSolutionTest) ... ok
testIsSolution (eightqueens.test_checker.SolutionTest) ... ok
testValidateContents (eightqueens.test_checker.ValidationTest) ... ok
testValidateQueens (eightqueens.test_checker.ValidationTest) ... ok
testValidateShape (eightqueens.test_checker.ValidationTest) ... ok

----------------------------------------------------------------------
XML: nosetests.xml
----------------------------------------------------------------------
Ran 8 tests in 0.590s

OK
Recording test results
Finished: SUCCESS
```

Figure 18-7. Nose's Output on Hudson

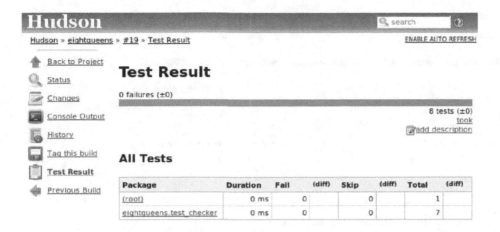

Figure 18-8. *Hudson's test reports*

Navigation on your test results is a very powerful feature of Hudson. But it shines when you have failures or tons of tests, which is not the case on this example. But we wanted to show it in action, so we fabricated some failures on the code to show you some screenshots. Look at Figure 18-9 and Figure 18-10 to get an idea of what you get from Hudson.

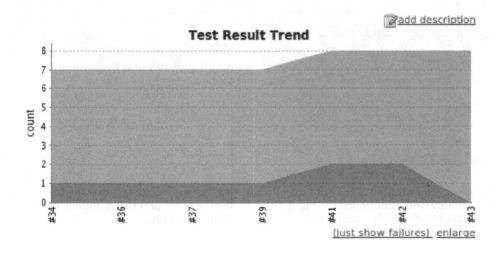

Figure 18-9. *Graph of test results over time*

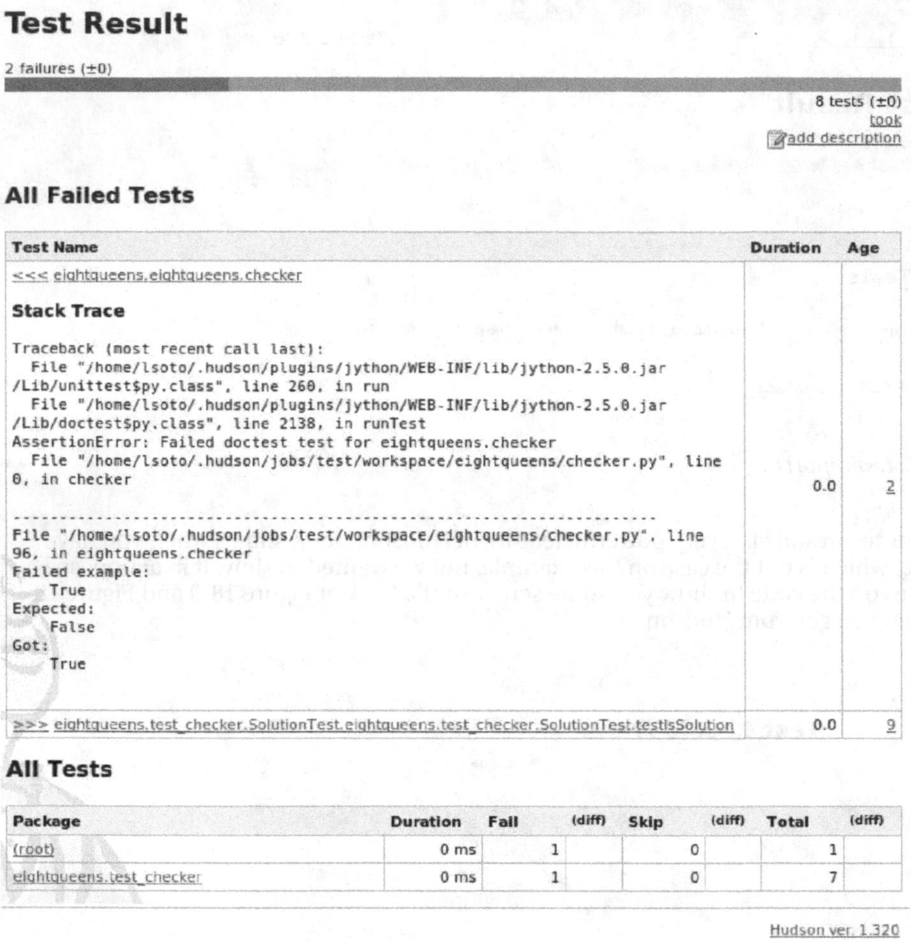

Test Result

2 failures (±0)

8 tests (±0)
took
✎add description

All Failed Tests

Test Name	Duration	Age
<<< eightqueens.eightqueens.checker		
Stack Trace		

Traceback (most recent call last):
  File "/home/lsoto/.hudson/plugins/jython/WEB-INF/lib/jython-2.5.0.jar
/Lib/unittest$py.class", line 260, in run
  File "/home/lsoto/.hudson/plugins/jython/WEB-INF/lib/jython-2.5.0.jar
/Lib/doctest$py.class", line 2138, in runTest
AssertionError: Failed doctest test for eightqueens.checker
  File "/home/lsoto/.hudson/jobs/test/workspace/eightqueens/checker.py", line
0, in checker
 	
-- 	
File "/home/lsoto/.hudson/jobs/test/workspace/eightqueens/checker.py", line
96, in eightqueens.checker
Failed example:
    True
Expected:
    False
Got:
    True
	0.0	2

>>> eightqueens.test_checker.SolutionTest.eightqueens.test_checker.SolutionTest.testIsSolution	0.0	9

All Tests

Package	Duration	Fail	(diff)	Skip	(diff)	Total	(diff)
(root)	0 ms	1		0		1	
eightqueens.test_checker	0 ms	1		0		7	

Hudson ver. 1.320

Figure 18-10. *Test report showing failures*

We had to use a slightly more complicated script to use Nose and Hudson together, but it has the advantage that it will probably work untouched for a long time, unlike the original script manually built the suite, which would have to be modified each time a new test module is created.

Summary

Testing is fertile ground for Jython usage, because you can exploit the flexibility of Python to write concise tests for Java APIs, which also tend to be more readable than the ones written with JUnit. Doctests in particular don't have a parallel in the Java world, and can be a powerful way to introduce the practice of automated testing for people who want it to be simple and easy.

Integration with continuous integration tools, and Hudson in particular, lets you get the maximum from your tests, avoid unnoticed test breakages and delivers a live history of your project health and evolution.

CHAPTER 19

■ ■ ■

Concurrency

Supporting concurrency is increasingly important. In the past, mainstream concurrent programming generally meant ensuring that the code interacting with relatively slow network, disk, database, and other I/O resources did not unduly slow things down. Exploiting parallelism was typically only seen in such domains as scientific computing with the apps running on supercomputers.

But there are new factors at work now. The semiconductor industry continues to work feverishly to uphold Moore's Law of exponential increase in chip density. Chip designers used to apply this bounty to speeding up an individual CPU. For a variety of reasons this old approach no longer works as well, so now chip designers are cramming chips with more CPUs and hardware threads. Speeding up execution means harnessing the parallelism of the hardware, and it is now our job as software developers to do that work.

The Java platform can help out here. The Java platform is arguably the most robust environment for running concurrent code today, and this functionality can be readily be used from Jython. The problem remains that writing concurrent code is still not easy. This is especially true with respect to a concurrency model based on threads, which is what today's hardware natively exposes.

This means we have to be concerned with thread safety, which arises as an issue because of the existence of mutable objects that are shared between threads. (Mutable state might be avoidable in functional programming, but it would be hard to avoid in any but the most trivial Python code.) If you attempt to solve concurrency issues through synchronization, you run into other problems: besides the potential performance hit, there are opportunities for deadlock and livelock.

■ **Note** Implementations of the JVM (like HotSpot) can often avoid the overhead of synchronization. We will discuss what's necessary for this scenario to happen later in this chapter.

Given all of these issues, it has been argued that threading is just too difficult to get right. We're not convinced by that argument. Useful concurrent systems have been written on the JVM, and that includes apps written in Jython. Key success factors in writing such code include:

- Keep the concurrency simple.
- Use tasks, which can be mapped to a thread pool.
- Use immutable objects where possible.
- Avoid unnecessary sharing of mutable objects.

- Minimize sharing of mutable objects. Queues and related objects -- like synchronization barriers -- provide a structured mechanism to hand over objects between threads. This can enable a design where an object is visible to only one thread when its state changes.

- Code defensively. Make it possible to cancel or interrupt tasks. Use timeouts.

Java or Python APIs?

One issue that you will have to consider in writing concurrent code is how much to make your implementation dependent on the Java platform. Here are our recommendations:

- If you are porting an existing Python code base that uses concurrency, you can just use the standard Python threading module. Such code can still interoperate with Java, because Jython threads are always mapped to Java threads. (If you are coming from Java, you will recognize this API, since it is substantially based on Java's.)

- Jython implements dict and set by using Java's ConcurrentHashMap. This means you can just use these standard Python types, and still get high performance concurrency. (They are also atomic like in CPython, as we will describe.)

- You can also any use of the collections from java.util.concurrent. So if it fits your app's needs, you may want to consider using such collections as CopyOnWriteArrayList and ConcurrentSkipListMap (new in Java 6). The Google Collections Library is another good choice that works well with Jython.

- Use higher-level primitives from Java instead of creating your own. This is particular true of the executor services for running and managing tasks against thread pools. So for example, avoid using threading.Timer, because you can use timed execution services in its place. But still use threading.Condition and threading.Lock. In particular, these constructs have been optimized to work in the context of a with-statement, as we will discuss.

In practice, using Java's support for higher level primitives should not impact the portability of your code so much. Using tasks in particular tends to keep all of this well isolated, and such thread safety considerations as thread confinement and safe publication remain the same.

Lastly, remember you can always mix and match.

Working With Threads

Creating threads is easy, perhaps too easy. This example downloads a web page concurrently.

Listing 19-1. test_thread_creation.py

```
from threading import Thread
import urllib2

downloaded_page = None # global

def download(url):
    """Download ``url`` as a single string"""
    global downloaded_page
```

```
        downloaded_page = urllib2.urlopen(url).read()
        print "Downloaded", downloaded_page[:200]

def main_work():
    # do some busy work in parallel
    print "Started main task"
    x = 0
    for i in xrange(100000000):
        x += 1
    print "Completed main task"

if __name__ == '__main__':
    # perform the download in the background
    Thread(target=lambda: download("http://www.jython.org")).start()
    main_work()
```

Be careful not to inadvertently invoke the function; target takes a reference to the function object (typically a name if a normal function). Calling the function instead creates an amusing bug where your target function runs now, so everything looks fine at first. But no concurrency is happening, because the function call is actually being run by the invoking thread, not this new thread.

The target function can be a regular function, or an object that is callable (implements __call__). This latter case can make it harder to see that the target is a function object!

To wait for a thread to complete, call join on it. This enables working with the concurrent result. The only problem is getting the result. As we will see, publishing results into variables is safe in Jython, but it's not the nicest way.

■ **Note** Daemon threads present an alluring alternative to managing the lifecycle of threads. A thread is set to be a daemon thread before it is started:

```
# create a thread t
t.setDaemon(True)
t.start()
```

Daemon status is inherited by any child threads. Upon JVM shutdown, any daemon threads are simply terminated, without an opportunity—or need—to perform cleanup or orderly shutdown.

This lack of cleanup means it's important that daemon threads never hold any external resources, such as database connections or file handles. Any such resource will not be properly closed upon a JVM exit. For similar reasons, a daemon thread should never make an import attempt, as this can interfere with Jython's orderly shutdown.

In production, the only use case for daemon threads is when they are strictly used to work with in-memory objects, typically for some sort of housekeeping. For example, you might use them to maintain a cache or compute an index.

Having said that, daemon threads are certainly convenient when playing around with some ideas. Maybe your lifecycle management of a program is to use "Control-C" to terminate. Unlike regular threads, running daemon threads won't get in the way and prevent JVM shutdown. Likewise, a later example demonstrating deadlock uses daemon threads to enable shutdown without waiting on these deadlocked threads.

With that in mind, it's generally best not use daemon threads. At the very least, serious thought should be given to their usage.

Thread Locals

The threading.local class enables each thread to have its own instances of some objects in an otherwise shared environment. Its usage is deceptively simple:simply create an instance of threading.local, or a subclass, and assign it to a variable or other name. This variable could be global, or part of some other namespace. So far, this is just like working with any other object in Python.

Threads can then share the variable, but with a twist: each thread will see a different, thread-specific version of the object. This object can have arbitrary attributes added to it, each of which will not be visible to other threads.

Other options include subclassing threading.local. As usual, this allows one to define defaults and specify a more nuanced properties model. But one unique, and potentially useful, aspect is that any attributes specified in __slots__ will be *shared* across threads.

However, there's a big problem when working with thread locals. Usually they don't make sense because threads are not the right scope, but an object or a function is, especially through a closure. If you are using thread locals, you are implicitly adopting a model where threads are partitioning the work. But then you are binding the given piece of work to a thread. This makes using a thread pool problematic, because you have to clean up after the thread.

■ **Note** In fact, we see this very problem in the Jython runtime. A certain amount of context needs to be made available to execute Python code. In the past, we would look this "ThreadState" up from the thread. Historically, this may have been in fact faster, but it now slows things down, and unnecessarily limits what a given thread can do. A future refactoring of Jython will likely remove the use of "ThreadState" completely, simultaneously speeding and cleaning things up. Having said that, thread locals might be useful in certain cases. One common scenario is where your code is being called by a component that you didn't write. Or you may need to access a thread-local singleton. And of course, if you are using code whose architecture mandates thread locals, it's just something you will have to work with.

But often this is unnecessary. Your code may be different, but Python gives you good tools to avoid action at a distance. You can use closures, decorators, even sometimes selectively monkey patching modules. Take advantage of the fact that Python is a dynamic language, with strong support for metaprogramming, and remember that the Jython implementation makes these techniques accessible when working with even recalcitrant Java code.

In the end, thread locals are an interesting aside. They do not work well in a task-oriented model, because you don't want to associate context with a worker thread that will be assigned to arbitrary tasks. Without a lot of care, this can make for a confused mess.

No Global Interpreter Lock

Jython lacks the global interpreter lock (GIL), which is an implementation detail of CPython. For CPython, the GIL means that only one thread *at a time* can run Python code. This restriction also applies to much of the supporting runtime as well as extension modules that do not release the GIL. (Unfortunately development efforts to remove the GIL in CPython have so far only had the effect of slowing down Python execution significantly.)

The impact of the GIL on CPython programming is that threads are not as useful as they are in Jython. Concurrency will only be seen in interacting with I/O as well as scenarios where computation is performed by an extension module on data structures managed outside of CPython's runtime. Instead, developers typically will use a process-oriented model to evade the restrictiveness of the GIL.

Again, Jython does not have the straightjacket of the GIL. This is because all Python threads are mapped to Java threads and use standard Java garbage collection support (the main reason for the GIL in CPython is because of the reference counting GC system). The important ramification here is that you can use threads for compute-intensive tasks that are written in Python.

Module Import Lock

Python does, however, define a *module import lock*, which is implemented by Jython. This lock is acquired whenever an import of any name is made. This is true whether the import goes through the import statement, the equivalent __import__ builtin, or related code. It's important to note that even if the corresponding module has already been imported, the module import lock will still be acquired, if only briefly.

So don't write code like this in a hot loop, especially in threaded code:

Listing 19-2.

```python
def slow_things_way_down():
    from foo import bar, baz
    ...
```

It may still make sense to defer your imports. Such deferral can decrease the start time of your app. Just keep in mind that thread(s) performing such imports will be forced to run single threaded because of this lock. So it might make sense for your code to perform deferred imports in a background thread.

Listing 19-3. background_import.py

```python
from threading import Thread
import time

def make_imports():
    import unicodedata

background_import = Thread(target=make_imports)
background_import.start()
```

```
print "Do something else while we wait for the import"
for i in xrange(10):
    print i
    time.sleep(0.1)
print "Now join..."
background_import.join()

print "And actually use unicodedata"
import unicodedata
```

So as you can see, you need to do at least two imports of a given module; one in the background thread; the other in the actual place(s) where the module's namespace is being used.

Here's why we need the module import lock: upon the first import, the import procedure runs the (implicit) top-level function of the module. Even though many modules are often declarative in nature, in Python all definitions are done at runtime. Such definitions potentially include further imports (recursive imports), and the top-level function can certainly perform much more complex tasks. The module import lock simplifies this setup so that it's safely published. We will discuss this concept further later in this chapter.

Note that in the current implementation, the module import lock is global for the entire Jython runtime. This may change in the future.

Working With Tasks

It's usually best to avoid managing the lifecycle of threads directly. Instead, the task model often provides a better abstraction.

Tasks describe the asynchronous computation to be performed. Although there are other options, the object you submit to be executed should implement Java's Callable interface (a call method without arguments), as this best maps into working with a Python method or function. Tasks move through the states of being created, submitted (to an executor), started, and completed. Tasks can also be canceled or interrupted.

Executors run tasks using a set of threads. This might be one thread, a thread pool, or as many threads as necessary to run all currently submitted tasks concurrently. The specific choice comprises the executor policy, but generally you want to use a thread pool so as to control the degree of concurrency.

Futures allow code to access the result of a computation -- or an exception, if thrown -- in a task only at the point when it's needed. Up until that point, the using code can run concurrently with that task. If it's not ready, a wait-on dependency is introduced.

We are going to look at how we can use this functionality by using the example of downloading web pages. We will wrap this up so it's easy to work with, tracking the state of the download, as well as any timing information.

Listing 19-4. downloader.py

```
import threading
import time
import urllib2
from java.util.concurrent import Callable

class Downloader(Callable):
    def __init__(self, url):
        self.url = url
        self.started = None
```

```
        self.completed = None
        self.result = None
        self.thread_used = None
        self.exception = None

    def __str__(self):
        if self.exception:
            return "[%s] %s download error %s in %.2fs" % \
                (self.thread_used, self.url, self.exception,
                    self.completed - self.started, ) #, self.result)
        elif self.completed:
            return "[%s] %s downloaded %dK in %.2fs" % \
                (self.thread_used, self.url, len(self.result)/1024,
                    self.completed - self.started, ) #, self.result)
        elif self.started:
            return "[%s] %s started at %s" % \
                (self.thread_used, self.url, self.started)
        else:
            return "[%s] %s not yet scheduled" % \
                (self.thread_used, self.url)

    # needed to implement the Callable interface;
    # any exceptions will be wrapped as either ExecutionException
    # or InterruptedException
    def call(self):
        self.thread_used = threading.currentThread().getName()
        self.started = time.time()
        try:
            self.result = urllib2.urlopen(self.url).read()
        except Exception, ex:
            self.exception = ex
        self.completed = time.time()
        return self
```

In Jython any other task could be done in this fashion, whether it is a database query or a computationally intensive task written in Python. It just needs to support the Callable interface.

Next, we need to create the futures. Upon completion of a future, either the result is returned, or an exception is thrown into the caller. This exception will be one of:

- InterruptedException

- ExecutionException. Your code can retrieve the underlying exception with the cause attribute.

(This pushing of the exception into the asynchronous caller is thus similar to how a coroutine works when send is called on it.)

Now we have what we need to multiplex the downloads of several web pages over a thread pool.

Listing 19-5. test_futures.py

```
from downloader import Downloader
from shutdown import shutdown_and_await_termination
from java.util.concurrent import Executors, TimeUnit
```

```
MAX_CONCURRENT = 3
SITES = [
    "http://www.cnn.com/",
    "http://www.nytimes.com/",
    "http://www.washingtonpost.com/",
    "http://www.dailycamera.com/",
    "http://www.timescall.com/",
    ]

pool = Executors.newFixedThreadPool(MAX_CONCURRENT)
downloaders = [Downloader(url) for url in SITES]
futures = pool.invokeAll(downloaders)

for future in futures:
    print future.get(5, TimeUnit.SECONDS)

shutdown_and_await_termination(pool, 5)
```

Up until the get method on the returned future, the caller runs concurrently with this task. The get call then introduces a wait-on dependency on the task's completion. (So this is like calling join on the supporting thread.)

Shutting down a thread pool should be as simple as calling the shutdown method on the pool. However, you may need to take into account that this shutdown can happen during extraordinary times in your code. Here's the Jython version of a robust shutdown function, shutdown_and_await_termination, as provided in the standard Java docs.

Listing 19-6. shutdown.py

```
from java.util.concurrent import TimeUnit

def shutdown_and_await_termination(pool, timeout):
    pool.shutdown()
    try:
        if not pool.awaitTermination(timeout, TimeUnit.SECONDS):
            pool.shutdownNow()
            if (not pool.awaitTermination(timeout, TimeUnit.SECONDS)):
                print >> sys.stderr, "Pool did not terminate"
    except InterruptedException, ex:
        # (Re-)Cancel if current thread also interrupted
        pool.shutdownNow()
        # Preserve interrupt status
        Thread.currentThread().interrupt()
```

The CompletionService interface provides a nice abstraction to working with futures. The scenario is that instead of waiting for all the futures to complete, as our code did with invokeAll, or otherwise polling them, the completion service will push futures as they are completed onto a synchronized queue. This queue can then be consumed, by consumers running in one or more threads.

Listing 19-7. test_completion.py

```
from downloader import Downloader
from shutdown import shutdown_and_await_termination
```

```
from java.util.concurrent import Executors, ExecutorCompletionService
import os
import hashlib

MAX_CONCURRENT = 3
SITES = [
    "http://www.cnn.com/",
    "http://www.nytimes.com/",
    "http://www.washingtonpost.com/",
    "http://www.dailycamera.com/",
    "http://www.timescall.com/",
    # generate a random web site name that is very, very unlikely to exist
    "http://" + hashlib.md5(
        "unlikely-web-site-" + os.urandom(4)).hexdigest() + ".com",
    ]

pool = Executors.newFixedThreadPool(MAX_CONCURRENT)
ecs = ExecutorCompletionService(pool)

# this function could spider the links from these roots;
# for now just schedule these roots directly
def scheduler(roots):
    for site in roots:
        yield site

# submit tasks indefinitely
for site in scheduler(SITES):
    ecs.submit(Downloader(site))

# work with results as soon as they become available
submitted = len(SITES)
while submitted > 0:
    result = ecs.take().get()
    # here we just do something unimaginative with the result;
    # consider parsing it with tools like beautiful soup
    print result
    submitted -= 1

print "shutting pool down..."
shutdown_and_await_termination(pool, 5)
print "done"
```

This setup enables a natural flow. Although it may be tempting to then schedule everything through the completion service's queue, there are limits. For example, if you're writing a scalable web spider, you would want to externalize this work queue, but for simple management, it would certainly suffice.

■ **Note** Why use tasks instead of threads? A common practice too often seen in production code is the addition of threading in a haphazard fashion:

Heterogeneous threads. Perhaps you have one thread that queries the database. And another that rebuilds an associated index. What happens when you need to add another query?

Dependencies are managed through a variety of channels, instead of being formally structured. This can result in a rats' nest of threads synchronizing on a variety of objects, often with timers and other event sources thrown in the mix.

It's certainly possible to make this sort of setup work—just debug away—but using tasks, with explicit wait-on dependencies and time scheduling, makes it far simpler to build a simple, scalable system.

Thread Safety

Thread safety addresses such questions as:

- Can the (unintended) interaction of two or more threads corrupt a mutable object? This is especially dangerous for a collection like a list or a dictionary, because such corruption could potentially render the underlying data structure unusable or even produce infinite loops when traversing it.

- Can an update get lost? Perhaps the canonical example is incrementing a counter. In this case, there can be a data race with another thread in the time between retrieving the current value, and then updating with the incremented value.

Jython ensures that its underlying mutable collection types -- dict, list, and set -- cannot be corrupted. But updates still might get lost in a data race.

However, other Java collection objects that your code might use would typically not have such no-corruption guarantees. If you need to use LinkedHashMap, so as to support an ordered dictionary, you will need to consider thread safety if it will be both shared and mutated.

Here's a simple test harness we will use in our examples. ThreadSafetyTestCase subclasses unittest.TestCase, adding a new method assertContended.

Listing 19-8. threadsafety.py

```
import threading
import unittest

class ThreadSafetyTestCase(unittest.TestCase):

    def assertContended(self, f, num_threads=20, timeout=2., args=()):
        threads = []
        for i in xrange(num_threads):
            t = threading.Thread(target=f, args=args)
            t.start()
            threads.append(t)
        for t in threads:
            t.join(timeout)
            timeout = 0.
        for t in threads:
            self.assertFalse(t.isAlive())
```

This new method runs a target function and asserts that all threads properly terminate. Then the testing code needs to check for any other invariants.

For example, we use this idea in Jython to test that certain operations on the list type are atomic. The idea is to apply a sequence of operations that perform an operation, then reverse it. One step forward, one step back. The net result should be right where you started, an empty list, which is what the test code asserts.

List 19-9. test_list.py

```python
from threadsafety import ThreadSafetyTestCase
import threading
import time
import unittest

class ListThreadSafety(ThreadSafetyTestCase):

    def test_append_remove(self):
        lst = []
        def tester():
            # preserve invariant by adding, then removing a unique
            # value (in this case, a reference to the worker thread
            # executing this function)
            ct = threading.currentThread()
            for i in range(1000):
                lst.append(ct)
                time.sleep(0.0001)
                lst.remove(ct)
        self.assertContended(tester)
        self.assertEqual(lst, [])

if __name__ == '__main__':
    unittest.main()
```

Of course these concerns do not apply at all to immutable objects. Commonly used objects like strings, numbers, datetimes, tuples, and frozen sets are immutable, and you can create your own immutable objects too.

There are a number of other strategies in solving thread safety issues. We will look at them as follows:

- Synchronization

- Atomicity

- Thread Confinement

- Safe Publication

Synchronization

We use synchronization to control the entry of threads into code blocks corresponding to synchronized resources. Through this control we can prevent data races, assuming a correct synchronization protocol. (This can be a big assumption!)

A threading.Lock ensures entry by only one thread. (In Jython, but unlike CPython, such locks are always reentrant; there's no distinction between threading.Lock and threading.RLock.) Other threads have to wait until that thread exits the lock. Such explicit locks are the simplest and perhaps most portable synchronization to perform.

You should generally manage the entry and exit of such locks through a with-statement; failing that, you must use a try-finally to ensure that the lock is always released when exiting a block of code.

Here's some example code using the with-statement. The code allocates a lock, then shares it amongst some tasks.

Listing 19-10. test_lock.py—LockTestCase.test_with_lock

```
def test_with_lock(self):
        counter = [0]
        lock = Lock()
        def loop100(counter):
            for i in xrange(100):
                with lock:
                    counter[0] += 1
                # sleeping helps ensures that all threads run in our test
                time.sleep(0.0001)

        self.assertContended(loop100, args=(counter,), num_threads=20)
        self.assertEqual(counter[0], 2000) # 20 threads * 100 loops/thread
```

Alternatively, you can do this with try-finally.

Listing 19-11. test_lock.py—LockTestCase.test_try_finally_lock

```
def test_try_finally_lock(self):
        counter = [0]
        lock = Lock()
        def loop100(counter):
            for i in xrange(100):
                lock.acquire()
                try:
                    counter[0] += 1
                finally:
                    lock.release()
                time.sleep(0.0001)

        self.assertContended(loop100, args=(counter,), num_threads=20)
        self.assertEqual(counter[0], 2000)
```

But don't do this. It's actually slower than the with-statement, and using the with-statement version also results in more idiomatic Python code.

Another possibility is to use the synchronize module, which is specific to Jython. This module provides a ``make_synchronized`` decorator function, which wraps any callable in Jython in a synchronized block.

Listing 19-12. test_synchronized.py

```
from synchronize import make_synchronized
from threadsafety import ThreadSafetyTestCase
import time
import unittest

@make_synchronized
def increment_counter(counter):
    counter[0] += 1
    # sleeping helps ensures that all threads run in our test
    time.sleep(0.0001)

class SynchronizedTestCase(ThreadSafetyTestCase):

    def test_counter(self):
        def loop100(counter):
            for i in xrange(100):
                increment_counter(counter)

        counter = [0]
        self.assertContended(loop100, args=(counter,), num_threads=20)
        self.assertEqual(counter[0], 2000) # 20 threads * 100 loops/thread

if __name__ == '__main__':
    unittest.main()
```

In this case, you don't need to explicitly release anything. Even in the case of an exception, the synchronization lock is always released upon exit from the function. Again, this version is also slower than the with-statement form, and it doesn't use explicit locks.

SYNCHRONIZATION AND THE WITH-STATEMENT

Jython's current runtime (as of 2.5.1) can execute the with-statement form more efficiently through both runtime support and how this statement is compiled. The reason is that most JVMs can perform analysis on a chunk of code (the *compilation unit*, including any inlining) to avoid synchronization overhead, so long as two conditions are met. First, the chunk contains both the lock and unlock. And second, the chunk is not too long for the JVM to perform its analysis. The with-statement's semantics make it relatively easy for us to do that when working with built-in types like `threading.Lock`, while avoiding the overhead of Java runtime reflection.

In the future, support of the new `invokedynamic` bytecode should collapse these performance differences.

The `threading` module offers portability, but it's also minimalist. You may want to use the synchronizers in `Java.util.concurrent` instead of their wrapped versions in `threading`. In particular, this approach is necessary if you want to wait on a lock with a timeout. Also, you may want to use factories like Collections.synchronizedMap, when applicable, to ensure the underlying Java object has the desired synchronization.

Deadlocks

But use synchronization carefully: this code will always eventually deadlock.

Listing 19-13. deadlock.py

```python
from __future__ import with_statement
from threading import Thread, Lock
from java.lang.management import ManagementFactory
import time, threading

def cause_deadlock():
    counter = [0]
    lock_one = Lock()
    lock_two = Lock()
    threads = [
        Thread(
            name="thread #1", target=acquire_locks,
            args=(counter, lock_one, lock_two)),
        Thread(
            name="thread #2 (reversed)", target=acquire_locks,
            args=(counter, lock_two, lock_one))]
    for thread in threads:
        thread.setDaemon(True) # make shutdown possible after deadlock
        thread.start()

    thread_mxbean = ManagementFactory.getThreadMXBean()
    while True:
        time.sleep(1)
        print "monitoring thread", counter[0]
        thread_ids = thread_mxbean.findDeadlockedThreads()
        if thread_ids:
            print "monitoring thread: deadlock detected, shutting down", list(thread_ids)
            break

def acquire_locks(counter, lock1, lock2):
    # Should eventually deadlock if locks are acquired in different order
    name = threading.currentThread().getName()
    while True:
        with lock1:
            with lock2:
                counter[0] += 1
                print name, counter[0]


if __name__ == '__main__':
    cause_deadlock()
```

Deadlock results from a cycle of any length of wait-on dependencies. For example, Alice is waiting on Bob, but Bob is waiting on Alice. Without a timeout or other change in strategy—Alice just gets tired of waiting on Bob!—this deadlock will not be broken.

Avoiding deadlocks can be done by never acquiring locks such that a cycle like that can be created. If we rewrote the example so that locks are acquired in the same order (Bob always allows Alice to go first), there would be no deadlocks. However, this ordering is not always so easy to do. Often, a more robust strategy is to allow for timeouts.

Other Synchronization Objects

The Queue module implements a first-in, first-out synchronized queue. (Synchronized queues are also called blocking queues, and that's how they are described in java.util.concurrent.) Such queues represent a thread-safe way to send objects from one or more producing threads to one or more consuming threads.

Often, you will define a poison object to shut down the queue. This will allow any consuming, but waiting, threads to immediately shut down. Or just use Java's support for executors to get an off-the-shelf solution.

If you need to implement another policy, such as last-in, first-out or based on a priority, you can use the comparable synchronized queues in java.util.concurrent as appropriate. (Note these have since been implemented in Python 2.6, so they will be made available when Jython 2.6 is eventually released.)

Condition objects allow for one thread to notify another thread that's waiting on a condition to wake up; notifyAll is used to wake up all such threads. Along with Queue, this is probably the most versatile of the synchronizing objects for real usage.

Condition objects are always associated with a Lock. Your code needs to bracket waiting and notifying the condition by acquiring the corresponding lock, then finally (as always!) releasing it. As usual, this is easiest done in the context of the with-statement.

For example, here's how we actually implement a Queue in the standard library of Jython (just modified here to use the with-statement). We can't use a standard Java blocking queue, because the requirement of being able to join on the queue when there's no more work to be performed requires a third condition variable.

Listing 19-15. Queue.py

```
"""A multi-producer, multi-consumer queue."""

from __future__ import with_statement
from time import time as _time
from collections import deque

__all__ = ['Empty', 'Full', 'Queue']

class Empty(Exception):
    "Exception raised by Queue.get(block=0)/get_nowait()."
    pass

class Full(Exception):
    "Exception raised by Queue.put(block=0)/put_nowait()."
    pass

class Queue:
    """Create a queue object with a given maximum size.
```

```python
    If maxsize is <= 0, the queue size is infinite.
    """
    def __init__(self, maxsize=0):
        try:
            import threading
        except ImportError:
            import dummy_threading as threading
        self._init(maxsize)
        # mutex must be held whenever the queue is mutating.  All methods
        # that acquire mutex must release it before returning.  mutex
        # is shared between the three conditions, so acquiring and
        # releasing the conditions also acquires and releases mutex.
        self.mutex = threading.Lock()
        # Notify not_empty whenever an item is added to the queue; a
        # thread waiting to get is notified then.
        self.not_empty = threading.Condition(self.mutex)
        # Notify not_full whenever an item is removed from the queue;
        # a thread waiting to put is notified then.
        self.not_full = threading.Condition(self.mutex)
        # Notify all_tasks_done whenever the number of unfinished tasks
        # drops to zero; thread waiting to join() is notified to resume
        self.all_tasks_done = threading.Condition(self.mutex)
        self.unfinished_tasks = 0

def task_done(self):
    """Indicate that a formerly enqueued task is complete.

    Used by Queue consumer threads.  For each get() used to fetch a task,
    a subsequent call to task_done() tells the queue that the processing
    on the task is complete.

    If a join() is currently blocking, it will resume when all items
    have been processed (meaning that a task_done() call was received
    for every item that had been put() into the queue).

    Raises a ValueError if called more times than there were items
    placed in the queue.
    """
    with self.all_tasks_done:
        unfinished = self.unfinished_tasks - 1
        if unfinished <= 0:
            if unfinished < 0:
                raise ValueError('task_done() called too many times')
            self.all_tasks_done.notifyAll()
        self.unfinished_tasks = unfinished

def join(self):
    """Blocks until all items in the Queue have been gotten and processed.

    The count of unfinished tasks goes up whenever an item is added to the
    queue. The count goes down whenever a consumer thread calls task_done()
    to indicate the item was retrieved and all work on it is complete.

    When the count of unfinished tasks drops to zero, join() unblocks.
```

```
        """
        with self.all_tasks_done:
            while self.unfinished_tasks:
                self.all_tasks_done.wait()

    def qsize(self):
        """Return the approximate size of the queue (not reliable!)."""
        self.mutex.acquire()
        n = self._qsize()
        self.mutex.release()
        return n

    def empty(self):
        """Return True if the queue is empty, False otherwise (not reliable!)."""
        self.mutex.acquire()
        n = self._empty()
        self.mutex.release()
        return n

    def full(self):
        """Return True if the queue is full, False otherwise (not reliable!)."""
        self.mutex.acquire()
        n = self._full()
        self.mutex.release()
        return n

    def put(self, item, block=True, timeout=None):
        """Put an item into the queue.

        If optional args 'block' is true and 'timeout' is None (the default),
        block if necessary until a free slot is available. If 'timeout' is
        a positive number, it blocks at most 'timeout' seconds and raises
        the Full exception if no free slot was available within that time.
        Otherwise ('block' is false), put an item on the queue if a free slot
        is immediately available, else raise the Full exception ('timeout'
        is ignored in that case).
        """
        with self.not_full:
            if not block:
                if self._full():
                    raise Full
            elif timeout is None:
                while self._full():
                    self.not_full.wait()
            else:
                if timeout < 0:
                    raise ValueError("'timeout' must be a positive number")
                endtime = _time() + timeout
                while self._full():
                    remaining = endtime - _time()
                    if remaining <= 0.0:
                        raise Full
                    self.not_full.wait(remaining)
            self._put(item)
```

```
            self.unfinished_tasks += 1
            self.not_empty.notify()

    def put_nowait(self, item):
        """Put an item into the queue without blocking.

        Only enqueue the item if a free slot is immediately available.
        Otherwise raise the Full exception.
        """
        return self.put(item, False)

    def get(self, block=True, timeout=None):
        """Remove and return an item from the queue.

        If optional args 'block' is true and 'timeout' is None (the default),
        block if necessary until an item is available. If 'timeout' is
        a positive number, it blocks at most 'timeout' seconds and raises
        the Empty exception if no item was available within that time.
        Otherwise ('block' is false), return an item if one is immediately
        available, else raise the Empty exception ('timeout' is ignored
        in that case).
        """
        with self.not_empty:
            if not block:
                if self._empty():
                    raise Empty
            elif timeout is None:
                while self._empty():
                    self.not_empty.wait()
            else:
                if timeout < 0:
                    raise ValueError("'timeout' must be a positive number")
                endtime = _time() + timeout
                while self._empty():
                    remaining = endtime - _time()
                    if remaining <= 0.0:
                        raise Empty
                    self.not_empty.wait(remaining)
            item = self._get()
            self.not_full.notify()
            return item

    def get_nowait(self):
        """Remove and return an item from the queue without blocking.

        Only get an item if one is immediately available. Otherwise
        raise the Empty exception.
        """
        return self.get(False)

    # Override these methods to implement other queue organizations
    # (e.g. stack or priority queue).
    # These will only be called with appropriate locks held
```

```
# Initialize the queue representation
def _init(self, maxsize):
    self.maxsize = maxsize
    self.queue = deque()

def _qsize(self):
    return len(self.queue)

# Check whether the queue is empty
def _empty(self):
    return not self.queue

# Check whether the queue is full
def _full(self):
    return self.maxsize > 0 and len(self.queue) == self.maxsize

# Put a new item in the queue
def _put(self, item):
    self.queue.append(item)

# Get an item from the queue
def _get(self):
    return self.queue.popleft()
```

There are other mechanisms to synchronize, including exchangers, barriers, latches, etc. You can use semaphores to describe scenarios where it's possible for multiple threads to enter, or use locks that are set up to distinguish reads from writes. There are many possibilities for the Java platform. In our experience, Jython should be able to work with any of them.

Atomic Operations

An atomic operation is inherently thread safe. Data races and object corruption do not occur, and it's not possible for other threads to see an inconsistent view.

Atomic operations are therefore simpler to use than synchronization. In addition, atomic operations will often use underlying support in the CPU, such as a compare-and-swap instruction. They may use locking too. The important thing to know is that the lock is not directly visible. Also, if synchronization is used, it's not possible to expand the scope of the synchronization. In particular, callbacks and iteration are not feasible.

Python guarantees the atomicity of certain operations, although at best it's only informally documented. Fredrik Lundh's article on "Thread Synchronization Methods in Python" summarizes the mailing list discussions and the state of the CPython implementation. Quoting his article, the following are atomic operations for Python code:

- Reading or replacing a single instance attribute

- Reading or replacing a single global variable

- Fetching an item from a list

- Modifying a list in place (e.g. adding an item using append)

- Fetching an item from a dictionary

- Modifying a dictionary in place (e.g. adding an item, or calling the clear method)

Although unstated, this also applies to equivalent ops on the builtin set type.

For CPython, this atomicity emerges from combining its Global Interpreter Lock (GIL), the Python bytecode virtual machine execution loop, and the fact that types like dict and list are implemented natively in C and do not release the GIL.

Despite the fact that this is in some sense accidentally emergent, it is a useful simplification for the developer. It's what existing Python code expects, so this is what we have implemented in Jython.

In particular, because dict is a ConcurrentHashMap, we also expose the following methods to atomically update dictionaries:

* ``setifabsent``

* ``update``

It's important to note that iterations are not atomic, even on a ConcurrentHashMap.

Atomic operations are useful, but they are pretty limited too. Often, you still need to use synchronization to prevent data races, and this has to be done with care to avoid deadlocks and starvation.

Thread Confinement

Thread confinement is often the best way to resolve problems seen in working with mutable objects. In practice, you probably don't need to share a large percentage of the mutable objects used in your code. Very simply put, if you don't share, then thread safety issues go away.

Not all problems can be reduced to using thread confinement. There are likely some shared objects in your system, but in practice most can be eliminated. And often the shared state can be someone else's problem:

- Intermediate objects don't require sharing. For example, if you are building up a buffer that is only pointed to by a local variable, you don't need to synchronize. It's an easy prescription to follow, so long as you are not trying to keep around these intermediate objects to avoid allocation overhead: don't do that.

- Producer-consumer. Construct an object in one thread, then hand it off to another thread. You just need to use an appropriate synchronizer object, such as a Queue.

- Application containers. The typical database-driven web application makes for the classic case. For example, if you are using modjy, then the database connection pools and thread pools are the responsibility of the servlet container. And they are not directly observable. (But don't do things like share database connections across threads.) Caches and databases then are where you will see shared state.

- Actors. The actor model is another good example. Send and receive messages to an actor (effectively an independent thread) and let it manipulate any objects it owns on your behalf. Effectively this reduces the problem to sharing one mutable object, the message queue. The message queue can then ensure any accesses are appropriately serialized, so there are no thread safety issues.

Unfortunately thread confinement is not without issues in Jython. For example, if you use StringIO, you have to pay the cost that this class uses list, which is synchronized. Although it's possible to further optimize the Jython implementation of the Python standard library, if a section of code is hot enough, you may want to consider rewriting that in Java to ensure no additional synchronization overhead.

Lastly, thread confinement is not perfect in Python, because of the possibility of introspecting on frame objects. This means your code can see local variables in other threads, and the objects they point to. But this is really more of an issue for how optimizable Jython is when run on the JVM. It won't cause thread safety issues if you don't exploit this loophole. We will discuss this more in the next section, on the Python Memory Model.

Python Memory Model

Reasoning about concurrency in Python is easier than in Java. This is because the memory model is not as surprising to our conventional reasoning about how programs operate. However, this also means that Python code sacrifices significant performance to keep it simpler.

Here's why. In order to maximize Java performance, it's allowed for a CPU to arbitrarily re-order the operations performed by Java code, subject to the constraints imposed by *happens-before* and *synchronizes-with* relationships. (The published Java memory model goes into more details on these constraints.) Although such reordering is not visible within a given thread, the problem is that it's visible to other threads. Of course, this visibility only applies to changes made to non-local objects; thread confinement still applies. In particular, this means you cannot rely on the apparent sequential ordering of Java code when looking at two or more threads.

Python is different. The fundamental thing to know about Python, and what we have implemented in Jython, is that setting any attribute in Python is a volatile write; and getting any attribute is a volatile read. This is because Python attributes are stored in dictionaries, and in Jython, this follows the semantics of the backing ConcurrentHashMap. So get and set are volatile. So this means that Python code has sequential consistency. Execution follows the ordering of statements in the code. There are no surprises here.

This means that *safe publication* is pretty much trivial in Python, when compared to Java. Safe publication means the thread safe association of an object with a name. Because this is always a memory-fenced operation in Python, your code simply needs to ensure that the object itself is built in a thread-safe fashion; then publish it all at once by setting the appropriate variable to this object.

If you need to create module-level objects—singletons—then you should do this in the top-level script of the module so that the module import lock is in effect.

Interruption

Long-threading threads should provide some opportunity for cancellation. The typical pattern is something like the following example.

Listing 19-16.

```
class DoSomething(Runnable):
    def __init__(self):
        cancelled = False

    def run(self):
        while not self.cancelled:
            do_stuff()
```

Remember, Python variables are always volatile, unlike Java. There are no problems with using a cancelled flag like this.

Thread interruption allows for even more responsive cancellation. In particular, if a thread is waiting on most any synchronizers, such as a condition variable or on file I/O, this action will cause the waited-on method to exit with an InterruptedException. (Unfortunately lock acquisition, except under certain cases such as using lockInterruptibly on the underlying Java lock, is not interruptible.)

Although Python's threading module does not itself support interruption, it is available through the standard Java thread API. First, let's import this class (we will rename it to JThread so it doesn't conflict with Python's version).

Listing 19-17.

```
from java.lang import Thread as JThread
```

As you have seen, you can use Java threads as if they are Python threads. So logically you should be able to do the converse: use Python threads as if they are Java threads. It would be nice to make calls like JThread.interrupt(obj).

■ **Note** Incidentally, this formulation, instead of obj.interrupt(), looks like a static method on a class, as long as we pass in the object as the first argument. This adaptation is a good use of Python's explicit self.

But there's a problem here. As of the latest released version (Jython 2.5.1), we forgot to include an appropriate __tojava__ method on the Thread class! So this looks like you can't do this trick after all.

Or can you? What if you didn't have to wait until we fix this bug? You could explore the source code -- or look at the class with dir. One possibility would be to use the nominally private _thread attribute on the Thread object. After all _thread is the attribute for the underlying Java thread. Yes, this is an implementation detail, but it's probably fine to use. It's not so likely to change.

But we can do even better. We can *monkey patch* the Thread class such that it has an appropriate __tojava__ method, but only if it doesn't exist. So this patching is likely to work with a future version of Jython because we are going to fix this missing method before we even consider changing its implementation and removing _thread.

So here's how we can monkey patch, following a recipe of Guido van Rossum.

Listing 19-18. monkeypatch.py

```
# http://mail.python.org/pipermail/python-dev/2008-January/076194.html
# - a recipe of Guido van Rossum

def monkeypatch_method(cls):
    def decorator(func):
        setattr(cls, func.__name__, func)
        return func
    return decorator

# and a useful variant, with a good ugly name

def monkeypatch_method_if_not_set(cls):
    def decorator(func):
        if not hasattr(cls, func.__name__):
            setattr(cls, func.__name__, func)
        return func
    return decorator
```

This monkeypatch_method decorator allows us to add a method to a class after the fact. (This is what Ruby developers call *opening* a class.) Use this power with care. But again, you shouldn't worry too much when you keep such fixes to a minimum, especially when it's essentially a bug fix like this one. In our case, we will use a variant, the monkeypatch_method_if_not_set decorator, to ensure we only patch if it has not been fixed by a later version.

Putting it all together, we have this code:

Listing 19-19. interrupt.py

```
from __future__ import with_statement
from threading import Condition, Lock, Thread
from java.lang import Thread as JThread, InterruptedException
from monkeypatch import monkeypatch_method_if_not_set
import time, threading

@monkeypatch_method_if_not_set(Thread)
def __tojava__(self, java_type):
    return self._thread

def be_unfair():
    unfair_condition = Condition()
    threads = [
        Thread(
            name="thread #%d" % i,
            target=wait_until_interrupted,
            args=(unfair_condition,))
        for i in xrange(5)]
    for thread in threads:
        thread.start()
    time.sleep(5)

    # threads should not be doing anything now, can verify by looking at some shared state

    # instead of notifying, we will interrupt the threads
    for thread in threads:
        JThread.interrupt(thread)
        # or you can use this equivalent op
        # thread.__tojava__(JThread).interrupt()
    for thread in threads:
        thread.join()

def wait_until_interrupted(cv):
    name = threading.currentThread().getName()
    with cv:
        while not JThread.currentThread().isInterrupted():
            try:
                print "Waiting pointlessly %s" % name
                cv.wait()
            except InterruptedException, e:
                break
    print "Finished %s" % name
```

```
if __name__ == '__main__':
    be_unfair()
```

(It does rely on the use of threading.Condition to have something to wait on.)

Lastly, you could simply access interruption through the cancel method provided by a Future. No need to monkey patch!

Summary

Jython can fully take advantage of the underlying Java platform's support for concurrency. You can also use the standard Python threading constructs, which in most cases just wrap the corresponding Java functionality. The standard mutable Python collection types have been implemented in Jython with concurrency in mind; and Python's sequential consistency removes some potential bugs.

But concurrent programming is still not easy to get right, either in Python or in Java. You should consider higher-level concurrency primitives, such as tasks, and you should be disciplined in how your code shares mutable state.

■ ■ ■

Using Other Tools with Jython

The primary focus of this appendix is to provide information on using some external Python packages with Jython, as well as providing information regarding the Jython registry. In some circumstances, the tools must be used or installed a bit differently on Jython than on CPython, and those differences will be noted. Because there is a good deal of documentation on the usage of these tools available on the web, this appendix will focus on using the tool specifically with Jython. However, relevant URLs will be cited for finding more documentation on each of the topics.

The Jython Registry

Because there is no good platform-independent equivalent of the Windows Registry or Unix environment variables, Java has its own environment variable namespace. Jython acquires its namespace from the following sources (later sources override defaults found in earlier places):

- The Java system properties, typically passed in on the command line as options to the java interpreter.

- The Jython "registry" file, containing prop=value pairs. Read on for the algorithm Jython uses to find the registry file.

- The user's personal registry file, containing similarly formatted prop/value pairs. The user's registry file can be found at "user.home"+"/.jython"

- Jython properties specified on the command line as options to the Jython class. See the -D option to the interpreter.

Registry Properties

The following properties are recognized by Jython. There may be others that aren't documented here; consult the comments in registry file for details.

python.cachedir

The directory to use for caches—currently just package information. This directory must be writable by the user. If the directory is an absolute path, it is used as given; otherwise, it is interpreted as relative to sys.prefix.

python.verbose

Sets the verbosity level for informative messages. Valid values in order of increasing verbosity are "error," "warning," "message," "comment," and "debug."

python.security.respectJavaAccessibility

Normally, Jython can only provide access to public members of classes. However if this property is set to false and you are using Java 1.2, then Jython can access nonpublic fields, methods, and constructors.

python.jythonc.compiler

The Java compiler to use with the JythonC tool, which now generates Java source code. This should be the absolute path to a Java compiler, or the name of a compiler on your standard PATH.

python.jythonc.classpath

Extensions to the standard java.class.path property for use with JythonC. This is useful if you use Jikes as your compiler.

python.jythonc.compileropts

Options to pass to the Java compiler when using JythonC.

python.console

The name of a console class. An alternative console class that supports GNU readline can be installed with this property. Jython already includes such a console class, and it can be enabled by setting this property to org.python.util.ReadlineConsole.

python.console.readlinelib

Allow a choice of backing implementation for GNU readline support. Can be either GnuReadline or Editline. This property is only used when python.console is set to org.python.util.ReadlineConsole.

Finding the Registry File

To find the Jython registry file and set the Python values for sys.prefix, you must first locate a root directory.

If a "*python.home*" exists, it is used as the root directory by default.

If "*python.home*" does not exist, "install.root" is used.

If neither of these exists, then Jython searches for the file "jython.jar" on the Java classpath, as defined in the system property java.class.path. (The actual file system isn't searched, only the paths defined on the classpath and one of them must literally include "jython.jar").

Once the root directory is found, sys.prefix and sys.exec_prefix are set to it, and sys.path has rootdir/Lib appended to it. The registry file used is then rootdir/registry.

Setuptools

Setuptools is a library that builds upon distutils, the standard Python distribution facility. It offers some advanced tools like easy_install, a command to automatically download and install a given Python package and its dependencies.

To get setuptools, download ez_setup.py from http://peak.telecommunity.com/dist/ez_setup.py. Then, go to the directory where you left the downloaded file and execute:

```
$ jython ez_setup.py
```

The output will be similar to the following:

```
Downloading http://pypi.python.org/packages/2.5/s/setuptools/setuptools-0.6c9-py2.5.egg
Processing setuptools-0.6c9-py2.5.egg
Copying setuptools-0.6c9-py2.5.egg to /home/lsoto/jython2.5.0/Lib/site-packages
Adding setuptools 0.6c9 to easy-install.pth file
Installing easy_install script to /home/lsoto/jython2.5.0/bin
Installing easy_install-2.5 script to /home/lsoto/jython2.5.0/bin

Installed /home/lsoto/jython2.5.0/Lib/site-packages/setuptools-0.6c9-py2.5.egg
Processing dependencies for setuptools==0.6c9
Finished processing dependencies for setuptools==0.6c9
```

As you can read on the output, the easy_install script has been installed to the bin directory of the Jython installation (/home/lsoto/jython2.5.0/bin in the example above). If you work frequently with Jython, it's a good idea to prepend this directory to the PATH environment variable, so you don't have to type the whole path each time you want to use easy_install or other scripts installed to this directory. From now on, we'll assume that this is the case. If you don't want to prepend Jython's bin directory to your PATH for any reason, remember to type the complete path on each example (i.e., type /path/to/jython/bin/easy_install when I say easy_install).

Okay, so now you have easy_install. What's next? Let's grab a Python library with it! For example, let's say that we need to access Twitter from a program written in Jython, and we want to use python-twitter project, located at http://code.google.com/p/python-twitter/.

Without easy_install, you would go to that URL, read the building instructions and, after downloading the latest version and executing a few commands, you should be ready to go. Except that libraries often depend on other libraries (as the case with python-twitter which depends on simplejson) so you would have to repeat this boring process a few times.

With easy_install you simply run:

```
$ easy_install python-twitter
```

And you get the following output:

```
Searching for python-twitter
Reading http://pypi.python.org/simple/python-twitter/
Reading http://code.google.com/p/python-twitter/
Best match: python-twitter 0.6
Downloading http://python-twitter.googlecode.com/files/python-twitter-0.6.tar.gz
Processing python-twitter-0.6.tar.gz
Running python-twitter-0.6/setup.py -q bdist_egg --dist-dir
/var/folders/mQ/mQkMNKiaE583pWpee85FFk+++TI/-Tmp-/easy_install-FU5COZ/python-twitter-
0.6/egg-dist-tmp-EeR4RD
zip_safe flag not set; analyzing archive contents...
Unable to analyze compiled code on this platform.
Please ask the author to include a 'zip_safe' setting (either True or False) in the
package's setup.py
Adding python-twitter 0.6 to easy-install.pth file

Installed /home/lsoto/jython2.5.0/Lib/site-packages/python_twitter-0.6-py2.5.egg
Processing dependencies for python-twitter
Searching for simplejson
```

```
Reading http://pypi.python.org/simple/simplejson/
Reading http://undefined.org/python/#simplejson
Best match: simplejson 2.0.9
Downloading http://pypi.python.org/packages/source/s/simplejson/simplejson-
2.0.9.tar.gz#md5=af5e67a39ca3408563411d357e6d5e47
Processing simplejson-2.0.9.tar.gz
Running simplejson-2.0.9/setup.py -q bdist_egg --dist-dir
/var/folders/mQ/mQkMNKiaE583pWpee85FFk+++TI/-Tmp-/easy_install-VgAKxa/simplejson-2.0.9/egg-
dist-tmp-jcntqu
**********************************************************************
WARNING: The C extension could not be compiled, speedups are not enabled.
Failure information, if any, is above.
I'm retrying the build without the C extension now.
**********************************************************************
**********************************************************************
WARNING: The C extension could not be compiled, speedups are not enabled.
Plain-Python installation succeeded.
**********************************************************************
Adding simplejson 2.0.9 to easy-install.pth file

Installed /home/lsoto/jython2.5.0/Lib/site-packages/simplejson-2.0.9-py2.5.egg
Finished processing dependencies for python-twitter
```

The output is a bit verbose, but it gives you a detailed idea of the steps automated by easy_install. Let's review it piece by piece:

```
Searching for python-twitter
Reading http://pypi.python.org/simple/python-twitter/
Reading http://code.google.com/p/python-twitter/
Best match: python-twitter 0.6
Downloading http://python-twitter.googlecode.com/files/python-twitter-0.6.tar.gz
```

We asked for "python-twitter," which is looked up on PyPI, the Python Package Index, which lists all the Python packages produced by the community (as long as they have been registered by the author, which is usually the case). The version 0.6 was selected since it was the most recent version at the time we ran the command.

Let's see what's next on the easy_install output:

```
Running python-twitter-0.6/setup.py -q bdist_egg --dist-dir
/var/folders/mQ/mQkMNKiaE583pWpee85FFk+++TI/-Tmp-/easy_install-FU5COZ/python-twitter-
0.6/egg-dist-tmp-EeR4RD
zip_safe flag not set; analyzing archive contents...
Unable to analyze compiled code on this platform.
Please ask the author to include a 'zip_safe' setting (either True or False) in the
package's setup.py
Adding python-twitter 0.6 to easy-install.pth file

Installed /home/lsoto/jython2.5.0/Lib/site-packages/python_twitter-0.6-py2.5.egg
```

Nothing special here: it ran the needed commands to install the library. The next bits are more interesting:

```
Processing dependencies for python-twitter
Searching for simplejson
```

```
Reading http://pypi.python.org/simple/simplejson/
Reading http://undefined.org/python/#simplejson
Best match: simplejson 2.0.9
Downloading http://pypi.python.org/packages/source/s/simplejson/simplejson-
2.0.9.tar.gz#md5=af5e67a39ca3408563411d357e6d5e47
```

As you can see, the dependency on simplejson was discovered and, since it is not already installed it is being downloaded. Next we see:

```
Processing simplejson-2.0.9.tar.gz
Running simplejson-2.0.9/setup.py -q bdist_egg --dist-dir
/var/folders/mQ/mQkMNKiaE583pWpee85FFk+++TI/-Tmp-/easy_install-VgAKxa/simplejson-2.0.9/egg-
dist-tmp-jcntqu
***********************************************************************
WARNING: The C extension could not be compiled, speedups are not enabled.
Failure information, if any, is above.
I'm retrying the build without the C extension now.
***********************************************************************
***********************************************************************
WARNING: The C extension could not be compiled, speedups are not enabled.
Plain-Python installation succeeded.
***********************************************************************
Adding simplejson 2.0.9 to easy-install.pth file

Installed /home/lsoto/jython2.5.0/Lib/site-packages/simplejson-2.0.9-py2.5.egg
```

The warnings are produced because the simplejson installation tries to compile a C extension which for obvious reasons only works with CPython and not with Jython.

Finally, we see:

```
Finished processing dependencies for python-twitter
```

Which signals the end of the automated installation process for python-twitter. You can test that it was successfully installed by running Jython and doing an import twitter on the interactive interpreter.

As noted above, easy_install will try to get the latest version for the library you specify. If you want a particular version, for example the 0.5 release of python-twitter then you can specify it in this way:

```
$ easy_install python-twitter==0.5
```

If new versions of python-twitter are released later, you can tell easy_install to upgrade it to the latest available version, by using the -U flag:

```
$ easy_install -U python-twitter
```

For debugging purposes, it is always useful to know where the bits installed using easy_install go. As you can stop of the install output, they are installed into <path-to-jython>/Lib/site-packages/<name_of_library>-<version>.egg which may be a directory or a compressed zip file. Also, easy_install adds an entry to the file <path-to-jython>/Lib/site-packages/easy-install.pth, which ends up adding the directory or zip file to sys.path by default.

Unfortunately, setuptools don't provide any automated way to uninstall packages. You will have to manually delete the package egg directory or zip file and remove the associated line on easy-install.pth.

Virtualenv

Often, it is nice to have separate versions of tools running on the same machine. The virtualenv tool provides a way to create a virtual Python environment that can be used for various purposes including installation of different package versions. Virtual environments can also be nice for those who do not have administrative access for a particular Python installation but still need to have the ability to install packages to it; such is often the case when working with domain hosts. Whatever the case may be, the virtualenv tool provides a means for creating one or more virtual environments for a particular Python installation so that the libraries can be installed into controlled environments other than the global site-packages area for your Python or Jython installation. The release of Jython 2.5.0 opened new doors for the possibility of using such tools as virtualenv.

To use virtualenv with Jython, we first need to obtain it. The easiest way to do so is via the Python Package Index. As you had learned in the previous section, easy_install is the way to install packages from the PyPI. The following example shows how to install virtualenv using easy_install with Jython.

```
jython easy_install.py virtualenv
```

Once installed, it is quite easy to use the tool for creation of a virtual environment. The virtual environment will include a Jython executable along with an installation of setuptools and its own site-packages directory. This was done so that you have the ability to install different packages from the PyPI to your virtual environment. Let's create an environment named JY2.5.1Env using the virtualenv.py module that exists within our Jython environment.

```
jython <<path to Jython>>/jython2.5.1/Lib/site-packages/virtualenv-1.3.3-
py2.5.egg/virtualenv.py JY2.5.1Env
New jython executable in JY2.5.1Env/bin/jython
Installing setuptools............done.
```

Now a new directory named JY2.5.1Env should have been created within your current working directory. You can run Jython from this virtual environment by simply invoking the executable that was created. The virtualenv tool allows us the ability to open a terminal and designate it to be used for our virtual Jython environment exclusively via the use of the *activate* command. To do so, open up a terminal and type the following:

```
source <<path-to-virtual-environment>>/JY2.5.1Env/bin/activate
```

Once this is done, you should notice that the command line is preceded by the name of the virtual environment that you have activated. Any Jython shell or tool used in this terminal will now be using the virtual environment. This is an excellent way to run a tool using two different versions of a particular library or for running a production and development environment side-by-side. If you run the easy_install.py tool within the activated virtual environment terminal then the tool(s) will be installed into the virtual environment. There can be an unlimited number of virtual environments installed on a particular machine. To stop using the virtual environment within the terminal, simply type:

```
deactivate
```

Now your terminal should go back to normal use and default to the global Jython installation. Once deactivated any of the Jython references made will call the global installation or libraries within the global site-packages area. It should be noted that when you create a virtual environment, it automatically inherits all packages used by the global installation. Therefore if you have a library installed in your global site-packages area then it can be used from the virtual environment right away. A good practice is to install only essential libraries into your global Jython environment and then install one-offs or test libraries into virtual environments.

It is useful to have the ability to list installations that are in use within a particular environment. One way to do this is to install the *yolk* utility and make use of its *-l* command. Such information may also be useful for purposes such as documentation of the dependencies contained in your *setup.py*.

In order to install *yolk*, you must grab a copy of the latest version of Jython beyond 2.5.1 as there has been a patch submitted that corrects some functionality which is used by *yolk*. You must also be running with JDK 1.6 or above as the patched version of Jython makes use of the *webbrowser* module. The *webbrowser* module makes use of some java.awt.Desktop features that are only available in JDK 1.6 and beyond. To install *yolk*, use the ez_install.py script as we've shown previously.

```
jython ez_install.py yolk
```

Once installed, you can list the package installations for your Jython installations by issuing the *-l* command as follows:

```
yolk -l
Django          - 1.0.2-final  - non-active development (/jython2.5.1/Lib/site-packages)
Django          - 1.0.3        - active development (/jython2.5.1/Lib/site-packages/Django-
1.0.3-py2.5.egg)
Django          - 1.1          - non-active development (/jython2.5.1/Lib/site-packages)
SQLAlchemy      - 0.5.4p2      - active development (/jython2.5.1/Lib/site-packages)
SQLAlchemy      - 0.6beta1     - non-active development (/jython2.5.1/Lib/site-packages)
django-jython   - 0.9          - active development (/jython2.5.1/Lib/site-
packages/django_jython-0.9-py2.5.egg)
django-jython   - 1.0b1        - non-active development (/jython2.5.1/Lib/site-packages)
nose            - 0.11.1       - active development (/jython2.5.1/Lib/site-packages/nose-
0.11.1-py2.5.egg)
setuptools      - 0.6c9        - active
setuptools      - 0.6c9        - active
snakefight      - 0.4          - active development (/jython2.5.1/Lib/site-
packages/snakefight-0.4-py2.5.egg)
virtualenv      - 1.3.3        - active development (/jython2.5.1/Lib/site-
packages/virtualenv-1.3.3-py2.5.egg)
wsgiref         - 0.1.2        - active development (/jython2.5.1/Lib)
yolk            - 0.4.1        - active
```

As you can see, all installed packages will be listed. If you are using yolk from within a virtual environment then you will see all packages installed in that virtual environment as well as those installed into the global environment.

Similarly to setuptools, there is no way to automatically uninstall virtualenv. You must also manually delete the package egg directory or zip file as well as remove references within easy-install.pth.

APPENDIX B

■ ■ ■

Jython Cookbook

There are a plethora of examples for using Jython that can be found on the web. This appendix is a compilation of some of the most useful examples that we have found. Those that were chosen are focused on topics that are not widely covered elsewhere on the web.

Unless otherwise noted, each of these examples have been originally authored for working on versions of Jython prior to 2.5.x, but we have tested each of them using Jython 2.5.1 and they function as advertised.

Logging

Using log4j with Jython, Josh Juneau
wiki.python.org/jython/JythonMonthly/Articles/August2006/1

Are you still using the Jython print command to show your errors? How about in a production environment, are you using any formal logging? If not, you should be doing so, and the Apache log4j API makes it easy to do so. Many Java developers have grown to love the log4j API, and it is utilized throughout much of the community. That is great news for Jython developers because we've got direct access to Java libraries! There are many Python logging libraries, such as the standard *logging* module. However, sometimes if you are working with Java code it is nice to have the option to integrate with APIs such as log4j.

Setting Up Your Environment

The most difficult part about using log4j with Jython is the setup. You must ensure that the log4j.jar archive resides somewhere within your Jython PATH (usually this entails setting the CLASSPATH to include necessary files). You then set up a properties file for use with log4j. Within the properties file, you can include appender information, where logs should reside, and much more. For more information, a good place to start is the log4j site manual: logging.apache.org/log4j/1.2/manual.html.

Listing B-1.

```
log4j.rootLogger=debug, stdout, R

log4j.appender.stdout=org.apache.log4j.ConsoleAppender
log4j.appender.stdout.layout=org.apache.log4j.PatternLayout

# Pattern to output the caller's file name and line number.
log4j.appender.stdout.layout.ConversionPattern=%5p [%t] (%F:%L) - %m%n

log4j.appender.R=org.apache.log4j.RollingFileAppender
log4j.appender.R.File=C:\\Jython\\testlog4j.log

log4j.appender.R.MaxFileSize=100KB
# Keep one backup file
log4j.appender.R.MaxBackupIndex=1

log4j.appender.R.layout=org.apache.log4j.PatternLayout
log4j.appender.R.layout.ConversionPattern=%p %t %c - %m%n
```

You are now ready to use log4j in your Jython application. As you can see, if you've ever used log4j with Java, it is pretty much the same.

Using log4j in a Jython Application

First, you must import the log4j packages:

Listing B-2.

```
from org.apache.log4j import *
```

Second, you obtain a new logger for your class or module and set up a PropertyConfigurator:

Listing B-3.

```
self.logger = Logger.getLogger("myClass")
# Assume that the log4j properties resides within a folder named "utilities"
PropertyConfigurator.configure(sys.path[0] + "/utilities/log4j.properties")
```

Lastly, use log4j:

Listing B-4.

```
# Example module within the class:
def submitDocument(self, event):
    try:
        # Assume we perform some SQL here
    except SQLException, ex:
        self.logger.error("docPanel#submitDocument ERROR: %s" % (ex))
```

Your logging will now take place within the file you specified in the properties file for log4j.appender.R.File.

Working with Spreadsheets

Creating and Reading Spreadsheets Using Apache Poi
Posted to the Jython-users mailing list by Alfonso Reyes on October 14, 2007

wiki.python.org/jython/PoiExample

What follows are a few Apache Poi examples. Apache Poi is a set of Java APIs for creating and manipulating various file formats based on the Office Open XML standards (OOXML) and Microsoft's OLE 2 Compound Document Format (OLE2). These APIs allow you to do things such as read and write spreadsheet files using Java. These examples require Apache Poi to be installed and on the classpath.

Create Spreadsheet
This is based on Java code at officewriter.softartisans.com/OfficeWriter-306.aspx and converted to Jython.

Listing B-5.

```
#jython poi example. from Jython mailing list

from java.io import FileOutputStream
from java.util import Date
from java.lang import System, Math
from org.apache.poi.hssf.usermodel import *
from org.apache.poi.hssf.util import HSSFColor
# Obtain the start time
startTime = System.currentTimeMillis()
# Create a new workbook, HSSFWorkbook is a high level representation of a workbook
wb = HSSFWorkbook()
# Create file if it doesn't exist
fileOut = FileOutputStream("POIOut2.xls")


# Create 3 sheets
sheet1 = wb.createSheet("Sheet1")
sheet2 = wb.createSheet("Sheet2")
sheet3 = wb.createSheet("Sheet3")
sheet3 = wb.createSheet("Sheet4")

# Create a header style
styleHeader = wb.createCellStyle()
fontHeader = wb.createFont()
fontHeader.setBoldweight(2)
fontHeader.setFontHeightInPoints(14)
```

```
fontHeader.setFontName("Arial")
styleHeader.setFont(fontHeader)

# Create a style used for the first column
style0 = wb.createCellStyle()
font0 = wb.createFont()
font0.setColor(HSSFColor.RED.index)
style0.setFont(font0)


# Create the style used for dates.
styleDates = wb.createCellStyle()
styleDates.setDataFormat(HSSFDataFormat.getBuiltinFormat("m/d/yy h:mm"))


# create the headers
rowHeader = sheet1.createRow(1)
# String value
cell0 = rowHeader.createCell(0)
cell0.setCellStyle(styleHeader)
cell0.setCellValue("Name")


# numbers
for i in range(0, 8):
    cell = rowHeader.createCell((i + 1))
    cell.setCellStyle(styleHeader)
    cell.setCellValue("Data " + str( (i + 1)) )

# Date
cell10 = rowHeader.createCell(9)
cell10.setCellValue("Date")
cell10.setCellStyle(styleHeader)
# Populate the columns of the spreadsheet
for i in range(0, 100):
    # create a new row
    row = sheet1.createRow(i + 2)
    for j in range(0, 10):
        # create each cell
        cell = row.createCell(j)
        # Fill the first column with strings
        if j == 0:
            cell.setCellValue("Product " + str(i))
            cell.setCellStyle(style0)
        # Fill the next 8 columns with numbers.
        elif j < 9:
            cell.setCellValue( (Math.random() * 100))
        # Fill the last column with dates.
        else:
            cell.setCellValue(Date())
            cell.setCellStyle(styleDates)
# Summary row
rowSummary = sheet1.createRow(102)
sumStyle = wb.createCellStyle()
```

```
sumFont = wb.createFont()
sumFont.setBoldweight( 5)
sumFont.setFontHeightInPoints(12)
sumStyle.setFont(sumFont)
sumStyle.setFillPattern(HSSFCellStyle.FINE_DOTS)
sumStyle.setFillForegroundColor(HSSFColor.GREEN.index)
cellSum0 = rowSummary.createCell( 0)
cellSum0.setCellValue("TOTALS:")
cellSum0.setCellStyle(sumStyle)


# numbers
# B
cellB = rowSummary.createCell( 1)
cellB.setCellStyle(sumStyle)
cellB.setCellFormula("SUM(B3:B102)")
```

Read an Excel File

This Jython code will open and read an existing Excel file.

Listing B-6.

```
"""     read.py
Read an existing Excel file (Book1.xls) and show it on the screen
"""
from org.apache.poi.hssf.usermodel import *
from java.io import FileInputStream
# Open an existing file and use HSSFWorkbook object to store it
file = "H:Book1.xls"
print file
fis = FileInputStream(file)
wb = HSSFWorkbook(fis)
# Obtain reference to the first sheet in the workbook
sheet = wb.getSheetAt(0)

# get No. of rows
rows = sheet.getPhysicalNumberOfRows()
print wb, sheet, rows

cols = 0 # No. of columns
tmp = 0

# This trick ensures that we obtain the data for future use even if it
# doesn't start from first few rows
for i in range(0, 10):
    row = sheet.getRow(i)
    if row:
        tmp = sheet.getRow(i).getPhysicalNumberOfCells()
        if tmp > cols:
            cols = tmp
print cols
```

```
for r in range(0, rows):
    row = sheet.getRow(r)
    print r
    if(row != None):
        for c in range(0, cols):
            cell = row.getCell(c)
            if cell != None:
                print cell

wb.close()
fis.close()
```

Jython and XML

Writing and Parsing RSS with ROME, Josh Juneau
wiki.python.org/jython/JythonMonthly/Articles/October2007/1

RSS is an old technology now. It has been around for years. However, it is a technology that remains very useful for disseminating news and other information. The ROME project on java.net is helping to make parsing, generating, and publishing RSS and Atom feeds a breeze for any Java developer.

Because I am particularly fond of translating Java to Jython code, I've taken simple examples from the Project ROME Wiki and translated Java RSS reader and writer code into Jython. It is quite easy to do, and it only takes a few lines of code.

Keep in mind that you would still need to build a front-end viewer for such an RSS reader, but I think you will get the idea of how easy it can be just to parse a feed with Project ROME and Jython.

Setting up the CLASSPATH

In order to use this example, you must obtain the ROME and JDOM jar files and place them into your CLASSPATH:

Listing B-7.

```
set CLASSPATH=C:\Jython\Jython2.2\rome-0.9.jar;%CLASSPATH%
set CLASSPATH=C:\Jython\Jython2.2\jdom.jar;%CLASSPATH%
OSX:
export CLASSPATH=/path/to/rome-0.9.jar:/path/to/jdom.jar
```

Parsing Feeds

Parsing feeds is easy with ROME. Using ROME with Jython makes it even easier with the elegant Jython syntax.

We took the FeedReader example from the ROME site and translated it into Jython (see the following). You can copy and paste the code into your own FeedReader.py module and run it to parse feeds. However, the output is unformatted and ugly. Creating a good looking frontend is up to you.

Listing B-8.

```
######################################
# File: FeedReader.py
#
# This module can be used to parse an RSS feed
######################################
from java.net import URL
from java.io import InputStreamReader
from java.lang import Exception
from java.lang import Object
from com.sun.syndication.feed.synd import SyndFeed
from com.sun.syndication.io import SyndFeedInput
from com.sun.syndication.io import XmlReader

class FeedReader(Object):
    def __init__(self, url=None):
        self.inUrl = url

    def readFeed(self):

        ######################################
        # If url passed in is blank, then use a default
        ######################################
        rssUrl = self.inUrl if self.inUrl else
        "http://www.dzone.com/feed/frontpage/java/rss.xml"

        ######################################
        # Parse feed located at given URL
        ######################################
        try:
            feedUrl = URL(rssUrl)
            input = SyndFeedInput()
            feed = input.build(XmlReader(feedUrl))
            ######################################
            # Do something here with feed data
            ######################################
            print(feed)

        except Exception, e:
            print 'An exception has occurred', e

if __name__ == "__main__":
    reader = FeedReader()
    reader.readFeed()
    print '***************Command Complete...RSS has been parsed*****************'
```

Creating Feeds

Similar to parsing a feed, writing a feed is also quite easy. When one creates a feed, it appears to be a bit more complex than parsing, but if you are familiar with XML and its general structure, then it should be relatively easy.

Creating a feed is a three step process. You must first create the feed element itself, then you must add individual feed entries, and lastly you must publish the XML.

Listing B-9.

```
######################################
# File: FeedWriter.py
#
# This module can be used to create an RSS feed
######################################
from com.sun.syndication.feed.synd import *
from com.sun.syndication.io import SyndFeedOutput
from java.io import FileWriter
from java.io import Writer
from java.text import DateFormat
from java.text import SimpleDateFormat
from java.util import ArrayList
from java.util import List
from java.lang import Object

class FeedWriter(Object):
    ######################################
    # Set up the date format
    ######################################
    def __init__(self, type, name):
        self.DATE_PARSER = SimpleDateFormat('yyyy-MM-dd')
        self.feedType = type
        self.fileName = name

    def writeFeed(self):

        try:
            ################################
            # Create the feed itself
            ################################
            feed = SyndFeedImpl()
            feed.feedType =self.feedType
            feed.title = 'Sample Feed (created with ROME)'
            feed.link = 'http://rome.dev.java.net'
            feed.description = 'This feed has been created using ROME and Jython'

            ################################
            # Add entries to the feed
            ################################
            entries = ArrayList()
            entry = SyndEntryImpl()
            entry.title = 'ROME v1.0'
            entry.link = 'http://wiki.java.net/bin/view/Javawsxml/Rome01'
            entry.publishedDate = self.DATE_PARSER.parse("2004-06-08")
            description = SyndContentImpl()
            description.type = 'text/plain'
            description.value = 'Initial Release of ROME'
            entry.description = description
```

```
            entries.add(entry)

            entry = SyndEntryImpl()
            entry.title = 'ROME v2.0'
            entry.link = 'http://wiki.java.net/bin/view/Javawsxml/Rome02'
            entry.publishedDate = self.DATE_PARSER.parse("2004-06-16")
            description = SyndContentImpl()
            description.type = 'text/plain'
            description.value = 'Bug fixes, minor API changes and some new features'
            entry.description = description
            entries.add(entry)

            entry = SyndEntryImpl()
            entry.title = 'ROME v3.0'
            entry.link = 'http://wiki.java.net/bin/view/Javawsxml/Rome03'
            entry.publishedDate = self.DATE_PARSER.parse("2004-07-27")
            description = SyndContentImpl()
            description.type = 'text/plain'
            description.value = '<p>More Bug fixes, mor API changes, some new features and
some Unit testing</p>'
            entry.description = description
            entries.add(entry)

            feed.entries = entries
            ################################
            # Publish the XML
            ################################
            writer = FileWriter(self.fileName)
            output = SyndFeedOutput()
            output.output(feed,writer)
            writer.close()

            print('The feed has been written to the file')


        except Exception, e:
            print 'There has been an exception raised',e



if __name__ == "__main__":
    ####################################
    # You must change his file location
    # if not using Windows environment
    ####################################
    writer = FeedWriter('rss_2.0','C:\\TEMP\\testRss.xml')
    writer.writeFeed()
    print '***************Command Complete...RSS XML has been created****************'
```

After you have created the XML, you'll obviously need to place it on a web server somewhere so that others can use your feed. The FeedWriter.py module would probably be one module among many in an application for creating and managing RSS Feeds, but you get the idea.

453

Summary

As you can see, using the ROME library to work with RSS feeds is quite easy. Using the ROME library within a Jython application is straightforward. As you have now seen how easy it is to create and parse feeds, you can apply these technologies to a more complete RSS management application if you'd like. The world of RSS communication is at your fingertips!

Working with CLASSPATH

Using the CLASSPATH, Steve Langer
wiki.python.org/jython/JythonMonthly/Articles/January2007/3

During October and November of 2006, there was a thread in the Jython-users group called "adding JARs to sys.path." More accurately, the objective was to add JARs to the sys.path at runtime. Several people asked the question, "Why would you want to do that?" Well there are at least two good reasons. The first is if you want to distribute a Jython or Java package that includes non-standard Jars in it. Perhaps you want to make life easier for the target user and not demand that they know how to set environment variables. A second even more compelling reason is when there is no normal user account to provide environment variables.

"What?" you ask. Well, in my case I came upon this problem in the following way. I am working on an open source IHE Image Archive Actor and needed a web interface. I'm using AJAX on the client side to route database calls through CGI to a Jython-JDBC enabled API. Testing the Jython-JDBC API from the command line worked fine; I had the PostgreSQL driver in my CLASSPATH. But when called via the web interface, I got "zxJDBC error, PostgreSQL driver not found" errors. Why? Because APACHE was calling the API and APACHE is not a normal account with environment variables.

What to Do?

The Jython-users thread had many suggestions, but none were found to work. Chapter 11 of O'Reilly's *Jython Essentials* mentions under "System and File Modules" that "to load a class at runtime, one also needs an appropriate class loader." Of course, no mention is made beyond that. After a while, it occurred to me that perhaps someone in the Java world had found a similar problem and had solved it. Then all that would be required is to translate that solution. And that is exactly what happened.

Method

For brevity, I will not repeat the original Java code here. The following shows how I call the Jython class (note that one can use either addFile or addURL depending on whether the Jar is on a locally accessible file system or remote server).

Listing B-10.

```
import sys
from com.ziclix.python.sql import zxJDBC

d,u,p,v = "jdbc:postgresql://localhost/img_arc2","postgres","","org.postgresql.Driver"

try :
    # if called from command line with .login CLASSPATH setup right,this works
```

```
        db = zxJDBC.connect(d, u, p, v)
except:
    # if called from Apache or account where the .login has not set CLASSPATH
    # need to use run-time CLASSPATH Hacker
    try :
        jarLoad = classPathHacker()
        a = jarLoad.addFile("/usr/share/java/postgresql-jdbc3.jar")
        db = zxJDBC.connect(d, u, p, v)
    except :
        sys.exit ("still failed \n%s" % (sys.exc_info()))
```

And here is the class "classPathHacker" which is what the original author called his solution. In fact, you can simply Google on "classPathHacker" to find the Java solution.

Listing B-11.

```
class classPathHacker :
######################################################
# from http://forum.java.sun.com/thread.jspa?threadID=300557
#
# Author: SG Langer Jan 2007 translated the above Java to this
#         Jython class
# Purpose: Allow runtime additions of new Class/jars either from
#         local files or URL
######################################################
    import java.lang.reflect.Method
    import java.io.File
    import java.net.URL
    import java.net.URLClassLoader
    import jarray

    def addFile (self, s):
        ###########################################
        # Purpose: If adding a file/jar call this first
        #         with s = path_to_jar
        ###########################################

        # make a URL out of 's'
        f = self.java.io.File (s)
        u = f.toURL ()
        a = self.addURL (u)
        return a

    def addURL (self, u):
        ##################################
        # Purpose: Call this with u= URL for
        #         the new Class/jar to be loaded
        ##################################

        parameters = self.jarray.array([self.java.net.URL], self.java.lang.Class)
        sysloader =  self.java.lang.ClassLoader.getSystemClassLoader()
        sysclass = self.java.net.URLClassLoader
        method = sysclass.getDeclaredMethod("addURL", parameters)
```

455

```
a = method.setAccessible(1)
jar_a = self.jarray.array([u], self.java.lang.Object)
b = method.invoke(sysloader, jar_a)
return u
```

Summary

That's it. Depressingly short for what it does, but then that's more proof of the power of this language. I hope you find this as powerful and useful as I have. It allows the possibility of distributing Jython packages with all their file dependencies within the installation directory, freeing the user or developer from the need to alter user environment variables, which should lead to more programmer control and thus higher reliability.

Ant

The following Ant example works with Jython version 2.2.1 and earlier, only due to the necessary jythonc usage. jythonc is no longer distributed with Jython as of 2.5.0. This example could be rewritten using object factories to work with current versions of Jython.

Writing Ant Tasks with Jython, Ed Takema

fishandcross.com/articles/AntTasksWithJython.html

Ant is the current tool of choice for Java builds. This is so partially because it was the first Java-oriented build tool on the scene and because the reigning champion *Make* was getting long in the tooth and had fallen out of favor with the Java crowd. But Java builds are getting more and more difficult, and these days there is general dissatisfaction with Ant. Note particularly Bruce Eckel's comments and Martin Fowler's further comments. The comments to Bruce Eckel's posting show similar frustrations. Fowler summarizes the issues like this:

> *Simple builds are easy to express as a series of tasks and dependencies. For such builds the facilities of Ant/Make work well. But more complex builds require conditional logic, and that requires more general programming language constructs. And that's where Ant/Make fall down. Ken Arnold's article, "The Sum of Ant," led me to Jonathon Simon's article, "Scripting with Jython Instead of XML," and got me thinking about extending Ant with Jython. Simon's article presents a technique to drive Ant tasks, testing, etc., all from Jython. What I am presenting is a technique to embed Jython scripts into Ant which is admittedly backwards from Simon's approach, but hopefully adds power and flexibility to Ant builds.*
>
> *My experience working with large builds automated through Ant is not dissimilar to what Fowler is referring to. Eventually, builds need to do either a lot of odd conditional logic in the xml file and ends up burying the logic in scripts, or in a large number of custom tasks written in Java. This is particularly the case if your builds include non-Java source that Ant just isn't smart about building. In one case in particular, the set of custom tasks for the build is really its own system with maintenance and staff costs that are quite substantial. A large number of scripts can quickly become a problem for enterprise build systems as they are difficult to standardize and cross platform issues are always looming.*
>
> *Fortunately, all is not lost. Ant continues to evolve and version 1.6 was a significant step forward for large build systems. Mike Spille, in his article, "ANT's Finally a Real Build Tool," demonstrates that the new <import> tag now allows build managers to write truly modular and standardized build systems based on Ant! As Ant grows up, more and more of these issues will get resolved.*

One of the strengths that Make always had was the ability to easily call scripts and command utilities. This is something that is definitely possible with Ant script/exec tasks, but it feels very un-Java. What we need is an elegant way to add ad-hoc behavior to Ant builds.

Writing Custom Ant Tasks

What I think can do the job is to take a more considered approach to using a scripting tool inside an Ant build. Rather than just create a mishmash of scripts that are called from exec or script tasks, I suggest that we write custom Ant build tasks in a high level scripting language. In this case, Jython.

Writing custom Ant tasks allows a build manager to leverage the huge number of already written tasks in their builds, while writing what naturally belongs in a more flexible tool in custom Ant tasks that can themselves then be reused, and are as cross-platform as Java itself, and wholly integrated into Ant. Because Ant uses Java introspection to determine the capabilities of custom tasks, Jython is the perfect tool to accomplish this. All we need to do is ensure that the methods that Ant expects are present in the Jython classes and Ant won't notice the difference.

What we will implement is the perennial SimpleTask which is nothing more than a "Hello World" for ant. It should be sufficient to demonstrate the key steps.

Setup Development Environment

To compile the Jython source you will need to add the ant.jar file to your classpath. This will make it available to Jython to extend which we'll do in the following. To do that, define your classpath:

Listing B-12.

```
<DOS>
set CLASSPATH=c:\path\to\ant\lib\ant.jar;%CLASSPATH%
<UNIX>
export CLASSPATH=/path/to/ant/lib/ant.jar:$CLASSPATH
```

SimpleTask Jython Class

The following is a very simple Ant task written in Jython. Save this as SimpleTask.py.

Listing B-13.

```
from org.apache.tools.ant import Task

class SimpleTask(Task):
  message = ""

  def execute(self):
      """@sig public void execute()"""
      Task.log(self, "Message: " + self.message)

  def setMessage(self, aMessage):
      """@sig public void setMessage(java.lang.String str)"""
      self.message = aMessage
```

This simple Jython class extends the Ant Task superclass. For each of the properties we want to support for this task, we write a setXXXXX method where XXXXX corresponds to the property we are

457

going to set in the Ant build file. Ant creates an object from the class, calls the setXXXXX methods to set up the properties and then calls the execute method (actually, it calls the perform method on the Task superclass which calls the execute() method). So let's try it out.

Compiling Jython Code to a Jar

To build this into a jar file for use in Ant, do the following:

Listing B-14.

```
jythonc -a -c -d -j myTasks.jar SimpleTask.py
```

This will produce a jar file myTasks.jar and include the Jython core support classes in the jar. Copy this jar file into your Ant installation's lib directory. In my case I copy it to c:toolsantlib.

Build.XML File to Use the Task

Once you've got that working, here is a very simple Ant test build file to test your custom Jython task.

Listing B-15.

```
<project name="ant jython demo" default="testit" basedir=".">

  <!-- Define the tasks we are building -->
  <taskdef name="Simple" classname="SimpleTask" />

  <!-- Test Case starts here -->
  <target name="testit">
    <Simple message="Hello World!" />
  </target>

</project>
```

A Task Container Task

All right, that is a pretty simple task. What else can we do? Well, the sky is the limit really. Here is an example of a task container. In this case, the task holds references to a set of other tasks (SimpleTask tasks in this case):

Listing B-16.

```
from org.apache.tools.ant import Task
from org.apache.tools.ant import TaskContainer

class SimpleContainer(TaskContainer):

  subtasks = []

  def execute(self):
    """@sig public void execute()"""
```

```
        for task in self.subtasks:
            task.perform()

    def createSimpleTask(self):
        """@sig public java.lang.Object createSimpleTask()"""

        task = SimpleTask()
        self.subtasks.append(task)
        return task

class SimpleTask(Task):

    message = ""

    def execute(self):
        """@sig public void execute()"""
        Task.log(self, "Message: " + self.message)

    def setMessage(self, aMessage):
        """@sig public void setMessage(java.lang.String str)"""
        self.message = aMessage
```

The SimpleContainer extends the TaskContainer Java class. Its createSimpleTask method creates a SimpleTask object and returns it to Ant so its properties can be set. Then when all the tasks have been added to the container and their properties have been set, the execute method on the SimpleContainer class is called, which in turn calls the perform method on each of the contained tasks. Note that the perform method is inherited from the Task superclass and it in turn calls the execute method which we have overridden.

Build.XML File to Use the TaskContainer

Here is an Ant build file to test your custom jython task container. Note that you don't need to include a task definition for the contained SimpleTask unless you want to use it directly. The createSimpleTask factory method does it for you.

Listing B-17.

```
<project name="ant jython demo" default="testit" basedir=".">

    <!-- Define the tasks we are building -->
    <taskdef name="Container" classname="SimpleContainer" />

    <!-- Test Case starts here -->
    <target name="testit">

        <Container>

            <SimpleTask message="hello" />
            <SimpleTask message="there" />

        </Container>
```

```
</target>

</project>
```

Things to Look Out For

As I learned this technique, I discovered that the magic doc strings are really necessary to force Jython to put the right methods in the generated Java classes. For example:

Listing B-18.

```
"""@sig public void execute()"""
```

This is primarily due to Ant's introspection that looks for those specific methods and signatures. These docstrings are required or Ant won't recognize the classes as Ant tasks.

I also learned that for Jython to extend a Java class, it must specifically import the Java classes using this syntax:

Listing B-19.

```
from org.apache.tools.ant import Task
from org.apache.tools.ant import TaskContainer

class MyTask(Task):
    ...
```
You can not use this syntax:

```
import org.apache.tools.ant.Task
import org.apache.tools.ant.TaskContainer

 class MyTask(org.apache.tools.ant.Task):
    ...
```

This is because, for some reason, Jython doesn't figure out that MyTask is extending this Java class and so doesn't generate the right Java wrapper classes. You will know that this working right when you see output like the following when you run the jythonc compiler:

Listing B-20.

```
processing SimpleTask

Required packages:
  org.apache.tools.ant

Creating adapters:

Creating .java files:
  SimpleTask module
    SimpleTask extends org.apache.tools.ant.Task <<<
```

Summary

Here is a quick summary then of why this is a helpful technique.

First, it is a lot faster to write Ant tasks that integrate with third party tools and systems using a glue language; Jython is excellent at that. That is really my prime motivation for trying out this technique.

Secondly, Jython has an advantage over other scripting languages (which could be run using Ant's exec or script tasks), because it can be tightly integrated with Ant (use the same logging methods, same settings, and so on). This makes it easier to build a standardized build environment.

Finally, and related to the last point, Jython can be compiled to Java byte code, which runs like any Java class file. This means you don't have to have Jython installed to use the custom tasks and your custom task, if written well, can run on a wide variety of platforms.

I think this is a reasonable way to add flexibility and additional integration points to Ant builds.

Developing Django Web Apps

Using Django in Netbeans, Josh Juneau

It is not a very straightforward task if you wish to develop Jython web applications utilizing a standard framework from within Netbeans. However, with a little extra configuration and some manual procedures, it is easy enough to do. In this section I will demonstrate how we can make use of Netbeans for developing a Django application without using any Netbeans plug-ins above and beyond the standard Python support. This section will cover the setup for a Django project within Netbeans, but it will not cover any Django features. For complete details on using Django with Jython, please refer to Chapter 14. You will see that Jython applications can be run, tested, and verified from within the IDE with very little work. Because there are a few steps in this section that may be more difficult to visualize, please use the provided screen shots to follow along if you are not using Netbeans while reading this text.

In order to effectively create and maintain a Django web site, you need to have the ability to run commands against *manage.py*. Unfortunately, there is no built-in way to easily do this within the IDE, so we have to use the terminal or command line along with the IDE to accomplish things. Once we create the project and set it up within Netbeans, we can work with developing it from within Netbeans and you can also set up the project *Run* feature to startup the Django server.

Assuming that you already have Django setup and configured along with the Django-Jython project on your machine, the first step in using a Django project from within Netbeans is actually creating the project. If you are working with a Django project that has already been created then you can skip this step, but if not then you will need to go to the terminal or command-line and create the project using *django-admin.py*. For the purposes of this tutorial, let's call our Django site *NetbeansDjango*.

Listing B-21.

```
django-admin.py startproject NetbeansDjango
```

Now we should have the default Django site setup and we're ready to bring it into Netbeans. To do this, start a new Python project within Netbeans using the *Python Project with Existing Sources* option, and be sure to set your Python Platform to Jython 2.5.1 so we are using Jython. After hitting the Next button, we have the ability to add sources to our project. Hit the Add button and choose the main project folder, so in our case select the *NetbeansDjango* folder. This will add our project root as the source root for our application. In turn, it adds our Django setup files such as *manage.py* to our project. After doing so your project should look something like Figure B-1.

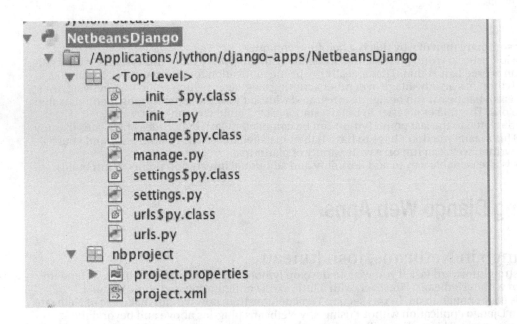

Figure B-1. Adding Django files to your project

In this next step, we will configure the Netbeans project *Run* option so that it starts up the Django web server for us. To do so, right-click (Cntrl+Click) on the newly created project and go to Properties. From there, choose the Python option in the left-hand menu and add the Django directory (containing the bin, conf, contrib, core, and so on files) to your path. For this tutorial we will also make use of the PostgreSQL database, so you'll want to also add the postgresql.jar to your Python path.

Next, select the Run option from the left-hand menu and add manage.py as the main module, and add *runserver* as the application argument. This will essentially hook up the Run project option to the Django manage.py such that it will invoke the Django web server to start up.

At this point, we are ready to begin developing our Django application. So with a little minor setup and some use of the terminal or command-line we are able to easily use Netbeans for developing Django projects. There are a few minor inconsistencies with this process; however, note that there is no real integrated way to turn off the webserver as yet so once it is started we can either leave it running or stop it via your system process manager. Otherwise you can hook up different options to the Netbeans Run project command such as syncdb by simply choosing a different application argument in the project properties. If you use this methodology, then you can simply start and stop the Django web server via the terminal as normal. I have also found that after running the Django web server you will have to manually delete the *settings$.py.class* file that is generated before you can run the server again or else it will complain.

In future versions of Netbeans, it is expected that Django functionality will be built into the Python support. We will have to take another look at using Django from within Netbeans at that time. For now, this procedure works and it does a fine job. You can make use of similar procedures to use other web frameworks such as Pylons from within Netbeans.

APPENDIX C

■■■

Built-in Functions

Much of this appendix was taken from the Python Documentation Set, which can be found at www.python.org/doc/. The Python Documentation is Copyright 2001, 2002, 2003, 2004, 2005, 2006 Python Software Foundation; all rights reserved. More information can be found at http://docs.python.org/copyright.html. Version references reflect both CPython and Jython releases. In cases where versions refer to 2.3 or 2.4, assume that these functions were implemented in Jython 2.5.0 because there was no Jython 2.3 or 2.4.

Constructor Functions

Constructor functions are used to create objects of a given type.

■ **Note** In Python, a type and its constructor function are the same thing. So you can use the type function, which we will discuss momentarily, to look up the type of an object, and then make instances of that same type.

First we will look at the constructor functions, which are more typically used for conversion. This is because there is generally a convenient literal syntax available for creating instances. In the case of *bool*, there just two constants, *True* and *False*.

bool([x])

Convert a value to a Boolean, using the standard truth-testing procedure. If *x* is false or omitted, this returns *False;* otherwise it returns *True*. As noted at the start of this section, *bool* is also a class, which is a subclass of *int*. Class *bool* cannot be subclassed further. Its only instances are *False* and *True*.

If no argument is given, this function returns *False*.

chr(i)

Return a string of one character whose ASCII code is the integer *i*. For example, chr(97) returns the string 'a.' This is the inverse of *ord*. The argument must be in the range [0..255], inclusive; *ValueError* will be raised if *i* is outside that range. See also *unichr*.

complex([real[, imag]])

Create a complex number with the value *real* + *imag**j or convert a string or number to a complex number. If the first parameter is a string, it will be interpreted as a complex number and the function must be called without a second parameter. The second parameter can never be a string. Each argument may be any numeric type (including complex). If *imag* is omitted, it defaults to zero and the function serves as a numeric conversion function like *int*, *long* and *float*. If both arguments are omitted, returns 0j.

dict([arg])

Create a new data dictionary, optionally with items taken from *arg*.

> For other containers see the built-in *list*, *set*, and *tuple* classes, and the *collections* module.
> There is a convenient literal for creating dict objects:

```
a_dict = { 'alpha' : 1, 'beta' : 2, 'gamma' : 3 }
```

> It can be more convenient to create dict objects using the dict function:

```
a_dict = dict(alpha=1, beta=2, gamma=3)
```

> In this latter case, keyword arguments are passed where the argument names become the keys. Similarly, you can pass an iterator to the dict function which produces pairs.

file(filename[, mode[, bufsize]])

Constructor function for the *file* type. The constructor's arguments are the same as those of the *open* built-in function described in the following.

> When opening a file, it's preferable to use *open* instead of invoking this constructor directly. *file* is more suited to type testing (for example, writing isinstance(f, file)).
> Version Added: 2.2.

float([x])

Convert a string or a number to floating point. If the argument is a string, it must contain a possibly signed decimal or floating point number, possibly embedded in whitespace. The argument may also be [+|-]nan or [+|-]inf. Otherwise, the argument may be a plain or long integer or a floating point number, and a floating point number with the same value (within Python's floating point precision) is returned. If no argument is given, returns 0.0.

frozenset([iterable])

Return a new frozenset object whose elements are taken from iterable. The elements of a set must be hashable. To represent sets of sets, the inner sets must be frozenset objects. If *iterable* is not specified, a new empty frozenset is returned.

int([x[, radix]])

Convert a string or number to a plain integer. If the argument is a string, it must contain a possibly signed decimal number representable as a Python integer, possibly embedded in whitespace. The *radix* parameter gives the base for the conversion (which is 10 by default) and may be any integer in the range

[2, 36], or zero. If *radix* is zero, the proper radix is determined based on the contents of string; the interpretation is the same as for integer literals. (See *numbers.*) If *radix* is specified and *x* is not a string, *TypeError* is raised. Otherwise, the argument may be a plain or long integer or a floating point number. Conversion of floating point numbers to integers truncates (towards zero). If the argument is outside the integer range a long object will be returned instead. If no arguments are given, returns 0.

iter(o[, sentinel])

Return an *iterator* object. The first argument is interpreted very differently depending on the presence of the second argument. Without a second argument, *o* must be a collection object, which supports the iteration protocol (the *__iter__* method), or it must support the sequence protocol (the *__getitem__* method with integer arguments starting at 0). If it does not support either of those protocols, *TypeError* is raised. If the second argument, *sentinel*, is given, then *o* must be a callable object. The iterator created in this case will call *o* with no arguments for each call to its *next* method; if the value returned is equal to *sentinel*, *StopIteration* will be raised, otherwise the value will be returned.

    Version Added: 2.2.

list([iterable])

Return a list whose items are the same and in the same order as *iterable*'s items. *Iterable* may be either a sequence, a container that supports iteration, or an iterator object. If *iterable* is already a list, a copy is made and returned, similar to iterable[:]. For instance, list('abc') returns ['a', 'b', 'c'] and list((1, 2, 3)) returns [1, 2, 3]. If no argument is given, returns a new empty list, [].

object()

Return a new featureless object. *Object* is a base for all new style classes. It has the methods that are common to all instances of new style classes.

    Version Added: 2.2.

    Version Changed: CPython 2.3, Jython 2.5.0.

    This function does not accept any arguments. Formerly, it accepted arguments but ignored them.

open(filename[, mode[, bufsize]])

Open a file, returning an object of the *file* type described previously. If the file cannot be opened, *IOError* is raised. When opening a file, it's preferable to use *open* instead of invoking the *file* constructor directly.

    The first *argument* is the file name to be opened, and *mode* is a string indicating how the file is to be opened.

    The most commonly-used values of *mode* are 'r' for reading, 'w' for writing (truncating the file if it already exists), and 'a' for appending (which on *some* Unix systems means that *all* writes append to the end of the file regardless of the current seek position). If *mode* is omitted, it defaults to 'r'. The default is to use text mode, which may convert '\n' characters to a platform-specific representation on writing and back on reading. Thus, when opening a binary file, you should append 'b' to the *mode* value to open the file in binary mode, which will improve portability. (Appending 'b' is useful even on systems that don't treat binary and text files differently, where it serves as documentation.)

    The optional *bufsize* argument specifies the file's desired buffer size: 0 means unbuffered, 1 means line buffered, any other positive value means use a buffer of (approximately) that size in bytes. A negative *bufsize* means to use the system default, which is usually line buffered for tty devices and fully buffered for other files. If omitted, the system default is used.

Modes 'r+', 'w+' and 'a+' open the file for updating (note that 'w+' truncates the file). Append 'b' to the mode to open the file in binary mode, on systems that differentiate between binary and text files; on systems that don't have this distinction, adding the 'b' has no effect.

In addition to the standard `fopen` values *mode* may be 'U' or 'rU'. Python is usually built with universal newline support; supplying 'U' opens the file as a text file, but lines may be terminated by any of the following: the Unix end-of-line convention '\n', the Macintosh convention '\r', or the Windows convention '\r\n'. All of these external representations are seen as '\n' by the Python program. If Python is built without universal newline support a *mode* with 'U' is the same as normal text mode. Note that open file objects also have an attribute called *newlines* which has a value of None (if no newlines have yet been seen), '\n', '\r', '\r\n', or a tuple containing all the newline types seen.

Python enforces that the mode, after stripping 'U', begins with 'r', 'w' or 'a'.

Python provides many file handling modules including *fileinput, os, os.path, tempfile,* and *shutil*.

range([start,] stop[, step])

This is a versatile function to create lists containing arithmetic progressions. It is most often used in *for* loops. However, we recommend the use of xrange instead.

The arguments must be plain integers. If the *step* argument is omitted, it defaults to 1. If the *start* argument is omitted, it defaults to 0. The full form returns a list of plain integers [start, start + step, start + 2 * step, ...]. If *step* is positive, the last element is the largest start + i * step less than *stop*; if *step* is negative, the last element is the smallest start + i * step greater than *stop*. *step* must not be zero (or else *ValueError* is raised). Some examples:

```
>>> range(10)
[0, 1, 2, 3, 4, 5, 6, 7, 8, 9]
>>> range(1, 11)
[1, 2, 3, 4, 5, 6, 7, 8, 9, 10]
>>> range(0, 30, 5)
[0, 5, 10, 15, 20, 25]
>>> range(0, 10, 3)
[0, 3, 6, 9]
>>> range(0, -10, -1)
[0, -1, -2, -3, -4, -5, -6, -7, -8, -9]
>>> range(0)
[]
>>> range(1, 0)
[]
```

set([iterable])

Return a new set, optionally with elements are taken from *iterable*.

For other containers see the built-in *dict, list,* and *tuple* classes, and the *collections* module.
Version Added: CPython 2.4, Jython 2.5.0.

slice([start,] stop[, step])

Return a *slice* object representing the set of indices specified by range(start, stop, step). The start and step arguments default to None. Slice objects have read-only data attributes *start, stop,* and *step,* which merely return the argument values (or their default). They have no other explicit functionality; however they are used by Numerical Python and other third party extensions. Slice objects are also generated when extended indexing syntax is used. For example: a[start:stop:step] or a[start:stop, i].

str([object])

Return a string containing a nicely printable representation of an object. For strings, this returns the string itself. The difference with repr(object) is that str(object) does not always attempt to return a string that is acceptable to *eval*; its goal is to return a printable string. If no argument is given, returns the empty string, ''.

tuple([iterable])

Return a tuple whose items are the same and in the same order as *iterable*'s items. *Iterable* may be a sequence, a container that supports iteration, or an iterator object. If *iterable* is already a tuple, it is returned unchanged. For instance, tuple('abc') returns ('a', 'b', 'c') and tuple([1, 2, 3]) returns (1, 2, 3). If no argument is given, returns a new empty tuple, ().

type(name, bases, dict)

Return a new type object. This is essentially a dynamic form of the *class* statement. The *name* string is the class name and becomes the *__name__* attribute; the *bases* tuple itemizes the base classes and becomes the *__bases__* attribute; and the *dict* dictionary is the namespace containing definitions for class body and becomes the *__dict__* attribute. For example, the following two statements create identical *type* objects:

```
>>> class X(object):
...     a = 1
...
>>> X = type('X', (object,), dict(a=1))
```
    Version Added: Jython 2.2.

unichr(i)

Return the Unicode string of one character whose Unicode code is the integer *i*. For example, unichr(97) returns the string u'a'. This is the inverse of *ord* for Unicode strings. The valid range for the argument depends how Python was configured—it may be either UCS2 [0..0xFFFF] or UCS4 [0..0x10FFFF]. *ValueError* is raised if i is outside this range. For ASCII and 8-bit strings see *chr*.
    Version Added: Jython 2.0.

unicode([object[, encoding [, errors]]])

Return the Unicode string version of *object* using one of the following modes:

If *encoding* and/or *errors* are given, unicode() will decode the object which can either be an 8-bit string or a character buffer using the codec for *encoding*. The *encoding* parameter is a string giving the name of an encoding; if the encoding is not known, *LookupError* is raised. Error handling is done according to *errors*; this specifies the treatment of characters which are invalid in the input encoding. If *errors* is 'strict' (the default), a *ValueError* is raised on errors, while a value of 'ignore' causes errors to be silently ignored, and a value of 'replace' causes the official Unicode replacement character, U+FFFD, to be used to replace input characters which cannot be decoded. See also the *codecs* module.

If no optional parameters are given, unicode() will mimic the behavior of str() except that it returns Unicode strings instead of 8-bit strings. More precisely, if *object* is a Unicode string or subclass it will return that Unicode string without any additional decoding applied.

For objects which provide a *__unicode__* method, it will call this method without arguments to create a Unicode string. For all other objects, the 8-bit string version or representation is requested and then converted to a Unicode string using the codec for the default encoding in 'strict' mode.

xrange([start,] stop[, step])

This function is very similar to *range*, but returns an "xrange object" instead of a list. This is an opaque sequence type which yields the same values as the corresponding list, without actually storing them all simultaneously. The advantage of *xrange* over *range* is minimal (since *xrange* still has to create the values when asked for them) except when a very large range is used on a memory-starved machine or when all of the range's elements are never used (such as when the loop is usually terminated with *break*).

■ **Note** *xrange* is intended to be simple and fast. Implementations may impose restrictions to achieve this. The C implementation of Python restricts all arguments to native C longs ("short" Python integers), and also requires that the number of elements fit in a native C long. If a larger range is needed, an alternate version can be crafted using the *itertools* module: `islice(count(start, step), (stop-start+step-1)//step)`.

Math Built-in Functions

Most math functions are defined in the `math` (or `cmath` for complex math) module. The following functions are built in: abs, cmp, divmod, pow, and round.

abs(x)

Return the absolute value of a number. The argument may be a plain or long integer or a floating point number. If the argument is a complex number, its magnitude is returned.

cmp(x, y)

Compare the two objects x and y and return an integer according to the outcome. The return value is negative if x < y, zero if x == y and strictly positive if x > y.

divmod(a, b)

Take two (noncomplex) numbers as arguments and return a pair of numbers consisting of their quotient and remainder when using long division. With mixed operand types, the rules for binary arithmetic operators apply. For plain and long integers, the result is the same as (a // b, a % b). For floating point numbers the result is (q, a% b), where q is usually math.floor(a / b) but may be 1 less than that. In any case q * b + a % b is very close to a, if a % b is non-zero it has the same sign as b, and 0 <= abs(a % b) < abs(b).

Changed in Jython 2.5.0: Using `divmod()` with complex numbers is deprecated.

pow(x, y[, z])

Return x to the power y; if z is present, return *x* to the power *y*, modulo z (computed more efficiently than pow(x, y) % z). The two-argument form pow(x, y) is equivalent to using the power operator: x**y.

The arguments must have numeric types. With mixed operand types, the coercion rules for binary arithmetic operators apply. For int and long int operands, the result has the same type as the operands (after coercion) unless the second argument is negative; in that case, all arguments are converted to float and a float result is delivered. For example, 10**2 returns 100, but 10**-2 returns 0.01. If the second argument is negative, the third argument must be omitted. If *z* is present, *x* and *y* must be of integer types, and *y* must be non-negative.

round(x[, n])

Return the floating point value *x* rounded to *n* digits after the decimal point. If *n* is omitted, it defaults to zero. The result is a floating point number. Values are rounded to the closest multiple of 10 to the power minus *n*; if two multiples are equally close, rounding is done away from 0 (for example, round(0.5) is 1.0 and round(-0.5) is -1.0).

Functions on Iterables

The next group of built-in functions operate on iterables, which in Jython also includes all Java objects that implement the java.util.Iterator interface.

all(iterable)

The *all()* function returns True if all elements of the *iterable* are true (or if the iterable is empty). It is equivalent to the following:

```
def all(iterable):
    for element in iterable:
        if not element:
            return False
    return True
```
Version Added: 2.5.

any(iterable)

The *any()* function returns *True* if any of the elements of the iterable are true (or *False* if iterable is empty). It is equivalent to the following:

```
def any(iterable):
    for element in iterable:
        if element:
            return True
    return False
```
Version Added: 2.5.

enumerate(sequence[, start=0])

Return an enumerate object. *sequence* must be a sequence, an iterator, or some other object which supports iteration. The next( ) method of the iterator returned by enumerate( ) returns a tuple containing a count (from *start* which defaults to 0) and the corresponding value obtained from iterating over *iterable*. enumerate( ) is useful for obtaining an indexed series: (0, seq[0]), (1, seq[1]), (2, seq[2]), ...

filter(function, iterable)

Construct a list from those elements of *iterable* for which *function* returns true. *Iterable* may be either a sequence, a container which supports iteration, or an iterator. If *iterable* is a string or a tuple, the result also has that type; otherwise it is always a list. If *function* is None, the identity function is assumed, that is, all elements of *iterable* that are false are removed.

Note that filter(function, iterable) is equivalent to [item for item in iterable if function(item)] if function is not **None** and [item for item in iterable if item] if function is None.

map(function, iterable, ...)

Apply *function* to every item of *iterable* and return a list of the results. If additional *iterable* arguments are passed, *function* must take that many arguments and is applied to the items from all iterables in parallel. If one iterable is shorter than another it is assumed to be extended with None items. If *function* is None, the identity function is assumed; if there are multiple arguments, map() returns a list consisting of tuples containing the corresponding items from all iterables (a kind of transpose operation). The *iterable* arguments may be a sequence or any iterable object; the result is always a list.

max(iterable[, key])or max([, arg, ...][, key])

With a single argument *iterable*, return the largest item of a non-empty iterable (such as a string, tuple or list). With more than one argument, return the largest of the arguments.

The optional *key* argument specifies a one-argument ordering function like that used for list.sort(). The key argument, if supplied, must be in keyword form (for example, max(a,b,c,key=func)).

Changed in version 2.5: Added support for the optional *key* argument.

min(iterable[, key]) or min([, arg, ...][, key])

With a single argument *iterable*, return the smallest item of a non-empty iterable (such as a string, tuple or list). With more than one argument, return the smallest of the arguments.

The optional *key* argument specifies a one-argument ordering function like that used for list.sort(). The key argument, if supplied, must be in keyword form (for example, min(a,b,c,key=func)).

Changed in version 2.5: Added support for the optional *key* argument.

reduce(function, iterable[, initializer])

Apply *function* of two arguments cumulatively to the items of *iterable*, from left to right, so as to reduce the iterable to a single value. For example, reduce(lambda x,y: x+y, [1, 2, 3, 4, 5]) calculates ((((1+2)+3)+4)+5). The left argument, *x*, is the accumulated value and the right argument, *y*, is the update value from the *iterable*. If the optional *initializer* is present, it is placed before the items of the iterable in the calculation, and serves as a default when the iterable is empty. If *initializer* is not given and *iterable* contains only one item, the first item is returned.

reversed(seq)

Return a reverse *iterator* (An iterator which gives you the elements of seq in reverse order). The argument *seq* must be an object which has a __reversed__ method or supports the sequence protocol (the __len__ method and the __getitem__ method with integer arguments starting at 0).

Version Added: CPython 2.4, Jython 2.5.

sorted(iterable[, cmp[, key[, reverse]]])

The sorted function returns a sorted list. Use the optional *key* argument to specify a key function to control how it's sorted. So for example, this will sort the list by the length of the elements in it:

```
>>> sorted(['Massachusetts', 'Colorado', 'New York', 'California', 'Utah'], key=len)
['Utah', 'Colorado', 'New York', 'California', 'Massachusetts']
```

And this one will sort a list of Unicode strings without regard to it whether the characters are upper or lowercase:

```
>>> sorted(['apple', 'Cherry', 'banana'], key=str.upper)
['apple', 'banana', 'Cherry']
```

Although using a *key* function requires building a decorated version of the list to be sorted, in practice this uses substantially less overhead than calling a *cmp* function on every comparison. We recommend you take advantage of a keyed sort.

sum(iterable[, start=0])

Sums *start* and the items of an *iterable* from left to right and returns the total. *start* defaults to 0. The *iterable*'s items are normally numbers, and are not allowed to be strings. The fast, correct way to concatenate a sequence of strings is by calling `''.join(sequence)`. Note that `sum(range(n), m)` is equivalent to `reduce(operator.add, range(n), m)` To add floating point values with extended precision, see `math.fsum()`.

zip([iterable, ...])

This function returns a list of tuples, where the *i*-th tuple contains the *i*-th element from each of the argument sequences or iterables. The returned list is truncated in length to the length of the shortest argument sequence. When there are multiple arguments which are all of the same length, *zip* is similar to *map* with an initial argument of None. With a single sequence argument, it returns a list of 1-tuples. With no arguments, it returns an empty list.

The left-to-right evaluation order of the iterables is guaranteed. This makes possible an idiom for clustering a data series into n-length groups using `zip(*[iter(s)]*n)`.

zip in conjunction with the * operator can be used to unzip a list:

```
>>> x = [1, 2, 3]
>>> y = [4, 5, 6]
>>> zipped = zip(x, y)
>>> zipped
[(1, 4), (2, 5), (3, 6)]
>>> x2, y2 = zip(*zipped)
>>> x == x2, y == y2
True
```

Version Added: 2.0.
Version Changed: CPython 2.4, Jython 2.5.
Formerly, zip required at least one argument and zip() raised a TypeError instead of returning an empty list.

■ **Note** Although `filter`, `map`, and `reduce` are still useful, their use is largely superseded by using other functions, in conjunction with generator expressions. The `range` function is still useful for creating a list of a given sequence, but for portability eventually to Python 3.x, using `list(xrange())` instead is better.

Some advice:

Generator expressions (or list comprehensions) are easier to use than `filter`.

Most interesting but simple uses of `reduce` can be implemented through `sum`. And anything more complex should likely be written as a generator.

Conversion Functions

hex(x)

Convert an integer number (of any size) to a hexadecimal string. The result is a valid Python expression.
    Version Changed: CPython 2.4, Jython 2.5.
    Formerly only returned an unsigned literal.

long([x[, radix]])

Convert a string or number to a long integer. If the argument is a string, it must contain a possibly signed number of arbitrary size, possibly embedded in whitespace. The *radix* argument is interpreted in the same way as for *int*, and may only be given when x is a string. Otherwise, the argument may be a plain or long integer or a floating point number, and a long integer with the same value is returned. Conversion of floating point numbers to integers truncates (towards zero). If no arguments are given, returns 0L.

oct(x)

Convert an integer number (of any size) to an octal string. The result is a valid Python expression.
    Version Changed: CPython 2.4, Jython 2.5.
    Formerly only returned an unsigned literal.

ord(c)

Given a string of length one, return an integer representing the Unicode code point of the character when the argument is a unicode object, or the value of the byte when the argument is an 8-bit string. For example, `ord('a')` returns the integer 97, `ord(u'\u2020')` returns 8224. This is the inverse of *chr* for 8-bit strings and of *unichr* for unicode objects. If a unicode argument is given and Python was built with UCS2 Unicode, then the character's code point must be in the range [0..65535] inclusive; otherwise the string length is two, and a *TypeError* will be raised.

Functions for Working with Code

classmethod(function)

Return a class method for *function*.

A class method receives the class as implicit first argument, just like an instance method receives the instance. To declare a class method, use this idiom:

```
class C:
    @classmethod
    def f(cls, arg1, arg2, ...): ...
```

The @classmethod form is a function *decorator*. See the description of function decorators in Chapter 4 for details.

It can be called either on the class (such as C.f()) or on an instance (such as C().f()). The instance is ignored except for its class. If a class method is called for a derived class, the derived class object is passed as the implied first argument.

Class methods are different than C++ or Java static methods. If you want those, see *staticmethod* in this section.

Version Added: 2.2.
Version Changed: CPython 2.4, Jython 2.5.
Function decorator syntax added.

compile(source, filename, mode[, flags[, dont_inherit]])

Compile the *source* into a code or AST object. Code objects can be executed by an *exec* statement or evaluated by a call to *eval*. *source* can either be a string or an AST object. Refer to the *ast* module documentation for information on how to work with AST objects.

The *filename* argument should give the file from which the code was read; pass some recognizable value if it wasn't read from a file ('<string>' is commonly used).

The *mode* argument specifies what kind of code must be compiled; it can be 'exec' if *source* consists of a sequence of statements, 'eval' if it consists of a single expression, or 'single' if it consists of a single interactive statement (in the latter case, expression statements that evaluate to something other than None will be printed).

The optional arguments *flags* and *dont_inherit* control which future statements (see PEP 236) affect the compilation of *source*. If neither is present (or both are zero) the code is compiled with those future statements that are in effect in the code that is calling compile. If the *flags* argument is given and *dont_inherit* is not (or is zero) then the future statements specified by the *flags* argument are used in addition to those that would be used anyway. If *dont_inherit* is a non-zero integer then the *flags* argument is it. The future statements in effect around the call to compile are ignored.

Future statements are specified by bits which can be bitwise ORed together to specify multiple statements. The bitfield required to specify a given feature can be found as the *compiler_flag* attribute on the _Feature instance in the __future__ module.

This function raises *SyntaxError* if the compiled source is invalid, and *TypeError* if the source contains null bytes.

■ **Note** When compiling a string with multi-line statements, line endings must be represented by a single newline character ('\n'), and the input must be terminated by at least one newline character. If line endings are represented by '\r\n', use str.replace to change them into '\n'.

Version Changed: CPython 2.3, Jython 2.5.
The flags and dont_inherit arguments were added.

eval(expression[, globals[, locals]])

The arguments are a string and optional globals and locals. If provided, *globals* must be a dictionary. If provided, *locals* can be any mapping object.

The *expression* argument is parsed and evaluated as a Python expression (technically speaking, a condition list) using the *globals* and *locals* dictionaries as global and local namespace. If the *globals* dictionary is present and lacks '__builtins__', the current globals are copied into *globals* before *expression* is parsed. This means that *expression* normally has full access to the standard *__builtin__* module and restricted environments are propagated. If the *locals* dictionary is omitted it defaults to the *globals* dictionary. If both dictionaries are omitted, the expression is executed in the environment where *eval* is called. The return value is the result of the evaluated expression. Syntax errors are reported as exceptions. Example:

```
>>> x = 1
>>> print eval('x+1')
2
```

This function can also be used to execute arbitrary code objects (such as those created by *compile*). In this case pass a code object instead of a string. If the code object has been compiled with 'exec' as the *kind* argument, *eval*'s return value will be None.

■ **Hints** Dynamic execution of statements is supported by the *exec* statement. Execution of statements from a file is supported by the *execfile* function. The *globals* and *locals* functions return the current global and local dictionary, respectively, which may be useful to pass around for use by *eval* or *execfile*.

Version Changed: CPython 2.4, Jython 2.5.
Formerly, *locals* was required to be a dictionary.

execfile(filename[, globals[, locals]])

This function is similar to the *exec* statement, but parses a file instead of a string. It is different from the *import* statement in that it does not use the module administration: it reads the file unconditionally and does not create a new module.

The arguments are a file name and two optional dictionaries. The file is parsed and evaluated as a sequence of Python statements (similarly to a module) using the *globals* and *locals* dictionaries as global and local namespace. If provided, *locals* can be any mapping object.

If the *locals* dictionary is omitted it defaults to the *globals* dictionary. If both dictionaries are omitted, the expression is executed in the environment where *execfile* is called. The return value is None.
Version Changed: CPython 2.4, Jython 2.5.
Formerly, *locals* was required to be a dictionary.

■ **Warning** The default locals act as described for function locals below: modifications to the default locals dictionary should not be attempted. Pass an explicit locals dictionary if you need to see effects of the code on locals after function execfile returns. execfile cannot be used reliably to modify a function's locals.

---

property([fget[, fset[, fdel[, doc]]]])

Return a property attribute for *new-style classes* (classes that derive from *object*).

fget is a function for getting an attribute value, likewise *fset* is a function for setting, and *fdel* a function for del'ing, an attribute. Typical use is to define a managed attribute x:

```
class C(object):
    def __init__(self):
        self._x = None

    def getx(self):
        return self._x
    def setx(self, value):
        self._x = value
    def delx(self):
        del self._x
    x = property(getx, setx, delx, "I'm the 'x' property.")
```

If given, *doc* will be the docstring of the property attribute. Otherwise, the property will copy *fget*'s docstring (if it exists). This makes it possible to create read-only properties easily using *property* as a *decorator*:

```
class Parrot(object):
    def __init__(self):
        self._voltage = 100000

    @property
    def voltage(self):
        """Get the current voltage."""
        return self._voltage
```

turns the *voltage* method into a "getter" for a read-only attribute with the same name.

A property object has *getter*, *setter*, and *deleter* methods usable as decorators that create a copy of the property with the corresponding accessor function set to the decorated function. This is best explained with an example:

```
class C(object):
    def __init__(self):
        self._x = None
```

```
@property
def x(self):
    """I'm the 'x' property."""
    return self._x

@x.setter
def x(self, value):
    self._x = value

@x.deleter
def x(self):
    del self._x
```

This code is exactly equivalent to the first example. Be sure to give the additional functions the same name as the original property (x in this case.)

The returned property also has the attributes fget, fset, and fdel corresponding to the constructor arguments.

Version Added: 2.2.
Version Changed: 2.5.

staticmethod(function)

Return a static method for *function*.

A static method does not receive an implicit first argument. To declare a static method, use this idiom:

```
class C:
    @staticmethod
    def f(arg1, arg2, ...): ...
```

The @staticmethod form is a function *decorator*. See the description of function definitions in Chapter 4 for details.

It can be called either on the class (such as C.f()) or on an instance (such as C().f()). The instance is ignored except for its class.

Static methods in Python are similar to those found in Java or C++. For a more advanced concept, see *classmethod* in this section.

Version Added: 2.2.
Version Changed: CPython 2.4, Jython 2.5.
Function decorator syntax added.

super(type[, object-or-type])

Return a proxy object that delegates method calls to a parent or sibling class of *type*. This is useful for accessing inherited methods that have been overridden in a class. The search order is same as that used by *getattr* except that the *type* itself is skipped.

The *__mro__* attribute of the *type* lists the method resolution search order used by both *getattr* and *super*. The attribute is dynamic and can change whenever the inheritance hierarchy is updated.

If the second argument is omitted, the super object returned is unbound. If the second argument is an object, isinstance(obj, type) must be true. If the second argument is a type, issubclass(type2, type) must be true (this is useful for classmethods).

■ **Note** *Super* only works for new-style classes.

There are two typical use cases for *super*. In a class hierarchy with single inheritance, *super* can be used to refer to parent classes without naming them explicitly, thus making the code more maintainable. This use closely parallels the use of *super* in other programming languages.

The second use case is to support cooperative multiple inheritance in a dynamic execution environment. This use case is unique to Python and is not found in statically compiled languages or languages that only support single inheritance. This makes it possible to implement "diamond diagrams" where multiple base classes implement the same method. Good design dictates that this method have the same calling signature in every case (because the order of calls is determined at runtime, because that order adapts to changes in the class hierarchy, and because that order can include sibling classes that are unknown prior to runtime).

For both use cases, a typical superclass call looks like this:

```
class C(B):
    def method(self, arg):
        super(C, self).method(arg)
```

Note that *super* is implemented as part of the binding process for explicit dotted attribute lookups such as super().__getitem__(name). It does so by implementing its own *__getattribute__* method for searching classes in a predictable order that supports cooperative multiple inheritance. Accordingly, *super* is undefined for implicit lookups using statements or operators such as super()[name].

Also note that *super* is not limited to use inside methods. The two argument form specifies the arguments exactly and makes the appropriate references.

Version Added: 2.2.

Input Functions

input([prompt])
Equivalent to eval(raw_input(prompt)).

■ **Warning** This function is not safe from user errors! It expects a valid Python expression as input; if the input is not syntactically valid, a SyntaxError will be raised. Other exceptions may be raised if there is an error during evaluation. (On the other hand, sometimes this is exactly what you need when writing a quick script for expert use.)

If the *readline* module was loaded, then *input* will use it to provide elaborate line editing and history features.

Consider using the *raw_input* function for general input from users.

raw_input([prompt])

If the *prompt* argument is present, it is written to standard output without a trailing newline. The function then reads a line from input, converts it to a string (stripping a trailing newline), and returns that. When EOF is read, *EOFError* is raised. Here's an example:

```
>>> s = raw_input('--> ')
--> Monty Python's Flying Circus
>>> s
"Monty Python's Flying Circus"
```

If the *readline* module was loaded, then *raw_input* will use it to provide elaborate line editing and history features.

Functions for Working with Modules and Objects

callable(object)

Return *True* if the *object* argument appears callable, *False* if not. If this returns true, it is still possible that a call fails, but if it is false, calling *object* will never succeed. Note that classes are callable (calling a class returns a new instance); class instances are callable if they have a *__call__* method.

delattr(object, name)

This is a relative of *setattr*. The arguments are an object and a string. The string must be the name of one of the object's attributes. The function deletes the named attribute, provided the object allows it. For example, delattr(x, 'foobar') is equivalent to del x.foobar.

dir([object])

Without arguments, return the list of names in the current local scope. With an argument, attempt to return a list of valid attributes for that object.

If the object has a method named *__dir__*, this method will be called and must return the list of attributes. This allows objects that implement a custom *__getattr__* or *__getattribute__* function to customize the way *dir* reports their attributes.

If the object does not provide *__dir__*, the function tries its best to gather information from the object's *__dict__* attribute, if defined, and from its type object. The resulting list is not necessarily complete, and may be inaccurate when the object has a custom *__getattr__*.

The default *dir* mechanism behaves differently with different types of objects, as it attempts to produce the most relevant, rather than complete, information:

- If the object is a module object, the list contains the names of the module's attributes.

- If the object is a type or class object, the list contains the names of its attributes, and recursively of the attributes of its bases.

- Otherwise, the list contains the object's attributes' names, the names of its class' attributes, and recursively of the attributes of its class' base classes.

The resulting list is sorted alphabetically. For example:

```
>>> import struct
>>> dir()   # doctest: +SKIP
['__builtins__', '__doc__', '__name__', 'struct']
>>> dir(struct)   # doctest: +NORMALIZE_WHITESPACE
['Struct', '__builtins__', '__doc__', '__file__', '__name__',
 '__package__', 'clearcache', 'calcsize', 'error', 'pack', 'pack_into',
 'unpack', 'unpack_from']
>>> class Foo(object):
...     def __dir__(self):
...         return ["kan", "ga", "roo"]
...
>>> f = Foo()
>>> dir(f)
['ga', 'kan', 'roo']
```

■ **Note** Because dir is supplied primarily as a convenience for use at an interactive prompt, it tries to supply an interesting set of names more than it tries to supply a rigorously or consistently defined set of names, and its detailed behavior may change across releases. For example, metaclass attributes are not in the result list when the argument is a class.

---

getattr(object, name[, default])

Return the value of the named attribute of *object*. *name* must be a string. If the string is the name of one of the object's attributes, the result is the value of that attribute. For example, getattr(x, 'foobar') is equivalent to x.foobar. If the named attribute does not exist, *default* is returned if provided, otherwise *AttributeError* is raised.

globals()

Return a dictionary representing the current global symbol table. This is always the dictionary of the current module (inside a function or method, this is the module where it is defined, not the module from which it is called).

hasattr(object, name)

The arguments are an object and a string. The result is *True* if the string is the name of one of the object's attributes, False if not. (This is implemented by calling getattr(object, name) and seeing whether it raises an exception or not.)

■ **Note** Java dynamic integration: The supporting special method for getattr is __getattr__. When Jython code is compiled, it actually uses __getattr__ for implementing attribute lookup. So x.y.z is actually compiled to the equivalent chain of x.__getattr__('y').__getattr__('z'). Alternatively for more efficient Java integration, __findattr__ is supported. It returns null instead of throwing an AttributeError if the attribute is not part of a given

---

object. But use __getattr__ if you are going to be chaining method calls together so as to maintain Python exception handling semantics.

If the given Jython class implements a Java interface (or extends a Java class, which is the less preferable case in Jython as it is in Java in general), then Java code that uses such instances can statically bind method lookup.

[The Clamp project supports an alternate way of exposing Java interfaces, such that the interfaces are created from Jython code. We're not certain about this approach as a best practice however. Java interfaces in Java are quite precise with respect to interoperability. Other parts are useful, such as AOT compilation of Java proxies for Jython classes.]

---

hash(object)

Return the hash value of the object (if it has one). Hash values are integers. They are used to quickly compare dictionary keys during a dictionary lookup. Numeric values that compare equal have the same hash value (even if they are of different types, as is the case for 1 and 1.0).

help([object])

Invoke the built-in help system. (This function is intended for interactive use.) If no argument is given, the interactive help system starts on the interpreter console. If the argument is a string, then the string is looked up as the name of a module, function, class, method, keyword, or documentation topic, and a help page is printed on the console. If the argument is any other kind of object, a help page on the object is generated.

This function is added to the built-in namespace by the *site* module. For more information on the site module, take a look at the Python documentation http://docs.python.org/library/site.html#module-site.

Version Added: 2.2.

id(object)

Return the "identity" of an object. This is an integer (or long integer) which is guaranteed to be unique and constant for this object during its lifetime. Two objects with non-overlapping lifetimes may have the same *id* value. (Implementation note: this is the address of the object.)

isinstance(object, classinfo)

Return true if the *object* argument is an instance of the *classinfo* argument, or of a (direct or indirect) subclass thereof. Also return true if *classinfo* is a type object (new-style class) and *object* is an object of that type or of a (direct or indirect) subclass thereof. If *object* is not a class instance or an object of the given type, the function always returns false. If *classinfo* is neither a class object nor a type object, it may be a tuple of class or type objects, or may recursively contain other such tuples (other sequence types are not accepted). If *classinfo* is not a class, type, or tuple of classes, types, and such tuples, a *TypeError* exception is raised.

Version Changed: 2.2.

Support for a tuple of type information was added.

issubclass(class, classinfo)

Return true if *class* is a subclass (direct or indirect) of *classinfo*. A class is considered a subclass of itself. *classinfo* may be a tuple of class objects, in which case every entry in *classinfo* will be checked. In any other case, a *TypeError* exception is raised.

Version Changed: CPython 2.3, Jython 2.5.

Support for a tuple of type information was added.

len(s)

Return the length (the number of items) of an object. The argument may be a sequence (string, tuple or list) or a mapping (dictionary).

locals()

Update and return a dictionary representing the current local symbol table.

■ **Warning** The contents of this dictionary should not be modified; changes may not affect the values of local variables used by the interpreter.

Free variables are returned by *locals* when it is called in a function block. Modifications of free variables may not affect the values used by the interpreter. Free variables are not returned in class blocks.

reload(module)

Reload a previously imported *module*. The argument must be a module object, so it must have been successfully imported before. This is useful if you have edited the module source file using an external editor and want to try out the new version without leaving the Python interpreter. The return value is the module object (the same as the *module* argument).

When reload(module) is executed:

- Python modules' code is recompiled and the module-level code reexecuted, defining a new set of objects which are bound to names in the module's dictionary. The init function of extension modules is not called a second time.

- As with all other objects in Python the old objects are only reclaimed after their reference counts drop to zero in CPython. However, in Jython once the object is no longer in use then it becomes garbage collected.

- The names in the module namespace are updated to point to any new or changed objects.

- Other references to the old objects (such as names external to the module) are not rebound to refer to the new objects and must be updated in each namespace where they occur if that is desired.

There are a number of other caveats: if a module is syntactically correct but its initialization fails, the first *import* statement for it does not bind its name locally, but does store a (partially initialized) module object in sys.modules. To reload the module you must first *import* it again (this will bind the name to the partially initialized module object) before you can *reload* it.

When a module is reloaded, its dictionary (containing the module's global variables) is retained. Redefinitions of names will override the old definitions, so this is generally not a problem. If the new version of a module does not define a name that was defined by the old version, the old definition remains. This feature can be used to the module's advantage if it maintains a global table or cache of objects. With a *try* statement it can test for the table's presence and skip its initialization if desired:

```
try:
    cache
except NameError:
    cache = {}
```

It is legal though generally not very useful to reload built-in or dynamically loaded modules, except for *sys*, *__main__* and *__builtin__*. In many cases, however, extension modules are not designed to be initialized more than once, and may fail in arbitrary ways when reloaded.

If a module imports objects from another module using *from ... import ...*, calling *reload* for the other module does not redefine the objects imported from it. One way around this is to re-execute the *from* statement, another is to use *import* and qualified names (*module.*name*) instead.

If a module instantiates instances of a class, reloading the module that defines the class does not affect the method definitions of the instances: they continue to use the old class definition. The same is true for derived classes.

repr(object)
Return a string containing a printable representation of an object. This is the same value yielded by conversions (reverse quotes). It is sometimes useful to be able to access this operation as an ordinary function. For many types, this function makes an attempt to return a string that would yield an object with the same value when passed to *eval*, otherwise the representation is a string enclosed in angle brackets that contains the name of the type of the object together with additional information often including the name and address of the object. A class can control what this function returns for its instances by defining a *__repr__* method.

setattr(object, name, value)
This is the counterpart of *getattr*. The arguments are an object, a string and an arbitrary value. The string may name an existing attribute or a new attribute. The function assigns the value to the attribute, provided the object allows it. For example, setattr(x, 'foobar', 123) is equivalent to x.foobar = 123.

type(object)
Return the type of an *object*. The return value is a type object. The *isinstance* built-in function is recommended for testing the type of an object.

With three arguments, *type* functions as a constructor as detailed earlier in this appendix.

vars([object])
Without arguments, return a dictionary corresponding to the current local symbol table. With a module, class or class instance object as argument (or anything else that has a *__dict__* attribute), returns a dictionary corresponding to the object's symbol table.

■ **Warning** The returned dictionary should not be modified: the effects on the corresponding symbol table are undefined.

__import__(name[, globals[, locals[, fromlist[, level]]]])

■ **Note** This is an advanced function that is not needed in everyday Python programming.

This function is invoked by the *import* statement. It can be replaced (by importing the *builtins* module and assigning to builtins.__import__) in order to change semantics of the *import* statement, but nowadays it is usually simpler to use import hooks (see PEP 302). Direct use of *__import__* is rare, except in cases where you want to import a module whose name is only known at runtime.

The function imports the module *name*, potentially using the given *globals* and *locals* to determine how to interpret the name in a package context. The *fromlist* gives the names of objects or submodules that should be imported from the module given by *name*. The standard implementation does not use its *locals* argument at all, and uses its *globals* only to determine the package context of the *import* statement.

level specifies whether to use absolute or relative imports. The default is -1 which indicates both absolute and relative imports will be attempted. 0 means only perform absolute imports. Positive values for *level* indicate the number of parent directories to search relative to the directory of the module calling *__import__*.

When the *name* variable is of the form package.module, normally, the top-level package (the name up till the first dot) is returned, *not* the module named by *name*. However, when a non-empty *fromlist* argument is given, the module named by *name* is returned.

For example, the statement import spam results in bytecode resembling the following code:

```
spam = __import__('spam', globals(), locals(), [], -1)
```

The statement import spam.ham results in this call:

```
spam = __import__('spam.ham', globals(), locals(), [], -1)
```

Note how *__import__* returns the toplevel module here because this is the object that is bound to a name by the *import* statement.

On the other hand, the statement from spam.ham import eggs, sausage as saus results in:

```
_temp = __import__('spam.ham', globals(), locals(), ['eggs', 'sausage'], -1)
eggs = _temp.eggs
saus = _temp.sausage
```

Here, the spam.ham module is returned from *__import__*. From this object, the names to import are retrieved and assigned to their respective names.

If you simply want to import a module (potentially within a package) by name, you can get it from *sys.modules*:

```
>>> import sys
>>> name = 'foo.bar.baz'
>>> __import__(name)
<module 'foo' from ...>
>>> baz = sys.modules[name]
>>> baz
<module 'foo.bar.baz' from ...>
```

Version Changed: 2.5.
The level parameter was added.
Version Changed: 2.5.
Keyword support for parameters was added.

Index

■ M